ALASTAIR SAWDAY'S

Special
places to stay

BRITISH BED & BREAKFAST

Edited by Jackie King

Typesetting, Conversion & Repro:	Avonset, Bath
Maps:	Maps in Minutes, Cornwall
Printing:	Midas Book Printers, UK
Design:	Caroline King & Springboard Design, Bristol
UK Distribution:	Portfolio, Greenford, Middlesex
US Distribution:	The Globe Pequot Press, Guilford, Connecticut

First published in October 2000

Alastair Sawday Publishing Co. Ltd
The Home Farm, Barrow Gurney, Bristol BS48 3RW

The Globe Pequot Press
P. O. Box 480
Guilford, Connecticut 06437
USA

Fifth edition 2000

Copyright © October 2000 Alastair Sawday Publishing Co. Ltd

A catalogue record for this book is available from the British Library.

Alastair Sawday has asserted his right to be identified as the author of this work.

ISBN 1-901970-10-8 in the UK

ISBN 0-7627-0770-4 in the US

Printed in Slovenia

The publishers have made every effort to ensure the accuracy of the information in the book at the time of going to press. However, they cannot accept any responsibility for any loss, injury or inconvenience resulting from the use of information contained in this guide.

Alastair Sawday's

Special

places to stay

British Bed & Breakfast

The Globe Pequot Press

Guilford
Connecticut, USA

Alastair Sawday Publishing
Bristol, UK

Contents

Contents

Acknowledgements

The best part of the editor's job is 'the people'. It is fun working with the delightful owners one finds in this book; so many of them are originals and there is a vast well of basic human kindness out there. But the final production process can be challenging, not least because there are many owners whom we do not accept and telling them so can be difficult. That is a painful process for them, for we are talking about their homes. So I salute Jackie who, with Sally's help, has worked so long and with such devotion on a complex and often tricky project. She has kept the integrity of the book while making it fresh and hugely interesting.

The most taxing part of the job is the sheer administration. Every detail has to be right and every house has to be re-assessed each year and inspected at least once every three years. So, again, I am grateful to Jackie and Sally for vanquishing such a mountain of detail.

Thank you, too, to Julia who calmly pulls us through the birth of each book - a masterful midwife, she ensures a high-tech, relatively pain-free delivery. Bridget Bishop deserves a mention too for so efficiently and good-humouredly managing the finances of the book.

The result of everybody's effort is probably our best book ever on B&B in the UK.

Series Editor: Alastair Sawday

Editor: Jackie King

Editorial Assistant: Sally George

Production Manager: Julia Richardson

Administration: Kate Harris

Inspections: Julie Albeson, Lindy Ball, Tom Bell, Jeremy Bolam, Fredena Burns, Gillian Charlton-Meyrick, Annie Coates, Jenny Colbourne, Lally Croggon, Trish Dugmore, Jonathan Goodall, Mary Harman, Caroline Heron, Richard Hogg, Marina King, Auriol Marson, Diana Morriss, Caroline Portway, James & Petrina Pugh, Jack Raymond, Margaret Paterson, Rosemary Piper, Anne Sorrell, Stephen Tate, Angela Whatley

Accounts: Bridget Bishop, Sheila Clifton, Sandra Hasell, Jenny Purdy

Symbols: Mark Brierley

Introduction

Is this book right for you? Here are a few questions to help you decide.

Are you unstuffy, open-minded and yet, in one way or another, quite demanding? Do you enjoy meeting new people and new ideas? Have you a yearning for beautiful places?

If so, then YES - this book is for you. A few more hints: if you are a little weary of the frenzied fantasies of our age - such as the ones that suggest we can all be happy if we shop a lot and use the Internet - then this book is for you, for it is full of real dreams realised in bricks and mortar. If you are weary, too, of the incessant hum of modern life - mobile phone conversation, traffic, muzak, computers, exhortations to be elsewhere and be somebody different - then devour this book, for everyone featuring in it has sought, and often found, their solutions.

It strikes me that the happiness quota among the owners in this book is unusually high. They often live in deeply peaceful places; many of them have taken bold decisions to change their lives, or have firmly stuck to places that they know and love. That, I suppose, is partly why we have selected them. Beyond that, they have great taste, interesting ideas, fine houses - in some combination. Yes, they are special, and I urge you to go and meet them. I have often gone off on a whim to visit these places and have never been anything other than absolutely delighted. They are beacons of light and I am proud to play a part in introducing you to them.

Alastair Sawday

Introduction

How do we choose our Special Places?

We look for owners and houses that we like. There are many reasons why a place may be deemed special – the setting, the architecture, the mix of lavish comfort and great value, the refreshing simplicity - and we understand that everybody travels with the hope of fulfilling their own little dream. We don't claim to be able to guide you always to perfect places, but to places where, at least, if there is a failing, there is also something special that makes up for it. We are proud of our collection of houses and their owners and believe that we have the richest and most satisfyingly eclectic variety of B&Bs of any guide book.

We have turned down many houses that have proudly claimed a high tourist board rating – sometimes, actually, the kiss of death. We celebrate individuals who have insisted on doing things their way, rather than those who breathlessly pursue an extra 'star' by knocking about a room to squeeze in a shower cubicle, or by replacing a faded but comfortable and beautiful old sofa with an over-stuffed Scotch-guarded, slouch-guarded matching three-piece suite. There is no objective measure of style, generosity, a genuine welcome or a breathtaking setting.

What to expect

With very few exceptions, you will be staying in somebody's home – 'real' people who have families, sometimes other jobs, maybe pets, friends, gardens or farms to look after. We choose them because we know that they will do a good job of looking after you, too – that they will be sensitive to your needs and respect the fact that you are paying to stay with them and will want to feel spoiled in some way.

We know from the hundreds of readers' letters we receive that our hosts do a fantastically professional job of looking after guests – there are numerous tales of unexpected generosity, heart-touching kindness and genuine care. If you are unhappy about anything, or if you are short of something do mention it, do just ask if you may have those fresh towels/extra blanket/more hot water; if you don't want your room disturbed in the daytime, simply say so.

Things can go awry. It is hard to 'complain' when you're in somebody else's house, but every owner would prefer to discuss what is wrong at the time rather than to receive a complaint afterwards. It's devastating for a owner to discover that a seemingly contented couple were in fact shivering in the night or sad not to get the double-cream porridge that we'd waxed so lyrical about.

Introduction

Finding the right place for you

It's our job to get you to a place that you will like. We give honest descriptions of our houses and owners and you should glean from the write-up what the owners are like or how formal the house is. Talk of beautiful things should alert you to the fact that this may not be the place to take your toddler; phrases such as 'dress for dinner' tell you that this isn't a 'come as you are' sort of place.

In each write-up there will be clues as to the mood of the house and the owners; we choose our words carefully. If you don't read carefully you may end up in the wrong place.

We have a huge variety of houses in the book – the older or larger properties may be more immediately appealing, but don't overlook the few modern houses – they often have huge style, too.

Quick reference indices

At the back of the book we have given at-a-glance information to help direct you to houses perfect for you if you prefer to eat home-grown food, take children or pets with you or travel alone. We can also direct you to houses that look after vegetarians or have facilities for those with impaired mobility or whose hosts will collect you from local stations.

How to use this book

Map

When you know where in Britain you want to stay, look at the map at the front of the book first, find your area and look for the houses nearest. Don't focus on counties, as this can be misleading. Maybe you're going to a wedding in Suffolk – don't just flip through the Suffolk section – look for your destination on the map and we'll maybe lead you to your perfect retreat just over the border in Norfolk. Please note that on the map which includes London, the flags are not placed geographically.

Rooms

We state if rooms are double/twin/single, and if beds are king-size or four-poster. If a bathroom is en suite, you don't have to go through public areas to get to it and we say if there is a bath or a shower. A private/shared bathroom means that it is not en suite and will have either a shower or a bath and a wc and a basin; the former you will have to yourself, the latter will be shared with other guests or family members.

Introduction

If you'd like your child in the room with you, ask at the time of booking if you may have a foldaway bed and what the charge will be.

Prices

We give the price per person, inclusive of full English breakfast, unless otherwise stipulated. Some owners do not offer cooked breakfast but, instead, include a substantial Continental version. We also show the supplement for single use of a double room.

Some owners do put up their prices during the year, so confirm on the telephone how much your particular room will be.

Symbols

We have an explanation of our symbols at the back of the book, on page 432. Use the symbols for each entry as a guide, not an unequivocal statement of fact. If an owner has a Pets Welcome symbol, tell her about your dog/parrot, so that she can consider the other guests that she has booked and make her decision.

Equally, if an owner doesn't have a symbol that you are looking for, it is worth discussing your needs – one that doesn't have a Child Welcome symbol, for example, may be happy to have your children to stay if you are booking all of the bedrooms.

Abbreviations

SSSI stands for Site of Special Scientific Interest (often rich in flora and fauna) and AONB stands for Area of Outstanding Natural Beauty.

Types of property

There are huge differences in the levels of luxury in our *Special Places*. Price is generally an indicator of how lavish your surroundings are likely to be; but we expect you to find value for money in each of our places. A huge, ancient farmhouse may have draughts, so packing an extra sweater may be a good idea; you may swelter in a city centre house and find that there is too much traffic noise to open the double-glazed window; if you are a light sleeper, take ear plugs. Glean as much information as possible from the owners beforehand if you are sensitive to noise/heat/whatever.

Practical Matters

Meals

We tell you if the owner does packed lunch/lunch/supper/dinner for guests, and the price per person. Do give advance warning if you'd like to

Introduction

eat in and tell your hosts about any dietary requirements. Many are wonderful cooks – competent and imaginative – who use the freshest and best local or home-produced food. It's often far more relaxing after a busy day or a long journey, to have a bath and amble downstairs to eat a fine meal rather than to have to get the car out again.

Seasons and public holidays

Bank holidays are, of course, the busiest times for our owners so book early if you want that four-poster/the room with a balcony that faces seawards. We are staggered at how far in advance some of the houses are booked.

Bookings and cancellations

Hosts will take bookings by post/fax/email although most like to chat on the phone – that way you can get a feeling for each other. Some will ask for a deposit – often non-refundable if you cancel and they can not re-let the room. Some London owners ask for hefty deposits to secure a room – they know that their visitors can be fickle and that they can be left with an empty room because of a last-minute cancellation or change of travel plan.

Do let your host know roughly what time you will be arriving and call if you are severely delayed. Most will want to be there when you arrive and to spend some time with you. It's especially important to be prompt if you have booked an evening meal – we do hear of owners fretting over dinner spoiling in the oven, having had no phone call to warn of a delay.

Owners vary in insistence upon arrival and departure times and we do complain about tales of guests being told to arrive after 5pm and leave by 10am; tell us if you have unreasonable demands made on you. It's understandable that you will want to make the most of your lovely surroundings, so ask if you may read in the garden, pack after you've made the most of some morning sun or arrive slightly earlier to swim in the pool that we've told you about.

Payment

All of our owners take cash and cheques with a cheque card. If they also take credit cards, we have given them the appropriate symbol – if yours is an obscure one, confirm on the phone that they can accept it.

Children

A thorny subject! We wanted to make this a child-friendly book, and have encouraged our hosts to accept children as run-of-the-mill guests rather than alien beings. The mere mention of children often illicits sharp intakes

Introduction

of breath from owners who know from experience how difficult it is to balance the needs of very different guests. They may be very happy to have you and your children if you are the only guests, but many find it exhausting trying to give the ideal stay to families at the same time as elderly guests or couples on a romantic break.

Many owners love children, even if they don't have the symbol, but don't want to advertise the fact for fear of putting others off. They therefore keep quiet about their climbing frames or cots for fear of portraying their elegant retreat as some sort of crèche.

Even in those houses that do have the child symbol, we do ask you to be sensitive to other guests and to be realistic about the behaviour of your little ones. If you have a child who often cries in the night you'll feel more comfortable in, say, a large farmhouse rather than in a small cottage where you'll be cheek-by-jowl with others.

Dogs

Many of you love to travel with your hound and many owners love dogs enough to make yours welcome. Some may have them in the house, a few accept them in the bedrooms, others may provide a kennel or ask that yours sleep in your car. Make absolutely sure what the house rules are before making your booking.

Smoking

The No-Smoking symbol means no smoking anywhere in the house. The absence of the symbol obviously doesn't mean that you may light up anywhere, rather that you ask the owner where you may smoke. And don't forget that other guests may have strong feelings.

Tipping

Few owners expect you to tip them. If you have encountered extraordinary kindness, you may like to leave a little gift or send a thank you card. It is rewarding for owners if you write to tell us of your good fortune – we record all feedback from readers.

Environment

We seek to reduce our impact on the environment where possible by:

• Planting trees to compensate for our carbon emissions (as calculated by Edinburgh University); we are officially a carbon-neutral publishing company.

Introduction

- Re-using paper, recycling stationery, tins, bottles, etc.

- Encouraging staff use of bicycles (they're given free) and encouraging car-sharing.

- Celebrating the use of organic, home and locally produced food.

- Publishing books that support, in however small a way, the rural economy and small-scale businesses.

- Encouraging our owners to follow recommendations made to them by the Energy Efficiency Centre to make their homes more environmentally friendly.

Subscriptions

Owners pay to appear in this guide, their fee goes towards the high production costs of an all-colour book.

We only include places and owners that we find special. It is not possible for anyone to buy their way in.

Special Places to Stay on the Internet

As we go to press, our web site is going through a radical regeneration, and by the time you read this, what was a growing collection of web pages will have become an online database with roughly a thousand entries. These are from the various titles in the *Special Places to Stay* series, so if you like the places in *British Bed and Breakfast*, why not browse some of those further afield?

We flatter ourselves that the 8,000 visitors a month who come to the site have good reason to, and we think you should join them! Not only do they have access to open, honest and up-to-date information about hundreds of places to stay across Europe, but they also know that if they want to buy any of our books, their best option is to come directly to our window on the world wide web:

www.sawdays.co.uk

Disclaimer

We make no claims to pure objectivity in judging our *Special Places to Stay*. They are here because we like them. Our opinions and tastes are ours alone and this book is a statement of them; we hope that you will share them.

Introduction

We have done our utmost to get our facts right but apologise unreservedly for any mistakes that may have crept in. Sometimes, too, prices shift, usually upwards and 'things' change. We should be grateful to be told of any errors or changes, however small.

Finally

Do let us know how you get on in these houses – feedback is vital to the continued success of the book. There is a report form at the back of the book, or email britishbandb@sawdays.co.uk.

We hugely enjoy putting together this guide and establishing relationships with our old and new friends. Put our judgement to the test – set forth with an open mind and enjoy these people who open their homes to share with you.

County page photographs

Thank you to those who allowed us to use their pictures:-

Lisa Saunders, Bridget Sudworth, Hildegard Owen, Ozric Armstrong, *Lancashire Life* magazine, Joanna Macinnes, Sally Barber, Andrew Dow, Louise Broughton, Sara Hay, Caroline Smith, Guy Griffiths, Inge Ford, Robert Bird, Chris Beaty, Ray Smith, Andrew Farmer, Rosalind Bufton, Caroline Flynn, Richard Freeland, Sheila Clifton.

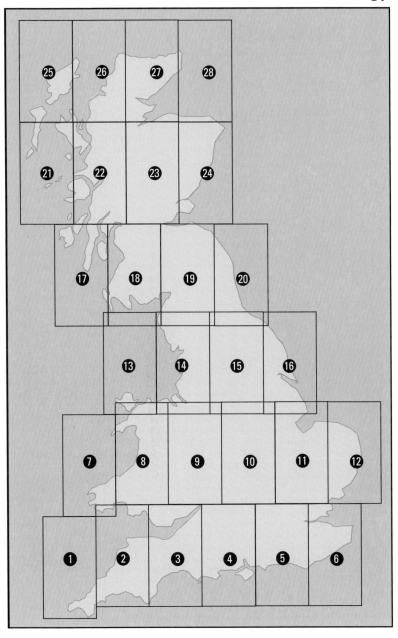

Guide to our map page numbers

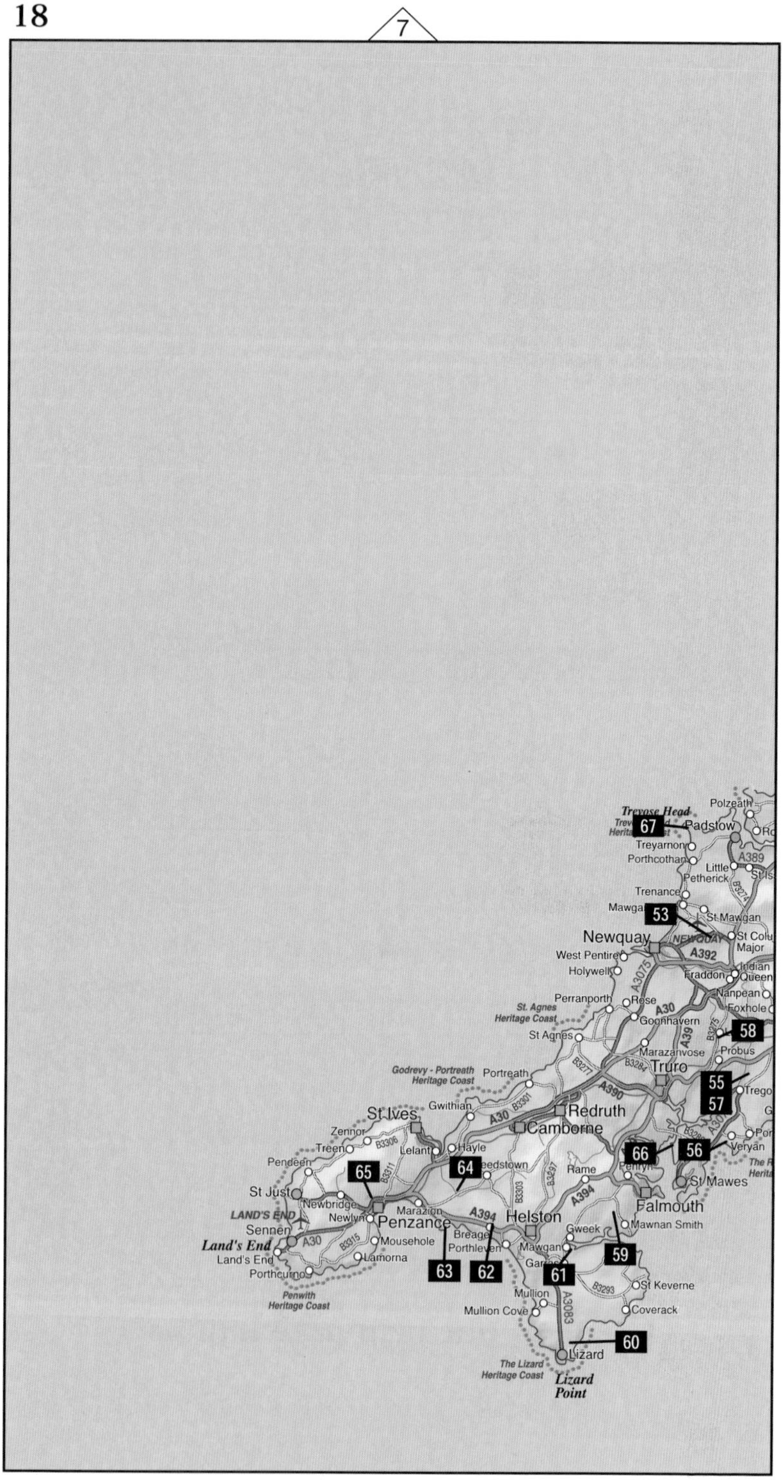

Map scale: 14.3 miles to 1 inch

Map 1

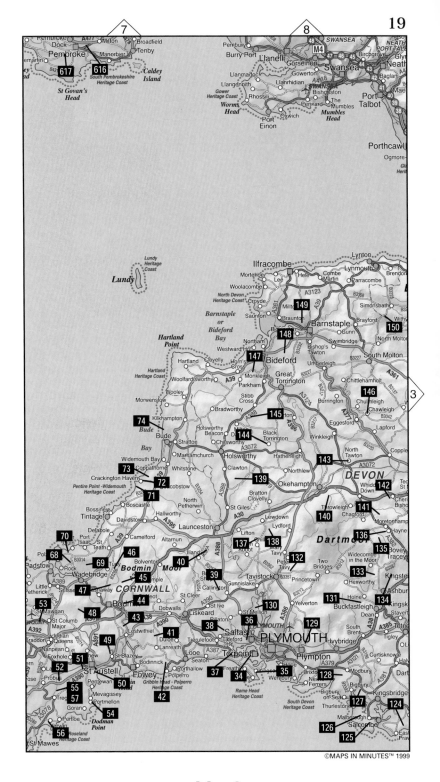

Map 2

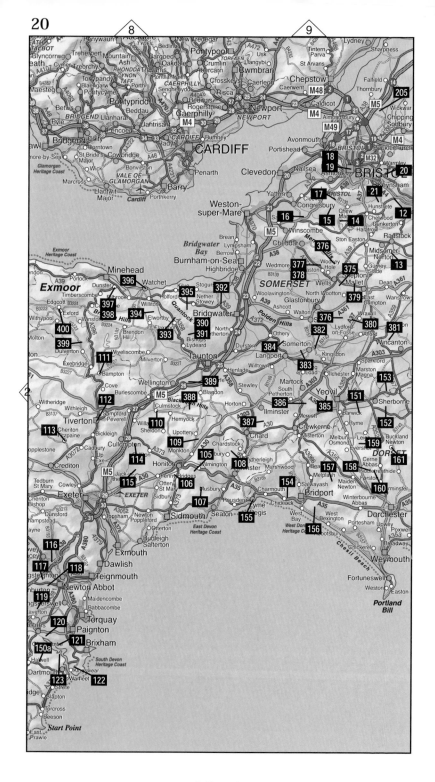

Map 3

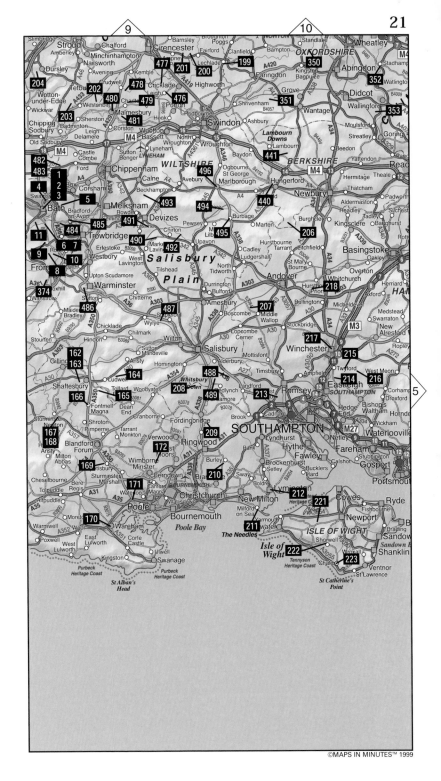

Map 4

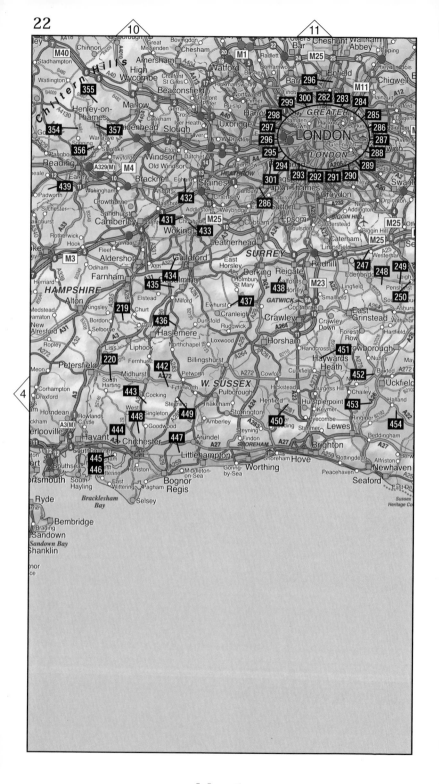

Map 5

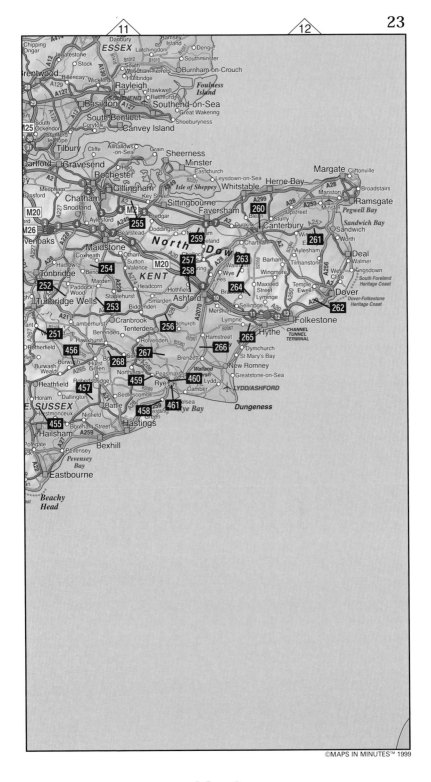

Map 6

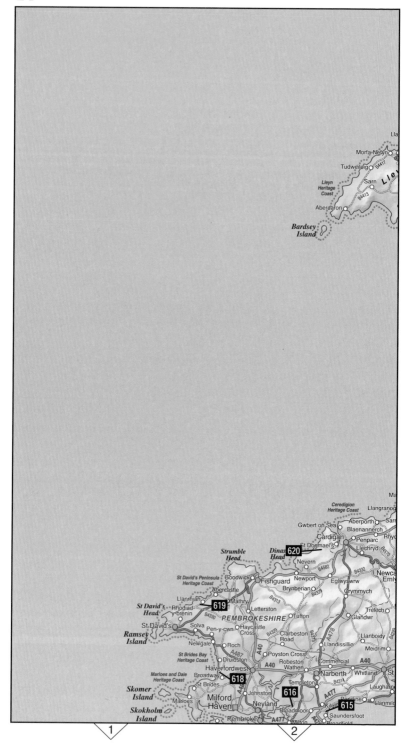

Map 7

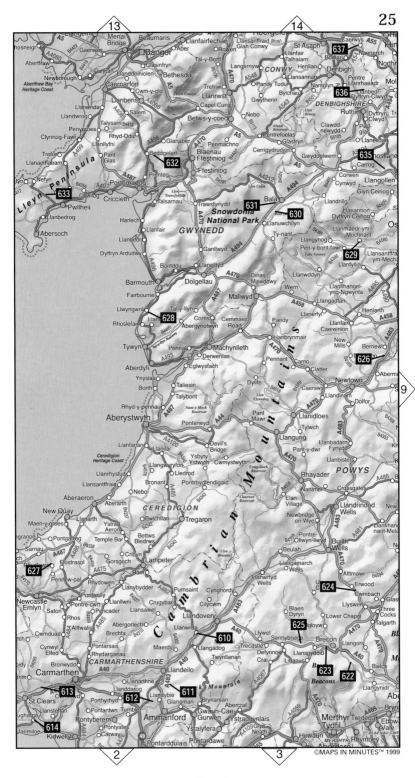

Map 8

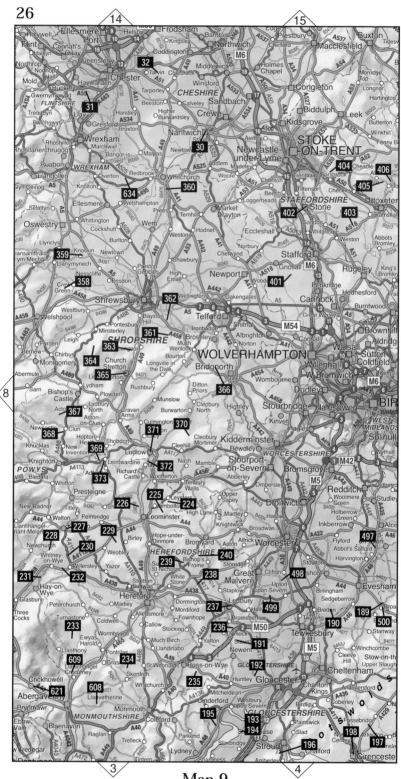

Map 9

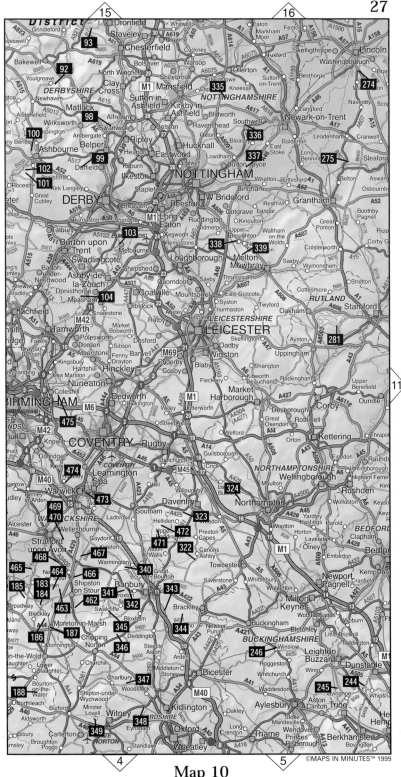

Map 10

©MAPS IN MINUTES™ 1999

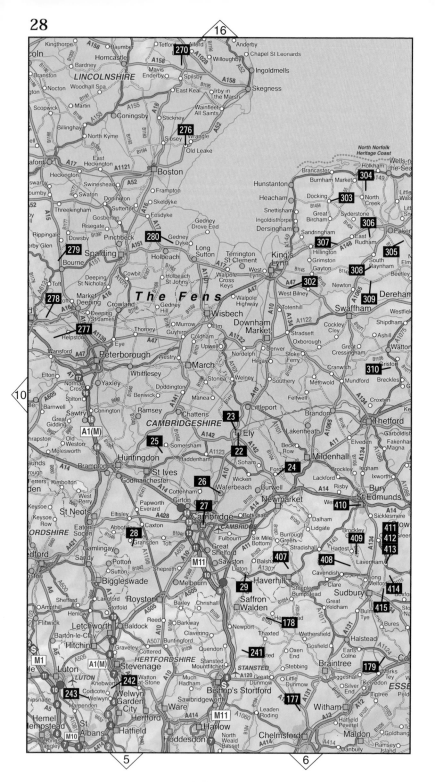

Map 11

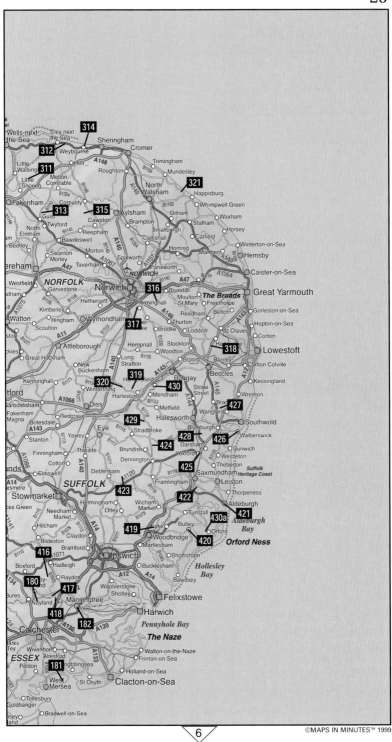

©MAPS IN MINUTES™ 1999

Map 12

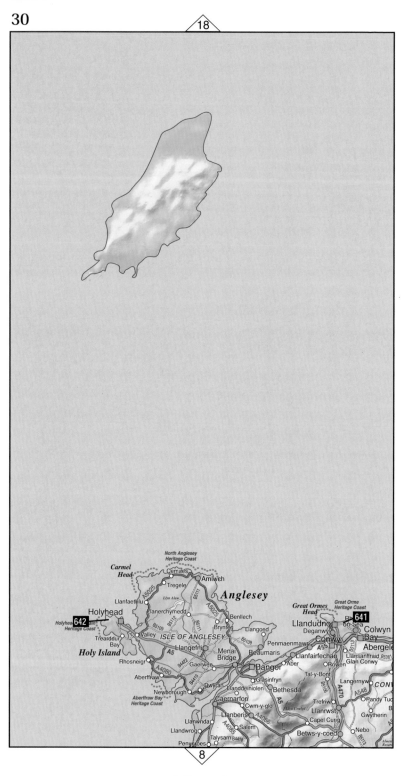

Map 13

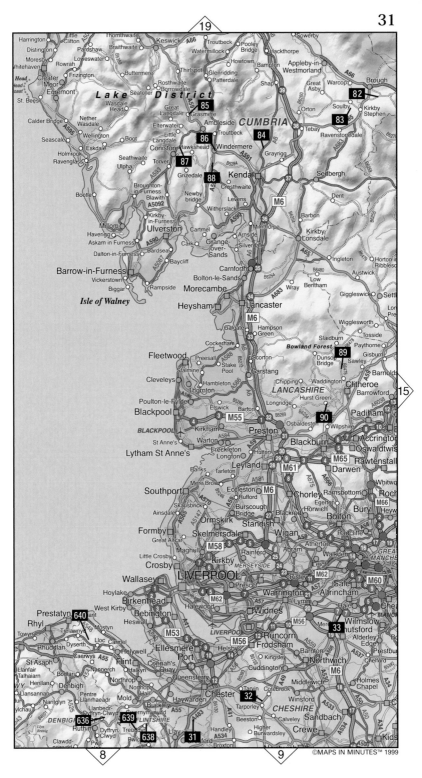

Map 14

©MAPS IN MINUTES™ 1999

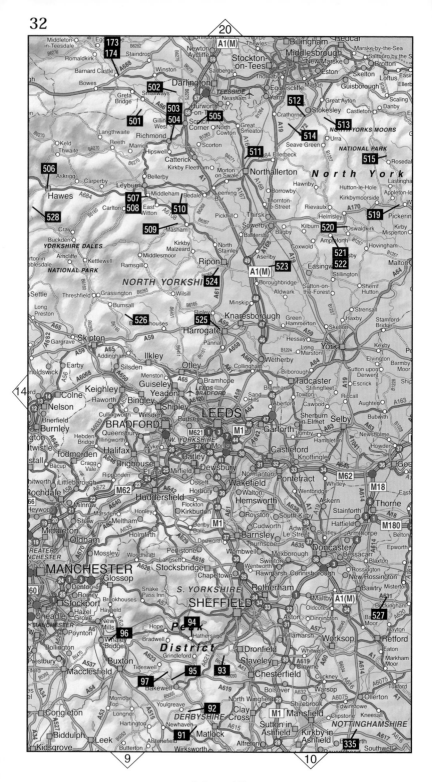

Map 15

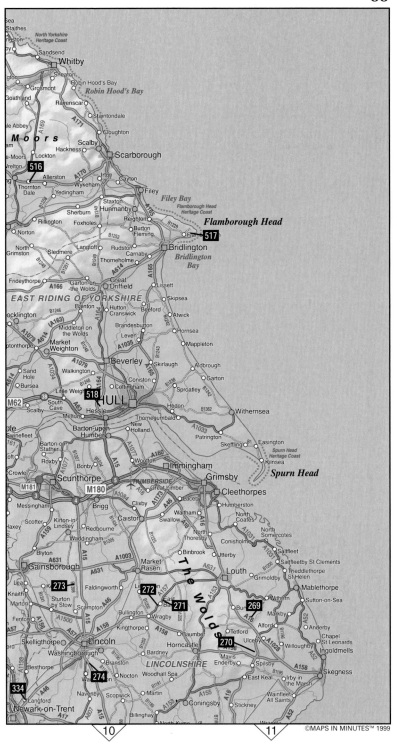

Map 16

©MAPS IN MINUTES™ 1999

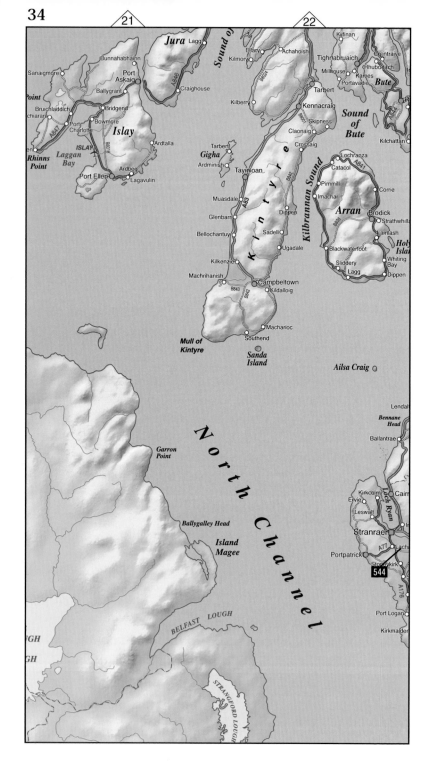

Map 17

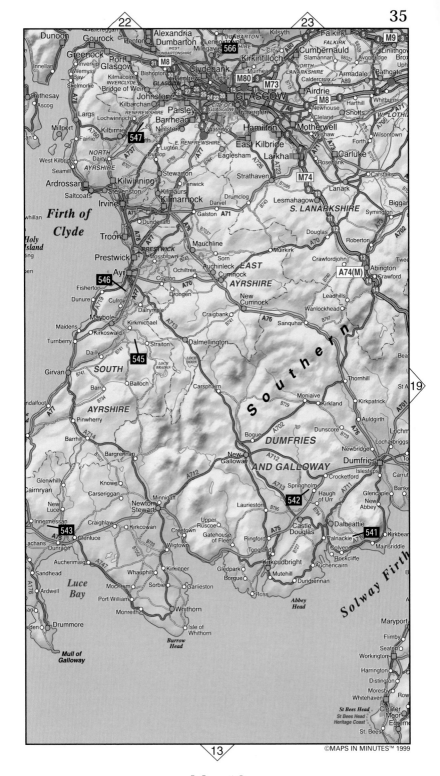

Map 18

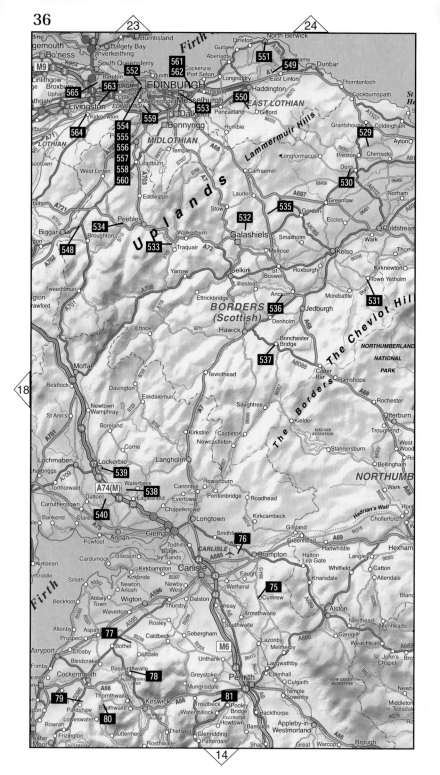

Map 19

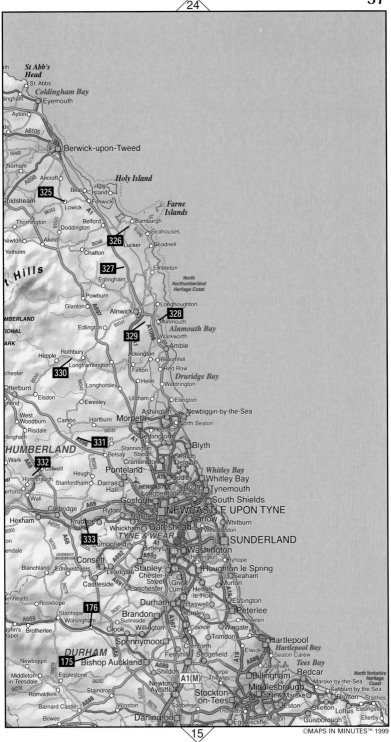

Map 20

©MAPS IN MINUTES™ 1999

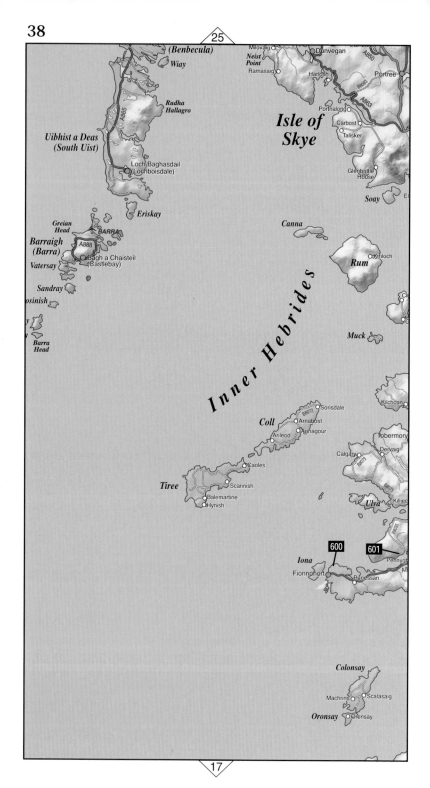

(Benbecula)
Wiay

Milovaig
Dunvegan

Neist
Point
Ramasaig
Harlosh

Isle of
Skye

Portree

Portnalong
Carbost
Talisker

Uibhist a Deas
(South Uist)

Rudha
Hallagro

Loch Baghasdail
(Lochboisdale)

Glenbrittle
House

Soay

Eriskay

Canna

Greian
Head
BARRA

Barraigh
(Barra)
A888

Vatersay

Bagh a Chaisteil
(Castlebay)

Rum

Kinloch

Sandray

osinish

Muck

Barra
Head

Inner Hebrides

Kilchoan

Sorisdale

Coll
B8072
Arnabost
Arinagour

Anleod

Tobermory

Calgary
Dervaig

Caoles

Tiree

Scarinish

Ulva
Killiec

Balemartine
Hynish

600   601

Pennyg

Iona

Fionnphort

Bunessan

Colonsay

Machrins
Scalasaig

Oronsay
Oronsay

Map 21

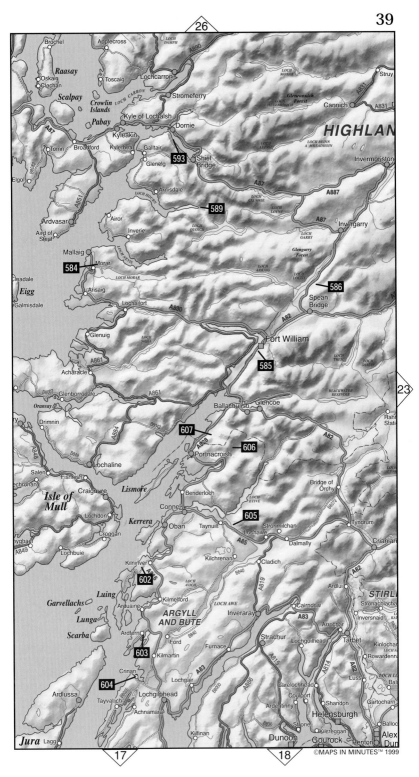

Map 22

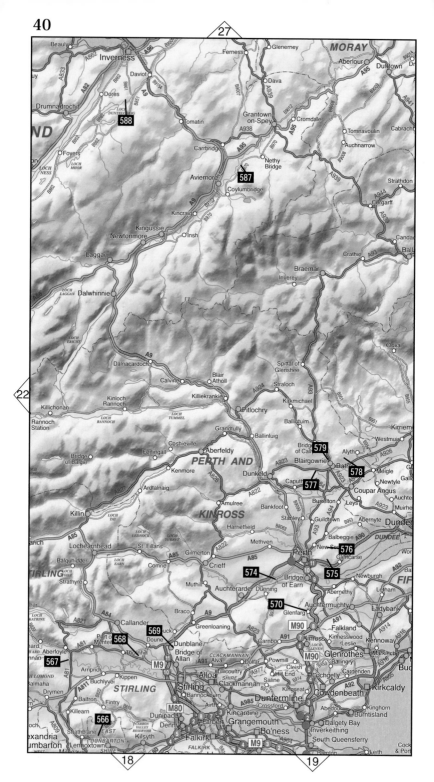

Map 23

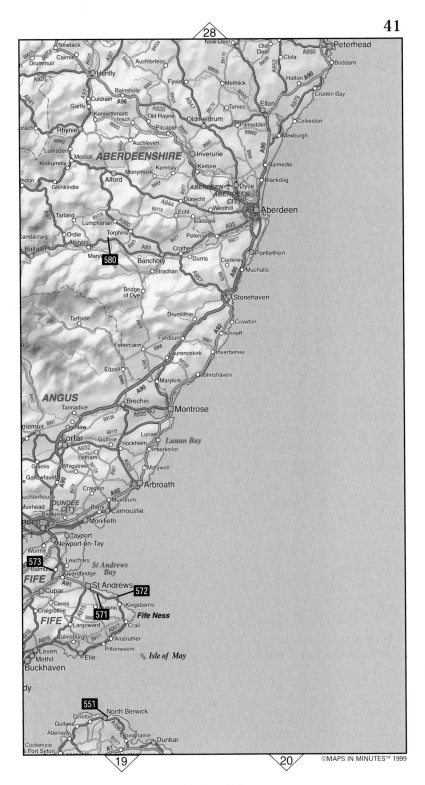

©MAPS IN MINUTES™ 1999

Map 24

Map 25

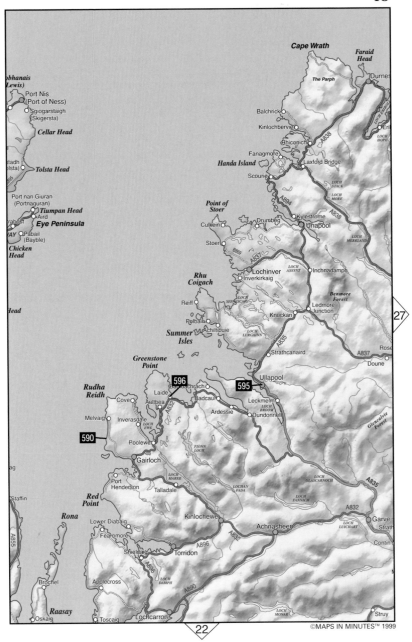

Cape Wrath

Faraid Head

The Parph

Durness

Balchrick

Kinlochbervie

Bhiconich

Fanagmore

Handa Island

Laxford Bridge

Scourie

LOCH STACK

LOCH MORE

Point of Stoer

Culkein

Drumbeg

Kylestrome

Uapool

LOCH MERKLAND

Stoer

B869

A837

B864

Lochinver

Inverkirkaig

LOCH ASSYNT

Inchnadamph

Rhu Coigach

Reiff

LOCH SIONASCAIG

BENMORE FOREST

Polbain

Achiltibuie

Knockan

Ledmore Junction

LOCH LURGAINN

Summer Isles

Strathcanaird

A835

A837

Rose

Doune

Greenstone Point

Ullapool

596 Badrachach

Rudha Reidh

Laide

Badcaul

595 Leckmelm

Cove

Aultbea

A832

Ardessie

Dundonnell

LOCH BROOM

Melvaig

Inverasdale

LOCH EWE

Glencalvie Forest

590

Poolewe

FIONN LOCH

Gairloch

LOCH MAREE

LOCH GLASCARNOCH

A835

Port Henderson

Talladale

LOCHAN FADA

LOCH FANNICH

Red Point

Lower Diabaig

Kinlochewe

Achnasheen

A832

Garve

LOCH LUICHART

Strath

Fearnmore

A896

A832

Contin

Rona

Shieldaig

Torridon

Brochel

A896

LOCH DAMPH

Applecross

A890

LOCH MONAR

Struy

Raasay

Oskaig

Toscaig

Lochcarron

©MAPS IN MINUTES™ 1999

Port Nis (Port of Ness)

Sgiogarstaigh (Skigersta)

Cellar Head

Tolsta Head

Port nan Giuran (Portnaguran)

Tiumpan Head

Eye Peninsula

Pabail (Bayble)

Chicken Head

27

Map 26

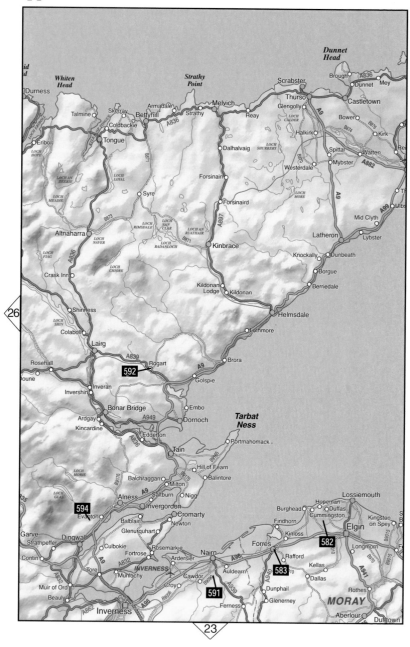

Map 27

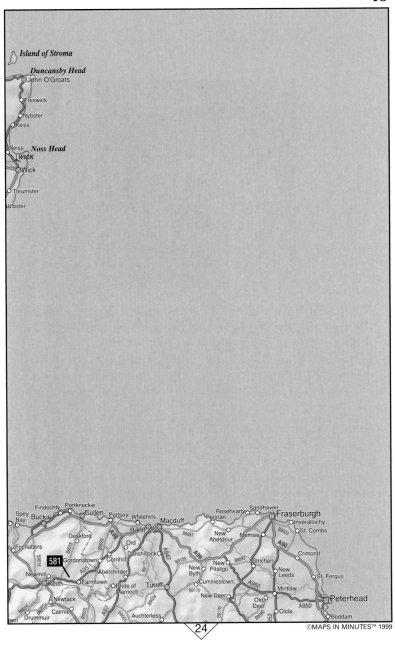

Island of Stroma

Duncansby Head
John O'Groats

Freswick

Nybster
Keiss

Reiss   Noss Head

WICK

Wick

Thrumster

Ulbster

Spey Bay   Findochty Portknockie
Buckie   Cullen Portsoy Whitehills   Macduff   Rosehearty Sandhaven   Fraserburgh
Pennan   Inverallochy
Fochabers   Deskford   Banff   St. Combs
              Ord   B9031   New Aberdour   Memsie
Gordonstown Cornhill Danshillock   Crimond
581   A947 A98 B9105
Newmill   Aberchirder   New Byth   New Pitsligo   B9093   Strichen   New Leeds
Keith   Farmtown   St. Fergus
       Bride of Marnoch   Turriff   Cuminestown   Mintlaw
Newtack   New Deer   Old Deer   Peterhead
Cairnie   B9024   B9170   Clola   A950
Drummuir   Auchterless   Boddam

24

©MAPS IN MINUTES™ 1999

Map 28

A word from Country Living

I'm delighted to welcome you to this new edition of *Special Places to Stay: British Bed & Breakfast*, produced by Alastair Sawday Publishing. Since its inception, *Country Living* magazine has celebrated the beauty and diversity of the countryside and has keenly supported the many rural businesses that are associated with it. We are therefore particularly pleased to be associated with this book which contains more than 600 different, mostly rural, enterprises.

From a Somerset retreat to a Scottish castle, from moated houses to self-catering barns, you'll find plenty of original and inspiring places to stay in whether you are planning a weekend for two or week away with the family. Many houses have large and beautiful gardens – one includes a sunken Italianate garden – and some have swimming pools; a few even host concerts and plays.

Country Living's idea of what makes a special place to stay is very similar to that of Alastair Sawday Publishing. So if you are looking for beautiful and often unusual settings, warm and comfortable bedrooms, delicious home-cooked breakfasts (often using organic or home-grown produce) and a thoroughly genuine welcome, then look no further. I hope you will enjoy this book and continue to enjoy reading *Country Living* magazine.

Susy Smith

Editor, *Country Living* magazine

ENGLAND

A journey is like a marriage. The certain way to be wrong is to think you control it.

John Steinbeck

The peace suggests rural retreat, the views of the floodlit Abbey remind you that you are in Bath. Simone's home is worthy of the glossiest magazines. It's sumptuous and luxurious; embroidered cotton bed linen, excellent bathroom fittings, fine cutlery. Haitian Simone spoils guests and does it with cross-cultural colour — breakfast here is Caribbean with fresh fruit, yoghurt, and cereals. The garden looks French and formal, with box parterre, lavender and roses. There are views across the canal to National Trust land, yet it's less than 15 minutes to the city centre. *Babies and children over 10 welcome.*

Rooms: 1 double, en suite; 1 twin and 1 single sharing en suite bathroom.

Price: From £27.50 p.p. Single occ. £40.

Breakfast: 7.30-9am.

Meals: Available close by.

Closed: Christmas Day.

Bristol, Bath & N.E. Somerset

From Bath city centre follow signs to American Museum. Pass Mercedes garage (300 yards up Bathwick Hill on right). Take first road on right after garage. House is 300 yards down on right.

Entry No: 1   Map no: 4

Mrs S. Johnson
Sydney Buildings
Bathwick Hill, Bath
Bath & N.E. Somerset BA2 6DB
Tel: 01225 463033
Fax: 01225 463033
e-mail: jeannette.lichner@pobox.com
Web: www.sawdays.co.uk

The Georgian and the Victorian blend seamlessly in this lovingly restored house built by a Bath merchant in 1778. Derek and Maria have decorated the rooms with colours authentic to the era, amassed period furniture and restored the veranda to its former glory. There is significant road noise in the two front bedrooms, but there is also a quiet room overlooking the rear garden and many guests have stayed here happily. Fires, a mahogany four-poster, garden ponds, canal-side walks and memorably charming, relaxed hosts. All this a 15-20 minute stroll by the canal from the wonders of Bath.

Rooms: 2 doubles, both en suite (shower); 1 twin with private bathroom.

Price: £30-£37.50 p.p. Single occ. £50-£55. Min. 2 nights stay.

Breakfast: Flexible.

Meals: Good food available locally.

Closed: Sometimes at Christmas.

Actually on the A4, towards city centre, near junction of A46. Opposite Bath Rugby Club training ground. Private locked car park on premises.

Entry No: 2   Map no: 4

Derek & Maria Beckett
Cedar Lodge
13 Lambridge
Bath
Bath & N.E. Somerset BA1 6BJ
Tel: 01225 423468

Built in 1820 and with lovely views over the city, this is a truly fine Bath stone 'residence'. It is beautifully furnished with pieces accumulated over the years; it feels evolved rather than designed. Mrs Bowman gives her guests the freedom to come and go and they also have the run of the large living room with French doors. Open these doors and step out onto an exceptional walled garden that she largely manages herself. In one bedroom there are a bow-fronted mahogany chest, a bureau, an arched alcove bookshelf and a bathroom across the hall. The second looks over the North lawn. *Children over 12 welcome.*

Rooms: 2 twins, each with separate bathroom (bath/shower).

Price: £25 p.p. Single supp. £3.

Breakfast: By arrangement.

Meals: Available locally.

Closed: Christmas & New Year.

From Bath city centre, 15 minute walk. Quarter way up Bathwick Hill. Pass Cleveland Walk on left, house is one of the big ones on the right.

Entry No: 3   Map no: 4

Mrs Elspeth Bowman
9 Bathwick Hill
Bath
Bath & N.E. Somerset BA2 6EW
Tel: 01225 460812

A grand, listed, Georgian hotel built in 1750 by John Wood the Elder, but it feels more like a happy family home. There are toys scattered about, a welcome absence of ceremony, and simple, unimposing bedrooms (pine and prints), some cottagey and some Georgian. At the heart of the house is a large, comfortable sitting room. Tea can be taken here, looking onto the garden (with tennis court) and overseen by court paintings of Charles I and II. Long, lush views — and the walled garden cottage is very special.

Rooms: 2 twins and 4 doubles, all en suite (bath); 2 singles, both en suite (shower), 1 with private wc.

Price: £25-£39 p.p. Single occ. £38-£48.

Breakfast: Until 10am. £3.50 p.p. extra for Full English.

Meals: Available locally.

Closed: 20-30 December.

Breakfast on the terrace and gaze over the honey-coloured collage of Regency Bath below, a stunning spectacle from this lofty vantage point. Much-travelled Anne's Cotswold stone house is an oriental excursion, enriched by batiks, silk paintings and other Malaysian memorabilia. Exotic plants and hand-painted pots fringe the garden pond that shimmers with fish. Anne, once a Far East head-hunter, now channels her considerable vitality and energy into caring for guests.

Rooms: 1 twin/family, en suite (shower); 1 double, en suite (bath & shower); 1 double/single with private shower room.

Price: From £25-£30 p.p. Single occ. £35.

Breakfast: Flexible.

Meals: Excellent pub within walking distance.

Closed: Occasionally.

M4, junc. 18, A46 (Bath) for 9 miles. Ignore A4 Bath sign. Right onto A363 (Bradford on Avon) for 150 yds, fork left (Bathford Hill). First right into Church St. House 200 yds on right with iron gates.

Entry No: 4   Map no: 4

Rosamund & John Napier
Eagle House
Church Street, Bathford
Bath & N.E. Somerset BA1 7RS
Tel: 01225 859946
Fax: 01225 859430
e-mail: jonap@eagleho.demon.co.uk
Web: www.eaglehouse.co.uk

M4 exit 18, A46. A46 joins A4, then left for Chippenham. At r'bout, A363 (Bradford on Avon). Bear left under bridge, into Bathford. 1.5 miles on, left after pub (Lower Kingsdown Rd). Bear right at bottom, house 300 yds on left.

Entry No: 5   Map no: 4

Anne Venus
Owl House
Kingsdown, Nr. Box
Bath & N.E. Somerset SN13 8BB
Tel: 01225 743883
Fax: 01225 744450
e-mail: venus@zetnet.co.uk
Web: www.owlhouse.co.uk

Bath stone from Combe Down was trundled down the hill to build all that celebrated Regency elegance. We defy you not to be hit by the 'wow' factor when you stand in the gorgeous garden and see the steep valley stretching out before you. The Sticklands do a professional job, yet haven't lost any of the personal, caring touch that has brought guests back time and time again. Organic eggs and proper bacon for breakfast, fluffy towels and a range of teas in the bedrooms. A peaceful retreat from the bustle of the city.

Rooms: 2 twins/doubles and 1 family room, all en suite (shower).

Price: From £30 p.p. Single occ. £35. £5 supp. per room for single night stay.

Breakfast: 7-9.30am.

Meals: Dinner, £18-£22 p.p., by prior arrangement. B.Y.O. wine.

Closed: Christmas.

200 years ago, it wasn't so much 'messing about in boats' — it was more a way of life; canals were arteries of the burgeoning Industrial Revolution. This lock-keeper's cottage was built in 1801 by the Somerset Coal Canal Company. The Wheeldons own the stretch of canal running through the garden carrying brightly-coloured narrow boats (hire an electric launch for a day's pootling) and there is a peaceful towpath walk to the local pub and to a café/restaurant. The cottage has kept its character, and the Wheeldons have 'fed and watered' guests for years.

Rooms: 1 double and 1 twin/double both with private bath and shower.

Price: £24-£26 p.p. Single supp. by arrangement.

Breakfast: Until 9am.

Meals: Available nearby.

Closed: Christmas & New Year.

From A36 about 3 miles out of Bath on the Warminster road, take uphill road by traffic lights and Viaduct Inn. Take 1st turn left (approx. 100 yds) signed Monkton Combe. After village (0.5 miles on) Grey Lodge first house on left.

Entry No: 6   Map no: 4

5 miles south of Bath just off the A36, 50 yds north of BP garage. (The entrance is at an oblique angle so it is wise to turn in the garage and approach the entrance from the south.)

Entry No: 7   Map no: 4

Jane & Anthony Stickland
Grey Lodge, Summer Lane
Combe Down, Bath
Bath & N.E. Somerset BA2 7EU
Tel: 01225 832069
Fax: 01225 830161
e-mail: greylodge@freenet.co.uk
Web: www.sawdays.co.uk

Tim & Wendy Wheeldon
Dundas Lock Cottage
Monkton Combe, Bath
Bath & N.E. Somerset BA2 7BN
Tel: 01225 723890
Fax: 01225 723890
e-mail: dundaslockcottage@freenet.co.uk
Web: www.sawdays.co.uk

Meandering lanes lead you to this 17th-century cottage; quintessentially English with roses round the door, a grandfather clock in the hall and an air of genteel tranquillity. Julia Naismith has updated the cottage charm with Regency mahogany in the inglenook dining room and sumptuous sofas in the sitting room. Bedrooms have long views over farmland and undulating countryside; behind is a conservatory and sloping, south-facing garden with pond and benches. Do ask your hostess about Bath (just 20 minutes away) — she knows the city well.

Rooms: 2 king-size doubles, sharing en suite (bath & shower), let only to members of same party; 1 twin, en suite (bath & shower); 1 single, en suite (bath & shower).

Price: From £25 p.p. No single supp. £75 per night family rate.

Breakfast: Until 9.30am.

Meals: Dinner, by arrangement, 3 courses, £18 p.p.

Closed: Never.

From Bath, A36 to Woolverton. Opposite Red Lion pub, take turning for Laverton. One mile to x-roads, and continue towards Faukland (signed). Downhill for 80 yards. House on left, just above farm entrance on right.

Entry No: 8   Map no: 4

Mrs Julia Naismith
Hollytree Cottage
Laverton
Bath
Bath & N.E. Somerset BA3 6QZ
Tel: 01373 830786
Fax: 01373 830786

So much to delight the eye — a Georgian corner cupboard, mellow elm floors, pottery, pictures and coloured glass within and, without, the quaintly symmetrical front elevation with Venetian windows. Built in 1760, the house was sold for £400 to Somerset Council in 1920 when it became a police house. Today a cottagey charm reigns — bedrooms are pretty and simple with cushions piled on patchwork quilts and the bathroom has new pine panelling. This is a fascinating village that oozes history; there are two famous pubs nearby — The George, where Judge Jeffries held court and the Fleur de Lys, where the worst of his villains were hung.

Rooms: 1 double and 1 single, sharing bathroom.

Price: £25 p.p.

Breakfast: Flexible.

Meals: Available locally.

Closed: Christmas.

From Bath or Warminster, Norton St Philip is signed (A366) off A36, approx. 7 miles south of Bath. After village sign, the house is soon on the left. If you come to the crossroads, you have gone too far.

Entry No: 9   Map no: 4

Judy Jenkinson
The Old Police House
Town Barton
Norton St. Philip
Bath & N.E. Somerset BA3 6LN
Tel: 01373 834308
e-mail: grahamjenkinson@cs.com

You may expect a formidable landlady but you get Jayne — bustling about in the friendliest way. Her welcome, and that of her dogs, is a stark counterpoint to the formality of the handsome corniced sitting room where you will be offered tea when you arrive. The lovely walled garden makes the perfect place to idle away a few moments on a summer afternoon. The rooms are comfortable enough, big and homely, but it is Jayne who adds something special.

Rooms: 2 main twins/doubles, both en suite (bath). 1 room is in flat with sitting and dining room and small kitchen. Folding beds available.

Price: £30 p.p. In flat, £32.50 p.p. £15 p.p. on extra beds. Single occ. £50.

Breakfast: Flexible.

Meals: Available locally.

Closed: Christmas & New Year.

"Yes, yes, yes", quoth the inspector. She loved the way it manages to combine elegance with a sense of cosiness. Logs burn in the fire, the colours are warm, the dresser is Welsh, the stones are flagged. The kitchen — Aga and terracotta tiles — is beamed and easy around the cherry wood refectory table. There is peace and comfort among the quirky internal touches, the winding stairs and old bread-oven. Angharad is an aromatherapist (treatment available). The bedroom is "pure magic", with gorgeous furniture. *Children over 5 welcome.*

Rooms: 1 double, en suite (shower).

Price: £24 p.p. No single supp.

Breakfast: Flexible.

Meals: Light supper by arrangement or local pubs.

Closed: Never.

From Bath follow A36 to Woolverton. Turn left at Woolverton House Hotel. After 1 mile cross bridge and take 3rd right. House is signed, 4th on right.

Entry No: 10   Map no: 4

Jayne & Oliver Holder
Irondale House
67 High Street
Rode
Bath & N.E. Somerset BA3 6PB
Tel: 01373 830730
Fax: 01373 830730
e-mail: holder@irondalebnb.freeserve.co.uk

From Bath A367 Exeter road. After 3 miles, left opposite Burnt House Inn, signed 'Wellow 3 miles'. There, park in the square by the Fox and Badger pub. House is 2 doors down.

Entry No: 11   Map no: 4

Angharad Rhys-Roberts
Honey Batch Cottage
Railway Lane, Wellow
Bath
Bath & N.E. Somerset BA2 8QG
Tel: 01225 833107

Come at the right time and the beautiful crops of sulphur-yellow rapeseed and vibrant blue linseed blanket the Addicotts' acres. The flax from linseed is used to heat the sturdy listed house — it has stone mullion windows, open fires and big bedrooms. Your hosts manage the mix of B&B-ing and farming with an easy-going humour. There are dressers with old china, Chinese rugs on wooden floors, swathes of Bath stone and a smattering of Africana. They are passionate supporters of Bath Rugby Club.

Rooms: 1 double, en suite (bath); 1 twin and 2 doubles with shared bathroom/shower.

Price: From £25 p.p. Single occ. £32.

Breakfast: Flexible.

Meals: Available locally.

Closed: Christmas & New Year.

From A4 W of Bath, A39 through Corston. 1 mile on, just before Wheatsheaf Pub (on right), turn right. Signposted 200m along lane on right.

Entry No: 12   Map no: 3

Gerald & Rosaline Addicott
Corston Fields Farm
Corston, Bath
Bath & N.E. Somerset BA2 9EZ
Tel: 01225 873305
Fax: 01225 873305
e-mail: corston.fields@btinternet.com
Web: www.sawdays.co.uk

A large old Mendip-style 'long cottage' with mullioned windows, beams made of ships' timbers and... a vineyard! The flavour is Somerset and old stone barns and you are temptingly close to the treasures of Bath and Wells, the gardens and concerts at Stourhead, Gregorian chant in Downside Abbey and Babbington House. Bedrooms are light and pretty, with fresh flowers and good towels. No sitting room but tea in the beautiful walled garden is a rich compensation. Interesting, child-friendly hosts. Excellent value.

Rooms: 1 twin/family, en suite (shower) and 1 small double/single with shared/private bathroom.

Price: £17-£18.50 p.p.

Breakfast: Flexible.

Meals: Available locally at excellent pubs.

Closed: Never.

From Bath take A367 Wells Rd through Radstock. After 3 miles, at large r'bout, take B3139 towards Trowbridge. After 1.1 miles, right up drive. Melon Cottage is at top, visible from road.

Entry No: 13   Map no: 3

Virginia & Hugh Pountney
Melon Cottage Vineyard
Charlton, Radstock
Nr. Bath
Bath & N.E. Somerset BA3 5TN
Tel: 01761 435090
e-mail: pountney@pountneyb.freeserve.co.uk

Only a short walk from the surprisingly beautiful Chew Valley lake. Sandra is as friendly as can be, offering you tea and biscuits on arrival. There are 130 acres of farmland and this is a much-loved house: stone fireplace, stone walls, oak beams and a glass-topped 18th-century well in the dining room. The rooms are entirely comfortable, the double has stripey wallpaper and chintzy bedspread and cushions. Pretty gardens around the farmhouse, two lovely Labradors and, often, new-born calves in the fields. Breakfasts are particularly good.

Rooms: 1 double and 1 family room (large double and 2 singles), both with basins and sharing shower room.

Price: From £20 p.p. for one night; £18 p.p. for longer stays. Single supp. £5.

Breakfast: Until 9am.

Meals: Packed lunch by arrangement. Other meals available locally.

Closed: December-March.

Smothered in clematis, jasmine, roses and honeysuckle — the scent wafts delectably through the bedroom window — it's hard to believe that Spring Farm, with its beautiful walled garden and lush meadow of wild flowers, is only a few miles from Bristol. Plump beds and lovely linen in light, airy bedrooms decorated with elegant country simplicity. Laze in the garden, lulled by the sound of summer bees. In winter, breakfast by an open fire, enveloped by the friendly, generous atmosphere of the Gallannaughs' impeccable English farmhouse with its Aga, terracotta tiles and antique pine.

Rooms: 1 large double, en suite (bath); 1 double with private bathroom.

Price: £20-£25 p.p. No single supp.

Breakfast: Until 9am.

Meals: Packed lunch £5 p.p.

Closed: Christmas.

From Chew Stoke village, take B3114 towards Compton Martin. 1 mile on, take small turning to right, then branch down 'No Through Road'. Farm is at end of lane.

Entry No: 14   Map no: 3

Sandra Hasell
Herons Green Farm
Compton Martin
Chew Valley
Bath & N.E Somerset BS40 6NL
Tel: 01275 333372
Fax: 01275 333041
e-mail: hasell@farmersweekly.net

From Bristol take A38 for airport. 5 miles out, turn left on B3130 towards Winford. On leaving village, bear right up Regil Lane. After Regil Stone, Spring Farm is 5th on right.

Entry No: 15   Map no: 3

Judy & Roger Gallannaugh
Spring Farm
Regil
Nr. Winford
Bristol BS40 8BB
Tel: 01275 472735
e-mail: bookings@springfarm.swest.co.uk
Web: www.sawdays.co.uk

Cool and uncluttered, with wooden floors and flagstones, a piano and an open fire. They are interesting people, he ex-business in Africa, she an English (EFL) teacher — with small, well-behaved children. The house is Grade II listed and has lovely views across the Vale of Wrington. The bedrooms are in a wooden-floored wing (built long and low, around 1760, for rope-making); it looks onto a paddock and a copse. You feel very private here. The bed is huge, made specially in Africa, with the best linen and there's a large bathroom with an old pine dresser stacked with books. Only five minutes from Bristol airport.

Rooms: 1 king-size room, en suite.

Price: £25 p.p. Single supp. £10.

Breakfast: 8-10am.

Meals: Supper from £12.50 p.p.

Closed: Christmas & New Year.

A retreat where you set your own agenda. Don't come in search of answers, but perhaps to forget the questions. You could try yoga or reflexology, or learn about 'Healing for Life' or 'The God Within' — just bring your toothbrush and an open mind; the ethos is entirely non-prescriptive. There are books everywhere, simple bedrooms (warm and spotless), communal dining, silent suppers, good food, open country all around and some of the nicest people you could hope to meet. A very special place indeed.

Rooms: 27 twins and 8 singles.

Price: Full board, £32.50-£37.50 p.p.

Breakfast: 8.30am.

Meals: All meals available, included in price.

Closed: Never.

From Bristol A38. Four miles past the airport, take right to Lower Langford/Wrington. 200 yards on, 5th, pink, house on left.

Entry No: 16   Map no: 3

Rebecca Wimshurst
Dring Cottage
Lower Langford
Bristol BS40 5BW
Tel: 01934 862243
Fax: 01934 862670
e-mail: wimshurst@dringcottage.fsnet.co.uk

On A38, south from Bristol, left onto B3130, signed Winford. There, 2nd right, manor is signed. House at top.

Entry No: 17   Map no: 3

James Fahey
Winford Manor Retreat
Winford
Bristol BS40 8DW
Tel: 01275 472262
Fax: 01275 472065
e-mail: omegatrust@aol.com
Web: www.winfordmanorretreat.com

Unabashedly 1920s mock-Tudor with an oak-panelled hall and a great engraved fireplace. This is a generous house on the edge of the Bristol Downs, perfectly placed for country quiet in the evening after city bustle in the daytime. Light from the garden floods in and Philippa, with long experience of five-star hotels, revels in doing a proper job. The breakfast menu is mouth-watering and the morning papers come with it. The guestrooms are 'fully-equipped', pastel-decorated and eminently comfortable; your hosts are affable and interested. *Children over seven welcome.*

Rooms: 1 twin, en suite (bath); 2 doubles, en suite shower and private wc; 1 single with private bathroom.

Price: £30 p.p. Single occ. £38-£48.

Breakfast: Flexible.

Meals: Available locally.

Closed: Christmas & New Year.

From M5, exit 17 onto A4018. At 4th r'bout take 3rd exit into Parry's Lane. Left into Saville Rd. 3rd right into Hollybush Lane. Turn 1st left immed. after 2nd road hump into Downs Edge. Drive to end.

Entry No: 18   Map no: 3

Alan & Philippa Tasker
Downs Edge
Saville Road, Stoke Bishop
Bristol BS9 1JA
Tel: 0117 968 3264
Fax: 0117 968 3264
e-mail: downsedge@sbishop99.freeserve.co.uk
www.sawdays.co.uk

An easy-going house and hostess — there's enough of a family feel to make you feel at home in the city and enough privacy to ensure a peaceful stay. Anne thoroughly enjoys meeting guests and has an easy-going humour. She has furnished rooms carefully with flowers, books, pretty china and good linen — the twins each have a double duvet to make them extra snug. Some strong colours — jade green in the double's shower room, terracotta in the dining room and a vibrant silk tablecloth. It's a short walk to Clifton village and Suspension Bridge and to Bristol's Harbourside. Excellent value for city convenience.

Rooms: 2 doubles and 1 twin, all en suite (shower).

Price: From £25 p.p. Single occ. £38.

Breakfast: Flexible.

Meals: Available locally.

Closed: Christmas Eve.

From M5 SW, junc. 18. Follow A4 signs to Bristol West and airport. Under suspension bridge & follow city sign painted on road. Then follow lane signed Clifton. Left into Clifton Vale just before church, & first right into Camden Terrace. House on right.

Entry No: 19   Map no: 3

Anne Malindine
14 Camden Terrace
Clifton Vale
Bristol BS8 4PU
Tel: 0117 914 9508
Fax: 0117 914 9508
e-mail: anne@amalindine.freeserve.co.uk

The house is full of books, paintings and character — a place that, rather than provide a kettle and telly in each room, provides the whole house for you to be at home in. Valerie is artistic and musical (there is a piano to play) and interested in people. John Wood the Younger lived here; it has an unusual entrance, a secret garden... and is right beside the (clockless) Saxon/Norman church. The atmosphere is cosy: Liberty curtains and a log fire, leaded windows, winding stairs, semicircular bathroom windows, open fireplaces and a walled garden. Booking essential. *Children over eight welcome.*

Rooms: 1 double with basin and 1 twin sharing bathroom and separate shower.

Price: From £16 p.p. No single supp.

Breakfast: Until 9.30am.

Meals: Dinner, 4 courses, £11 p.p. with notice (not Thurs). B.Y.O. wine. Good pub food locally. Packed lunch possible.

Closed: December, January & February.

An exceptional house in a quiet, secluded hamlet, yet minutes from Bath and Bristol. Julia exudes warmth and enthusiasm and is utterly natural. Both she and Patrick love their garden — immaculate lawns, deep herbaceous borders, croquet lawn, masses of roses and clematis, burgeoning fruit and vegetable garden and views to the Mendips. "I could hardly tear myself away," wrote our inspector. On warm days breakfast is served on the terrace and guests have exclusive use of the drawing room. Julia has deep local knowledge. *Children over 12 welcome.*

Rooms: 1 twin/double, with extra single bed, en suite (bath & shower).

Price: £30 p.p. No single supp.

Breakfast: Flexible.

Meals: Dinner, £15-£20 p.p., by prior arrangement. Good food available locally, too.

Closed: Mid-December-mid-January.

From A420, A431 into Bitton, right beside White Hart. Church on left, 25 yards of garden wall, then 3 entrances on left. Take middle one. Mrs Atkins would like to talk you through these instructions on booking.

Entry No: 20   Map no: 3

Valerie Atkins
Granchen
Church Road
Bitton
Bristol BS30 6LJ
Tel: 0117 932 2423

From Bath, A4 west. At r'bout by Globe Inn, left onto A39 towards Wells. Through Corston (ignore Burnett sign), after 0.5 miles take B3116, SHARP right. After 1 mile left signed Burnett and next right. House 100 yds on left.

Entry No: 21   Map no: 3

Patrick & Julia Stevens
Brooklands
Burnett
Keynsham
Bristol BS31 2TF
Tel: 0117 986 8794
Fax: 0117 986 8794

Cathedral views from the walled garden and lots of ancient, narrow streets and medieval buildings to discover in this bustling market town. Sheila runs her large, peaceful 17th-century house with care; she serves locally-baked bread and home-made marmalade at the long mahogany dining table. The feel is traditional English. The south-facing bedrooms have country antiques and lovely views of the beautiful walled garden. The sublime Cathedral is a mere five minutes' walk away and Cambridge 15 miles.

Rooms: 1 double with private bathroom; 1 twin, en suite (bath).

Price: £24 p.p. Single supp. £16.

Breakfast: Until 9.30am.

Meals: Available locally.

Closed: 20 December-2 January and for annual holiday.

Cambridgeshire

Entering Ely from Cambridge on A10, turn left at lights by Lamb Hotel. Left again at next lights, after 200m into Egremont St. House is last on left with off-street parking just beyond.

Entry No: 22   Map no: 11

Sheila Friend-Smith
Old Egremont House
31 Egremont Street
Ely
Cambridgeshire CB6 1AE
Tel: 01353 663118
Fax: 01353 66968

A Grade II-listed house whose period elegance clearly encourages long stays — only three owners since a doctor built it in the 1800s. Lots of original features — high ceilings, tall windows, wood floors, cast-iron baths, an enormous log-burning fireplace — yet it all feels open and light; white prevails, fresh and bright. Breakfast is at the old pine farmhouse table where the food is "brilliant". Robin and Jenny slipped the leash and left London for the Isle of Ely, where everything, everybody, slows down. Join them, and see one of England's loveliest Cathedrals, too.

Rooms: 1 double suite, 1 family suite and 1 twin, all en suite (bath).

Price: From £25 p.p. Single occ. from £40. Short break rates available. Min. 2 nights stay at weekends.

Breakfast: 8.30-9.30am; or times by arrangement.

Meals: Good restaurants nearby.

Closed: Christmas & New Year.

It's a racing cert — you'll find an engaging style running alongside the most delicious of breakfasts here in the wistful *Waterland* world of Graham Swift's novel. (Malcolm's an equine buff). We cannot overstate the quality of the breakfast: locally sourced fresh produce, soft cheeses, hams, black puddings, kippers, haddock. Jan, formerly an illustrator, cooks and attends to the décor — old pine, huge cushions, handsome wallpapers and fresh flowers. A Georgian home, croquet lawn and conservatory — a winner!

Rooms: 1 twin/double and 1 single sharing bathroom; 1 double, en suite (shower).

Price: Double from £25 p.p. Single occ. £30-£35. Min. 2 nights in high season.

Breakfast: Flexible.

Meals: Available locally.

Closed: Christmas.

Cathedral House is 75 yards down from Tourist Information Centre, in the centre of Ely, near the Cathedral.

Entry No: 23   Map no: 11

Robin & Jenny Farndale
Cathedral House
17 St. Mary's Street, Ely
Cambridgeshire CB7 4ER
Tel: 01353 662124
Fax: 01353 662124
e-mail: farndale@cathedralhouse.co.uk
Web: www.cathedralhouse.co.uk

Take A142 Newmarket to Ely road, through Fordham and turn right at Murfitts Lane; at the end, right into Carter St and Queensberry is 200m on left next to Fordham Moor Rd.

Entry No: 24   Map no: 11

Jan & Malcolm Roper
Queensberry
196 Carter Street
Fordham, Ely
Cambridgeshire CB7 5JU
Tel: 01638 720916
Fax: 01638 720233

Some of the finest sunsets and an observatory for star-gazers. It is also marvellous bicycling country, flat and gentle (you may hire bikes). Freda is an ex-teacher, married to a local GP, and there is an aura of quiet decency, added to by the home-made jams and breads, the organic meat, the old cream earthenware tiles and the low-ceilinged dining room with Welsh dresser and oak chest. Your small bedroom is in a converted barn — there are books and music, fresh space of your own and a two-acre garden with summerhouse to enjoy. You can stay in the barn and self-cater if you wish.

Rooms: 1 double with private bathroom, sitting room and kitchen.

Price: From £25 p.p. Single supp. £5. Self-catering £250 p.w.

Breakfast: Until 9.30am.

Meals: Available locally.

Closed: Christmas & New Year.

A 1780s Adam-style house tucked quietly away at the edge of the village and with a lovely garden and water features. The sitting room, with Tudor brick walls, drain-brick floors, fireplace and old velvet sofas is the former coach-house, and Sally and Phil add thoughtful touches to make you feel at home, newspapers and soft drinks among them. It is a beautifully kept house, with a grand piano, deeply comfortable chairs and lots of books and games in the guest sitting room. *Children by arrangement.*

Rooms: 2 doubles, both en suite (shower).

Price: £30-£40 p.p. Single occ. £50.

Breakfast: 8-9.30am.

Meals: Dinner £27.50 p.p. Supper £15 p.p. Picnics £15 p.p. B.Y.O. wine.

Closed: Never.

From St. Ives take A1123 for Bluntisham. On nearing village, over bridge and turn first left into High Street. House is 500 yards on, on left.

Entry No: 25   Map no: 11

Freda Carlyle
Holmefields
16 High Street, Bluntisham
Huntingdon
Cambridgeshire PE283LD
Tel: 01487 841435
e-mail: roycarlyle@compuserve.com

A14 north of Cambridge and A10 towards Ely. Right into Waterbeach. Bear left at village green. Last house at end of High St before bend. Opposite 2 white houses, through white gates.

Entry No: 26   Map no: 11

Phil & Sally Myburgh
Berry House
High Street
Waterbeach
Cambridgeshire CB5 9JU
Tel: 01223 860702
Fax: 01223 860702
e-mail: sal@berryhouse.demon.co.uk

Just 10 minutes' walk from Kings College Chapel — services during term time — No 46 is, among the whooshing bicycles and swishing gowns, an oasis of peace, good taste and good conversation. Once home to college staff, the cottage has been lovingly converted and has a wonderful collection of paintings. Pride of place goes to one of the eccentric professors riding through the oh-so-recognisable streets. It is by Ophelia Redpath, who did the painting, too, of the house. No sitting room, but Alice is a marvellous hostess and a fount of information. *Children over 12 welcome.*

Rooms: 1 twin/double with private bathroom; 1 double, en suite (shower).

Price: £35 p.p. Single occ. £50.

Breakfast: Until 9am.

Meals: Available locally.

Closed: Never.

Nice people in an equally nice house; "take us as you find us" — a refreshing change from anxious hostesses making a lip-stiffening effort. It is all large, open, warm and friendly. One cosy and very private bedroom is up its own spiral staircase — a lovely conversion and sure winner of 1st prize in any Loo With A View competition. Sheep graze in the fields around the house and barn, bees slave to make your breakfast honey... this is a proper working farm, with both crops and sheep. Perfectly quiet, yet so close to Cambridge.

Rooms: 1 double and 1 family room, both en suite (shower).

Price: £22.50 p.p. Single occ. £25.

Breakfast: Until 9.30am.

Meals: Not available, but good local pubs.

Closed: 22 December-2 January.

Follow signs for city centre, BR station & Botanical Gardens. Panton St is one-way and should be approached via Bateman St from either Hills Rd or Trumpington Rd.

Entry No: 27   Map no: 11

Alice Percival
46 Panton Street
Cambridge
Cambridgeshire CB2 1HS
Tel: 01223 365285/568305
Fax: 01223 461142

Turn off the A1198 at Longstowe. The house is exactly 3 miles along the B1046, between Little Gransden and Longstowe.

Entry No: 28   Map no: 11

Sue Barlow
Model Farm
Little Gransden
Cambridgeshire SG19 3EA
Tel: 01767 677361
Fax: 01767 677883
e-mail: modelfarm@f1racing.co.uk

A large, elegant 1840 Regency-style house hugs the bend of a river on the edge of the quiet, historic village of Linton. Rooms are elegant and country squire-ish, with glass doors overlooking the large gardens. Some have river views. The lovely conservatory, draped with mimosa and with red and black tile floors, is for summer breakfasts, while in winter one repairs to the dark green dining room. Bedrooms are comfortable and well-equipped, and stocked with books. Judith looks after all this and two teenage children, yet still finds time to be a charming and helpful hostess.

Rooms: 2 doubles, 1 en suite (bath); 1 with private bathroom.

Price: £22.50-£25 p.p. Single supp. £27-£30.

Breakfast: 7.30-9.30am.

Meals: Available locally.

Closed: Never.

A1307 from Cambridge, left into High Street. First right after The Crown (on left) into Horn Lane. House on right next to chapel and before ford.

Entry No: 29   Map no: 11

Judith Rossiter
Springfield House
14-16 Horn Lane
Linton
Cambridgeshire CB1 6HT
Tel: 01223 891383
Fax: 01223 890335

The Elizabethan oak and walnut staircase is among the finest you'll see. The Grade II*-listed house survived the great fire of Nantwich in 1583 and is reputed to be the finest in this medieval town; the 14th-century church next door is the oldest building. There are panelled rooms, large fireplaces and excellent breakfasts — organic stoneground bread, comb honey and free-range eggs. The guests' dining room is elegant but the family kitchen enticing, with its Provençal tiled floor and happy bustle. Bedrooms are homely — one is pink and floral, the other has bamboo bedheads with blue painted panelling. The Pearsons are lovely.

Rooms: 1 twin with basin and 1 double, sharing bathroom.

Price: £27.50 p.p. Single occ. £30.

Breakfast: Flexible.

Meals: Available locally.

Closed: Never.

M6 junc. 16 for Nantwich. There, over railway crossing, straight over 1st r'bout and 2nd left. 3rd right into 'Historic Town Centre'. Follow road round and house is on left (only one with front garden).

Entry No: 30   Map no: 9

Mrs Jean A. Pearson
Kiltearn House
33 Hospital Street
Nantwich
Cheshire CW5 5RL
Tel: 01270 628892
Fax: 01270 626646

Cheshire

"Our guests seem to oversleep". This is peace indeed. A haven for garden buffs, walkers, birdwatchers — Britain at its best with rare trees planted in 1860, flowers everywhere, a pond, a fruitful vegetable garden and a warm welcome from Rachel, a passionate gardener. She also embroiders her own designs which can be seen around the house. It is furnished in elegant, traditional style and the proportions of the light-filled drawing room and the big, high-ceilinged dining room feel just right. The bedrooms are light and large and there's tennis, too.

Rooms: 1 double and 1 twin/double, both en suite (bath). 1 single, half-tester, en suite (shower).

Price: £24 p.p. Single supp. £4.

Breakfast: Before 10.30am.

Meals: Dinner, £18 p.p., on request. B.Y.O. wine. Good village pubs within walking distance.

Closed: Christmas week-3 January.

From Chester, A55 west, then A5104 to Broughton. Left at 2nd r'bout to Pennyffordd on A5104. Through Broughton & over A55. First left to Kinnerton down Lesters Lane. House on right, opposite Mount Farm.

Entry No: 31   Map no: 9

Jonathan & Rachel Major
The Mount
Higher Kinnerton
Chester
Cheshire CH4 9BQ
Tel: 01244 660275
Fax: 01244 660275
Web: www.sawdays.co.uk

You quickly get the feel of Roughlow, planted as it is in the very hillside — it is simple, solid, authentic, and greatly loved. The cobbled entrance yard is a treasure box of carefully-nurtured natural textures and materials and flowering trees and shrubs. From the terrace, on a clear day, you can see for 40 miles. Bedrooms are big and furnished with great artistic flair; the suite is vast. Sally was once an interior designer and has an eye for colour and the ability to create a calming, uncluttered space. There's a tennis court and they both collect art — you will enjoy discovering it all.

Rooms: 3 twins/doubles, all en suite and 1 with sitting room.

Price: £25-£35 p.p. Single supp. £10.

Breakfast: 8-9am.

Meals: Dinner, £20 p.p., on request for minimum of 4 people. Good pubs & hotels nearby.

Closed: Never.

A51 from Chester. Cross r'bout at Tarvin & take A54 to Manchester (not Tarporley). Pass Elf garage. Take second right & follow signs to Willington. Straight over x-roads & up Chapel Lane. Farm on right at top of hill.

Entry No: 32   Map no: 9

Sally & Peter Sutcliffe
Roughlow Farm
Willington, Tarporley
Cheshire CW6 0PG
Tel: 01829 751199
Fax: 01829 751199
e-mail: sutcliffe@roughlow.freeserve.co.uk
Web: www.roughlow.freeserve.co.uk

A lovely little guest house on a quiet country lane with the village pub at the end of the drive, Dunham Massey Deer Park five minutes' walk away, and only six miles from Manchester. The rooms are modern and almost sumptuous (TV and video hidden in wooden cabinets) and have great country views. David designed the furniture. One bed is vast enough to deserve nine pillows. Janice is a trained cook, specialising in vegetable dishes. David, the 'Silver Fox', was a professional snooker player. Marvellous value so close to the city yet so rural. *Children over 12 welcome.*

Rooms: 1 7ft 6in bed, en suite (shower); 1 four-poster, en suite (bath and shower) and 1 double with large, private bathroom.

Price: From £30 p.p. Single occ. from £46.

Breakfast: Until 9.30am.

Meals: Dinner, 3 courses, from £17.50 p.p. Private dinner parties available on request.

Closed: Christmas & New Year.

Take A556 NE to Manchester, then left on A56 towards Lymm. At first pub turn right down Park Lane. House is next to The Swan With Two Nicks.

Entry No: 33   Map no: 14

David & Janice Taylor
Ash Farm Country Guest House
Park Lane
Little Bollington, nr. Altrincham
Cheshire WA14 4TJ
Tel: 0161 929 9290
Fax: 0161 928 5002

Two hundred years ago the Navy used to test cannons in the creek at the bottom of the garden, but now you hear only wildlife. Clive and Button have lovingly tended their 1744 house and created a comfortable home. They'll bring you scones in a sitting room alive with colour and light, and you eat your morning kippers and free-range eggs from a walnut table that cleverly conceals a snooker table. Cranberry covers on the old oak beds, wonderful views from a high brass bed and from the antique four-poster — there's an understated elegance here.

Rooms: 1 four-poster, 1 twin/double, both en suite (shower); 1 double with private bath.

Price: £32.50-£47.50 p.p. (for 2 night stays). Single person/single night supp. from £15.

Breakfast: Until 10.30am.

Meals: Available locally.

Closed: Occasionally.

A38 over Tamar Bridge. After 7 miles, A374 left towards Torpoint at Ring O'Bells pub in Antony. Right round back of pub, then 1st left to St. John. Left at small green. House 1st on right.

Entry No: 34   Map no: 2

Cornwall

Clive & Button Poole
The Old Rectory
St John-in-Cornwall
Nr. Torpoint
Cornwall PL11 3AW
Tel: 01752 822275
Fax: 01752 823322
e-mail: clive@oldrectory-stjohn.co.uk

Very special and intriguing, surrounded by tidal estuaries on three sides, Erth Barton is a Grade II-listed manor house that has its own chapel in which a 14th-century fresco clings to the walls. Its many rooms are filled with thousands of books and pictures. Guy is eccentric, often very funny and passionate about horses — bring your own, or some may be available to competent riders. Rooms, reached via four staircases, are simple and bright with old rugs, scattered books and fine views. "Fantastic views, fantastic house," said our inspector. *Children over 12 welcome.*

Rooms: 1 twin with separate private bathroom; 2 doubles, both en suite.

Price: £34 p.p. Single supp. £5.

Breakfast: Until 9.30am.

Meals: Dinner £20 p.p. B.Y.O wine.

Closed: Never.

Bring your own music... there's a boudoir grand to be played as well as a music centre you can use. Ann is fun and a natural entertainer. Wonderfully comfortable house with touches of luxury and matchless views over Plymouth Sound. It is at the top of a steep hill overlooking a charming village of 600 souls. Ann cooks superb meals with wholefood ingredients and local produce. She also makes her own muesli, bread, yoghurt and ice-cream and can even cater for vegans.

Rooms: 1 twin/double and 1 twin, both en suite (shower); 1 double, en suite (bath).

Price: £21-£27.50 p.p. Single supp. by arrangement.

Breakfast: Until 9.30am.

Meals: Dinner £20 p.p. Light supper £9 p.p.

Closed: Never.

From Plymouth take A38 & cross Tamar Bridge. Through bypass tunnel over r'bout. On top of next hill left to Trematon; through village to Elmgate. Take middle of 3 roads marked 'dead end'.

Entry No: 35   Map no: 2

Guy Bentinck
Erth Barton
Saltash
Cornwall PL12 4QY
Tel: 01752 842127
Fax: 01752 842127

B3247 towards Mount Edgcumbe. Turn right before the school, signposted Kingsand. Down hill to right, left fork on bend into Kingsand, 2nd left, then left again. House on left with yellow door. Avoid single track road.

Entry No: 36   Map no: 2

Ann Heasman
Cliff House
Devonport Hill, Kingsand
Cornwall PL10 1NJ
Tel: 01752 823110
Fax: 01752 822595
e-mail: info@cliffhse.abel.co.uk
Web: www.sawdays.co.uk

This is 'Cornwall's Forgotten Corner', in gorgeous countryside. The house is opposite the church, rooted in time and space; the massive walls echo their 400 years of history. There's great style everywhere, with farmhouse charm in the kitchen — Aga, pine chairs, chequered tablecloth, Welsh dresser — and sheer elegance in the flagstoned sitting room, with Farrow and Ball Library Red walls contrasting with heavy calico curtains, off-white sofas and church candles. Bedrooms have crisp cotton and great comfort. Your hosts are easy and relaxed and there is a games room, too, with bar billiards and table tennis. Excellent value.

Rooms: 1 king-size with extra single, en suite (shower) and 1 double, en suite (bath & shower); 1 double with private bathroom.

Price: £20 p.p. Single supp. £5.

Breakfast: Flexible.

Meals: Available locally.

Closed: Christmas & Boxing Day.

To Sheviock Barton on A374. House is opposite church.

Entry No: 37   Map no: 2

Carol & Tony Johnson
Sheviock Barton
Sheviock
Torpoint
Cornwall PL11 3EH
Tel: 01503 230793
Fax: 01503 230793

The setting will bowl you over, and so will the Walkers' warmth and talent (Nicky is an artist who will share her studio or give you lessons). This lovely old Georgian farmhouse has breathtaking views over undulating countryside, streams and wooded valleys — wander along a track beside the leat. Delicious breakfasts in the walled garden in summer, log fires, a good collection of books and two grand pianos inside. Lantallack is an inspiration for musicians, artists or anyone wanting to combine fun with peace and tranquillity. Cottage with stunning views for self-catering, too.

Rooms: 1 double, en suite (shower); 1 twin with basin, next to private bathroom. Cottage: sleeps 6/7.

Price: £25-£27.50 p.p. No single supp. Cottage from £255 per week.

Breakfast: Flexible.

Meals: Good pubs and restaurants nearby.

Closed: Never.

A38 through Saltash and on for 3 miles. At Landrake 2nd right signed New Barton. After 1 mile, left at white cottage signed Tideford, and house is 150 yds on, on right.

Entry No: 38   Map no: 2

Nicky Walker
Lantallack Farm
Landrake, Nr. Saltash
Cornwall PL12 5AE
Tel: 01752 851281
Fax: 01752 851281
e-mail: lantallack@ukgateway.net
Web: www.lantallack.co.uk

An old corn mill with the original water wheel now in the kitchen and with views down the garden to the salmon/sea trout river from the bedrooms. Richard is a keen fly fisherman and can fix up rods for visitors. Mariebel is a professional portrait painter who taught for many years; she's still happy to teach individuals or groups. Bicton is informal, comfortable and relaxed. Meals are eaten in the huge farmhouse kitchen or in the impressive slate-floored dining room. The Lynher Valley is unspoilt and enchanting, with lovely walks all round. *Children by arrangement.*

Rooms: 1 double, en suite (shower); 1 double with private, adjacent bathroom and wc.

Price: £25-£30 p.p. Single supp. by arrangement.

Breakfast: Flexible.

Meals: Dinner, £18 p.p., by arrangement.

Closed: Never.

The house is named after the hill and the peace within is as deep as the valley. You have utter privacy; a private entrance to your own fresh, elegant suite: a twin-bedded room and a large, square, high sitting room with double doors giving onto the wooded valley. There's a CD player, plus music, chocolates and magazines and you can have tea in the rambling garden that wraps itself around the house. Jos and Mary-Anne really want you to enjoy your stay; you will. Butcher's sausages and free-range eggs for breakfast. Perfect.

Rooms: 1 twin, en suite (bath/shower) with sitting room and adjoining single for child if needed.

Price: £30 p.p. Single supp. £10.

Breakfast: Flexible.

Meals: Dinner, 3 courses, £18 p.p., by prior arrangement. B.Y.O wine.

Closed: Christmas.

On A388 Callington-Launceston, left at Kelly Bray (opp. garage) to Maders. 400 yds after Maders, left to Golberdon and left at x-roads. After 400 yds, right down unmarked lane. Mill 0.75 miles on.

Entry No: 39   Map no: 2

Richard & Mariebel Allerton
Bicton Mill
Bicton
Nr. Liskeard
Cornwall PL14 5RF
Tel: 01579 383577
Fax: 01579 383577
Web: www.sawdays.co.uk

From Launceston, B3254 towards Liskeard. Go through Daw's House and South Petherwin, down steep hill and take last left before little bridge. House is first on left.

Entry No: 40   Map no: 2

Jos & Mary Anne Otway-Ruthven
Hornacott
South Petherwin
Launceston
Cornwall PL15 7LH
Tel: 01566 782461
Fax: 01566 782461

A happy extended family farm down a wild-flowered drive in a hidden fold of the Cornish countryside. Richard and Helen are your young hosts. There are ducks, a goat and a cat. Helen, an aromatherapist and reflexologist (you can book a treatment) is enthusiastic and gentle. Fabulous breakfasts, tea and home-made biscuits at the scrubbed pine table. Fresh fish is a dinner speciality. Bedrooms with lovely brass beds, crisp linen and soft towels — simplicity and charm. Botelet is a treasure house, highly original.

Rooms: 1 double and 1 twin (small double with single), both with basins and shared use of private bathroom.

Price: £25 p.p. Single supp. by arrangement.

Breakfast: Flexible.

Meals: Dinner, £20-£30 p.p. Packed lunch, cream teas and drinks are also available.

Closed: Occasionally.

Leave Liskeard on the A38. At Dobwalls take left fork, A390 signed St. Austell. After East Taphouse, turn left onto B3359 signed Looe. After 2 miles, turn right signed Botelet.

Entry No: 41   Map no: 2

The Tamblyn Family
Botelet
Herodsfoot, Liskeard
Cornwall PL14 4RD
Tel: 01503 220225
Fax: 01503 220225
e-mail: stay@botelet.co.uk
Web: www.botelet.co.uk

At the head of the old smuggling route — Polperro is just two miles away — sits this 14th-century Grade II*-listed hall house. The original smoke-blackened trusses tower over the canopied bed; ancient charm blended perfectly with comfort. There are three dressing gowns in descending order of size and you have your own sitting room with woodburner. The Macartneys have breathed new life into the house with passion and style. Food is organic and free-range where possible and guests have been in raptures — many saying that this is the best B&B they have stayed in.

Rooms: 1 double and 1 single with shared use of private bathroom and sitting room.

Price: £25-£30 p.p.

Breakfast: Flexible.

Meals: Dinner, £12.50-£17 p.p., by arrangement.

Closed: Never.

A387 through Looe and approx. 3 miles beyond, then B3359 signed Pelynt. Just less than a mile on, 2nd of two turnings on left. After 0.5 miles, left at T-junc., then fork left, signed.

Entry No: 42   Map no: 2

Michael & Ann Macartney
Penellick
Pelynt, Nr. Looe
Cornwall PL13 2LX
Tel: 01503 272372
Fax: 01503 272372
e-mail: penellick@hotmail.com
Web: www.sawdays.co.uk

The Black Prince — Cornwall's first Duke — owned this land in the 12th century and the Crusaders sailed from here to France. Now it's a family home, full of laughter. The kitchen is homely — and the Aga has hatched many a bantam's egg. Rob, a retired Admiral, was in command of the Royal Yacht Britannia; Restormel ("with a less submissive crew") is his new ship. Bedrooms are traditional, not frilly — three doubles in the house and two doubles and a bunk room in the self-contained wing. Views are to the salmon and trout river below. Golf, fishing, garden visits, bicycle trails, beaches, walking...

Rooms: 1 double/family room, en suite (shower); 2 doubles sharing private bathroom. Self-catering also available, sleeps 4/6.

Price: From £23 p.p. No single supp. Self-catering from £250 p.w. Short breaks available.

Breakfast: Flexible.

Meals: Packed lunch from £5 p.p.

Closed: Never.

On entering Lostwithiel on A390, take heritage signs to Restormel Castle. Stone gateposts on right 1 mile on. Follow drive to back of house.

Entry No: 43   Map no: 2

Roz Woodard
Restormel Manor
Lostwithiel
Cornwall PL22 OHN
Tel: 01208 873444
Fax: 01208 873455

See the world in writer-explorer Robin's 18th- and 19th-century manor house, chock-a-block with exotic artefacts and Louella's sumptuous hand-stencilled fabrics and furniture. Rich, dark colours, wonderful quilts, cushions and rugs, old beams, and books floor-to-ceiling. A sensuous mix of old-English country life, the 'global village' and atelier — with comfort that swaddles you. Here on the edge of Bodmin Moor, red deer roam; closer to home there is a splendid conservatory looking onto elegant lawns, gardens, a tennis court and views to make your heart leap — and an opera house in a converted barn at the bottom of the garden.

Rooms: 3 doubles, 1 en suite (bath), 2 with private bathrooms.

Price: £30 p.p. No single supp. Reduced rates for children.

Breakfast: Flexible.

Meals: Dinner, 3 courses, £18 p.p., by arrangement. Packed lunch from £5 p.p.

Closed: Christmas & New Year.

6 miles after Jamaica Inn on A30, left signed Cardinham/Mount. Straight on, ignore Cardinham sign. After 2.5 miles, left to Maidenwell. House is 400 yds on right, after cattle grid.

Entry No: 44   Map no: 2

Robin & Louella Hanbury-Tenison
Cabilla Manor
Nr. Mount, Bodmin
Cornwall PL30 4DW
Tel: 01208 821224
Fax: 01208 821267
e-mail: robin@cabilla.co.uk
Web: www.sawdays.co.uk

One of the most exquisite houses we've seen — parts are 15th century and the setting is magical. There are 30 acres with ancient woods, an unrestored water garden, three Celtic crosses and a holy well; the scent of the wisteria is heady. The magic continues inside. Catherine — the loveliest of ladies — has matched fabrics, antique pieces, colours and bed linen with enormous care and flair. One of the bedrooms was part of the old chapel and has ancient stone lintels — all are sunny and have proper bathrooms with lovely old baths. The guest sitting room has a piano, books, beautiful art and fresh flowers. There's a heated outdoor pool, too. *Children over 10 welcome.*

Rooms: 1 twin, en suite (bath); 2 doubles, each with private bathroom.

Price: £30-£35 p.p. No single supp.

Breakfast: Flexible.

Meals: Dinner, £15 p.p., by arrangement.

Closed: Occasionally.

From A30, take turning for Blisland. In village, past church on left and pub on right, and take lane at bottom left of village green. 0.25 miles on, drive is on left (granite pillars and cattle grid).

Entry No: 45   Map no: 2

Christopher & Catherine Hartley
Lavethan
Blisland
Bodmin
Cornwall PL30 4QG
Tel: 01208 850487
Fax: 01208 851387
e-mail: chish@lavethan.fsnet.co.uk

Your children can collect their breakfast eggs, climb in the garden, visit the animals or miniature farmyard, or watch a video. Nursery teas begin at 5pm (you can have a cream tea in the garden) and Lucy will babysit while you slink off to the local pub — the highest in Cornwall. One bedroom is jolly with new pine, the other two more traditional. Celtic crosses in the garden and original panelling hint at the house's 500-year history. Lucy sets aside weeks for walkers and anglers, too.

Rooms: 1 double, en suite (shower) and 1 family room (double and bunk beds), en suite (bath).

Price: £23-£26 p.p. Special breaks available. Children under 5 free in term-time.

Breakfast: Flexible.

Meals: Packed lunch £5 p.p., nursery tea £3.50 p.p., supper £8 p.p., evening meal £13.50 p.p.

Closed: Christmas.

From Launceston, A395, then A39 through Camelford. Left onto B3266 to Bodmin. 4 miles on, left (signed Wenfordbridge Pottery). Over bridge, past pottery and on brow of hill, left into a lane. House at top.

Entry No: 46   Map no: 2

Lucy Finnemore
Higher Lake Farm
St Breward
Bodmin
Cornwall PL30 4NB
Tel: 01208 850716

A place for peaceful time away. You have your own entrance at the side of the farmhouse (14th-century in parts) to two bedrooms, a dining room and a sitting room with an open fire and bread oven. There's also a loggia for summer breakfasts. The feel is traditional, with antiques and quilting; the Hurleys are keen for you to feel happy, yet are unobtrusive. Their adorable black Labradors will give you the most enthusiastic welcome. Rock is just 15 minutes away — the Hurley's cottage for six with Aga is here, too. *Children and pets by arrangement.*

Rooms: 1 double with private bathroom; second double available.

Price: £25 p.p. Single supp. £5. Cottage for 6, £350-£600 p.w.

Breakfast: Until 9.30am.

Meals: Dinner, from £12.50 p.p., by arrangement. Packed lunch from £5 p.p.

Closed: Occasionally.

A30 towards Bodmin. 6 miles after Jamaica Inn, right for St. Breward. Follow signs for St. Mabyn, left over bridge. Penwine is 2.5 miles on, on right, on bend with trees, before B3266.

Entry No: 47   Map no: 2

Heather & George Hurley
Penwine Farmhouse
St. Mabyn
Nr. Bodmin
Cornwall PL30 3DB
Tel: 01208 841783
Fax: 01208 841783

At the head of the beautiful Ruthern Valley, there are stunning views, grassy fields and grazing cattle and horses all around this 450-acre dairy farm. Lay back in the garden hammock to take in the undulating view and drink in the peace. Gelda has decorated the house with flair and attention to detail. Swathes of designer fabrics hang in thick folds at the windows, bathroom towels are large and fluffy and sofas are satisfyingly squishy. Breakfast can be served in the garden in summer and Gelda's suppers are delicious. *Children by arrangement.*

Rooms: 2 doubles, each with private bathroom.

Price: £25-£35 p.p. Special rates available.

Breakfast: Flexible.

Meals: Dinner, 3 courses, £20 p.p. or 2 courses, £14 p.p., both by arrangement.

Closed: Never.

M5 to Exeter. Follow A30 to r'bout at end of Bodmin bypass. Take A30 for Redruth. 2.2 miles on, right to Withiel. Through Withiel (do not fork right), down hill, over bridge, left at T-junc., signed Wadebridge. Approx. 0.5 miles on, drive on right.

Entry No: 48   Map no: 2

Gelda & Michael Madden
Higher Tregawne
Withiel
Bodmin
Cornwall PL30 5NS
Tel: 01208 831257
Fax: 01208 831257

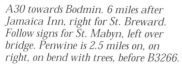

An architecturally elegant 16th-century manor house, generous in size and full of light, Nanscawen sits in five lush acres in the wooded Luxulyan valley. Indeed, you come for the setting; there is utter peace and the views are marvellous. The Martins' hospitality is lavish in modern luxuries such as hot tub, swimming pool, ruffled towels and bathtime goodies and they care deeply that you should be comfortable. Prize-winning sausages and locally-smoked salmon for breakfast if you wish. Bedrooms with lots of peaches and pinks, some modern furniture, elaborate drapes and even teddies on the beds.

Rooms: 1 twin/double, 1 four-poster and 1 double, all en suite (bath).

Price: £27-£42 p.p. Single supp. by arrangement.

Breakfast: Until 9am.

Meals: Available locally.

Closed: Never.

Step from the bedroom balcony and throw a stone into the sea — you are that close. "I can't believe how lovely this is," wrote our inspector. The house was to be Georgian but things took so long to arrive from London that it slid into Regency. You eat in a Tuscan pink kitchen; wooden floors shine, there are pictures, deep sofas to curl up in — all flooded with natural light. Beds are big with generous swathes of material at the windows. Walk barefoot from the heavenly garden onto the sandy beach and swim or launch a boat. Idyllic, and the Harveys are lovely. *Children by arrangement.*

Rooms: 1 twin/double with private bathroom; 1 twin/double and 1 double, both en suite (bath) and each with sitting room.

Price: £30-£38 p.p. Single supp. by arrangement.

Breakfast: Flexible.

Meals: Occasionally available.

Closed: Christmas & New Year.

From A390 beyond St. Austell, left for Mevagissey and Pentewan, past Mount Edgecombe Hospice. Left signed Porthpean Beach. Down narrow lane, second big house at bottom, with balls on pillars.

A390 south towards St. Austell. In St. Blazey take right immediately after railway. House is 0.75 miles on right.

Entry No: 49   Map no: 2

Mr & Mrs Keith & Fiona Martin
Nanscawen Manor House
Prideaux Road, Luxulyan Valley,
nr. St. Blazey, Cornwall PL24 2SR
Tel: 01726 814488
Fax: 01726 814488
e-mail: keithmartin@compuserve.com
Web: www.nanscawen.co.uk

Entry No: 50   Map no: 2

Christine & Michael Harvey
Tredeague
Porthpean
St. Austell
Cornwall PL26 6AX
Tel: 01726 72142
Fax: 01726 73084
e-mail: tredeague@compuserve.com

Come and go as you please, to and from the beaches, gardens — particularly Heligan — and coastal walks of the area. For children the place is heaven — chickens to feed, ponies to ride, a games room, toys and a lovely, brand new indoor swimming-pool. Floral bedrooms come with pots of potpourri and pastoral views; breakfasts are Cornish and hearty. If you choose to self-cater, four beamy, stone-walled cottages are available. Separate tables in dining room; unsophisticated and friendly.

Rooms: 2 doubles, en suite (shower); 1 double, en suite (bath); 1 twin with private bathroom; 1 family room, en suite (bath/shower). Also 4 self-catering cottages, sleep 2/6.

Price: Family room £70. Double £23-£25 p.p. Single occ. £28-£30. Self-catering £175-£695 p.w.

Breakfast: Until 9am.

Meals: Available locally.

Closed: Christmas.

A classical late Regency English country house with the occasional hint of Eastern promise. In the drawing room, where tea is served, a beautiful Chinese cabinet occupies one wall and pale yellows and light blues sit comfortably together. In the dining room, a mahogany oval table is surrounded by exquisite furniture and a Malaysian inscribed tapestry — a thank-you present from the days of Empire. Upstairs, the comfortable bedrooms have antique furniture, garden views and generous baths. The garden is your hosts' first love; you'll see why. *Children by arrangement.*

Rooms: 1 four-poster, en suite (bath), 1 twin, en suite (bath) and 1 double with private bath.

Price: £30-£38 p.p. Single supp. £10.

Breakfast: Until 9.30am.

Meals: Dinner, 4 courses, £22.50 p.p., by arrangement. B.Y.O. wine.

Closed: Christmas & Easter.

In St. Austell follow signs to Truro on A390. From Texaco garage on left, climb long hill, just after brow of hill turn right at St. Mewan school. After 0.5 miles, 2nd farmhouse on left.

Entry No: 51   Map no: 2

Judith Nancarrow
Poltarrow Farm
St. Mewan, St. Austell
Cornwall PL26 7DR
Tel: 01726 67111
Fax: 01726 67111
e-mail: enquire@poltarrow.co.uk
Web: www.poltarrow.co.uk

A30 towards Truro, then left for Grampound Rd. After 3 miles, right onto A390 towards Truro. House is 200 yds on down private lane, on right, by reflector posts.

Entry No: 52   Map no: 2

Alison O'Connor
Tregoose
Grampound
Truro
Cornwall TR2 4DB
Tel: 01726 882460
Fax: 01872 222427

All the tranquillity of the countryside is here with the drama of the sea close by. Traditional farmhouse hospitality and quiet nights in this solid old house. Jacqui used to be head chef for the National Trust, so cooks well; her home-made soups and breads are delicious. You can enjoy carriage rides and even learn to harness and drive a horse and carriage. This is cosy, with a certain elegance; it has antiques and a fine collection of paintings, as well as four-posters, big bathrooms, good china and kind and welcoming hosts.

Rooms: 2 doubles and 1 family room, all en suite (1 shower and 2 bath/shower). 1 children's room.

Price: £24 p.p. Single supp. by arrangement.

Breakfast: 8-8.30am.

Meals: Dinner from £14 p.p.

Closed: Never.

Sir Henry de Bodrugan lived here — he was a renowned host and, 500 years on, Tim and Sally uphold the tradition with sackfuls of enthusiasm. Everything's freshly decorated, there are family antiques, the promise of home-made bread and good food. In the dining room, even with sofas, woodburner and piano, you could turn a cartwheel. An ancient lane flanked by flowers leads you to Colona Bay: small, secluded and full of rock pools where Robin, their son, catches 'blemmies' by hand. It's blissful. There's an indoor heated pool and sauna, too. Heligan and the Eden project are nearby.

Rooms: 1 large double and 1 twin, both with private bathrooms; 1 double, en suite (shower).

Price: £25-£30 p.p. No single supp.

Breakfast: Until 9.30am.

Meals: Supper/dinner, £12/£20 p.p., by arrangement. Packed lunch from £3.50 p.p.

Closed: Christmas & New Year.

A3059 west to Newquay. 0.5 miles on, follow signs to Tregaswith. Farm is second on right.

Entry No: 53   Map no: 1

From St. Austell to Mevagissey. Through village, up steep hill and down into Portmellon. Up steep hill, left-hand bend, entrance is 100 yards on.

Entry No: 54   Map no: 2

John & Jacqui Elsom
Tregaswith Farmhouse
Tregaswith
Nr. Newquay
Cornwall TR8 4HY
Tel: 01637 881181
Fax: 01637 881181

Sally & Tim Kendall
Bodrugan Barton
Mevagissey
Cornwall PL26 6PT
Tel: 01726 842094
Fax: 01726 844378
e-mail: bodruganbarton@ukonline.co.uk
Web: www.sawdays.co.uk

In Lally and William's garden — one of Cornwall's loveliest and occasionally open to the public — there's a comforting sense that all is well in England's green and pleasant land. St. Crida's church rises on tiptoes above treetops while the murmur of a lazy stream reaches your ears. Inside the 1730s house, shimmering wooden floors are covered with rugs and light pours into every elegant corner. Breakfast at the mahogany table has a habit of turning into an early-morning house-party, such is Lally's sense of fun and spontaneity. The big guestrooms exude taste and simplicity. *Children over eight welcome.*

Rooms: 3 twins/doubles, 1 en suite (bath/shower), 2 with private bathrooms.

Price: £30-£35 p.p. Single supp. by arrangement.

Breakfast: Until 9.30am.

Meals: Available locally.

Closed: Christmas & New Year.

From St Austell, A390 to Grampound. Just beyond the clock tower, left into Creed Lane. After 1 mile left at grass triangle opposite church. House is behind 2nd white gate on left.

Entry No: 55   Map no: 1

Lally & William Croggon
Creed House
Creed
Grampound, Truro
Cornwall TR2 4SL
Tel: 01872 530372

A lovely Queen Anne manor house with the elegance and warmth of old-time country-house hospitality. Afternoon tea if you arrive in time. No packed lunches but great hampers; no simple suppers but candlelit dinner parties in the panelled dining room then coffee in the drawing room under the eye of Admiral Sir Arthur Kemp, reputed to haunt Crugsillick. He was responsible for the magnificent plaster ceiling moulded by his French Napoleonic prisoners. The bedrooms are stylish and comfortable. A smugglers' path takes you to the sea three-quarters of a mile away. *Children over 12 welcome.*

Rooms: 1 twin, en suite (shower); 1 twin/double, en suite (bath/shower); 1 four-poster with private bathroom. 3 self-catering cottages (4-7 people), 1 suitable for wheelchair users.

Price: £40-£48 p.p. Single occ. £60.

Breakfast: Until 9.30am.

Meals: Dinner £25 p.p. Hampers £15 p.p., by arrangement.

Closed: Never.

Take A390 from St. Austell, left on B2387 to Tregony. A3078 through Ruan High Lanes. Sharp first left towards Veryan, right after 180 metres.

Entry No: 56   Map no: 2

Oliver & Rosemary Barstow
Crugsillick Manor, Ruan High Lanes
Nr. St. Mawes, Truro
Cornwall TR2 5LJ
Tel: 01872 501214
Fax: 01872 501228
e-mail: barstow@adtel.co.uk
Web: www.adtel.co.uk

An old barn has been joined to the main house to create a courtyard and luxurious guestrooms, all done with great attention to fabric and detail and with a firm eye on authenticity. It is a very old farmhouse, in the family since the 1600s, and only now becoming a B&B... impeccably. A stable door opens from the main bedroom onto the garden with its prettily planted shrubs and banked lawns. A delightful young couple with charming children. The village, too, is lovely and here you are in the geographic centre of Cornwall.

Rooms: 1 large twin with connecting sitting room/small bedroom.

Price: £30 p.p.

Breakfast: A tray will be laid with fruit salad, cereal, toast, etc.

Meals: Available locally.

Closed: Christmas, New Year & Easter.

Barbara is genuinely keen on doing B&B; they have built Oxturn specifically for welcoming guests. The interior is all beiges and creams, fitted furniture, impeccable modernity. So don't expect anything rustic or traditional Cornish (apart from the excellent breakfasts). You come for Barbara, for the views, for the care and attention to detail and comfort. Nothing whacky, eccentric or old here, just plain, solid B&B of the best kind, bright, light and in a good position above the village. *Children over 12 welcome.*

Rooms: 1 double with private bathroom and 1 twin/double, en suite.

Price: £22-£25 p.p. Single supp. by arrangement.

Breakfast: 8-9am

Meals: Dinner sometimes available. Good food in village pub.

Closed: Christmas & New Year.

From Truro, A390 for St Austell. 6 miles on, through Grampound; on leaving village, at top of hill, turn right at speed limit sign into Bosillion Lane. House is 150 yds on left.

Entry No: 57   Map no: 1

Jonathon & Annabel Croggon
Bosillion Farmhouse
Bosillion Lane, Grampound
Truro
Cornwall TR2 4QY
Tel: 01726 883327

From A30, B3275 south to Ladock. There, turn opposite the Falmouth Arms and follow road uphill for 200 yards. Right opposite Public Footpath sign to West Gate. House is on right.

Entry No: 58   Map no: 1

Ian & Barbara Holt
Oxturn House
Ladock
Truro
Cornwall TR2 4NP
Tel: 01726 884348

Begun in the 13th century, 'modernised' in the 16th century, the house has sweeping views to open country and the distant Helford river. Country house elegance entwines with a higgledy-piggledy lived-in feel, warm woods, warm kitchen, lots of antiques, dark oak, open fireplace, granite-walled, deep green, candlelit dining room... all in perfect taste. Bedrooms are cosy and stocked with good books, jugs of fresh water and home-made biscuits. Judy makes her own bread and preserves; both she and Mike are easy hosts.

Rooms: 1 twin with private bathroom; 2 doubles, both en suite (1 bath & shower, 1 bath). Extra shower room also available. Self-catering cottage available.

Price: £23.50-£28.50 p.p. Single supp. in high season, £12.

Breakfast: Until 10am.

Meals: Dinner, 4 courses, with wine £19 p.p.

Closed: Christmas.

The view of garden to church to sea to headland is heart-stopping and the ever-changing light casts a spell over the landscape. The dining room is illuminated by fire and candle; the yellow drawing room, with wooden floors and deep sofas, is perfect. Cascading drapes, immaculate linen, a regal four-poster and a luxurious half-tester — the bedrooms are exquisite. Marion speaks with passion and humour of her piece of England. Her garden is a delight — swim in the sheltered pool, or breathe deeply of the clean Cornish air while walking the three minutes to the sea. Irresistible.

Rooms: 1 four-poster, 1 half-tester, 1 twin/double, all en suite (bath & shower).

Price: £40-£46 p.p. Single supp. £10.

Breakfast: Until 9.30am.

Meals: Dinner, 3 courses, £26 p.p., by arrangement.

Closed: Christmas.

From Truro, take Falmouth Rd (A39). At Hillhead roundabout follow sign to Constantine. 0.5 miles after High Cross garage turn left to Port Navas. House is opposite the granite mushrooms.

Entry No: 59   Map no: 1

Judy Ford
Treviades Barton
High Cross, Constantine,
nr. Falmouth, Cornwall TR11 5RG
Tel: 01326 340524/340143
Fax: 01326 340524/340143
e-mail: treviades.barton@btinternet.com
Web: www.btinternet.com/~treviades.barton/

From Helston, A3083 south. Just before Lizard, left to Church Cove. Follow signs for about 0.75 miles. House on left behind blue gates.

Entry No: 60   Map no: 1

Peter & Marion Stanley
Landewednack House
Church Cove
The Lizard
Cornwall TR12 7PQ
Tel: 01326 290909
Fax: 01326 290192
e-mail: landewednack.house@virgin.net

What a stunning position! The house sits in a secluded spot at the top of a wooded valley, just minutes from the coast and the Helford River. The Leiths are attentive and charming hosts who want you to leave feeling refreshed and well looked after. The Georgian rectory, restored with enormous care and style, is both elegant and comfortable with lots of space, light and views. Breakfast, all organic from the farm shop, is served in the beautiful turquoise dining room — the magnificent table is a family heirloom. Bedrooms are exceptionally comfortable with lovely colours and great views.

Rooms: 2 twins/doubles, both en suite (bath & shower).

Price: £35 p.p. No single supp.

Breakfast: 8.15-9.15am.

Meals: Available locally.

Closed: Occasionally.

Built of sturdy granite from two, or even three, 200-year-old miners' cottages, this home in a quiet hamlet is a typically Cornish blend of inglenooks, narrow staircases, low ceilings, stripped pine doors with touches of unpretentious, flowery decoration and needlework. Moira, a retired midwife, has a passion for gardening — Goff, a potter, is currently creating a potager for her — and the herbs from her beautifully tended garden are delicious. Flowers are fresh, sheets are crisp and cotton, and beds have patchwork and quilted bedspreads. Goff and Moira are immensely kind.

Rooms: 1 double, en suite (bath/shower); 1 twin/double with private bathroom; 1 double, en suite (shower).

Price: £18-£22 p.p. No single supp.

Breakfast: Flexible.

Meals: Packed lunch and evening meal by arrangement.

Closed: Christmas & New Year.

From Helston, A3083 for the Lizard. Left onto B3293 for St. Keverne. Left at Mawgan Cross, past post office, and right into tiny slip road. Pass Old Court House pub, house is 2nd on right.

Entry No: 61   Map no: 1

Susan Leith
The Old Rectory
Mawgan
Helston
Cornwall TR12 6AD
Tel: 01326 221261
Fax: 01326 221797

From A394 Helston to Penzance, second right after Ashton Post Office for Tresowes Green. After 0.25 miles, you will see a sign for the house (with three chimneys) on the right.

Entry No: 62   Map no: 1

Moira & Goff Cattell
The Gardens
Tresowes
Ashton, Helston
Cornwall TR13 9SY
Tel: 01736 763299

Roomy, artistic interior and stunning coastal setting. Set foot in the slate-flagged hallway of this converted barn and feel calmed by the whitewashed stone walls and honey-coloured timbers. Your hosts — busy and efficient — are horsey people. Richly-coloured rugs and Liberty sofas piled high with cushions coax you into comfortable decline; there are fresh flowers, fruit and toiletries and a four-poster, too. From your private terrace, the wild blue yonder and views across the sea to St. Michael's Mount.

Rooms: 3 doubles, 2 en suite (bath/shower), 1 en suite (bath).

Price: £22.50-£35 p.p. Single occ. £45-£60.

Breakfast: Until 9am.

Meals: Available within walking distance.

Closed: 25 & 26 December.

From A30 after Crowlas roundabout, A394 to Helston. 0.25 miles after next roundabout, 1st right towards Perranuthnoe. Ednovean Farm drive on left, signed.

Entry No: 63   Map no: 1

Christine & Charles Taylor
Ednovean Farm
Perranuthnoe
Nr. Penzance
Cornwall TR20 9LZ
Tel: 01736 711883
Fax: 01736 710480
Web: www.ednoveanfarm.co.uk

Windswept walks are within easy reach; seabird acrobatics will dazzle and magical Prussia Cove will enchant you. The road ends at Ennys, so the rural bliss is entirely yours. Gill has responded to the existing magic of the house and added a dash of her own with artefacts and curios from her extensive travels, designer fabrics and antique pieces. Stone floors lead you to a sumptuous log-fired sitting room; complimentary afternoon tea is laid out in the kitchen; bedrooms have great views. You can play tennis or swim in the heated pool. *Children over three welcome.*

Rooms: 1 twin, en suite (bath); 2 four-posters, en suite (shower). 2 family suites in barn and 3 luxury self-catering apartments sleeping 2-4.

Price: £27.50-£35 p.p. Single supp. £12.50. Self-catering: 1 bedroom £225-£400 p.w.; 2 bedroom £400-£750 p.w.

Breakfast: Until 9.15am.

Meals: Available locally.

Closed: November, December & January.

2 miles east of Marazion on B3280, look for sign leading down Trewhella Lane between St Hilary and Relubbus. Keep going to Ennys.

Entry No: 64   Map no: 1

Gill Charlton
Ennys
St. Hilary, Penzance
Cornwall TR20 9BZ
Tel: 01736 740262
Fax: 01736 740055
e-mail: ennys@zetnet.co.uk
Web: www.ipl.co.uk/ennys.html

A thoroughly unpretentious and completely relaxing house full of the sound of laughter. Sally enjoys entertaining and the arts and receives guests with vivacious good humour in her large, rambling, supremely comfortable family house with big rooms. Nothing sumptuous, all entirely natural. Old toys lie around for new children to play with and a barbecue is set up in the garden for fine weather, otherwise bedrooms have high beds, warm rugs and views of the wooded valley.

Rooms: 1 twin, en suite (shower); 1 double, en suite (bath); 2 cottage suites for 2-4 people.

Price: £25-£30 p.p. Cottage suite £27.50-£30 p.p. Children under 5, £5; 5-15, £15.

Breakfast: Until 9am.

Meals: Available locally.

Closed: Christmas & New Year. Cottage suites available all year.

Take Penzance bypass for Land's End. Right at r'bout to Heamoor. Through village, right at x-roads signed to Gulval, 1st left signed Bone Valley/New Mill. House on right after 0.5 miles.

Entry No: 65   Map no: 1

Sally Adams
Tremearne
Bone Valley, Penzance
Cornwall TR20 8UJ
Tel: 01736 364576
Fax: 01736 364576
e-mail: sally@threesfilms.com
Web: www.sawdays.co.uk

Trelissick Mansion, next door, was bought by the Copeland family in 1920; the gardens were developed by Peter's grandparents, who then gave the whole lot to the National Trust in the '50s. The estate's bailiff used to live here at Trevilla — and what a stunning position; the Fal Estuary, the sea and the peninsula wrap around you. You have a small sitting room next to your bedroom; the high, antique basketwork twin beds have French polished frames — nothing frilly, but entirely comfortable and with sea views. Jinty and Peter are special and the King Harry Ferry will take you to the Roseland Peninsula.

Rooms: 1 twin with basin, private bathroom and small private sitting room. Can sleep 3rd person.

Price: £25 p.p.

Breakfast: Until 9.30am.

Meals: Available locally.

Closed: Christmas & New Year.

A390 to Truro, left onto A39 to Falmouth. At double roundabout with Shell garage, left off 2nd roundabout (B3289). Pass pub on left. At crossroads, left (still B3289). 200 yards on, fork right to Feock. Keep going to T-junction, then left. House first on right.

Entry No: 66   Map no: 1

Jinty & Peter Copeland
Trevilla House
Feock
Truro
Cornwall TR3 6QG
Tel: 01872 862389
Fax: 01872 870088
e-mail: trevilla@clara.co.uk

You are almost at sea — crashing surf and Atlantic winds in a stunning Daphne du Maurier setting. The cottage, in the family for four generations, was once a 'fish cellar' for processing catches. Today it is a homely refuge with family furniture and oil paintings and so intimately close to the sea that you might spot dolphins or a lazy basking shark. The drawing room, with woodburner, greets you. The bedrooms are simple and unfussy but it will be the views that rivet you.

Rooms: 2 twins, both en suite. A single can be added to one to make a family room.

Price: From £22.50 p.p. No single supp.

Breakfast: Flexible.

Meals: Dinner from £12 p.p. Packed lunch from £5 p.p.

Closed: Never.

The grandeur is so soft, and Sarah and her family so natural, that you'll feel at home immediately. The Empire sofa, good oils on the walls, faded rugs on wooden floors, lovely lamps and an oak chest are just what you might hope for. They, and Sydney the polar bear, all sit beautifully in the 1780s, creeper-clad vicarage. Good period furniture, fresh flowers and quilted bedspreads in the bedrooms; in one a Napoleonic four-poster. The children's room, off the twin, with its miniature beds is utterly charming. *Children over five welcome.*

Rooms: 1 four-poster, 1 twin with children's room and 1 suite, all en suite (bath).

Price: £20-£27 p.p. Single supp. £5.

Breakfast: Until 10.30am.

Meals: Available locally.

Closed: Christmas Day.

From St. Merryn, right for Trevose Head/Harlyn. Continue towards Trevose Head, over sleeping policemen. After toll gate ticket machine right through farm gate. Continue towards sea; cottage gate is at the end, on right.

Entry No: 67   Map no: 1

Phyllida & Antony Woosnam-Mills
Mother Ivey Cottage
Trevose Head
Padstow
Cornwall PL28 8SL
Tel: 01841 520329
Fax: 01841 520329
e-mail: woosnammills@compuserve.com

From Wadebridge, B3314 towards Rock and Polzeath. After 3.5 miles, left signed St. Minver. In village, left into cul-de-sac just before Four Ways Inn. House at bottom on left.

Entry No: 68   Map no: 2

Mrs Sarah Tyson
The Old Vicarage
St. Minver
Nr. Rock
Cornwall PL27 6QH
Tel: 01208 862951
Fax: 01208 863578
Web: www.sawdays.co.uk

John Betjeman and A.L. Rowse, the historian, both loved Bokelly and often wrote about the 15th-century manor house. The Elizabethan tithe barn, your hosts and the garden are absolutely marvellous, too, and a tennis court, small pond, croquet lawn and a folly add to the magic. The house is relaxed and easy and is beautiful without making any effort. There's an exhilarating mix of the exotic (a papier-mâché ship used in a film that Lawrence directed) and the familiar (squishy sofas and traditional carpets). A very special place indeed.

Rooms: 1 double, en suite (bath); 1 double, with private bathroom.

Price: £30 p.p.

Breakfast: Flexible.

Meals: Dinner, 1st night only, £15 p.p. Packed lunch from £7.50 p.p.

Closed: Never.

On A39, 7 miles South of Camelford at St. Kew Highway, right through village on Trelill Rd. (Do not go to St. Kew). 1 mile on, pass white cottage on right, left over cattle grid past white bungalow, house is 0.25 miles down drive.

Entry No: 69   Map no: 2

Maggie & Lawrence Gordon Clark
Bokelly
St. Kew
Bodmin
Cornwall PL30 3DY
Tel: 01208 850325

As one visitor said, "Some barn!" Lovingly converted with original beams and exposed granite walls, it hunkers down in its own secluded valley and a path leads you through the woods to Epphaven Cove. The inside is elegantly uncluttered and cool; seagrass contrasts strikingly with old oak and the downstairs bedrooms have good period furniture, fresh flowers and quilted bedspreads. The shower room — a mixture of rusty reds and Italian marble — is quite magnificent. Jo's daughter is an aromatherapist — book an appointment. *Children over 12 welcome.*

Rooms: 1 double and 2 twins sharing 1 bathroom and 1 shower room.

Price: £28 p.p. Single supp. by arrangement.

Breakfast: Until 9.30am.

Meals: Available locally.

Closed: Christmas.

A39 to Wadebridge. At r'bout follow signs to Polzeath, then to the Porteath Bee Centre. Go through the Bee Centre shop car park, down farm track; house signed on right after 150 yards.

Entry No: 70   Map no: 2

Jo Bloor
Porteath Barn
St. Minver, Wadebridge
Cornwall PL27 6RA
Tel: 01208 863605
Fax: 01208 863954
e-mail: mbloor@ukonline.co.uk
Web: www.sawdays.co.uk

You get the peace and privacy of self catering, yet can eat in the farm's award-winning restaurant. Samphire House feels mediterranean with two open plan sitting rooms and a balcony overlooking its swimming pool. There are equally large sitting rooms, and a huge garden, in Samphire Cottage and Eastern Gate, a converted barn, is a charming retreat with an oak staircase and gallery. Walk along the donkey path — two moorland ponies will probably follow you — to National Trust coastline, Strangles beach and High Cliff. You can get married here, too.

Rooms: Samphire House and Samphire Cottage each sleep 10. Eastwood cottage sleeps 4.

Price: Samphire House, from £850 p.w., Samphire Cottage, from £650 p.w. and Eastern Gate, from £350 p.w.

Breakfast: Self-catering.

Meals: Available in farmhouse restaurant.

Closed: Never.

From Crackington Haven follow the coastal road keeping the sea on your right. Up hill and turn right signed Trevigue. Farm is 1.5 miles on the left on top of the cliffs.

Entry No: 71   Map no: 2

Gayle Crocker
Trevigue
Crackington Haven
Bude
Cornwall EX23 0LQ
Tel: 01840 230418
Fax: 01840 230418
e-mail: trevigue@talk21.com

Considered one of the loveliest houses in the area, Manor Farm was the Domesday-listed property of Duke William's half brother. Ancient stone, manicured lawns and rolling countryside outside, sober luxury inside where your hostess, who runs the house with irreproachable efficiency, knows well how to look after visitors. If you stay in to eat, you change for dinner and meet fellow guests for drinks before dining in dinner-party style. There are fine paintings, stone-silled windows onto garden views, carefully-decorated rooms. It is a house of character, totally English, elegant and peaceful.

Rooms: 3 twins/doubles, en suite (1 bath, 2 showers).

Price: £30 p.p. Single occ. £35.

Breakfast: 8.30am.

Meals: Dinner £16 p.p.

Closed: Christmas Day.

From Wainhouse Corner on A39, follow sign to Crackington Haven. At beach, turn inland for 1 mile, left into Church Park Road and first right into lane.

Entry No: 72   Map no: 2

Muriel Knight
Manor Farm
Crackington Haven
Bude
Cornwall EX23 0JW
Tel: 01840 230304

The road twists and turns, the driveway falls through the spring-fed wooded valley and, suddenly, the secret is yours. The former vicarage — part 16th century with Georgian and Edwardian additions — is beautiful and within its intriguing garden you are neighbour only to sea, coastal path and fields; nearby are sandy beaches. Lots of light, sea views, seagrass matting, paintings, comfy sofas, pretty fabrics and the feel of a family home. Perfect. Bedrooms are fresh and peaceful, bathrooms charming. What's more, Jane and Anthony share their house without fuss. *Children over five welcome.*

Rooms: 1 double and 1 twin, each with basin and private bathroom and 1 other twin let to members of same party. Small single for child.

Price: £22-£30 p.p. Single supp. £10.

Breakfast: Flexible.

Meals: Simple supper or 3-course dinner, from £12 p.p., by arrangement.

Closed: Christmas.

Leave A39 at Wainhouse Corner, south of Bude, to Crackington Haven & St. Gennys Church. 2 miles on, fork right by white cottage signed St. Gennys Church. Before church, right into lane/drive.

Entry No: 73   Map no: 2

Anthony & Jane Farquhar
St. Gennys House
St. Gennys
Bude
Cornwall EX23 0NW
Tel: 01840 230384
Fax: 01840 230537
Web: www.sawdays.co.uk

The house hunkers down at the foot of the cliffs and you are virtually *on* the beach. Low tide reveals miles of soft sand and rockpools. At high tide you can watch the drama of the crashing waves from the coastal path. The Shaker simplicity of the wrought iron and brass beds, slate floors and stone walls, mixed with contemporary checks feels just right. The fully-glazed Upper Room gives a 270° view of the surrounding National Trust SSSI coastline. Excellent breakfasts — in the courtyard if fine — and exceptionally gentle and genuine hosts. Perfect. *Children by arrangement.*

Rooms: 1 double with connecting single and private bathroom; 1 twin, en suite (shower).

Price: £22-£27 p.p. Single supp. £5. Supp. for single night's stay £5.

Breakfast: By arrangement until 9am.

Meals: Good pubs/restaurants nearby.

Closed: Christmas & New Year.

On A39 Bideford-Camelford, turn off to Poughill. Right by post office in village, signed Northcott Mouth. Continue past 'No through road' sign to entrance to beach. House is 2nd on right, through five-bar gate.

Entry No: 74   Map no: 2

Bob & Lyn French
The White Cottage
Northcott Mouth
Bude
Cornwall EX23 9ED
Tel: 01288 353859
Fax: 01288 353859

The house echoes the enthusiasm and love poured into it by the Duffs. A converted shooting lodge fashioned from local Eden sandstone, the 1750s house has seven acres and is surrounded by fell and field. Bedrooms feel new and fresh and bathrooms are modern and bright; each has far-reaching views. The gardens, with working walled kitchen garden, paddock and colourful borders, is the current project. Fishing and shooting are available, and the Duffs can advise you on some great local walks & rides, too.

Rooms: 2 doubles, both en suite (bath).

Price: £25 p.p. Single occ. £32.50.

Breakfast: Flexible.

Meals: Dinner and packed lunch by arrangement.

Closed: Christmas & New Year.

Cumbria & Lancashire

From M6 junc. 41, follow A6 to High Hesket, right to Armathwaite and follow signs to Newbiggin. At Newbiggin turn left. 0.5 miles to Cumrew, turn right, house behind stone wall and yew hedge.

Entry No: 75   Map no: 19

Roddy Duff
Cumrew House
Cumrew, Heads Nook
Brampton, nr. Carlisle
Cumbria CA8 9DD
Tel: 01768 896115
e-mail: rabduff@aol.com
Web: www.countrysport-lodge.com

Imagine the dreamy evenings — tennis or croquet under the setting sun, a cool drink on the terrace, a stroll through the gardens down to the River Irthing. *And* this thoroughly English country house can be entirely yours. You cater for yourself (the owners live in a wing to the rear of the house) and have the run of four bedrooms and large dining and sitting room with log fires. There's a summer house in the garden, too, and you're well placed for Northumberland, the Pennines and the Lakes — whether you will be able to stir yourself to explore are another matter. There's wine and a breakfast hamper waiting for you.

Rooms: 2 doubles, each with private bathroom; 2 twins, each en suite (shower).

Price: Lowest: £430 for 3 night short winter break (6 people); highest: £1448 for one week (8 people) high season.

Breakfast: Welcome hamper provided.

Meals: Self-catering.

Closed: Never.

The setting of this lovely old house could hardly be more beautiful. Many of its rooms face south and have superb views of peaceful countryside with the mountains and fells of Lakeland beyond. The house dates from c.1360 but bedrooms are sumptuous and large and the mood is of a tranquil, elegant, country way of living almost forgotten. Anthony, a tenor soloist, and Kathleen, a talented flower arranger, love sharing their home. Their food is legendary and, with a list of over 60 fine wines, dining in the 17th-century oak-beamed dining room is a memorable experience.

Rooms: 3 doubles: 2 en suite (shower), 1 with private bath.

Price: £38-£39 p.p. Single supp. £10.

Breakfast: 8.30-9am.

Meals: Dinner £19.50 p.p.

Closed: Christmas & New Year.

You will receive an information pack, including directions, when booking.

From M6, junc. 41, B5305 for Wigton. At A595, left (signed Cockermouth). After 6 miles, left for Boltongate: up and down the hill and left at bottom to Ireby. Out of the village and down the hill, pass between two white buildings and left into drive after 50 yds.

Entry No: 76   Map no: 19

Entry No: 77   Map no: 19

Beanlands
Irthington
Cumbria
Tel: 01386 701177
Fax: 01386 701178
e-mail: info@ruralretreats.co.uk
Web: www.ruralretreats.co.uk/2000

Anthony & Kathleen Peacock
Boltongate Old Rectory
Nr. Ireby
Cumbria CA5 1DA
Tel: 016973 71647
Fax: 016973 71798
e-mail: boltongate@aol.com

It is a real cosy/comfy picture-book cottage, far prettier than you expect. There is a cottage garden with sweet peas, herbs, veg and flowers, perfectly rambling. They kept most of the original features (old farming tools remain on idiosyncratic display), and there is wood everywhere. There are dried flowers, cast-iron tubs, antique linen and patchwork quilts, all against a background of wooden floorboards, high bedroom ceilings and a palpable keenness to make it work. Television is delightfully absent, classical music plays, there are home-laid eggs for a walker's breakfast, and you can see Skiddaw from the house.

Rooms: 1 double, en suite (bath); 1 twin, en suite (cast-iron bath).

Price: £22-£25 p.p. Reduction for weekly booking. Single supp. £10.

Breakfast: Until 9am.

Meals: Available locally.

Closed: 18-28 December.

From Keswick A591 to Carlisle (approx. 6.5 miles). Right at Bassenthwaite Chapel into village (0.5 miles). Straight on at village green for 170 yds.

Entry No: 78   Map no: 19

Roy & Chris Beaty
Willow Cottage
Bassenthwaite
Keswick
Cumbria CA12 4QP
Tel: 017687 76440

Rare wild flowers line the bank and salmon splash in Sandy Beck, the SSSI stream at the bottom of the garden. Water, hills, mountains and wildlife surround you and after a day's exploring you can slip into a state of oblivion — Janet is an aromatherapist and reflexologist. Cooking is imaginative — red onion and pepper quiche with cheese pastry; smoked haddock and parmesan omelette — and their advice informed. Bedrooms are beamed with new pine furniture and white-tiled bathrooms with charming handmade pottery basins. *Children over five welcome.*

Rooms: 1 family, en suite (Continental bath); 1 double, en suite (shower).

Price: From £24 p.p. Single supp. £8.

Breakfast: 8.30-9.30am.

Meals: Dinner, 3 courses, from £16.50 p.p. Packed lunch, £3.50 p.p.

Closed: Occasionally.

From A66 take A5086, signed to Egremont, at r'bout just outside Cockermouth. After 1 mile turn left at crossroads by school. Then 1st right signed Brandlingill. House is on the right after 1 mile.

Entry No: 79   Map no: 19

Mike & Janet Wright
Toddell Cottage
Brandlingill
Nr. Cockermouth
Cumbria CA13 0RB
Tel: 01900 828696
Fax: 01900 828696
e-mail: toddell@waitrose.com

Hazel's family are hoteliers — she knows what she is doing and will do a professional job of looking after you. Beds are hotel-big, too, and a dish of fresh fruit is placed in each room. Oak beams, flagged floors and stone fireplaces have been preserved in this 1650s house. The views are such that each of the five bedrooms is named after the mountain view that it has; Swinside brings the house its own spring water. Next door is a converted milking parlour where you can take lunch or tea. *Children over eight welcome. Self-catering also available in the valley.*

Rooms: 2 doubles and 3 twins/doubles, all en suite.

Price: From £39 p.p. Single supp. £15. (Lower weekly and winter rates).

Breakfast: Flexible.

Meals: Packed lunch £6.50 p.p. Dinner £22 p.p. There are tea rooms next door, open April-October.

Closed: Never.

Wordsworth's brother-in-law lived here and the great man came over frequently. The views that he enjoyed over to Barton Fell are as glorious as ever. The mood is genuine, simple, country hospitality at its best, with communal dining and no ceremony. Much of the atmosphere comes from Mary herself; she is great fun, down-to-earth and friendly, a real farmer's wife. The home-made biscuits in the rooms are a typical gesture. The bedrooms are simple and unfussy, and with those views. There are 300 acres, 850 sheep and a lovely walled garden... all in the National Park.

Rooms: 2 twins/doubles, both en suite (shower). Another bathroom also available.

Price: £21 p.p. Single supp. £1.

Breakfast: Until 8.30am unless previously arranged.

Meals: Available locally.

Closed: 1 November-31 March.

From M6 junc. 40 west on A66. Past Keswick and continue on A66 for Cockermouth. Left at Braithwaite onto B5292, Whinlatter Pass. Through forest to Lorton. Left onto B5289 to farm, 1.5 miles on.

Entry No: 80   Map no: 19

Hazel Thompson
New House Farm
Lorton, Cockermouth
Cumbria CA13 9UU
Tel: 01900 85404
Fax: 01900 85404
e-mail: hazel@newhouse-farm.co.uk
Web: www.sawdays.co.uk

From M6 junc. 40, A66 west. At r'bout left on A592. Follow signs to Dalemain house, go through car park into courtyard ignoring 'No car' signs. Right for 0.5 miles and right again, at farm building.

Entry No: 81   Map no: 19

Mrs Mary Milburn
Park House Farm
Dalemain
Penrith
Cumbria CA11 0HB
Tel: 01768 486212
Fax: 01768 486212
Web: www.sawdays.co.uk

This is a Victorian folly. Walk through the panelled hall to the vast drawing room and wonder at the courage of Simon and Wendy in rekindling the magic. Here are a grand piano, great tumbling curtains and rugs galore on wooden floors. The meals at the huge dining room table are informal feasts. The bold, south-facing bedrooms elaborate the fantasy. As for the wardrobes — look in the turrets. And take in the gilded, vaulted ceilings, the oak panelling, the soaring stained-glass windows. Perhaps, in summer, you may carry your dinner across the field to sit beside the pond, with the ducks.

Rooms: 1 four-poster, 1 double, 4 twins/doubles, all en suite (bath & shower).

Price: £40 p.p.

Breakfast: Until 12 noon.

Meals: Dinner (inc. wine) £22.50 p.p., by arrangement. Picnics £10 p.p.

Closed: Never.

Paradise in the Eden Valley. In her restoration, Anne has given sweet voice to the echoes of the past; there has been little external alteration since modernisation in 1719. From the superb, 1740-panelled dining room to the glorious four-poster with sloping floor and working gramophone, the house is a box of delights. Flagstones, wooden floors with good rugs, some pale yellow walls, oak everywhere, a great rug tumbling down a wall, superb furniture and stacks of character... it is a dream. One bathroom was once a stage-set for an Alan Ayckbourn play. The self-catering cottage is a lovely place to stay, too.

Rooms: 1 four-poster, en suite (shower); 1 twin/double, en suite (bath). Self-catering in the Old Wash House, sleeps 2.

Price: Up to £30 p.p. Single supp. £10. Cottage from £160-£255 p.w.

Breakfast: Flexible.

Meals: Dinner £18 p.p., B.Y.O wine. Packed lunch available on request.

Closed: Christmas & New Year.

M6 junction 38, then A685 through Kirkby Stephen. Just before Brough, right signed South Stainmore and house signed on left after 1 mile.

Entry No: 82   Map no: 19

Simon & Wendy Bennett
Augill Castle
Brough, Kirkby Stephen
Cumbria CA17 4DE
Tel: 017683 41937
Fax: 017683 41936
e-mail: augill@aol.com
Web: www.sawdays.co.uk

In Kirkby Stephen, 100 yds N of main square, left to Crosby Garrett. After 3 miles, left to Crosby Garrett. After 0.75 miles, left again. 1st left in village, and immediate left through gates.

Entry No: 83   Map no: 14

Anne McCrickard
The Old Rectory
Crosby Garrett, Kirkby Stephen
Cumbria CA17 4PW
Tel: 017683 72074
Fax: 017683 72074
e-mail: alexandanne@crosbygarrett.freeserve.co.uk
Web: www.crosbygarrett.freeserve.co.uk

Guests are immediately wrapped in the Midwinters' cheerful enthusiasm, just as Low Jock Scar itself is folded into the comforting slopes of the valley. This is a spotless guest house, run with equal amounts of friendliness and efficiency. From the conservatory you are lured out to ramble in the flourishing gardens, the pride of your green-fingered hosts. Listen out for the burbling beck and rest on its banks in the evening to recover from the five-course feast at dinner.

Rooms: 1 twin and 2 doubles, en suite (2 with bath and 1 with shower); 1 twin and 1 double sharing bathroom.

Price: £23.50-£29 p.p. Single supp. £10.

Breakfast: Until 9am.

Meals: Dinner £17 p.p. Packed lunch, by arrangement, £3.50 p.p.

Closed: 31 October-mid-March.

A Victorian Lakeland house, all set about with gables and chimney stacks and light-filtering bay windows, in three supremely peaceful acres on the edge of Grasmere. Rooms are pristine, big and comfortable, with some new pine furniture, matching floral wallpapers and cushions and brass bedside lamps — from two you can see the lake across the wildflower meadow cultivated by the Kirkbrides. There's a payphone, and a boot-and-drying room, too. Walk from the house, row round the lake or make a pilgrimage to Wordsworth's cottage and grave. *Children over 10 welcome. Exclusively for non-smokers.*

Rooms: 1 four-poster, en suite (bath/shower); 2 doubles, en suite (1 bath & 1 shower). Self-catering cottage also available.

Price: £30-£35 p.p. Single occ. £45. Check for price of cottage.

Breakfast: Until 8.45am.

Meals: Available locally.

Closed: November-February.

From Kendal take A6 to Penrith. After 5 miles you see the Plough Inn on left. Turn into lane on left after 1 mile.

Entry No: 84   Map no: 14

Alison & Philip Midwinter
Low Jock Scar
Selside, Kendal
Cumbria LA8 9LE
Tel: 01539 823259
Fax: 01539 823259
e-mail: philip@low-jock-scar.freeserve.co.uk
Web: www.sawdays.co.uk

Enter Grasmere from A591, turn opposite St. Oswald's church. After 100 yds, right into Langdale road. House is on left.

Entry No: 85   Map no: 14

Lyn & John Kirkbride
Ryelands
Grasmere
Cumbria LA22 9SU
Tel: 015394 35076
Fax: 015394 35076
Web: www.sawdays.co.uk

You won't find another B&B like this in the Lakes. It is run by a young couple who have escaped London. Splashes of colour — Barbie pink, lemon, peppermint — give a fresh, exciting feel to the house. Blinds, no frills, modern art, black-and-white checked hallway and the odd Conran piece set it apart from other B&Bs on Windermere's 'Golden Mile'. Jeremy, an ex-editor and very easy-going, has big plans for the terraced back garden which leads to a stream and, beyond that, woodland protected from development. The house is 1890s, the feel 1990s — how refreshing!

Rooms: 5 doubles, all en suite (shower).

Price: From £27 p.p. Single supp. £10.

Breakfast: Flexible.

Meals: Light evening meals, by arrangement.

Closed: Never.

Bonnie Prince Charlie rested here. The River Rothay (you cross it on a private bridge to reach the house) flows by and the scenery is glorious. The house, more guest-house than private home, has simple country cottage comforts, with stone-flagged floors wrapped in rugs, beamed ceilings, a clothes-drying room for walkers, a small sitting room and small dining room, too. The pastel and chintz rooms are modest but comfortable and all have views of the river. Alan and Gillian are sweet and down-to-earth.

Rooms: 1 twin and 2 doubles, all en suite (bath); 2 doubles, en suite (shower).

Price: £26-£35 p.p. No singles.

Breakfast: Until 9am.

Meals: Available locally.

Closed: 24-26 December.

A591 to Windermere. Left by Tourist Information and through village. House on right after less than 0.5 miles, opposite modern church.

Entry No: 86   Map no: 14

Jane Sowerby & Jeremy Davies
The Coach House
Lake Road, Windermere
Cumbria LA23 2EQ
Tel: 015394 44494
Fax: 015394 43476
e-mail: info@coachhouse.net1.co.uk
Web: www.lakedistrictbandb.com

From Ambleside, A593 Coniston road to Rothay Bridge (approx. 500 yards). Cross bridge and turn immediately into house entrance.

Entry No: 87   Map no: 14

Alan & Gillian Rhone
Riverside Lodge
Nr. Rothay Bridge, Ambleside
Cumbria LA22 0EH
Tel: 015394 34208
Fax: 015394 31884
e-mail: alanrhone@riversidelodge.co.uk
Web: www.riversidelodge.co.uk

Guests have been very happy here in this big, light house where you'll find a smiling welcome and not a hint of stuffiness — the Broughtons have a great sense of fun. Bedrooms have big, comfy beds — there is lots of attention to detail — and the suite is a lovely hideaway in the loft. You'll find it easy to relax by the fire in the winter with a glass of wine, or in the garden in summer — it's sunny and secluded. After a splendid cooked breakfast — there's organic home-made bread and Aga pancakes, too — walk to the lakes, fells and village, all a mere five-minute stroll away.

Rooms: 1 family suite (1 double, 1 twin), en suite (bath); 1 twin/double, en suite (shower).

Price: £26-£28 p.p. Single supp. £10. Half price for children.

Breakfast: 8.30-9.30am.

Meals: Available locally.

Closed: Christmas & New Year.

From Kendal, A591 to Windermere and follow signs to Bowness. There, bear left at bottom of hill and first left opposite church. Follow road past garage on left. House is 50 yards on, on right.

Entry No: **88**   Map no: 14

Louise & Steve Broughton
Low Fell, Ferney Green
Bowness-on-Windermere
Cumbria LA23 3ES
Tel: 015394 45612
Fax: 015394 48411
e-mail: hotpancake@low-fell.co.uk
Web: www.low-fell.co.uk

The stream meanders and the wild deer roam — the Ribble Valley, an AONB, feels like a time-locked land. The Queen is a frequent visitor to the local royal estate and she knows well the charm of the area. The Smiths are easy and comfortable to be with and here, in their former 18th-century tithe barn where church rafters hold up the guest sitting room, you settle among plump sofas, antiques, and some lace and flounces. You have the whole of the top floor and your own entrance. Breakfast is a feast — the jams and the muesli are home-made — and the garden is a peaceful retreat, full of interesting plants and wildlife.

Rooms: 1 twin/double, en suite (shower); 1 double, en suite (bath/shower); 1 double with private bath.

Price: From £23 p.p. Single supp. £5.

Breakfast: 7.15-9.15am.

Meals: Available locally at good pubs.

Closed: Christmas & New Year.

M6 junc. 31, A59 to Skipton, left to Clitheroe. Through Clitheroe and Waddington, further 0.5 miles, turn left along Cross Lane. 0.75 miles past Colthurst Hall. Peter Barn is on left.

Entry No: **89**   Map no: 14

Jean & Gordon Smith
Peter Barn Country House
Cross Lane/Rabbit Lane
Waddington, Clitheroe
Lancashire BB7 3JH
Tel: 01200 428585

On the Stonyhurst Estate — the school is just across the playing fields — Timothy Cottage is attractive, oak beamed and unpretentious. Bedrooms are small and pretty, with old pine furniture and crisp white sheets. The only disturbance here is likely to be from the sheep, yet there are three pubs within walking distance. You'll breakfast well (local sausages, home-made jams and fruit compote, for example), in the tiled conservatory with views of the well-kept garden and the Pendle Hills. Pauline is lively and fun. She's also a keen walker and has stacks of local knowledge to share. *Children over 10 welcome.*

Rooms: 1 twin, en suite (shower); 1 double, sharing bathroom.

Price: From £21.50 p.p. Single occ. £26.

Breakfast: Flexible.

Meals: Not available.

Closed: Christmas & New Year.

Take B6243 from Clitheroe for Longridge. On entering Hurst Green, turn right opposite cottages, up the drive to St. Joseph's primary school. At top, bear left — cottage is at bottom of lane.

Entry No: 90   Map no: 14

Pauline Cook
Timothy Cottage
Whalley Road
Clitheroe
Lancashire BB7 9QJ
Tel: 01254 826337
Fax: 07070 600902

This house hasn't always had such easy-going hosts as Marsha and John; in 1821 its owner was involved in the last fatal illegal duel in England. Entering the 16th-century mellow limestone house, one feels the warmth of the beamed sitting room with its unusual low stone fireplace and part-flagged floor. The elegant dining room looks out to the walled country garden and you can dine on Marsha's freshly prepared meals, including farm-cured bacon. Large bedrooms look down the conservation village towards the National Trust market hall. Freshly renovated bathrooms have a William Morris theme.

Rooms: 1 double, en suite (bath/shower); 1 double, 1 twin, both with private bathroom.

Price: £35-£37.50 p.p. Single occ. £50-£52.50.

Breakfast: Flexible.

Meals: Dinner £25 p.p. Packed lunch £3.50 p.p.

Closed: Never.

Three miles from Matlock on A6 towards Bakewell. Left on B5057 signed Winster for 3 miles. House at end of Main Street, looking down village.

Entry No: 91   Map no: 15

Derbyshire

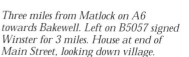

John & Marsha Biggin
The Dower House
Main Street
Winster
Derbyshire DE4 2DH
Tel: 01629 650931
Fax: 01629 650932
e-mail: fosterbig@aol.com

A 300-million-year-old Tufa rockface guards this Grade II-listed home, once part of the Duke of Rutland's estate. Rural delights of the Peak National Park start at the gate, so bring walking boots. Trout laze in the gin-clear waters of twin rivers nearby. Jan works very hard to make you happy — it's all spotless, elegant and comfortable. Books, magazines, 'smellies' in the bathroom, guide books and electric blankets add to your comfort. A stone-flagged, beamed hall-sitting room gives you space to read or chat. Breakfast varies daily and includes home-baked muffins.

Rooms: 1 double and 1 twin, each with private bathroom; 1 twin, en suite (shower) and separate w.c.

Price: £23 p.p.

Breakfast: 8.30-9am.

Meals: Available locally.

Closed: Never.

If you love gardens you'll wallow in this one. Within the two acres are herbaceous beds, a lily-pool and a lovely terraced garden of stone walls, hidden patios, even hidden sculptures and streams... exquisitely planned and unfussy. Hens, ponies and doves cluck, strut and coo in a charming, old stable yard. The house is elegant yet relaxed and full of antique country furniture and subtle colours. Breakfast is served in the old schoolroom and is a carefully prepared feast of organic eggs, honey, home-made jams and garden fruit. Glorious setting... and place. *Children over five welcome.*

Rooms: 1 double, en suite (bath/shower); 1 family and 1 twin sharing bathroom & wc.

Price: £21-£23 p.p. Single occ. from £25.

Breakfast: Until 9am.

Meals: Available locally.

Closed: 23 December-4 January.

A6 E of Bakewell, right onto B5056 to Ashbourne. Follow signs to Youlgrave and Alport, 1.75 miles. House is first on right in hamlet — sign at gateway.

Entry No: 92   Map no: 10

Jan Statham
Rock House
Alport
Bakewell
Derbyshire DE45 1LG
Tel: 01629 636736
Web: www.sawdays.co.uk

Leave the M1 at junction 29 and take the A617 to Chesterfield, then the B6051 to Millthorpe. Horsleygate Lane is 1 mile on, on right.

Entry No: 93   Map no: 15

Margaret Ford
Horsleygate Hall
Horsleygate Lane
Holmesfield
Derbyshire S18 7WD
Tel: 0114 289 0333
Web: www.sawdays.co.uk

People come from far away for the magic of this beautifully restored farmhouse. Such are the views of moor, valley and heather from the bedrooms that guests rarely use the curtains. It is deeply cared for, from the yellow hall with ticking grandfather clock to the pretty drawing room with sky-blue walls and clouds of cream damask at the windows. Flowers everywhere, oak furniture, fine rugs and ancestral bits and pieces, Chippendale chairs and a Louis XV rosewood bed. The terraced garden is a fine place for star-gazing. Drink — even bathe — in pure spring water. Mary is a delight and the house emanates a nourishing peace.

Rooms: 1 double and 1 four-poster, both en suite (shower).

Price: From £30 p.p. Single occ. from £45.

Breakfast: Until 9am.

Meals: Dinner available locally.

Closed: Christmas.

Elisabeth, immensely kind, is an avid gardener and bird lover and has designed her garden to encourage wildlife; it works. She also bakes bread, buys 'best local' and has generally made this big country house a real pleasure to visit. The double bedroom has walnut furniture, chintz, silk flowers and a superb view; you bathe in a cast iron bath. The twin shares the fabulous view and its Victorian/Edwardian furniture fits with the period of that part of the house; the rest is 150 years older. Great walking all around and Chatsworth is 10 minutes away.

Rooms: 1 double, opposite private bathroom; 1 twin next to private shower room.

Price: £22.50 p.p. Single occ. £40.

Breakfast: Until 9am.

Meals: Available locally.

Closed: Christmas & New Year.

From Sheffield A625 into Hathersage. Right into School Lane. After 100 yards, left fork up 'Church Bank'. 50 yards on, right fork, then 0.5 miles. Over cattle grid. Signed.

Entry No: 94   Map no: 15

Mary Bailey
Carrhead Farm
Hathersage
Hope Valley
Derbyshire S32 1BR
Tel: 01433 650383
Fax: 01433 651441

On A6, 1.5 miles from Bakewell, right to Ashford-in-the-Water. Right to Monsal Head and right at Monsal Head Hotel into Little Longstone. Pass Pack Horse pub on left. House is almost opposite.

Entry No: 95   Map no: 15

Elisabeth Chadwick
The Hollow
Little Longstone
Bakewell
Derbyshire DE45 1NN
Tel: 01629 640746

Mineral water from the crystal-clear spring, lavish breakfasts with eggs and fruit from the farm, local sausages, oat cakes and home-made preserves — this is farmhouse life at its luxurious best in the heady surroundings of the Peak District. The farmhouse was built by the family in 1880 and is traditionally decorated throughout — antler horns on the landings, grand piano, marble fireplaces. Bedrooms are homely and one has wonderful views across the Derbyshire Peaks. Pam serves home-made cake and tea on arrival and will instantly put you at your ease.

Rooms: 2 doubles, en suite (1 shower, 1 bath); 1 twin/double room, en suite (bath/shower).

Price: £23-£30 p.p. No single supp.

Breakfast: Flexible.

Meals: Plenty of local pubs & restaurants.

Closed: December, January & February.

A magnificent William IV property built on the precipice of a spectacular limestone gorge. Beyond the formal gardens and 30 acres of parkland there are panoramic views over the River Wye and to the green hillside of Brushfield beyond. Inside, sympathetic renovation is complete — you'll marvel at the ornate, delicate plasterwork on the ceilings. Imposing though it is, this former mill owner's house today buzzes with family life. Four generations of Hull-Baileys live here. Bobby cares for guests and family alike with efficient kindness.

Rooms: 2 doubles and 1 twin, all en suite (bath & shower).

Price: From £32.50-£47.50 p.p.

Breakfast: Flexible.

Meals: Dinner & packed lunch by arrangement.

Closed: Christmas & New Year.

From A6 follow Chinley signs. At Squirrels Hotel leave B6062, over bridge, left into Stubbins Lane. After 0.25 miles take left fork onto farm road, over cattle grid and almost 0.5 miles into farmyard.

Entry No: 96   Map no: 15

Pamela & Nick Broadhurst
Cote Bank Farm
Buxworth
High Peak
Derbyshire SK23 7NP
Tel: 01663 750566
Fax: 01663 750566
e-mail: cotebank@btinternet.com.

From Ashford-in-the-Water, B6465 to Monsal Head. Left at Monsal Head Hotel, follow valley to The Old Mill, fork left. Left, at lodge building with white fence and 'Private Drive' sign.

Entry No: 97   Map no: 15

Bobby & Len Hull-Bailey
Cressbrook Hall
Cressbrook, Nr. Buxton
Derbyshire SK17 8SY
Tel: 01298 871289
Fax: 01298 871845
e-mail: stay@cressbrookhall.co.uk
Web: www.cressbrookhall.co.uk

Standing on a steep hillside between the Dales and the Peaks, this converted chapel has enormous views. The top floor is open-plan, loft style with huge leaded windows with distinctive coloured panels around the edges. You can dine on the balcony or at two long pine tables which overlook the surrounding countryside. The feel is contemporary — wrought iron light fittings, candelabras, very large beds; each have garden views. Outside there's wooden decking, pretty terraces and a small lily pond. It's easy, fun and completely without pretension.

Rooms: 1 family room with twin/king-size, en suite (shower); 1 twin/king, en suite (bath & shower).

Price: £25 p.p. Single occ. £30. Children, up to £10.

Breakfast: Flexible.

Meals: Dinner, 3 courses, £17.50 p.p.

Closed: Christmas & New Year.

From junc. 26 on M1 take A610 towards Ripley/Matlock. At Sawmills, right under railway bridge, signposted Crich/National Tramway. Right at market place onto Bowns Hill. Chapel is 200m on the right. Can collect from station.

Entry No: 98   Map no: 10

Fay & Steve Whitehead
Mount Tabor House
Bowns Hill
Crich
Derbyshire DE4 5DG
Tel: 01773 857008
e-mail: mountabor@email.msn.com

A solid Victorian farmhouse and the only place to stay in the area, it has its name because it looks over the Kedleston Hall estate and you can gaze across fields to the Robert Adam masterpiece. Back at the farm, you are received in a drawing room with yellow walls, pale blue ruching and darker blue curtains, blue sofas and an Adam fireplace. New-laid eggs for breakfast, fresh fruits and home-made breads accompany the full monty. Beds are antique four-posters. Perfect peace in 370 acres. *Children over eight welcome.*

Rooms: 2 doubles, en suite (1 bath/shower and 1 shower); 1 double with private bathroom.

Price: £27.50-£30 p.p. Single supp. £10.

Breakfast: Flexible.

Meals: Good food available locally.

Closed: Christmas Eve/Day.

From A52/A38 roundabout west of Derby, take A38 north. 1st left for Kedleston Hall. House is 1.5 miles past Park on crossroads in Weston Underwood.

Entry No: 99   Map no: 10

Linda & Michael Adams
Park View Farm
Weston Underwood
Ashbourne
Derbyshire DE6 4PA
Tel: 01335 360352
Fax: 01335 360352
e-mail: parkviewfarm@hotmail.com

Gateposts topped with stone pineapples (symbols of hospitality) and huge copper beeches lead to a glorious Georgian house set in 50 acres with grass terraces leading to the River Dove. Polished floors and attractive carpets, but still very much a family home; one bedroom has a four-poster with golden coverlet, another a French bed and pale peach walls. Your host is a keen country sportsman and can arrange fly-fishing. Perfect for all that the Dales have to offer. A magnificent house with the kindest of hostesses.

Rooms: 1 twin and 1 four-poster, both with private bathrooms.

Price: From £35 p.p. Single occ. from £40. Two nights' minimum stay at weekends.

Breakfast: Flexible.

Meals: Many good local pubs & restaurants.

Closed: 1 December-1 January.

There are long views over the Dove Valley towards Alton Towers (a comfortable five miles away!) and the house is up a tiny country lane in a fine garden. An ancestor of Peter was Lord Mayor of London in 1681, hence the memorabilia. Cynthia is Australian; is that why they are such a delightful and friendly couple? Although elegant, the house is a home and guests really are treated as friends. The hall sets the tone: white tiles, Indian rugs, woodburning stove and ancestral paintings. There is a small, book-lined sitting room for you, and the bedrooms are impeccable.

Rooms: 2 doubles, 1 en suite and 1 with private bathroom.

Price: £23-£25 p.p. Single occ. £30.

Breakfast: Flexible.

Meals: Good local pubs & restaurants nearby.

Closed: Christmas.

From Derby on A52, or Lichfield on A515, take Ashbourne bypass, direction A52 Leek. Turn right after Queen's Arms to Okeover/Mappleton. Through park, over bridge and turn left out of village. House on right with white gate.

Entry No: 100   Map no: 10

Cedric & Rosemaré Stevenson
Hinchley Wood
Mappleton
Nr. Ashbourne
Derbyshire DE6 2AB
Tel: 01335 350219
Fax: 01335 350580

From Ashbourne, A515 Lichfield road. After 4 miles, right onto B5033. After approx. 1 mile, take second lane on right. Rose Cottage is about 0.5 miles on, on right (cream coloured).

Entry No: 101   Map no: 10

Peter & Cynthia Moore
Rose Cottage
Snelston
Ashbourne
Derbyshire DE6 2DL
Tel: 01335 324230
Fax: 01335 324651
Web: www.sawdays.co.uk

Rose walkways, a brook and lawns that open onto fields — a lovely setting for afternoon tea; the teapot will be silver, the cakes home-made. Sue's competence has not overshadowed her sense of humour; she's frank and friendly. Guests have the run of the downstairs — two sitting rooms, stacks of books and oriental and antique pieces. The twin has mahogany beds and a Regency chair; the double has rose-patterned, cotton fabrics and a deep cast-iron bath next door. Fruit platter and scrambled eggs and smoked salmon will tempt you to get out of bed.

Rooms: 1 twin and 1 double, both with private, next door, bathrooms. Coach House sleeps 4.

Price: From £30 p.p.

Breakfast: Flexible.

Meals: Dinner, by arrangement, £22 p.p. (including wine).

Closed: Christmas & New Year.

Le Patron races vintage cars, Madame tends the beautiful garden, both are gracious and supremely welcoming hosts. Their splendid Georgian mansion, listed by Pevsner, was 'improved' in 1850 with pillars and later with a high Victorian conservatory where breakfast, overlooking the beautiful garden, is not to be missed. The house has the elegance of Georgian proportions with shutters, antique furniture and fine country or garden views. The bedrooms are in keeping, with excellent bathrooms. Welcoming and most interesting hosts. *Children over 14 welcome.*

Rooms: 1 twin, en suite (shower); 2 doubles, en suite (bath/shower).

Price: £28.50-£32 p.p. Single occ. £35-£40.

Breakfast: Until 9.15am.

Meals: Dinner, 3 courses, £20 p.p., available on request.

Closed: Christmas & Boxing Day.

From Ashbourne A515 towards Lichfield. 3 miles on, right to Snelston. Follow road for 1.25 miles to centre of village. House is opposite stone War Memorial. Drive round to rear of house.

Entry No: 102   Map no: 10

Edmund & Sue Jarvis
Oldfield House
Snelston, Ashbourne
Derbyshire DE6 2EP
Tel: 01335 324510
Fax: 01335 324113
e-mail: suejarvis@beeb.net
Web: www.sawdays.co.uk

Leave M1 at junc. 23a. Past airport. Right to Melbourne. Out of village on Ashby road. Right at Melbourne Arms on to Robinsons Hill. Or leave A/M42 at junc. 13, follow signs to Calke Abbey. Left at Melbourne Arms; house is on right.

Entry No: 103   Map no: 10

Robert & Patricia Heelis
Shaw House
Robinsons Hill
Melbourne
Derbyshire DE73 1DJ
Tel: 01332 863827
Fax: 01332 865201
e-mail: robert.heelis@tinyonline.co.uk

A former monastery dating from 1642, this Grade II* rambling family house is set in 18 acres of rolling lakeside gardens and woodland. Rooms are large but cosy, spotless and flower-filled with views over the gardens and surrounding countryside. Bold chintzy fabrics complement the classic English furniture, and bathrooms have Victorian claw-footed baths. Meals are eaten in the panelled dining room overlooking the gardens where you may stroll, play croquet or just relax and enjoy the friendly, peaceful atmosphere. Can you resist?

Rooms: 1 twin with private bathroom; 2 doubles, both en suite (bath).

Price: From £26-£28 p.p.; single from £28-£35.

Breakfast: Flexible.

Meals: Dinner, from £16 p.p., & packed lunch, available by arrangement.

Closed: Christmas & New Year.

M42, junc. 11, A444 towards Burton on Trent for approx. 2 miles, then left immediately before Cricketts Inn. The house is 0.5 miles on, 2nd house on right before church, immediately before 30mph speed limit sign.

Entry No: 104   Map no: 10

Clemency Wilkins
The Old Hall, Netherseal
Swadlincote, Ashby de la Zouche
Derbyshire DE12 8DF
Tel: 01283 760258
Fax: 01283 762991
e-mail: clemencywilkins@hotmail.com
Web: www.sawdays.co.uk

After a lot of travelling, these ex-TV producers had a clear vision of what made a perfect place to stay: privacy, stylish comfort and peace in stunning surroundings. Here you have it. Each bedroom is self-contained and has a private 'deck' dotted with pots; the woodland views are glorious. No expense has been spared: chrome shower heads are the size of dinner plates, the beds new and firm, the linen luxurious. They have used local craftsmen and much local material in the renovation. Judging by Frank's take on Jamie Oliver's nut torte, his breakfasts will be excellent. Valley, woodland and bluebell walks start from your terrace.

Rooms: 3 king-size, en suite (shower).

Price: £30 p.p. 10% discount for 3 or more nights.

Breakfast: Flexible.

Meals: Packed lunch from £5 p.p. Restaurants in Honiton, 3 miles away.

Closed: Christmas.

Offwell is 3 miles from Honiton and is signed off A35 Honiton to Axminster road. In centre of village, at church, go downhill. Farm 0.5 miles on.

Entry No: 105   Map no: 3

Frank & Carol Hayes
West Colwell Farm
Offwell, Honiton
Devon EX14 9SL
Tel: 01404 831130
Fax: 01404 831769
e-mail: west.colwell.farm@which.net
homepages.which.net/~west.colwell.farm/

Devon

From your free-standing bath you can look straight onto the church; a fine view from a fine bathroom. Floors slope and the peace hums. It is part of the Combe estate (Grade II*) with magnificent thatch and cruck beams, a 1600 date-stone and a 17th-century extension. The house is full of flowers and music and the Hills — artistic, fun and hugely welcoming — will look after you with the same attention to detail that was lavished on the renovation of the house. The drawing room is very pretty, with bright colours, shutters and leaded windows.

Rooms: 1 double & 1 twin, sharing bathroom.

Price: £25 p.p. No single supp.

Breakfast: Flexible.

Meals: Supper, £15 p.p., by arrangement.

Closed: Christmas.

Ian, a solicitor, has recently retired to concentrate on looking after his prize-winning Berkshire pigs and guests — he likes both equally! He and Maggie will give you the full Devon B&B experience — home-reared, additive-free sausages and bacon with newly-baked bread for breakfast. 'Combe' means valley and the downstairs bedroom with pink-flowered duvet and valance has a heart-healing view up the valley — it also has its own living room. Upstairs there is another pretty double room, plus a family suite of two adjoining rooms. Both enjoy the same lovely views and there is a large sitting and dining room, too.

Rooms: 1 twin, 1 double and 1 family suite, each en suite (bath/shower). Self-catering options available in these rooms, too.

Price: £20-£25 p.p. Single supp. £5.

Breakfast: Flexible.

Meals: Packed lunch £3 p.p. Dinner £11.50 p.p.

Closed: Never.

From Honiton High St, turn into New St by Lloyds Bank. At mini-r'bout, left, then first right. Up hill to golf course and on towards Colyton. Take 3rd left signed Slade. Farm in bottom of valley on right.

A30 through Honiton, and follow signs to Gittisham. In village, right over bridge — large house, last on left.

Entry No: 106   Map no: 3

Entry No: 107   Map no: 3

Andrew & Meriel Hill
Town House
Gittisham
Honiton
Devon EX14 3AJ
Tel: 01404 851041
Fax: 01404 851289

Maggie Todd
Smallicombe Farm
Northleigh, Colyton
Devon EX24 6BU
Tel: 01404 831310
Fax: 01404 831431
e-mail: maggie_todd@yahoo.com
Web: www.smallicombe.com

The nine-acre gardens are wonderful. The orchard has damsons and cherries, there are trees galore (ghinkos, meta sequoia, magnolia, jacaranda and Chinese shrubs). There are even three ponds and a bamboo valley, ewes, lambs, ponies, geese and free-range hens. The cottage suites have stripped pine, Laura Ashley-style linen and curtains and oak kitchens. But it is for the gardens that you come, and for the food: organic and local, traditional and delicious. Up to 16 can eat at separate tables.

Rooms: 1 twin/double, en suite (bath). Two cottage suites available on B&B or half-board basis.

Price: £28-£30 p.p. Single supp. £3.50-£5 in high season. Gourmet packages for special occasions available.

Breakfast: Until 8.45am.

Meals: Dinner, inc. aperitif, £19.50 p.p.

Closed: Mid-November-Christmas Eve & 3 January-12th February.

From Chard, A30 Honiton road for 0.25 miles. At top of hill fork left for Wambrook and Ferne Animal Sanctuary. After 3 miles, right after animal sanctuary. Follow signs left for Furley/Membury. At T-junc., left to Ford, then bear right. House on left.

Entry No: 108   Map no: 3

Robert & Pat Spencer
Goodmans House
Furley
Membury
Devon EX13 7TU
Tel: 01404 881690

The Buxtons look after hundreds of guests each year — lots of them stopping off en route to Cornwall. They enjoy what they do and have it down to a fine art. They are friendly folk who love their bit of Devon surrounded by the Blackdown Hills. The kitchen is vast, with terracotta tiles and an Aga which Rosalind uses to produce her generous breakfasts. The bedrooms are bright and airy. Fresh flowers and lovely views and a chance to sample the many French wines which Bob imports.

Rooms: 1 family (sleeps 4), 1 double and 1 twin, all en suite (shower).

Price: From £20 p.p.

Breakfast: 8.30am, or by arrangement.

Meals: Available locally.

Closed: Christmas.

At M5 junction 25 take A358 to Ilminster then A303 towards Honiton. After A30 merges from left, farm is 0.5 miles ahead on the right (directly off the A30).

Entry No: 109   Map no: 3

Rosalind & Bob Buxton
Courtmoor Farm
Upottery, Nr. Honiton
Devon EX14 9QA
Tel: 01404 861565
Fax: 01404 861474
e-mail: courtmoor.farm@btinternet.com
Web: www.btinternet.com/~courtmoor.farm

"An Irish attitude to life dominates this house," says Charlotte — that means friends, family and guests mingle indiscernibly. There's plenty of company and activity (friendly family, polo ponies — you can even have tuition — horses, fishing and the garden to explore) or complete peace and privacy in your room. Bedrooms have traditional furniture, fat pillows, sumptuous bedspreads and curtains and a tray with whisky decanter, mineral water and biscuits. Breakfasts offer no relief — home-reared organic sausages and bacon, and even home-grown melons in season. Charlotte scatters her magic over the whole place. *Children over six welcome.*

Rooms: 1 double and 1 twin, each en suite (bath). In the wing, an adjoining double and twin, en suite (bath), let only to members of same party.

Price: £20-£35 p.p. Single supp. £10.

Breakfast: Until 9.30am.

Meals: Picnic lunch, £15 p.p. Dinner, £25 p.p.

Closed: Christmas & New Year.

This Bampton-stoned, slate-roofed house was once the town mill — it dates back to the early 1600s. The expected beams, inglenook fireplaces and stream are still here, along with a fully co-ordinated look. The bedrooms are cosy, not large, and you may find a teddy on your bed. Kathy puts a lot of thought into creating a memorable breakfast and uses as much local, organic and home-grown produce as she can. The garden slopes down to the River Batherm and you are welcome to fish for trout. *Children over 12 welcome.*

Rooms: 1 four-poster, 1 king-size double, 1 twin, all en suite (shower).

Price: £24 p.p. For 3 nights or more: £22 p.p. £147 p.p. per week.

Breakfast: Flexible.

Meals: Available locally.

Closed: Never.

From M5, junc. 26 or 27, A38 towards Exeter for 6 miles, then take left to Culmstock. There, over bridge, 1st right into Silver St. Last drive on right.

Entry No: 110   Map no: 3

Mrs Charlotte Horne
Woodhayne Barton
Culmstock, Devon EX15 3JG
Tel: 01884 840708
Fax: 01884 841479
e-mail:
rogercharlotte@hornewoodhayne.demon.co.uk
Web: www.hornewoodhayne.demon.co.uk

From Tiverton take A396/B3227 to Bampton. There, turn right just before bridge over river. House is cream property opposite.

Entry No: 111   Map no: 3

Chris & Kathy Ayres
Manor Mill House
Bampton
Devon EX16 9LP
Tel: 01398 332211
Fax: 01398 332009
e-mail: stay@manormill.demon.co.uk
Web: www.manormill.demon.co.uk

The top of a steep hill seems an odd place for a coaching inn — the horses must have toiled. Now reap the panoramic rewards over the Exe valley. High ceilings and large windows bring light and space to this unpretentious family house. Barbara is an efficient, kind, no fuss hostess. Dining room, with beautiful dresser, and drawing room with antiques, have a subdued grandness. One flowery bedroom has a Victorian four-poster; another on the ground floor (good for those with impaired mobility) opens onto the gardens. A good place for breaking a journey or for those on business in Tiverton. *Children over 12 welcome.*

Rooms: 1 double, en suite (shower); 1 four-poster with private bathroom; 1 twin with private bathroom (bath/shower).

Price: From £22 p.p. Single occ. £25.

Breakfast: Until 9am.

Meals: Dinner, 3 courses, £12.50 p.p., by arrangement.

Closed: Never.

At junction 27 (M5) take A361 for approx. 4.5 miles. Turn off at Gornway Cross, for Grand Western Canal. At Canal Hill take 1st right into Exeter Hill. House is at top on left.

Entry No: 112   Map no: 3

Barbara Pugsley
Hornhill
Exeter Hill, Tiverton
Devon EX16 4PL
Tel: 01884 253352
Fax: 01884 253352
e-mail: hornhill@tinyworld.co.uk
Web: www.hornhill.fsnet.co.uk

You go down a very long lane and, more than likely, will wonder if you have lost your way. But what reward for your adventurousness! Mediterranean, surprising, bright, fresh, vibrant — Jellicoe's is an exceptional find. Michael is widely travelled, he cooks all kinds of food with passion and only copper pots and pans separate the master at work in his kitchen from your dining area; his three-course meals must be the best value food in this book. Bedrooms are exceptional with polished wooden floors, whitewashed walls and bathrooms are rag-rolled and fluorescent (lime green, for example). Come for restorative peace and excellent value.

Rooms: 2 doubles, en suite (shower); 1 twin, en suite (bath).

Price: £22 p.p. No single supp.

Breakfast: 7.30-9.30am.

Meals: Dinner, 3 courses, £12 p.p. Packed lunch £2.50 p.p.

Closed: Rarely. Please check.

Leave A396 at Bickleigh, turn right for Crediton, then immediate right again for Cadeleigh & Upham. Straight through Cadeleigh. Turn left at 'Post Box Cross', and right signed Upham. House is 2nd on left.

Entry No: 113   Map no: 3

Michael Jellicoe
Jellicoe's, Higher Holn
Upham, Cheriton Fitzpaine
Crediton, Devon EX17 4HN
Tel: 01363 866165
Fax: 01363 866165
e-mail: enquiries@jellicoes.co.uk
Web: www.jellicoes.co.uk

Their great love in life is horses, breeding and racing. There are 180 acres of farm and parkland around a 300-year-old house in lovely grounds. There is a grand horse-chestnut on parade in the parkland — a big attraction here. The house is well restored with a recently-revealed inscription dated 1760 and all bedrooms are charmingly furnished with timbered walls and good views. Breakfast, with home-made marmalade and fresh fruit, is served in the oak-panelled dining room which has a conservatory leading from it. Within a short walk is a lovely lake for fishing.

Rooms: 1 twin and 1 double, both en suite (shower); 1 double, en suite (bath). Another bath & shower available.

Price: £20-£25 p.p. Single supp. £2.

Breakfast: Flexible.

Meals: Great pubs within 2 miles.

Closed: Christmas.

Much-travelled and multi-lingual, Denise and Peter settled in this tranquil corner of East Devon after 10 years in France. Both history and walking buffs, they are a mine of information on the region. Their 1860s barn is large and airy with white oak doors, flagstones and French country furniture — there are hints of Provence. Bedrooms are light and unfussy with flowers, chocolates, farmland views and a lovely sea-green bathroom with a huge Victorian tub. The Italianate, gravelled garden is a peaceful sun trap; next door is an excellent farm shop and there's a great 16th-century pub nearby.

Rooms: 1 double and 1 twin, sharing private bathroom.

Price: From £25 p.p. No single supp.

Breakfast: Flexible.

Meals: Packed lunch, from £5 p.p., by arrangement.

Closed: Never.

M5, junc. 28, head for Cullompton, then left for Exeter. Through town and left at Sports Centre sign. Right at T-junc. and cross over m-way bridge. Next left (signed Plymtree). House is next lane on left.

Fay Down
Upton House
Cullompton
Devon EX15 1RA
Tel: 01884 33097
Fax: 01884 33097
Web: www.sawdays.co.uk

On A30 from Honiton or Exeter take Fenny Bridges/Fairmile exits and follow signs for Fairmile. At Fairmile Inn, right towards Talaton. Straight over at Beacon Hill x-roads (1.5 miles on). 1st right signed Plymtree. Downhill over bridge (300 yds). First house on right.

Peter & Denise Goss
Wayside
Lashbrook, Talaton
Exeter
Devon EX5 2RU
Tel: 01404 851231
Fax: 01404 850856
e-mail: osco@btinternet.com

It isn't easy to make people feel at home while still giving them space to be alone; the Rooths succeed. The comfortable rooms and bathroom are in their own private 'wing', but once you come downstairs in the morning you will be warmly greeted by Gina and her black Labrador. Breakfast is delicious, early only if you ask for it to be so. There are huge roses in the dining room window, a tennis court and green fields beyond. Gina, by the way, is very knowledgeable about the nearby gardens to be visited.

Rooms: 1 twin and 1 double, with private bathroom plus second wc. You can have exclusive use of 'wing' at no extra charge.

Price: £25 p.p. Single occ. £27.50.

Breakfast: Flexible.

Meals: Excellent food available locally.

Closed: Christmas & Easter.

The seductive charm of this hideaway miner's cottage will soothe even the most stressed souls. At the end of a long track criss-crossed by bridal paths, you find a lush oasis carved out of woodland. Mary, gently-spoken, loves to see guests unwind; both she and Dick have a finely-judged sense of humour. There's a pretty American patchwork quilt on the brass double bed and a small bathroom leads to a twin room. The sound of the river (they have their own water supply) and birdsong fill each room. Local sausages and bacon for breakfast, excellent dinners, easy company, a pool and 12 acres to explore — you'll want to return.

Rooms: 1 double, en suite; 1 twin with private bathroom.

Price: From £20 p.p.

Breakfast: Flexible.

Meals: Packed lunch by arrangement.

Closed: Christmas.

Turn off A38, going south to Chudleigh Knighton. Turn right just before village, and right at white thatched cottage. House is signed.

Entry No: 116   Map no: 3

The Rooth Family
Culver Combe
Chudleigh
Newton Abbot
Devon TQ13 0EL
Tel: 01626 853204
Fax: 01626 853204

From A38 take A382 at Drumbridges for Newton Abbot & Bovey Tracey. 4th left at raised r'bout for Bickington. There, down hill & past garage on left. Right for Haytor. Under bridge and left, then down long, bumpy farm track, past thatched cottage to house.

Entry No: 117   Map no: 3

Mrs Mary Lloyd-Williams
Hooks Cottage
Bickington
Nr. Ashburton
Devon TQ12 6JS
Tel: 01626 821312
Fax: 01626 821312
e-mail: hookscottage@yahoo.com

Clough Williams-Ellis (of Portmeirion) designed this elegant country house, set in five acres of wooded gardens in the Dartmoor National Park; test his genius yourself. It works: the spaces, the light and the soft, warm colours, the all-embracing atmosphere of elegant homeliness. There's comfort at every turn, antiques and heirlooms, and chats with well-travelled Madeleine and Mike are full of fun and a broad perspective. Enjoy the views of the Devon hills from the enchanting gardens and play tennis on the all-weather court.

Rooms: 1 twin/double with private bathroom; 1 double with private shower.

Price: £25-£28 p.p. Single supp. by arrangement.

Breakfast: Flexible.

Meals: Available locally.

Closed: Never.

A38 west to Plymouth. Take A382 turnoff, and 3rd turning off r'bout, signed Bickington. There, right at junc. (to Plymouth), right again (to Sigford/Widecombe). Over top of A38. Penpark is 1st entrance on right.

Entry No: 118   Map no: 3

Madeleine & Michael Gregson
Penpark, Bickington
Newton Abbot
Devon TQ12 6LH
Tel: 01626 821314
Fax: 01626 821101
e-mail: gregson.penpark@ukgateway.net
Web: www.sawdays.co.uk

You can feel that this elegant, Devon farmhouse (part 14th-century) has always been a happy family home. Sarah is capable and jolly and she and husband Michael clearly enjoy guests. The two bedrooms are large — the linen has that lovely, fresh, garden-dried smell — and each has a tray with pretty china, two types of tea, coffee and local spring water. By the bed you'll find a thoughtful selection of bedtime reading but sleep comes too easily for you to get through much of it. There's a pond, orchard, a few sheep and hens that give breakfast eggs and excellent food in the pub just up the road.

Rooms: 1 king-size, en suite (bath/shower); 1 twin with private bathroom.

Price: £22-£26 p.p.

Breakfast: Flexible until 9.30am.

Meals: Dinner and packed lunch by arrangement.

Closed: Christmas.

From Newton Abbot, A381, signed Totnes. After approx. 2.5 miles, right for Broadhempston. Through Ipplepen to Broadhempston, where village sign faces you as lane turns sharp right. Down hill & 2nd left. Pass pub on right & turn left 170 yds on into courtyard.

Entry No: 119   Map no: 3

Sarah Clapp
Manor Farm
Broadhempston
Nr. Totnes
Devon TQ9 6BD
Tel: 01803 813260
Fax: 01803 813260
e-mail: clappfamily@shines.swis.net

An extravagant nature hide, it is a converted summer house built and originally thatched for grand Sharpham House and feels like a 'garden with a room'. Your bedroom has a balcony that catches the morning sun and gazes over huge rhododendrons, magnolia, fuchsia, a lily-strewn pond and down to a bend in the River Dart far below. The two Richards are gifted gardeners, and the archetypal gardener's modesty and calm have penetrated to the house itself. It is uncluttered, serene... and very comfortable, with a huge bath, thick rugs, a fine bedroom, and birdsong to wake you. *Pets by arrangement.*

Rooms: 1 twin, en suite (bath).

Price: £25 p.p. Single supp. £5.

Breakfast: Flexible.

Meals: Excellent pub in village.

Closed: Never.

Tiny lanes twist down steep hills, suddenly giving onto great views of the Dart as it approaches the sea. Little villages are somehow built into the slopes. The surprisingly large house goes up and up, twisting and turning. Gillie is a landscape architect and costume designer — her flair is visible. Great brass beds, fat duvets and electric blankets add comfort to lovely, snug bedrooms. This is great value for a bright welcome in a special area of England.

Rooms: 1 twin, en suite (shower), 1 double, en suite (bath); 1 double sharing bathroom.

Price: £20-£25 p.p. No single supp.

Breakfast: Flexible.

Meals: Good food in local pubs.

Closed: January/February.

From Totnes follow signs to Kingsbridge (A381) for 0.5 miles. Left, signed Ashprington. Into village then left by pub (Dead End sign). House 0.25 miles.

Entry No: 120   Map no: 3

Richard Soans & Richard Pitts
Avenue Cottage
Ashprington
Totnes
Devon TQ9 7UT
Tel: 01803 732769
Fax: 01803 732769

From Totnes, follow Kingsbridge Road (A 381) for 1 mile, then left, signed Tuckenhay. After village, follow sign for Cornworthy. Turn left at Hunter's Lodge sign; house opposite inn.

Entry No: 121   Map no: 3

Gillie Brock
Hall House
Cornworthy
Totnes
Devon TQ9 7ES
Tel: 01803 732325

The view from Nonsuch is staggering. From your wicker seats in the conservatory you can spy the whole of Dartmouth below, a thousand yachts at their moorings (and marinas). To your left the mouth of the Dart is guarded on both points by ancient castles. But Nonsuch does not rest on its natural laurels; everything about it is captivating. The guests' sitting room has its own balcony. Great fresh breakfasts, large and extremely comfortable beds in big airy bedrooms, top quality bathrooms, views and more views. *Children over 10 welcome.*

Rooms: 5 twins/doubles, 2 en suite (bath), 1 with private bathroom, 2 en suite (shower).

Price: £35-£40 p.p. Single supp. £10.

Breakfast: Flexible.

Meals: Dinner, 3 courses, £19.50 p.p. Cheese course, £3.50 p.p.

Closed: Never.

Yachts bob at anchor on the sparkling Dart estuary below this 18th-century home, renamed The White House by American soldiers during World War II. The maritime theme plays throughout, with pebble collections and a flotilla of model ships. In one of the bright, cheerful, flower-filled bedrooms you can gaze snugly down at the Dart from the warmth of your double bed. You have your own sitting/breakfast room with an open fire, comfortable chairs and French windows opening onto the terrace. The views are magical and Hugh and Jill revel in having guests. *Children by arrangement.*

Rooms: 2 doubles: 1 en suite (bath & shower), 1 with private bathroom; 1 twin, en suite (shower).

Price: £27.50-£30 p.p. Single occ. £30-£45.

Breakfast: Flexible.

Meals: Not available.

Closed: Christmas.

2 miles before Brixham on A3022, take A379. After r'bout, fork left (A3205) downhill, through woods, left up Higher Contour Rd, down Ridley Hill. Nonsuch House at hairpin-bend.

Entry No: 122   Map no: 3

Christopher Noble
Nonsuch House, Church Hill
Kingswear, Dartmouth
Devon TQ6 0BX
Tel: 01803 752829
Fax: 01803 752357
e-mail: enquiries@nonsuch-house.co.uk
Web: www.nonsuch-house.co.uk

Coming downhill into Dittisham, turn sharp right immediately before Red Lion Inn. Go along The Level, up narrow hill and the house entrance is opposite at junction of Manor St and Rectory Lane.

Entry No: 123   Map no: 3

Hugh & Jill Treseder
The White House
Manor Street
Dittisham
Devon TQ6 0EX
Tel: 01803 722355
Fax: 01803 722355
Web: www.sawdays.co.uk

We defy you not to wax lyrical over the setting. The house clings to the hillside before the manicured fields give way to shallow, grassy cliffs, a private beach and tennis court. From the balcony in the four-poster room you can take in the National Trust land that wraps around this stretch of coastland and the views towards Lannacombe Bay. Freshly pressed cotton bed linen, muslin drapes and Laura Ashley fabrics. The lapping of waves and the occasional foghorn is all you'll hear. *Heated indoor swimming pool and sauna. Children by arrangement.*

Rooms: 1 four-poster, en suite. Luxury self-catering also available, sleeps 6.

Price: From £35-£45 p.p. Single supp. by arrangement. Self-catering from £285-£840 p.w.

Breakfast: Flexible.

Meals: Packed lunch by arrangement, from £5 p.p.

Closed: Never.

From Kingsbridge, A379 towards Dartmouth. In Frogmore, right over bridge. Follow signs to East Prawle. On entering village, left by school. Continue to 'phone box and turn left. Right 200 yds on, and follow signs down very steep drive to house.

Entry No: 124   Map no: 2

Sally & Peter Barber
Maelcombe House
East Prawle
Kingsbridge
Devon TQ7 2DE
Tel: 01548 511521
Fax: 01548 511501
e-mail: barber.maelcombe@talk21.com

The house is one of the few remaining thatched Devon longhouses in the area and sits at the head of its own valley with wonderful walking and beaches nearby. More like an hotel than a private house, you will be pampered. Lots of attention to detail — a fridge for drinks, Molton Brown toiletries in the bathroom, boxed stationery, lavender-scented linens and tea on arrival. Every window is dressed with swags, tails and tie-backs. Breakfast will be free-range, organic, local and seasonal. Bread is baked daily and jam and muesli are home-made. *Children by arrangement.*

Rooms: 1 king-size twin/double and 1 double, both en suite (shower); 1 four-poster, en suite (bath).

Price: £37.50-£47.50 p.p.

Breakfast: Until 10am or by arrangement.

Meals: Dinner £25 p.p., minimum 6 people, by arrangement.

Closed: Christmas.

In Marlborough village, take turning opp. Texaco garage into Collaton Rd. After approx. 0.3 miles, left signed Collaton. Keep left at grass island, signed Higher Collaton. House at end of private lane.

Entry No: 125   Map no: 2

Mark Andrews
The Yeoman's Country House
Collaton, Salcombe
Devon TQ7 3DJ
Tel: 01548 560085
Fax: 01548 562070
e-mail: yeomanshouse@easicom.com
Web: www.yeomanshouse.co.uk

A cottage and a bakery used to sit side-by-side — 200 years later, the dividing walls have gone. You are less than a mile from the coastal path at Hope Cove (smugglers used to use this as a den) and local materials have been sourced in the renovation — beams made from wood from Plymouth docks and panelling in the bedrooms from Dartmouth church. You have breakfast in a small book-filled, geranium-scented conservatory. There are stripped pine doors, a tongue-and-groove panelled bathroom and some lovely oak and pine furniture; bedrooms are cosy and low ceilinged. Paddy and Griselda, who used to run a restaurant in Salcombe, are delightful.

Rooms: 2 doubles, both en suite (bath); 1 twin, en suite (shower).

Price: £20-£24 p.p. Single supp. £10.

Breakfast: Flexible.

Meals: Dinner, by arrangement, £15 p.p.

Closed: Christmas.

Lesley and Ann are immensely caring people, which is reflected in the relaxed atmosphere here. You approach the house up a long drive to a mini-hamlet on top of a hill, four houses surrounded by hills and fields with views to the Avon estuary and a wedge of blue sea. The house is an ancient monument recorded in the Domesday Book, yet there is stacks of comfort: thick carpets, big rooms with big views, whitewashed walls and wonderful food. You can be free-range.

Rooms: 1 double, en suite (bath) and 1 twin, en suite (bath/shower).

Price: £22.50 p.p. Supp. for single night's stay £5 extra per room.

Breakfast: Flexible.

Meals: Dinner, 2 courses, from £10 p.p.; 3 courses, from £14 p.p., cheese £2 p.p. B.Y.O. wine.

Closed: Never.

From Kingsbridge on A381, take right to Hope Cove. In Galmpton, cottage is 200 yards on left, past village sign.

From Kingsbridge, A379 towards Plymouth for 4 miles. At top of hill, turn left immed. before gradient sign marked Stadbury (before Aveton Gifford). Long private road; take top fork and house on right.

Entry No: 126   Map no: 2

Entry No: 127   Map no: 2

Mr N.P. & Mrs G.M. Daly
Rose Cottage
Galmpton
Salcombe
Devon TQ7 3EU
Tel: 01548 561953
Fax: 01548 561953
Web: www.wsfb.co.uk/rosecottage

Lesley Dawson & Ann Kinning
Lower Stadbury
Aveton Gifford
Kingsbridge
Devon TQ7 4BD
Tel: 01548 852159
Fax: 01548 852159
Web: www.sawdays.co.uk

The woodpecker comes at 8.10 every morning; this is a haven for wildlife. Even the cat enters the mood, keen to join you in your room if that is her latest chosen spot and there are two goats to take for walks. The house used to be part of the Flete estate, and has big, bright bedrooms with cheerful colours, floor-length windows and velux; beds have pretty tapestry bedspreads or American quilts. Carol and Peter couldn't be nicer — they are clearly happy in their chosen spot in Devon. Cream tea if you arrive before 5pm, gin and tonic after. *Children over 10 welcome.*

Rooms: 2 doubles and 1 twin/double, all en suite (bath & shower).

Price: £25 p.p. No single supp. Reduction for 2 nights or more.

Breakfast: Flexible.

Meals: Dinner, £15 p.p., by arrangement. Packed lunch, £5 p.p.

Closed: Never.

The Tagerts are utterly charming and have a wonderful sense of humour. They enjoy looking after guests and this is communicated in the consummate ease with which they do it. You can relax in your own bit of the garden yet they will be there to mix you the perfect gin and tonic and later serve a delicious dinner — home-cured salmon, followed by local lamb, maybe. Beds are covered in real American patchwork quilts and the rooms are fresh and spotless and not a bit clinical. The Victorian barn sits in an AONB and is one of the best that we have seen; it seems to sing of the love and care with which it has been converted.

Rooms: 2 twins and 1 small double/single, en suite (bath/shower).

Price: £30-£35 p.p. No single supp.

Breakfast: Until 9.30am.

Meals: Dinner, £21.50 p.p., by arrangement.

Closed: Christmas & New Year.

From Modbury, A379 towards Plymouth. After 1.5 miles, take left to Orcheton. Right after 50 yds (Flete estate sign). Cottage is 3rd on right.

Entry No: 128   Map no: 2

Peter Foster & Carol Farrand
Goutsford, Ermington
Nr. Ivybridge
Devon PL21 9NY
Tel: 01548 831299
Fax: 01752 601728
e-mail: needham@exchange.uk.com
Web: www.sawdays.co.uk

From A38 take B3416 and follow signs to Hemerdon. There, pass pub and bear left after 'phone box. Continue past cottages on right. 300 yds down lane first right, gate on right over cattle grid.

Entry No: 129   Map no: 2

Bob & Frances Tagert
The Barn, Windwhistle Farm
Hemerdon
Plymouth
Devon PL7 5BU
Tel: 01752 347016
Fax: 01752 335670
e-mail: frances@tagert.freeserve.co.uk

What a fascinating place! The tide of the Tamar is magnetic and there's an old mine count house from the days when lead and silver were mined here. Trish, immensely warm, is winning the battle against nature, using Martha, the reluctant donkey that prefers to have her front feet in the kitchen. Home-grown veg and free-range eggs depend on the rabbits and the fox. You can sail off down the Tamar (this part is a SSSI and an AONB); there are moorings and a jetty for visiting boats. It's glorious, loaded with character, fun and real quality. Local branch line connects with Plymouth.

Rooms: 1 double, en suite (bath); 1 twin/double, en suite (bath) with extra single/dressing room.

Price: £25 p.p. for single night, £23 p.p. for longer stays. No single supp.

Breakfast: Flexible.

Meals: Supper, £12.50 p.p.; dinner, £15 p.p.; packed lunch, £5 p.p.; all by arrangement.

Closed: Never.

Into Bere Alston on B3257, turn left for Weir Quay. Over x-roads. Follow Hole's Hole sign, then right for Hooe. Fork left for South Hooe Farm. 300 yds on, turn sharply back to your left and down track.

Entry No: 130   Map no: 2

Trish Dugmore
South Hooe Mine
Hole's Hole
Bere Alston, Yelverton
Devon PL20 7BW
Tel: 01822 840329
e-mail: southhooe@aol.com
Web: www.sawdays.co.uk

"Very special people and a lovely place to stay in the middle of nowhere," says our inspector. The Hendersons' 17th-century longhouse has a gorgeous cobbled yard, a bridge across to the island (shades of Monet), goats and a lovely family atmosphere. They produce their own moorland water, all their fruit and vegetables and even make cheese. The rooms are simple country-style, the attitude very 'green' (hedge-laying, stone wall-mending) and the conversation fascinating. You can wander through two acres of young woodland, too.

Rooms: 2 twins and 2 singles, all with basins and sharing 1 bathroom.

Price: Twins £20 p.p.; single £20 p.p. Under 2s free, under 5s half-price in parents' room.

Breakfast: Flexible.

Meals: Evening meal occasionally available, £10 p.p.; also good pub.

Closed: Christmas.

Leave A38 at second Ashburton turning; follow signs for Dartmeet. After 2 miles, fork left to Holne. Pass church and inn on right. After 240 yds, right; after another 150 yds, left to Michelcombe. Left at foot of hill.

Entry No: 131   Map no: 2

John & Judy Henderson
Dodbrooke Farm
Michelcombe
Holne
Devon TQ13 7SP
Tel: 01364 631461
Web: www.sawdays.co.uk

An enchanted guest wrote: "If your life is full of stress, there is no better place to recover". Everything is geared to your comfort: enticing four-poster and half-tester beds in cottagey rooms and deep, free-standing baths. It is Joanna and Graham, though, who give that extra something. A lovely Devon couple, they have worked hard to restore the former gardener's bothy; Graham made much of the furniture. The guest sitting room has a slate floor, pine Victorian fireplace and leather sofas. There's a thriving organic vegetable garden, ponds, a stream and Nelson, newly retired from the rigours of the pony club.

Rooms: 1 four-poster, 1 half-tester, both with private bathroom (bath/shower); further single available.

Price: From £25 p.p.

Breakfast: Flexible.

Meals: Dinner, 3 courses, £12 p.p.

Closed: Never.

Pure ancient magic! Ann is wiry, twinkly and kind. She has restored this listed Devon longhouse with its Bronze Age foundation, keeping the shippon end (where her gentle giant shire horses live) and creating an engagingly chaotic haven for innumerable furry friends and the B&B guests she so enjoys. Simple but snug bedrooms, one with a four-poster. Her shire horses will pull you in a wagon to discover the secret lanes and picnic spots of the Dartmoor she knows and loves so deeply. The house is right by the Two Moors Way footpath. *Children over 10 by arrangement.*

Rooms: 1 four-poster and 1 twin, sharing private bathroom.

Price: £20 p.p. No single supp.

Breakfast: Flexible.

Meals: Packed lunch by arrangement.

Closed: Christmas.

From Tavistock B3357 to Princetown. 0.25 miles on, at Mount House School, take next left turning. Drive past the lake to the house.

Entry No: 132   Map no: 2

Mr & Mrs G.H. Moule
Mount Tavy Cottage
Tavistock
Devon PL19 9JL
Tel: 01822 614253
Web: www.mounttavy.freeserve.co.uk

From A38 take 2nd Ashburton turning towards Dartmeet & Princetown. In Poundsgate pass pub on left & take 3rd signposted turning right towards Corndon. Straight over x-roads, 0.5 miles further & farm is on left.

Entry No: 133   Map no: 2

Ann & William Williams
Corndonford Farm
Poundsgate
Newton Abbot
Devon TQ13 7PP
Tel: 01364 631595
Web: www.sawdays.co.uk

Restoring Bagtor House has been a labour of love; the family feel a deep attachment to their 'friendly, happy' house. The kitchen and the breakfast room are tangibly ancient — 14th century — and the latter contains a huge fireplace and oak panelling. Among this ancient beauty — where John Ford, the dramatist contemporary of Shakespeare, was born — there is no stinting on modern comforts; bedrooms, beds and bathrooms are big. You breakfast on home-laid eggs and here, in a leafy, lush spot of the Dartmoor National Park, you can watch fat sheep graze, wander in the garden or walk to Bagtor, just behind the house.

Rooms: 1 double & 1 king-size with extra single, both with private bathroom.

Price: From £25 p.p. Single supp. by arrangement.

Breakfast: Flexible.

Meals: Available locally at excellent pubs.

Closed: Christmas.

From Bovey Tracy, B3387 for Widecombe in the Moor. After 2.5 miles, left for Ilsington. After 0.75 miles, fork right to Bickington. Next right to Bagtor. House on right 0.75 miles on.

Entry No: 134   Map no: 2

Nigel & Sue Cookson
Bagtor House
Ilsington
Newton Abbot
Devon TQ13 9RT
Tel: 01364 661538
Fax: 01364 661538

A little green lane goes up beyond this cottage to the moor and Easdon Tor — this is a great place for walking and riding. A great place to relax, too. Liza and Hugh both have such an easy, calm manner. They are also vegetarian and dedicated users of organic produce. The rooms in the cottage and the barn, which is also let for self-catering, have a successful mix of pictures, oriental rugs, books, beams, views, plants, pine, granite walls, cool linen and some handsome Victorian finds, like the bath and the dining room fireplace. *Children by arrangement.*

Rooms: 1 twin/double, en suite (bath). In barn: double with sofa bed and bunk, with private bathroom.

Price: £23 p.p. No single supp. Barn from £150-£250 p.w.

Breakfast: Flexible (vegetarian/vegan).

Meals: Available locally.

Closed: Christmas & New Year.

A38 SW from Exeter, A382 to Bovey Tracey. Left at 2nd r'bout in Bovey for Manaton. Through Manaton and, 2 miles on, right at Heatree Cross, signed Moretonhampstead. 0.5 miles on, look for name of cottage in hedge. Cottage is up track, to the right.

Entry No: 135   Map no: 2

Liza & Hugh Dagnall
Easdon Cottage
Long Lane
Manaton
Devon TQ13 9XB
Tel: 01647 221389
Fax: 01647 221389
Web: www.sawdays.co.uk

Through the reigns of 25 monarchs, Gate House has stood solidly on this beautiful corner of Dartmoor. Unusually for a 15th-century hall house, a brightness finds its way inside, making everything gleam. You dine by candlelight off crisp white table linen and have your own sitting room with a vast, granite fireplace. There's a pool in the large, secluded gardens that overlooks woodlands and the moor. John and Sheila love having guests and take such care with everything that you will feel truly spoiled.

Rooms: 2 twins/doubles, both en suite (1 bath/shower and 1 shower); 1 twin/double, next to private bathroom.

Price: £28 p.p. Single supp. £7.

Breakfast: Flexible.

Meals: Packed lunch available. Dinner, 4/5 courses, £16 p.p., by arrangement. B.Y.O wine.

Closed: Never.

Luxury touches at every turn — as if the rare solitary stream-side setting of this longhouse wasn't enough. Maureen pampers you imaginatively: champagne on occasions, toiletries, bedside bags of truffles, soft towels and robes in huge bedrooms — one with its own conservatory, the other two with private terraces. Outdoors, a swimming pool is colourfully lit at night. Renowned for inspired vegetarian and traditional cooking, Maureen serves breakfast in the (fountained) sunroom. She is gregarious yet unobtrusive. Moors, not fairies, at the bottom of the gardens. But there is magic here....

Rooms: 3 garden rooms, each with private garden or private conservatory, 2 doubles, 1 twin/double, all en suite (bath or shower).

Price: £49 p.p. Single occ. £76. Minimum 2 nights. Special winter breaks November-March. Please book ahead.

Breakfast: Until 9.30am.

Meals: Restaurant nearby.

Closed: Christmas & New Year.

The Gate House is 25 yards off North Bovey's village green, down Lower Hill past the village inn.

Entry No: 136   Map no: 2

John & Sheila Williams
The Gate House
North Bovey
Devon TQ13 8RB
Tel: 01647 440479
Fax: 01647 440479
e-mail: gatehouseondartmoor@talk21.com

In Chillaton keep pub and P.O. on your left, up hill towards Tavistock. After 300 yds, right turn (Bridlepath sign). Cottage at end of lane.

Entry No: 137   Map no: 2

Maureen Rowlatt
Tor Cottage
Chillaton, Nr. Tavistock
Devon PL16 0JE
Tel: 01822 860248
Fax: 01822 860126
e-mail: info@torcottage.demon.co.uk
Web: www.torcottage.demon.co.uk

Devon is awash with the good things of nature, but this delightful house is worth a trek via those softly folded valleys and high-sided lanes. The outside is less interesting than the inside, so persevere. Sara-Jane has the gift of drawing you into the bosom of the family. The beds have embossed sheets, towels as large as they are fluffy and the bathrooms have Floris soaps. The garden fits the house — beautifully tended and comfortable. Lush country, unspoilt and rural. Come. *Children over nine welcome.*

Rooms: 1 twin with basin, and 1 small double, sharing private bathroom.

Price: £18.50 p.p.

Breakfast: Flexible.

Meals: Packed lunch from £5 p.p.

Closed: Occasionally.

Walk, ride, sail (on Roadford Reservoir) to your heart's content from your base in this lovely, converted mill in the heart of Devon. The Archers have lived all over the world (Hong Kong, Canada, India...) and have settled among the natural treasures of this delectable region. It is perfect for Sonia's landscape painting and she hopes other painters will join her. They offer you glasses of wine in their large, homely kitchen, fold you in human warmth, advise you how to explore the area, and practise their Cantonese on you if you wish. *Children by arrangement.*

Rooms: 1 twin, en suite (bath & shower) with sitting room.

Price: £25 p.p. Infants free; 7 years & under £2.50.

Breakfast: Flexible.

Meals: Dinner £15 p.p. (not on Sundays).

Closed: Christmas & New Year.

From A30, A386 to Tavistock. Right to Lydford. Through Lydford and on to Brentor. Right at Liddaton turning and fork right, follow hill down and right for Coryton. Over r'way bridge, bear left and house in front.

Sara-Jane & Robert Cumming
Broad Park Farm
Coryton
Okehampton
Devon EX20 4AA
Tel: 01822 860281
Fax: 01822 860281
e-mail: rpcumming@nascr.net

Follow signs out of Ashwater to Clawton/Holsworthy. After 1 mile, just by Thorney Cross, mill entrance is inside Renson Farm driveway.

Geoffrey & Sonia Archer
Renson Mill
Ashwater
Devon EX21 5ER
Tel: 01409 211665
Fax: 01409 211665
Web: www.sawdays.co.uk

This 14th-century, Grade II-listed, thatched Dartmoor longhouse, within Dartmoor National Park, was recently home of author Doris Lessing. Its history goes on and on... enchantingly pervasive in the architecture, interiors, gardens — and atmosphere. Sleep resplendent in four-posters in low-ceilinged, beamy rooms, all with views of the very English country garden, whence come copious fresh flowers. Your hosts are adventurously well-travelled and interesting. There's a petanque pitch outside and just one field away lies the moor with all its wild treasures.

Rooms: 3 four-posters, 2 en suite (1 shower, 1 bath), 1 with private shower room.

Price: £32.50-£35 p.p. Single supp. £10.

Breakfast: Until 9.30am.

Meals: Packed lunch £5 p.p.

Closed: Christmas & New Year.

There are few traces of its 13th-century origins but the house is listed and there are pieces of fine old oak and granite everywhere, to which the Merchants have added their own antiques and old photographs. The age of this magnificent house (tiny corridors and doorways) has yielded to modern comfort in a most sensitive way. The bedrooms, particularly, are wondrously cosy, with thick carpets and wooden furniture. Treat yourself to a Devon farmhouse dinner with home-grown meat and vegetables. This is a working Dartmoor farm, with 50 milking cows and a pedigree Aberdeen Angus herd.

Rooms: 1 twin, 1 double and 1 four-poster, all en suite (shower).

Price: £22-£24 p.p. Single supp. by arrangement.

Breakfast: Flexible.

Meals: Dinner £13 p.p.

Closed: Never.

From M5, take A30 for Okehampton. After 23 miles exit to Okehampton & Belstone. Left, pass garage & immediately right opp. lay-by into lane. After 1 mile, left at T-junc. Gate on right after 50 yards.

Entry No: 140   Map no: 2

John & Maureen Pakenham
Tor Down House
Belstone
Okehampton
Devon EX20 1QY
Tel: 01837 840731
Fax: 01837 840731
e-mail: tordownhouse@appleonline.net

From Bovey Tracey A382. After Moretonhamstead, look for signs to farm.

Entry No: 141   Map no: 2

Trudie Merchant
Great Sloncombe Farm
Moretonhampstead
Devon TQ13 8QF
Tel: 01647 440595
Fax: 01647 440595
e-mail: hmerchant@sloncombe.freeserve.co.uk

Only 900 years old and still humming with life: there's a goat in love with a goose, a pony in the rambling gardens, dogs, cats, guinea fowl, rabbits and foxes. Sally-Anne is artistic, slightly zany and adventurous, as are her family. The farm is in the Domesday Book and is steeped in history with huge flagstone fireplaces, interesting contemporary art, books, pianos and wellies by the front door where you leave your stress on arrival. Not a road in sight, perfect quiet and sweeping views.

Rooms: 1 twin and 1 double, sharing bathroom.

Price: £25 p.p. Single occ. £30.

Breakfast: Flexible.

Meals: Available nearby.

Closed: Christmas & New Year.

A house of strong tastes and opinions, perfect for the young at heart looking for a touch of luxury of an unusual kind. It's full of surprises: strong colours, huge curtains, touches of Baroque and Rococo (he's an antique dealer), stone Buddhas by the door, soft music, lots of mirrors, paint-effect doors, Gothic touches. Yes, there is a trouser press, too. The beds are splendid four-posters; you will be comfortable. Catherine, once an air hostess, loves cooking and so does Edward, a Londoner. They are friendly, cheerful, zappy and hospitable. *Children over five welcome*

Rooms: 1 double with private bathroom; 1 double, en suite (shower).

Price: From £25 p.p. No single supp.

Breakfast: Flexible.

Meals: Dinner, by arrangement, £20 p.p. Packed lunch, £5 p.p.

Closed: Never.

A30 to Okehampton. After 10 miles left exit into Cheriton Bishop, second left between 2 cottages. Go down & up hill. Road turns sharp left. Go down lane; farm signed.

Entry No: 142   Map no: 2

Sally-Anne Carter-Johnson
Higher Eggbeer Farm
Cheriton Bishop
Nr. Exeter
Devon EX6 6JQ
Tel: 01647 24427

From Exeter/M5, follow the A30 Okehampton road. Take B3219 for North Tawton. There, at Market Square right at clock tower and house is 100 yds on left.

Entry No: 143   Map no: 2

Edward & Catherine Henson
The Old Rectory
Essington
North Tawton
Devon EX20 2EX
Tel: 01837 82866
Fax: 01837 82866
e-mail: oldrectory@hensone.freeserve.co.uk

Stewart & Jennie gave up working in London to take over the estate that has been in the family for 900 years. They valiantly look after the house (Georgian with Victorian façade) and 150 acres almost single-handedly. You'll find a real country home rather than an anodyne hotel, with history oozing in every stone, painting, piece of furniture and panelling. Stewart is an engaging guide to it all. The large twin room has padded headboards, peach, piped covers and a big bathroom. The breakfast room is lined with ancient books; the snooker room has a grand piano and a log fire in winter. Walk along the old carriage drive to Black Torrington.

Rooms: 1 twin, en suite (bath).

Price: £25 p.p. Single supp. £2.50.

Breakfast: Flexible.

Meals: Available locally.

Closed: Christmas & New Year.

Rolling fields and gentle hills stretch up to Dartmoor and you'll not spot another house. Everything feels exactly right — fresh flowers, shiny silver, comfy sofas, lovely oak furniture. The bedrooms are just as good — white, crisp cotton duvets, soft chairs and books. The views are unbeatable. The façade is Georgian, but the house's origins are 16th century. Valerie loves gardening and is retrieving this pretty garden from its former ignored state. She is great fun and delights in having guests. A great place to escape from it all. *Children over 12 welcome.*

Rooms: 1 king-size double and 1 twin, sharing private bathroom.

Price: £20 p.p. No single supp.

Breakfast: Flexible.

Meals: Dinner, £12.50 p.p., by arrangement.

Closed: Never.

From Okehampton, A386 towards Hatherleigh. There, left onto B3072 towards Holsworthy. After 4 miles, pass through Highampton, then take right to Black Torrington. Left at Post Office. Entrance is 700/800 yds on right.

Entry No: 144   Map no: 2

Mr & Mrs Stewart Coham-MacLaren
Coham Manor
Black Torrington
Beaworthy
Devon EX21 5HT
Tel: 01409 231514
Fax: 01409 231514
e-mail: maclaren.4@cwcom.net

From Holsworthy, A388 for Bideford. Through Milton Damerel and past Woodford Bridge Hotel on left, then right to Newton St. Petrock. 1 mile on, near church, straight on signed Shebbear. House is round bend in lane on left.

Entry No: 145   Map no: 2

Mrs Valerie Lampen
The Old Rectory
Newton St. Petrock
Holsworthy, Devon EX22 7LR
Tel: 01409 281225
Fax: 01409 281225
e-mail: vlampen@netscapeonline.co.uk
members.netscapeonline.co.uk/vlampen

The Weeks have brought a vibrancy to this 300-year-old longhouse with old pine pieces, real candelabras, pretty fabrics and bright colours, yet the old bones of the place — wood, stone floors and beams — are allowed to breathe. The brass double bed is pure farmhouse charm, with Laura Ashley fabrics and papers. Pillows and cushions are stacked high and there are home-made biscuits and an electric blanket. The sparkling bathroom gives onto blossom trees and the garden. Shelley loves cooking and is such easy company.

Rooms: 1 double, en suite (bath); 1 extra double for children.

Price: £20-£22.50 p.p. Single supp. by arrangement.

Breakfast: Flexible.

Meals: Dinner from £12 p.p., packed lunch from £5 p.p.

Closed: Occasionally.

The bleat of a lost lamb was the only sound we heard at the 16th-century stone-and-cob Devon longhouse. Ann and Richard — vastly talented and artistic — have worked in harmony to restore it all. Ann has laid brick paths, stencilled, stitched and painted with striking Jane Churchill colours; Richard a restoration builder and carpenter, has renovated brass beds, made the dresser and uncovered everything of ancient beauty. The beds are so inviting that you can't resist the urge to collapse on them. *Children by arrangement.*

Rooms: 1 double, en suite (shower); 1 twin, en suite (bath/shower).

Price: £23.50 p.p. No single supp.

Breakfast: Flexible.

Meals: Dinner, 2 courses, £12.50 p.p., by arrangement.

Closed: 20 December-5 January.

From Eggesford, turn right off A377, signed Chawleigh. At very top, bear right through village. 2-3 miles out other side of village, at Burridge Moor Cross, left signed Cheldon. Less than 0.25 mile, on S-bend, concrete drive straight ahead.

Entry No: 146   Map no: 2

Mrs S. Weeks
Great Burridge Farm
Chawleigh
Chulmleigh
Devon EX18 7HY
Tel: 01363 83818
e-mail: shelleyweeks@smartone.co.uk

From A39, left into Bideford, round quay, passing old bridge on left. Follow signs to Torrington. 1.5 miles on, right at Crystal Centre, signed Buckland Brewer. 2.5 miles on, left, also signed. Beara is on right, 0.5 miles on.

Entry No: 147   Map no: 2

Ann & Richard Dorsett
Beara Farmhouse
Buckland Brewer
Bideford
Devon EX39 5EH
Tel: 01237 451666

Horwood is a 40-acre beef and sheep farm on the edge of a small hamlet, but you'd never know. Pure peace. Gill is a working interior designer so the house was always off to a flying start... with the help of three acres of lovely gardens, including a walled kitchen garden and a lake. There are long southerly views over open countryside and the Grade II-listed Georgian house has some wonderful rooms: big hall, library, both dining room and sitting room. The bedrooms are big, the wallpaper and drapes co-ordinated, the bathrooms tremendous.

Rooms: 1 double (5ft four-poster) and 1 twin, both en suite (bath/shower).

Price: £30-£40 p.p. Single occ. £40.

Breakfast: Until 9am.

Meals: Available locally.

Closed: Christmas & New Year.

You can't keep the tea trays upstairs for there is little furniture straight enough to put them on! The house is a creaky, lived-in, 17th-century barn conversion with good country taste. There is a bathroom with a huge bath under a long sloping ceiling, views of a hilltop crowned with trees, a handsome main bedroom with wiggly walls and wicker furniture, a fire in the elegant-but-homely drawing room and a drying area for wet walkers. The flower garden and lawn stretch up the hill. Very nice, easy and unstuffy people.

Rooms: 2 doubles and 1 twin, all with basins and sharing bathroom and shower room.

Price: £17-£20 p.p. No single supp.

Breakfast: Flexible.

Meals: Good pubs nearby.

Closed: Christmas & New Year.

M5 junction 27. At r'bout turn to Bideford. At second r'bout left to Newton Tracey. After about 2.5 miles right for Horwood. After 0.25 miles house sign & 2 white entrance pillars on left over cattle grid.

Entry No: 148   Map no: 2

Gill Barriball
Horwood House
Horwood
Nr. Bideford
Devon EX39 4PD
Tel: 01271 858231
Fax: 01271 858231

From Barnstaple, A361 towards Braunton. At 2nd set of lights, right signed Bradiford. Next T-junc., sharp left, over bridge, up hill for 50m, 2nd lane to right. House 1st on left.

Entry No: 149   Map no: 2

Jane & Tony Hare
Bradiford Cottage
Halls Mill Lane, Bradiford, Barnstaple
Devon EX31 4DP
Tel: 01271 345039
Fax: 01271 345039
e-mail: tony@humesfarm.co.uk
Web: www.humesfarm.co.uk

You eventually come to a deep, 'secret' valley to discover the rambling Georgian farmhouse of artist John and wife Penny. Crisp and white outside, it's homely and informal inside, with an oak-panelled dining room, antiques and paintings everywhere. Long views down the wooded valley from the rooms across the gardens, a haven with tree houses and waterfalls. John is proud of his musically gifted family — Penny sings and their daughter is a harpist; they stage concerts here each year. The en suite bedroom is large and lovely; the other two rooms are much smaller. *Children over 12 welcome.*

Rooms: 1 twin and 1 double with basins, sharing bathroom; 1 king-size, en suite (bath/shower). Also 3 self-catering units, sleep 4/5/6.

Price: From £25-£30 p.p. Single occ. £30-£35. Self-catering £250-£550 pw.

Breakfast: 8.30-9am.

Meals: Dinner, 3 courses, £18 p.p. Packed lunch by arrangement.

Closed: Christmas.

A361 to Barnstaple. Right at junction of South/North Molton. Through N. Molton, over bridge, onto moor signed Sandyway. After 3.5 miles, left at x-roads to Simonsbath; after 400 yds, right down lane, signed.

Entry No: 150   Map no: 2

John & Penny Adie
Barkham
Sandyway, South Molton
Devon EX36 3LU
Tel: 01643 831370
Fax: 01643 831370
e-mail: adie.exmoor@btinternet.com
Web: www.sawdays.co.uk

The house is old but the Coopers have unleashed their arty, bohemian taste to create an impressionistic ancient-and-modern interior that is a heady mix of laid-back informality and surprising touches of luxury. They are interesting people, green-leaning farmers who produce horses, poultry and organic food. (Jackie's breakfasts — platters of fruits and meats or full English are quite something.) The house is lovely, the outdoor pool is heated, some rooms have distant sea views. Come for a wonderful time rather then hotelly perfection.

Rooms: 2 king-size beds, and 1 double, all en suite (bath/shower); 1 twin with basin and private jacuzzi bath.

Price: £30-£40 p.p. Children is same room as parents, £5. No single supp.

Breakfast: Flexible.

Meals: Dinner by arrangement.

Closed: Christmas.

Follow A3122 to Forces Tavern, then follow signpost to Cornworthy. At Tideford Cross turn right, and then left over cattle grid.

Entry No: 150a   Map no: 3

Jackie Cooper
Higher Tideford
Cornworthy, Totnes
Devon TQ9 7HL
Tel: 01803 712387
Fax: 01803 712388

Robin and Wendy ran a ski chalet for 11 years — they've swapped the Alps for this thatched Dorset dream of a village and here, too, they tread the middle line between care and professionalism. Much modern comfort has been added in sympathy with the old stones — some date from 1750. Bedrooms are charming — Victorian with brass bedstead, Farmhouse with pale, painted panelling and Nautical with an ancient ship's wheel. You breakfast next to a range, dine in the conservatory and have your own sitting room. Look for The Lion, The Witch and The Wardrobe surprise and the wild Heartsease pansy which thrives in the garden.

Rooms: 1 double, en suite (shower); 2 twins, sharing bathroom (can have exclusive use of bathroom if you wish).

Price: £22-£27 p.p. Single occ. £28.

Breakfast: Flexible.

Meals: Light supper and packed lunch, each £4.50 p.p. Dinner, 2 courses, £12 p.p., 3 courses, £15 p.p.

Closed: Christmas.

From Yeovil, A30 for Sherborne. On dual carriageway, ignore 1st right for Bradford Abbas — take 2nd. Down narrow lane & over x-roads. Take 1st right, then 1st left into North St. House on right, with 5-bar gate.

Entry No: 151   Map no: 3

Robin & Wendy Dann
Heartsease Cottage
North Street
Bradford Abbas, Sherborne
Dorset DT9 6SA
Tel: 01935 475480
Fax: 01935 475480
e-mail: heartsease@talk21.com

Dorset

The Benjamins have returned from working in the States and imported the country's high standard of B&B. Bedrooms are more 'le grand luxe' than cottagey and, naturally, the beds are big and of the finest quality; the four-poster has steps up to it. Lovely toile de jouy curtains throughout and a general feeling of opulence. State of the art bathroom fittings, power showers (of course) and generous, fluffy towels. The garden was designed by the 'sculptural' member of the Gardener's World team, Ivan Hicks, and there is much of interest. Sylvia's other passion is antiques — you can buy some of her finds if you wish.

Rooms: 4 doubles, all en suite (bath & shower); 2 twins, both en suite (bath & shower). Studio with kitchenette & shower room, suitable for family use.

Price: £30-£40 p.p. Single supp. £9.

Breakfast: Flexible.

Meals: Available locally.

Closed: Never.

From Sherborne follow signs to A3030, then to Alweston, 2 miles on. There, past post office on right, "P" for parking sign on left, and next left into Munden Lane. House behind Oxford Bakery.

Entry No: 152   Map no: 3

Sylvia & Joe Benjamin
Munden House
Alweston, Sherborne
Dorset DT9 5HU
Tel: 01963 23150
Fax: 01963 23153
e-mail: sylvia@mundenhouse.demon.co.uk
Web: www.mundenhouse.demon.co.uk

Jorgen and Anthony fled London for Wessex peace. Their refuge is this imposing, hydrangea-clad mock Gothic house — built by the Lord of the Manor for a vicar son — where excellent food and a striking mixture of décor dramatically blend east and west. At weekends, a chef from an acclaimed local restaurant prepares dinner. The open, light drawing room is a melange of sofas, oriental antiques and heavy, traditional curtains. Upstairs, design is at its showiest in the Chinese room where half-tester bed and furniture are black and gold lacquer. *Children over five welcome. Vegetarians catered for by prior arrangement.*

Rooms: 3 twins, 3 doubles and 1 single, all en suite (bath with shower).

Price: £25-£45 p.p. Single occ. £32-£55.

Breakfast: Until 10am.

Meals: Dinner available on Fri & Sat, £17-£22 p.p.

Closed: January and/or February.

From Sherborne A30 to Milborne Port. The Old Vicarage is 2nd on right on entering village.

Entry No: 153   Map no: 3

Mr Anthony Ma & Jorgen Kunath
The Old Vicarage
Milborne Port
Sherborne
Dorset DT9 5AT
Tel: 01963 251117
Fax: 01963 251515
Web: www.sawdays.co.uk

The Royal Commission included this house in its inventory on Historical Monuments in England. Dorset with its softly-folding hills and leafy lanes is the perfect backdrop for the listed, 17th-century house. There's stacks of atmosphere — original beams, flagstones, window seats and numerous family treasures. The bedrooms have been generously furnished with fine pieces such as an elegant sofa and a tall, dark wood chest. National Trust colours throughout. The garden is lovely — there is a seat for you — and Mrs Tennant is a quiet, thoughtful hostess. *Children over 14 welcome.*

Rooms: 1 double with private bathroom; 1 twin sharing bathroom, let only to members of same party.

Price: £25-£35 p.p. Single supp. £5.

Breakfast: Flexible.

Meals: Many pubs & restaurants nearby.

Closed: Christmas & New Year.

I could look at this view for hours: clear across Lyme Bay and along the Dorset coast for 30 miles — it is spectacular. Behind me is the Normans' large 1920s house where years of travel and naval lifestyle lie behind their meticulous and old-fashioned hospitality. The rooms are thoroughly comfortable and the dining room refurbished in keeping with the period of the house itself. Two of the guestrooms are large with wonderful coastal views, the third more cottagey; all have chairs, a writing desk and fresh flowers. *Children over eight welcome.*

Rooms: 1 family room and 2 twins, all en suite (bath).

Price: £22-£27 p.p. Single occ. £33-£40.

Breakfast: Until 9am.

Meals: Supper tray on first night, ordered in advance, £8 p.p.

Closed: Mid-November-early March.

From Bridport, A35 into Chideock. Right just before church. 0.75 miles up 'No Through Road' to T-junc. Turn right, house is 7th on right (thatched with 2 porches). Drive to end of house, through gate to car park.

Entry No: 154   Map no: 3

Mrs M. Tennant
Champ's Land
Brighthay Lane
North Chideock, nr. Bridport
Dorset DT6 6JZ
Tel: 01297 489314

On A3052 to Lyme, house is 1st left after 'Welcome to Lyme' sign on right. From Lyme: up Sidmouth Rd, past Morgan's Grave & Somers Rd, and enter first driveway on right, opposite junc. sign.

Entry No: 155   Map no: 3

Tony & Vicky Norman
The Red House
Sidmouth Road, Lyme Regis
Dorset DT7 3ES
Tel: 01297 442055
Fax: 01297 442055
e-mail: red.house@virgin.net
Web: www.sawdays.co.uk

This is a perfect place. Outside, 10 acres of orchard, valley and wooded hills, wrapped in peace and quiet; inside, 17th-century stone walls, low-beamed ceilings and a warm French flair. Sydney and Jayne are easy-going Francophiles who share a gift for unwinding stressed souls. Bedrooms have antique French beds, bold colours and crisp linen; in the sitting room there are books, open fire and soft, deep chairs. Eat on the terrace and soak up the beauty of the sunsets. Jayne makes compotes from the orchard fruit; you'll see them at breakfast along with 100%-meat sausages and, perhaps, cured ham and kippers. Cliff walks, beaches and fields are yours, too.

Rooms: 1 twin and 3 doubles, all en suite (bath).

Price: £32.50-£37.50 p.p. Single occ. (weekdays only) £45.

Breakfast: 8.45-9.30am.

Meals: Dinner, 3 courses, £16.50 p.p. Hot supper tray £13.50 p.p.

Closed: 24 December-2 January.

From Dorchester A35 towards Bridport. After 13 miles take second road signed left to Shipton Gorge and Burton Bradstock. First left to farmhouse.

Entry No: 156   Map no: 3

Sydney & Jayne Davies
Innsacre Farmhouse
Shipton Gorge
Nr. Bridport
Dorset DT6 4LJ
Tel: 01308 456137
Fax: 01308 456137

Stand on the cowslip and orchid-strewn ramparts of Eggardon's hill fort and you gaze across a valley to this romantically-secluded farmhouse. It is set in a maze of paths amongst wildflower meadows and medieval woodland. Follow the sleepy flower-decked lanes to the former shooting lodge with its enormous flagstones, stripped floors, chunky studded doors and exposed beams. The tranquillity of the bedrooms complements Rosie's vibrant paintings. Explore the enchanting secret valleys and bumpety hills of West Dorset or the spectacular Heritage coast.

Rooms: 1 twin, en suite (bath); 1 double/family, en suite (bath/shower).

Price: From £22.50 p.p. Single supp. by arrangement.

Breakfast: Flexible.

Meals: Award-winning pubs within short drive.

Closed: Occasionally.

On A356 from Dorchester, turn at first sign for Toller Porcorum. Through village & up hill. At tiny x-roads, right signed Powerstock, under r'way bridge. Track to farm 0.5 miles on left, opp. unmarked lane. House at end, on left.

Entry No: 157   Map no: 3

Rosie & Roger Britton
Grays Farmhouse
Toller Porcorum
Dorchester
Dorset DT2 0EJ
Tel: 01308 485574
e-mail: rosie-roger@freenetname.co.uk
Web: www.farmhousebnb.co.uk

You could scarcely find a more picture-book 'English cottage'. A lovely village, fields and hills all around, a 400-year lifespan, a thatched roof, a stream to cross, a pretty flowery garden. The house, from the outside, is impossibly pretty. Inside there's a stone-flagged hall and bedrooms that are functional — nothing fancy at all. Nicky, independent, enthusiastic and most knowledgeable about walks and visits in Hardy Country, will leave you to your own devices once you are properly advised. *Children over eight welcome.*

Rooms: 2 doubles (1 with room for extra bed) and 1 twin, all with basins and sharing 2 bathrooms.

Price: £21 p.p. Single supp. £5.

Breakfast: Until 9.30am.

Meals: Good food locally available.

Closed: Christmas.

You are deeply in Hardy Country here; the bedrooms are traditionally pretty and beamy with fresh flowers everywhere. There is an inglenook fireplace in the dining room with log fires that are coaxed into flame at the faintest hint of cold. Anita and André have travelled widely and Anita is very knowledgeable about health food; she loves this work and can produce almost anything you want for breakfast. There is a small sitting area in the dining room if you want to be private, with ample books, or a very pretty garden to sit in.

Rooms: 1 twin and 1 double, both en suite (bath); 2 singles, sharing bathroom. Cot bed & extra bed available on request.

Price: £24 p.p. Single £18 p.p.

Breakfast: 8-9.30am.

Meals: Occasionally by special request.

Closed: 20 December-3 January.

From Dorchester, A37 north. After 5 miles, in Grimstone, right under railway bridge to Sydling St. Nicholas. Lamperts is first thatched cottage on right, in village.

Entry No: 158   Map no: 3

Nicky Willis
Lamperts Cottage
Sydling St. Nicholas
Dorchester
Dorset DT2 9NU
Tel: 01300 341659
Fax: 01300 341699
e-mail: nikywillis@aol.com

From Holywell Cross (midway between Yeovil & Dorchester on A37) turn towards Batcombe; 50 yards on, left into small lane to Chetnole. Follow for 0.75 miles. House on right.

Entry No: 159   Map no: 3

André & Anita Millorit
Brambles
Woolcombe
Melbury Bubb, nr. Dorchester
Dorset DT2 0NJ
Tel: 01935 83672

Sally is a Thomas Hardy enthusiast and John Schlesinger's *Far From The Madding Crowd*'s church scene was filmed in the village. The Regency house is light with National Trust pink in the porch/hallway, a pale blue sitting room with comfy sofas and mahogany display cabinets and a flower-filled conservatory with wicker chairs. Above, cheerful, bright bedrooms with Provençal/Laura Ashley fabrics and cast-iron fireplaces overlook village roofs and sheep-grazed hills. Far from the madding crowd, indeed. *Children over 12 welcome.*

Rooms: 1 double, en suite (shower); 1 twin next to private bathroom.

Price: £27 p.p. Single occ. £32.

Breakfast: Flexible.

Meals: Good pub 50 yards away.

Closed: Occasionally.

The family Labrador, Holly, will greet you at this warm and friendly country house with owners to match. There is a walled half-acre garden and herbaceous border (Tia's passion). All rooms are beautifully decorated and have stunning views. After a day out or a good walk feel at home and hunker down with a pile of their books in front of a blazing log fire. And in the morning enjoy a memorable breakfast with free-range eggs and home-made jams and marmalades in the elegant dining room (again with log fire in winter). On a quiet road, this is a lovely old house, comfortable and easy.

Rooms: 1 twin/double en suite; 1 double and 1 single with private bathrooms.

Price: £22.50-£25 p.p.

Breakfast: Until 9am.

Meals: Dinner, £12.50 p.p., by prior arrangement.

Closed: 23-27 December.

From Dorchester A37 towards Yeovil. 3 miles on, through Grimstone and right for Sydling St. Nicholas. Under r'way viaduct and on for 4 miles to Sydling. House on right just past Greyhound pub.

Entry No: 160   Map no: 3

Mrs F. A. Anderson
Upper Mill
Sydling St. Nicholas
Dorchester
Dorset DT2 9PD
Tel: 01300 341230
Fax: 01300 341230

From Dorchester, B3143 into Buckland Newton over crossroads; Holyleas is on the right opposite village cricket pitch.

Entry No: 161   Map no: 3

Tia Bunkall
Holyleas House
Buckland Newton
Dorchester, Dorset DT2 7DP
Tel: 01300 345214
Fax: 01305 264488
e-mail: tiabunkall@holyleas.co.uk
Web: www.sawdays.co.uk

So close to the centre of town and so quiet, thanks to the massive walls and walled garden — open to the public once a year. The house is a Regency gem, of which there are many in this impressive little historic town. Inside the hall there is a marvellously odd statue of a man, made from motorbike parts, and an intricate model of a navy craft. Similarly unexpected is the breakfast: kippers, home-made jams (the garden is rich with fruit), eggs every way... One bedroom has views of the church and hills beyond, a vast and luxurious bathroom and a desk. A complete delight.

Rooms: 2 twins, both en suite (bath).

Price: £26-£30 p.p. Single occ. £40-£45.

Breakfast: Until 9.30am.

Meals: Good restaurants locally.

Closed: Christmas Day.

Your welcome begins as you step through the door to find an antique stove in a hall full of intriguing curios and, perhaps, the scent of freshly-baked bread. The elegant, 18th-century listed house is palpably 'English' — warm, Regency stripes and rugs in the drawing room, polished wood and china and pretty, comfortable, bedrooms. It is at ease in this delectable village, half a mile's stroll from the old town of Shaftesbury. The walled garden gives quiet seclusion, with views to the Dorset hills beyond.

Rooms: 1 double and 2 twins/doubles, all en suite (bath).

Price: £33-£35 p.p. Single occ. £45.

Breakfast: Flexible.

Meals: Dinner, 4 courses, £22.50 p.p., by arrangement.

Closed: Christmas.

From Shaftesbury, take B3091 towards Sturminster Newton. After 0.25 miles down St. John's Hill, Cliff House is first on the right, with parking next to garage.

Entry No: 162   Map no: 4

From Shaftesbury take B3091 towards Sturminster Newton. After 0.5 miles down St. John's Hill the Old Rectory is on right at bottom of hill, with parking on left.

Entry No: 163   Map no: 4

Diana Pow
Cliff House
Breach Lane, Shaftesbury
Dorset SP7 8LF
Tel: 01747 852548
Fax: 01747 852548
e-mail: dianaepow@aol.com
Web: www.cliff-house.co.uk

Rose-Marie & Tony Haines
The Old Rectory
St. James, Shaftesbury
Dorset SP7 8HG
Tel: 01747 853658
Fax: 01747 854276
e-mail: old.rec@btinternet.com
Web: www.sawdays.co.uk

A perfect spot for an untroubled retreat. Ella is well-travelled, friendly and very keen for you to settle easily into this soft, green corner of Dorset. She keeps her four-acre garden immaculately and has a small vineyard of German grapes; the peace and the birdsong find their way into the house through the French doors. There are bold colours — apple green in the bedroom, sunny yellow in the sitting room and red in the bathroom — books, family portraits and paintings. Breakfast is Aga-cooked; if you can stir yourself afterwards there are lots of walks from the house.

Rooms: 1 twin/double with private bathroom.

Price: £20 p.p. Single occ. £25.

Breakfast: Until 9.30am.

Meals: Available locally.

Closed: Never.

The sounds linger: the raucous babble of early morning birds, the gentler sound of running water, the creaking of the great iron wheel as it responds to the rush of water from the pond. The visual memories are equally intense: the millpond at dusk, the setting and views, the beamed bedrooms, and even a kingfisher. Some bedrooms are in the main house, others in the more recently renovated mill house and grain loft. Guests have a sitting room with a window over the pond.

Rooms: 3 twins/doubles, all en suite (1 bath, 2 shower).

Price: From £25 p.p. Single occ. £36.

Breakfast: Until 9am.

Meals: Pubs and restaurants locally.

Closed: Never.

From A30 between Shaftesbury and Salisbury, right at Berwick St. John & Alvediston sign, then along for 0.5 miles. Right, and continue until you see drive in front of you. House on left.

Entry No: 164   Map no: 4

Ella Humphreys
Ferne Park Cottage
Ferne
Shaftesbury
Dorset SP7 0EU
Tel: 01747 828767
Web: www.sawdays.co.uk

From Blandford Forum take A350 and take sign for Melbury Abbas. At bottom of hill, left for West Melbury. Just before village hall turn right, down hill, house on left, 10m after forking left.

Entry No: 165   Map no: 4

Richard & Tavy Bradley-Watson
Melbury Mill
Melbury Abbas
Shaftesbury
Dorset SP7 0PD
Tel: 01747 852163

Tim is a post-war classic car restorer and has just put the finishing touches to a 1934 Lagonda. Lucy does long-distance on her Arab horse. They and their four children all enjoy entertaining guests in the beloved cottage and wheelwright's workshop that they've carefully restored. The attic bedrooms are snug, with Lucy's quilts, country antiques and sparkling bathrooms. Breakfasts include organic sausages and bacon, eggs from the Kerridges' free-ranging chickens and ducks. The Downs beckon keen walkers, warm corners invite readers. A lovely setting.

Rooms: 1 double/family room, en suite (shower); 1 double and 1 single (let to same party) sharing bathroom. 1 self-catering cottage to sleep 2/3.

Price: £22.50-£25 p.p. Single £40. Supp. for single night's stay £2.50 p.p.

Breakfast: Until 9am.

Meals: Good food available locally.

Closed: Never.

General Pitt-Rivers, of famously eclectic tastes, lived here. Across the road the water meadows descend to the river that winds round Sturminster Newton. Australian Margie is fun and easy-going; the house is the same, with a huge fireplace in the hall and a smaller one in the snug sitting room. Bedrooms are big and unpretentiously attractive with plain Wilton carpets. Breakfasts, served from the vast and friendly kitchens, are feasts of local sausage, home-made marmalade and fruit salad, etc. A wonderful house.

Rooms: 1 double, en suite (bath); 1 double with private bathroom; 1 twin and 2 singles sharing 1 bathroom and another wc.

Price: From £23 p.p.

Breakfast: Flexible.

Meals: Not available. Good pub within walking distance.

Closed: Christmas.

From Shaftesbury, A350 to Compton Abbas. The Old Forge is the first property on left before Compton Abbas sign. Turn left; entrance on left through five-bar gate.

Tim & Lucy Kerridge
The Old Forge, Fanners Yard
Compton Abbas, Shaftesbury
Dorset SP7 0NQ
Tel: 01747 811881
Fax: 01747 811881
e-mail: theoldforge.kerridge@virgin.net
Web: www.heartofdorset.easynet.county.uk/cot6

On A357 Sherborne to Blandford road. House is 0.25 miles west of Sturminster Newton Bridge, on south side of road.

Charles & Margie Fraser
Newton House
Sturminster Newton
Dorset DT10 2DQ
Tel: 01258 472783
Web: www.sawdays.co.uk

A magical place. Complete peace: the garden runs down to the River Stour and has uninterrupted views over the water meadows. The millhouse, 16th-century and Grade I-listed, is as warm and interesting as the owners. The inside is no surprise: an original moulded plaster ceiling, half-tester bed in one room, a real four-poster in another, rich decoration and large table in the dining room. There is no sitting room for guests but the rooms are big and who cares when the house is so magnificent? *Children over 12 welcome.*

Rooms: 1 double, en suite (bath); 1 double and 1 four-poster sharing bathroom.

Price: £22.50-£30 p.p. Single occ. from £30.

Breakfast: Flexible.

Meals: Available locally.

Closed: Never.

Below is the River Stour which winds through the valley and under the medieval, nine-arched bridge; above is an Iron Age hillfort, between is Crawford House. Soft and pretty, the house has floor-length windows in the sitting room and dining room that allow sun to stream through in the most uplifting way. Bedroom colours are neutral and calm, offsetting floral curtains. One room has charming four-poster twin beds with chintzy drapes. Downstairs, there are lovely oils on the walls and Andrea brings you breakfast in the pale green dining room.

Rooms: 1 twin, en suite (bath); 2 twins sharing bathroom.

Price: £25 p.p.

Breakfast: Flexible.

Meals: Available locally.

Closed: Mid-October-mid-April.

House is on A357 between Sturminster Newton and Blandford. Look for well-marked turning on north side between Lydlinch and Fiddleford.

Entry No: 168   Map no: 4

Mr & Mrs A & J Ingleton
Fiddleford Mill
Fiddleford
Sturminster Newton
Dorset DT10 2BX
Tel: 01258 472786

First gateway on left after crossroads (B3075) on A350 going north after entering Spetisbury.

Entry No: 169   Map no: 4

Andrea Lea
Crawford House
Spetisbury
Blandford
Dorset DT11 9DP
Tel: 01258 857338
Fax: 01258 858152

If you ever stayed with the Hipwells in Affpuddle you will want to spoil yourself again. Their new home, rebuilt in 1762 after a great fire, on the foundations of a 13th-century goldsmith's house, is just as lovely as the old one. It is in the square of this attractive town and the views are soft and lush. The mood is of restrained luxury and uncluttered, often beautiful, good taste. Bedrooms are cream with old mahogany furniture and beams. There's a large drawing room and good paintings are all around. The Hipwells are easy; the house, and the garden, are a refuge. *Children over 10 welcome.*

Rooms: 3 twins/doubles, each with private bathroom.

Price: £22.50-£25 p.p. Single occ. £28-£30.

Breakfast: Flexible.

Meals: Dinner, sometimes available in winter, £10-£12 p.p.; otherwise, many good restaurants nearby.

Closed: Christmas-New Year.

Puzzle no more... a 'hard' is firm ground up which you drag a boat; 'lytchett' is a strip of land. The eclectic delights of this 1935 home include a 1662 court cupboard in the dining room, a conservatory sheltering exotic plants and fruit, home-made jams and produce, a telescope for bird and deer watching in one of the roomy bedrooms and mattresses of the type the Queen insists on. In good weather, breakfast in the conservatory or in the spectacular garden looking out towards Poole harbour. The Collinsons are easy-going.

Rooms: 1 king-size four-poster, en suite (bath & shower); 1 twin, en suite (bath); 1 small double, en suite (shower).

Price: £21-£33 p.p. No single supp. in small double. 10% off for 3 nights, 15% for a week.

Breakfast: Flexible.

Meals: Dinner, £12-£18 p.p., by arrangement

Closed: Hardly ever.

From Upton x-roads (0.5 miles S.E. of A35/A350 interchange), turn west into Dorchester Rd, 2nd left into Seaview Rd, over Sandy Lane into Slough Lane, then 1st left into Beach Rd. House is 150 yds on, on right.

From A35, take A351 to Wareham. Follow signs to town centre. In North St, go over lights into South St. 1st left into St John's Hill and house on SW side.

Entry No: 170   Map no: 4

Entry No: 171   Map no: 4

Anthea & Michael Hipwell
Gold Court House
St. John's Hill
Wareham
Dorset BH20 4LZ
Tel: 01929 553320
Fax: 01929 553320
Web: www.sawdays.co.uk

David & Elizabeth Collinson
Lytchett Hard
Beach Road
Upton, Poole
Dorset BH16 5NA
Tel: 01202 622297
Fax: 01202 632716

The Turnbulls are as thoroughly English as their 1930s thatched house and their huge and engaging country garden. Sara keeps a large, welcoming home with an impeccable mix of family portraits, landscape paintings and some silk paintings from Hong Kong and she successfully mixes antique and modern furniture, whites and pastels. She also pays attention to detail such as a new toothbrush for the forgetful, linen table napkins and three sorts of tea. Every view is into green Hardy Country. Bring your racquets — there's a tennis court in the garden.

Rooms: 1 double, 1 twin and 1 single sharing 2 bathrooms. Possible use of private bathroom.

Price: From £22 p.p.

Breakfast: Until 9.30am.

Meals: Good food available locally.

Closed: Never.

From Wimborne B3078 to Cranborne. Turn right to Holt. After 2 miles Thornhill is on the right, 200 yards beyond Old Inn.

Entry No: 172   Map no: 4

John & Sara Turnbull
Thornhill
Holt
Wimborne
Dorset BH21 7DJ
Tel: 01202 889434

Sarah-Jane, with energy and good humour, is breathing new life into her 10-bedroomed, 7-bathroomed Regency house. There's a large guest sitting room with two enormous sofas; murals remind you that this doubles as a nursery for the little ones when no one is visiting. Fresh flowers in the bedrooms, which have plain emulsioned walls and pretty floral curtains. The mature gardens envelop the house and merge with a buttercup field. Explore the rose garden and parkland and delight in finding the many rare plants in the woods.

Rooms: 1 double, en suite (shower); 2 twins, 1 en suite (bath), 1 with private bathroom.

Price: £20-£25 p.p. Single supp. £5.

Breakfast: Until 9.30am.

Meals: Available locally.

Closed: Christmas & New Year.

Durham

From A1, at Scotch Corner, A66 for Barnard Castle. 7 miles on, approaching 1st section of dual carriageway, 1st right for Barnard Castle to traffic lights. Right over bridge. At T-junc, left for Barnard Castle Town. Pass school and museum, then through iron gates on left.

Entry No: 173   Map no: 15

Sarah-Jane Ormston
Spring Lodge
Newgate, Barnard Castle
Co. Durham DL12 8NW
Tel: 01833 638110
Fax: 01833 638110
e-mail: ormston@telinco.co.uk
Web: www.springlodgebandb.co.uk

This is an ancient dwelling — mind your head on the beams. Philip and Judy run the antique shop downstairs and have clearly furnished the house from stock, creating a pretty, homely, atmosphere. Breakfast is a lavishly-supplied 'help-yourself' affair and, if you want the full works, you have only to pop over the road to 'The Old Well'. From the front of the house you step into the busy life of Barnard Castle; from the back onto an old cart-track which takes you along the Tees towards Egglestone Abbey.

Rooms: 1 large twin/double with sitting room & private bathroom.

Price: £20 p.p. Single occ. £35.

Breakfast: Flexible.

Meals: Available locally.

Closed: Christmas, New Year, March & April.

From A1 Scotch Corner, A66 to Barnard Castle over Egglestone bridge; past Bowes Museum to Butter market straight ahead of you. Turn left half way down The Bank.

Entry No: 174   Map no: 15

Philip & Judy Brown
Brown's Antiques
No. 34 The Bank
Barnard Castle
Co. Durham DL12 8PN
Tel: 01833 637891
Fax: 01833 637891

Drive for two miles through the forest to get here; there are 5,000 acres of mixed woodland, moors and becks, a valley with two small rivers, old oaks and beeches... fabulous. It is a walker's paradise, with pure air, birds aplenty, deer, and woodpeckers in the garden. The Georgian shooting lodge is in an open glade with views of the moors, almost Swiss in its prettiness. Helene — an exceptional cook — has lived here all her life. There are comfy sofas, big downstairs rooms, open fires, books and games. Dine among oils and Art-Nouveau fittings, sleep well in comfortable bedrooms. An enchanted spot. *Children over eight welcome.*

Rooms: 2 doubles, en suite (bath & shower); 1 twin, en suite (shower).

Price: £24-£30.50 p.p. Single supp. £1 (May-Sept & Easter).

Breakfast: Until 9am.

Meals: Dinner £19.50 p.p. Packed lunch £4 p.p.

Closed: 14 December-14 January.

A68 from Darlington, left to Hamsterley village. Continue for 2 miles (ignore forest signs), then right, signed The Grove, then left. Right (signed), after 3 miles, over stone bridge, house faces you.

Entry No: 175   Map no: 20

Helene Close
Grove House
Hamsterley Forest, Bishop Auckland
Co. Durham DL13 3NL
Tel: 01388 488203
Fax: 01388 488174
e-mail: xov47@dial.pipex.com
come.to/grovehouse

Just 12 miles from Durham, one of England's jewels, and one of only 20 similarly listed farmhouses in the county. It is way off the beaten track in magical scenery, a Grade II* early 17th-century building with later additions, with huge charm. The kitchen has the original bread oven and in it, Marguerite produces mouth-watering meals — and enjoys doing so. It is also sybaritically comfortable, with deep sofa and armchairs below beams in the sitting room and before the open fire in the dining room. Higgledy-piggledy and comfortable — perfect.

Rooms: 1 twin next to private bathroom.

Price: £32 p.p. Single supp. £10.

Breakfast: Flexible.

Meals: Dinner, 4 courses, £22 p.p., by arrangement.

Closed: Never.

Going west on A689, approx. 1 mile west of Wolsingham, left opp. brown caravan sign. Over bridge, sharp left over disused railway line. 0.5 miles up track, fork right through ford. House 200 yds further on.

Entry No: 176   Map no: 20

Anthony & Marguerite Todd
Coves House Farm
Wolsingham
Weardale
Co. Durham DL13 3BG
Tel: 01388 527375
Fax: 01388 526157

Floors slant and the old elm creaks —
this timber-framed Essex hall house is
tangibly old; it's 13th century and
Grade II* listed. You can be looked
after as a cherished only guest, or thing
can be moved around to accommodate
large group or family; Ros is flexible an
easy. Those who rush on through Esse
to get to Stansted airport (20 minutes)
miss the ruralness of it all. The tennis
court is hard by open fields and there
are ponds, an island and a boat. Strong
(Designers' Guild) colours in the twin
and a charming, more chintzy double.
You have a private drawing room.

Rooms: 1 double & 1 twin, both with
private bathroom.

Price: £28-£35 p.p.

Breakfast: Flexible.

Meals: Dinner, £20 p.p., by
arangement.

Closed: Occasionally.

*From Chelmsford, follow signs for
Broomford A&E Hospital. Approaching
Little Waltham, left for Great
Waltham. Left again beside Beehive
pub. On for 1.3 miles, then right on
concrete track in between two cottages.
(Meads and Ishael's).*

Entry No: 177   Map no: 11

Mrs Roslyn Renwick
Fitzjohns Farmhouse
Mashbury Road
Great Waltham, Chelmsford
Essex CM3 1EJ
Tel: 01245 360204/361224
Fax: 01245 361724
e-mail: rosrenwick@aol.com

Essex

An Elizabethan jewel! Exposed timber ceilings, open fireplaces, endless nooks and crannies: this farmhouse trumpets its history at every turn. The garden even has 'old-fashioned' roses and ponds. The Wordsworths (yes, they are related to the poet) are engaging and solicitous people, delighting in their home and guests. Little Brockholds Farm is no longer a working farm but all vegetables are organically home-grown and the hens and bantams are organically fed.

Rooms: 1 twin with private bathroom; 1 double, en suite.

Price: £32.50 p.p.

Breakfast: Flexible.

Meals: Dinner £15-£22.50 p.p.

Closed: Never.

As fascinating as the area it lives in, the Grade II* 'Old Hall' House has two mainly 14th-century cross wings, and a 'new' 15th-century wing where you breakfast in front of the log fire. A forest fell, surely, to provide the beams. The bedrooms are cosy and welcoming, with undulating floors and 'museum corners' enshrining original features. The road goes close by but there is an enchanting two-acre garden and good insulation. The interior is as beguiling as the house itself, with wonderfully strong colours. Think of beams, sofas, handsome furniture, books and a sense of history, and immensely likeable hosts.

Rooms: 1 double/family room, en suite (bath); 1 twin with private bathroom; 1 single with separate shower room & wc.

Price: Family room £45-£55, with £5 supp. for camp bed. Twin £20-£25 p.p. Single £27.50-£32.50.

Breakfast: Flexible.

Meals: Good local pubs close by.

Closed: Never.

From Saffron Walden take B1053 (George Street) to Radwinter. Turn right at church and first left after 1 mile (at grass triangle on sharp right-hand bend). Follow signs for Little Brockholds Farm.

Entry No: 178   Map no: 11

On A1124, 2.5 miles west of A12 junction. House is on left beyond the Cooper's Arms and opposite Queens Head. Parking in courtyard.

Entry No: 179   Map no: 11

Antony & Anne Wordsworth
Little Brockholds Farm
Radwinter
Saffron Walden
Essex CB10 2TF
Tel: 01799 599458
Fax: 01799 599458
e-mail: as@brockholds99.freeserve.co.uk

Patricia & Richard Mitchell
Old House
Fordstreet
Aldham, Colchester
Essex CO6 3PH
Tel: 01206 240456
Fax: 01206 240456
Web: www.sawdays.co.uk

The cattle seem perilously close; it is the ha-ha that does it, a dominant feature of the garden with its pond, lush greenery and tennis court. The entrance hall is surprisingly large and elegant for a '60s house; the drawing room is traditionally furnished and has fine windows looking over the garden to Dedham Vale. The walls are soft yellow, the carpet blue-grey. The dining room has a parquet floor, open fire and terracotta walls, hunting prints and candlelit dinners. Play the baby grand piano, let your conversation range wide with two delightful and widely-travelled people.

Rooms: 1 family and 1 twin, both en suite (bath/shower); 1 double with private bathroom.

Price: From £24-£30 p.p. Single occ. £35.

Breakfast: Flexible.

Meals: Packed lunch £7 p.p. Dinner, £22.50 p.p., by prior arrangement, B.Y.O wine.

Closed: Never.

Listen to the sea. It murmurs across the saltings where the Brent geese wheel and the great Constable skies stretch. The house is minutes from wild walking this island of Mersea is secluded, surprising. The house began in 1343, a hall house nearly as old as the exquisite church. The Georgians added their bit, but the venerable beams and uneven old construction shine through. It is a sunny, comfortable, beautiful house. There is a snug, book-filled, sitting room and a terracotta-floored conservatory gazing over the large garden. It is a privilege to stay here, among such nice people.

Rooms: 1 twin with private bathroom; 2 twins sharing a bathroom.

Price: £22.50 p.p. Single occ. £25-£30.

Breakfast: Until 9am.

Meals: Restaurant 1 mile away & pub within walking distance.

Closed: Never.

From A134 (Colchester/Sudbury road), at Great Horkesley, take Boxted Church Road for 2 miles east. House is 200 yards beyond turning to church.

Entry No: 180   Map no: 12

Jeremy & Mary Carter
Round Hill House
Parsonage Hill
Boxted, Colchester
Essex CO4 5ST
Tel: 01206 272392
Fax: 01206 272392
e-mail: jermar@appleonline.net

From Colchester take B1025, over causeway, then bear left. After 3 miles, pass Dog & Pheasant pub. Take 2nd right into Bromans Lane. House 1st on left.

Entry No: 181   Map no: 12

Ruth Dence
Bromans Farm
East Mersea
Essex CO5 8UE
Tel: 01206 383235
Fax: 01206 383235

Behind that gorgeous 1700s house, close to the Suffolk border, is an equally gorgeous garden. There is light and space, air and silence, both in and out. The house has been renovated in Lutyens style. The first thing you see is the hall decorated with painted panels. The drawing room has a grand piano, fireplace and big windows onto the rose garden; croquet on the lawn, midge-swatting by the hidden pond, then Coral's afternoon tea complete the picture. Bedrooms are bright and full of goodies; bathrooms have all you could wish for and one of the longest baths we know.

Rooms: 1 double and 1 twin with private bathroom; 1 single/twin with separate bathroom.

Price: £22.50-£25 p.p. Single occ. £30-£35.

Breakfast: Until 9.30am.

Meals: Available locally.

Closed: 22 December-2 January.

From A12 north of Colchester, follow A120 towards Harwich for approx. 7.5 miles. Left to Lt Bromley & follow for 2.9 miles. House set back on right.

Entry No: 182   Map no: 12

Christopher & Coral McEwen
Aldhams
Bromley Road
Lawford, Manningtree
Essex CO11 2NE
Tel: 01206 393210
Fax: 01206 393210
e-mail: coral.mcewen3@which.net

Once you've arrived in this quintessentially English village, you can forget about your car; walks on the Cotswolds Way and cycle rides start from your front door and for supper you need go no further than the famous Churchill Inn next door. Clare will do the same excellent job of caring for guests here as she used to in her Devon *Special Place*. Bedrooms are charming — one terracotta with a star pattern and the other creamy with floral curtains; there's an antique freestanding bath and wooden floors in the bathroom. Your breakfast room opens onto the garden.

Gloucestershire

Rooms: 2 doubles, 1 en suite (shower) and 1 en suite (bath).

Price: £27.50 p.p. Single supp. £5.

Breakfast: Flexible.

Meals: Available in the village.

Closed: Never.

From Chipping Campden, B4035. 1.5 miles on, right to Paxford and right at T-junction. Left at Churchill Inn — Vine cottage is on the left.

Entry No: 183   Map no: 10

Clare Shaw
Vine Cottage
Paxford
Chipping Campden
Gloucestershire GL55 6XH
Tel: 01386 593266
Fax: 01386 593266

It's homely and comforting, yet stylish, too. There's huge attention to detail and much to recommend the home of the Knotts, not least the captivating view up the stairs of a complex forest of beams, timber posts and bannisters. Interesting shapes everywhere, a split-level bathroom, honey-coloured stone windows with seats, Tudor bricks and handmade furniture crafted by Robin in his workshop. You'll feel at ease with this small family.

Rooms: 2 doubles, 1 en suite (bath), 1 with private bathroom.

Price: £27.50 p.p. Single supp. £5.

Breakfast: Until 9.30am.

Meals: Available at acclaimed inn across the road.

Closed: Christmas & New Year.

Fascinating conjecture: the Kettle may be the oldest continuous business premises in Britain. The Kettle refers to the Blacksmith's trade, but it has been a coaching inn, brewery, grocer's and pottery. Susie now runs an antique shop downstairs and the mood is set by stripped wooden doors, coir carpets, beams, leaded windows and white linen. Guests go through a little alleyway and up an iron staircase onto a platform that overlooks Cotswold rooftops to the church. You could almost be in France. You can breakfast on the platform and there's a dear little sitting room, too.

Rooms: 2 doubles, en suite (shower); 2 twins sharing bathroom. Guests share sitting room.

Price: £30 p.p. Single occ. £32.50.

Breakfast: Until 9am Mon-Fri. Until 10am Sat-Sun.

Meals: Excellent restaurants nearby.

Closed: Mid-January-mid-February.

Take A44 (Oxford-Evesham Rd). Turn off to B4018 for Chipping Campden, approx. 2 miles. The house is at the top of the village on the right-hand side heading towards Stratford-on-Avon.

In centre of Paxford opposite church.

Entry No: **184**   Map no: 10

Entry No: **185**   Map no: 10

Lisa & Robin Knott
Wells Farmhouse
Paxford
Chipping Campden
Gloucestershire GL55 6XH
Tel: 01386 593429
e-mail: lisa@clockrobin.co.uk
Web: www.wellsfarmhouse.co.uk

Charles & Susie Holdsworth-Hunt
The Kettle House
High Street, Chipping Campden
Gloucestershire GL55 6HN
Tel: 01386 840328
Fax: 01386 841740
e-mail: bed&breakfast@kettlehouse.co.uk
Web: www.kettlehouse.co.uk

The manor, originally a church on the site of an extinct medieval village mentioned in the Domesday Book, was converted in 1610 with Georgian additions. (Moseley and Mitford stayed here during the war.) The gardens are glorious, with a lake and wonderful views. The hall and ground floor are stone-flagged, with rugs for colour, and there are delightful touches of exotica everywhere. One bedroom is massive, with bathroom across the corridor. A wonderful place; John and Camilla are easy-going and entertaining. Our inspector didn't want to come home. *Children over seven welcome.*

Rooms: 2 doubles, both en suite (bath); 1 single with private bathroom.

Price: £38 p.p. Single supp. £10.

Breakfast: Until 9.30am.

Meals: Supper by arrangement. Excellent pub and restaurant nearby.

Closed: Christmas.

Astonishing! It feels palpably old — Elizabethan even — with superb mullioned windows, gables, acres of stoned slated and Norfolk reed thatched roofs, and those unexpected corners which make old buildings so fascinating. Yet it was started in 1951 and gradually added to as the family grew. Cecil, a retired builder, has flung the house open to guests, with huge generosity and bonhomie. There's an outdoor summer heated swimming pool for your use, an all-weather tennis court, croquet, billiard room, terraces and lawns, together with a superb prize-winning garden with a 10-acre arboretum. It's immaculate and sumptuous, but fun and rather special.

Rooms: 2 doubles, en suite (bath) and 1 double with private bathroom.

Price: £40 p.p. Single supp. £20.

Breakfast: Flexible.

Meals: Available locally.

Closed: Never.

4 miles north of Moreton-in-Marsh on A429, left to Aston Magna. At first building, turn immediately right & house is 0.75 miles on the right, up 0.5 mile drive.

Entry No: 186   Map no: 10

John & Camilla Playfair
Neighbrook
Aston Magna, Moreton-in-Marsh
Gloucestershire GL56 9QP
Tel: 01386 593232
Fax: 01386 593500
e-mail: johnplayfair@neighbrook.freeserve.co.uk
Web: www.sawdays.co.uk

From Stow-on-the-Wold on A424, opp. Coach & Horses pub, turn right by postbox. Entrance 100 yards on left.

Entry No: 187   Map no: 10

C.J. Williams
Windy Ridge
Longborough, Moreton-in-Marsh
Gloucestershire GL56 0QY
Tel: 01451 830465
Fax: 01451 831489
e-mail: cjw@windy-ridge.co.uk
Web: www.windy-ridge.co.uk

Look over the garden wall as you breakfast on home-made jams and enjoy those wonderful, long views. The garden, too, is worth a long look — James and Karin are passionate about it. The 16th- and 17th-century manor house has a flagstoned hall, huge fireplaces, sit-in inglenooks and Cotswold stone mullioned windows. One of the bedrooms has a secret door that leads to a stunning, surprising fuchsia-pink bathroom. The other, though smaller, has wonderful garden views. An easy-going and lovely house with owners to match.

Rooms: 1 double, en suite (bath/shower); 1 twin/double, en suite (bath).

Price: £30 p.p. Single supp. £15.

Breakfast: Usually 8-9.30am.

Meals: Menus available for local pubs & restaurants.

Closed: Christmas.

Guarding the beautiful 11th-century church at the end of the lane, this honey-stoned Cotswold beauty is an idyllic starting point for forays into the countryside by foot or bike; Liz thoughtfully gives maps to guests. A mulberry tree in the garden gives fruit at summer's end for breakfast served in the elegantly Georgian dining room. Bedrooms are beautifully decorated, so you can luxuriate. This is a period house to which the glossiest magazine couldn't do justice, in a perfect Cotswold village. *Children over eight welcome.*

Rooms: 5 rooms (3 four-posters), all en suite.

Price: From £44.50 p.p.

Breakfast: 8.15-9.15am.

Meals: Packed lunch available.

Closed: 22-27 December.

From Cirencester, A429 towards Stow. Turn right at Apple Pie House Hotel, signed Clapton. Follow signs. In village, down hill and left at green-doored 3-storey house. Manor is left of the church.

Entry No: 188   Map no: 10

Karin & James Bolton
Clapton Manor
Clapton-on-the-Hill
Nr. Bourton-on-the-Water
Gloucestershire GL54 2LG
Tel: 01451 810202
Fax: 01451 821804

From Broadway, B4632 Stratford road for 1.5 miles. At Willersey, right into Church Street. House is at end of lane opposite church. Car park at the rear.

Entry No: 189   Map no: 9

Liz & Chris Beauvoisin
The Old Rectory, Church Street
Willersey, Broadway
Gloucestershire WR12 7PN
Tel: 01386 853729
Fax: 01386 858061
e-mail: beauvoisin@btinternet.com
homepages.tesco.net/~j.walker

A magnificent Georgian manor in 15 acres, a delightful marriage of the formal and the wild, with tennis court, pool, croquet, and with a mill and a dovecote recorded in the Domesday Book. The two-acre lake is always active with wildfowl. Life here is elegant, comfortable and peaceful. The delightful owners have filled the house with gorgeous things. It stands behind the parish church. An excellent pub is a two-minute walk up the lane and there are attractive self-catering cottages in the old coaching yard. A good place for house parties.

Rooms: 4 four-posters, all en suite (1 with shower, 1 with bath & shower and 2 with bath); 1 twin and 1 twin/double, both en suite (bath). Cottages sleep from 2-8.

Price: From £42.50 p.p. Single occ. up to £65.

Breakfast: Flexible — served in bed at no extra cost!

Meals: Dinner, from £30 p.p., by arrangement.

Closed: Christmas.

From Cheltenham, A435 north, then B4079. About 1 mile after A438 crossroads, sign to Kemerton on right. Leave road at War Memorial. House is behind parish church.

Entry No: 190   Map no: 9

Bill & Diana Herford
Upper Court
Kemerton, Tewkesbury
Gloucestershire GL20 7HY
Tel: 01386 725351
Fax: 01386 725472
e-mail: uppercourt@compuserve.com
Web: www.sawdays.co.uk

Sit on the terrace — which is candlelit in the evenings — and take in the views of undulating hills and vineyards. Michael and Jo will bring you a glass of wine and supper. They are genuine, kind and so settled into their corner of England that you will relax immediately. Michael loves old cars — the Puma racing car was made right here — and is a guide at the vineyard. He also delivers organic bread to the neighbours. Jo makes excellent flapjacks and caters for special diets. The pretty and immaculate bedrooms are in a converted grain barn and have a soaring A-frame ceiling.

Rooms: 1 twin, en suite (bath); 1 double with private bath/shower. In cottage: 1 twin (with wheelchair access)

Price: £28-£30 p.p. No single supp.

Breakfast: Flexible.

Meals: Dinner, 3 courses (inc. bottle of wine) £18-£21 p.p.

Closed: Never.

From Gloucester A40 to Ross-on-Wye, right onto B4215 signed Newent. After approx. 7 miles, right (signed Dymock). After '3 Choirs Vineyard', next right (before M50). House 1 mile on right.

Entry No: 191   Map no: 9

Jo & Michael Kingham
The Old Winery
Welsh House Lane
Dymock
Gloucestershire GL18 1LR
Tel: 01531 890824
Fax: 01531 890824

Petrina is a natural and imaginative cook; eating here is something special. Your hosts thrive on the bustle and conversation of guests, young and old. You'll feel at ease, for the house is big enough for everyone to have some space. Very early risers can help themselves to tea and coffee, having let the dogs out! Bedrooms are large and airy; the beds are Emperor-size, no less. Large gardens with rolling lawns and sweeping views — an attractive and elegant house to which the Pughs bring a real sense of fun. Petrina loves young children.

Rooms: 2 king-size twins/doubles en suite; 1 double next to shower room and wc.

Price: £30 p.p.

Breakfast: Flexible.

Meals: Dinner £17.50 p.p. Gourmet dinner £22.50 p.p.

Closed: Never.

A superb Grade I-listed house, delectably old-fashioned, in a fascinating village. The family has lived at Frampton since the 11th century. The house speaks the elegant language of Vanburgh, is beautifully crafted and has a Strawberry Hill Gothic orangery (self-catering). Choose between two large rooms: one with Flemish tapestry, four-poster bed with hand-embroidered curtains and own dressing-room; the other a twin with views, antiques and panelling. Dutch ornamental canal, water lilies, lake, superb views... gorgeous!

Rooms: 1 double, en suite; 1 double with tester bed, dressing room and single bed.

Price: £45 p.p.

Breakfast: Flexible.

Meals: Good restaurant opposite & 2 pubs on the village green.

Closed: Never.

Take A40 from Gloucester towards Ross-on-Wye, then B4215 towards Highnam. 2 miles on left is Whitehall Lane. House is approx. 0.5 miles down lane, on right, behind laurel hedge.

Entry No: 192   Map no: 9

James & Petrina Pugh
Whitelands
Whitehall Lane
Rudford
Gloucestershire GL2 8ED
Tel: 01452 790406
Fax: 01452 790676
e-mail: pughwhitelands@talk21.com

From M5 junc. 13 west, then B4071. Left through village green, then just look to the left! Entrance is between two large chestnut trees 200 yds on left.

Entry No: 193   Map no: 9

Mrs Henriette Clifford
Frampton Court
Frampton-on-Severn
Gloucestershire GL2 7EU
Tel: 01452 740267
Fax: 01452 740698
e-mail: cliffordfce@farming.co.uk
Web: www.sawdays.co.uk

A perfect English scene... a late 18th-century house tucked down a lane off one of the country's longest village greens. White-clad cricketers smack leather off willow as bees buzz and the peace hums. The house, with its beautiful garden and orchards beyond, is equally tranquil; the bedrooms merge seamlessly with a family home where visitors take the engaging Carol and William as they find them. Carol, a talented flower arranger, has decorated big bedrooms in muted lemon yellows and rich velvety plums. Dogs and cats roam free. *Children over 10 welcome.*

Rooms: 1 twin/double and 1 twin, both en suite (bath/shower).

Price: £25 p.p. No single supp.

Breakfast: Until 9am.

Meals: Available locally.

Closed: Christmas & New Year.

Boards creak and you duck — it is a farmhouse of the best kind, simple, small-roomed, stone-flagged, beamed and delightful. The walls are white, the furniture is good and there are pictures everywhere. In spite of great age (16th century) there are lots of windows and good light. They farm 400 acres organically (cows and sheep) and your horse can come, too. Your welcome will be as generous as your farmer's breakfast. The views across the Severn estuary to the Cotswolds are "devastating" and there is, simply, no noise — unless the guinea fowl are in good voice.

Rooms: 1 double and 1 twin, sharing private bathroom and/or private shower room.

Price: £20-£25 p.p.

Breakfast: Flexible.

Meals: Packed lunch £10 p.p.

Closed: Christmas & New Year.

From A38 towards Bristol, turn west onto B4071. First left and drive the length of village green. 300 yards after it ends, right into Whittles Lane. House is last on right.

Entry No: 194   Map no: 9

Carol & William Alexander
The Old School House
Whittles Lane
Frampton-on-Severn
Gloucestershire GL2 7EB
Tel: 01452 740457
Fax: 01452 741721
e-mail: bedandbreakfast@f-o-s.freeserve.co.uk

2 miles south of Newnham on A48, opposite turning for Bullo Pill, there is large 'pull-in' with phone box on right. Turn here and follow farm track to end.

Entry No: 195   Map no: 9

Penny & David Hill
Grove Farm
Bullo Pill
Newnham
Gloucestershire GL14 1DZ
Tel: 01594 516304
Fax: 01594 516304

The large lake at the side of the house is at windowsill level, giving you a strange feeling of being underwater! The lake, the mill race and Judy — who's down-to-earth and friendly — make this place special. The independent will like having their own sitting room, own wing and front door. Bedrooms are newly and simply decorated and have modern furniture. With lots of space to sit outside, hills to climb and a genuinely warm welcome from Judy; you really should bring the family.

Rooms: 1 twin/double (extra single if needed) and 1 twin, both en suite (shower).

Price: £22-£25 p.p. Single supp. £5-£10.

Breakfast: Flexible.

Meals: Good pubs for supper within walking distance.

Closed: Christmas.

Little has changed in 500 years: only birdsong fractures the peace of the old stone house in the appropriately named hamlet of Calmsden ('place of calm'). The alcoved stone fireplace in the living room is what sold the house to the delightful Baxters — that and the wonky floors, the beams that go the wrong way and the ceilings that need ducking. Unwind in the bedrooms among fat pillows and magazines. The smell of home-baked bread will lure you from your room for breakfast. You eat in the dining room; wood panelled from top to toe, it's like a captain's study. *Children by arrangement.*

Rooms: 1 twin/double, en suite (bath/shower); 1 twin/double and 1 single, sharing private bathroom.

Price: £25-£35 p.p.

Breakfast: Until 9am.

Meals: Excellent pub 1.5 miles away.

Closed: 1 December-28 February.

From Stroud take A46 towards Bath. After 2 miles turn right to North Woodchester then 2nd left, down the hill, sharp right up short drive.

Entry No: 196   Map no: 9

Mrs Judy Sutch
Southfield Mill
Southfield Road
Woodchester, Nr. Stroud
Gloucestershire GL5 5PA
Tel: 01453 872896
Fax: 01452 872896

From Cirencester A429 north. After 5 miles, take the second turning signed to Calmsden, just before Hare and Hounds pub. Continue for 1.5 miles. Third house on right.

Entry No: 197   Map no: 9

Bridget Baxter
The Old House
Calmsden
Nr. Cirencester
Gloucestershire GL7 5ET
Tel: 01285 831240
Fax: 01285 831240
e-mail: baxter@calmsden.freeserve.co.uk

So quiet! In Cirencester's oldest street, it's hard to believe that just a few minutes away from this home is the pleasing bustle of the delightful market town. The Langtons have renovated their 17th-century (with later alterations) wool stapler's house with a deft hand and the rich red and ochre of the hall heralds the fact that you've arrived somewhere special. The panelled dining room has a vast Bath stone fireplace, candelabras and wall sconces. Stephen cooks an excellent breakfast and Anna has created sumptuous bedrooms; guests have waxed lyrical about the comfort.

Rooms: 2 twins and 1 double, each en suite (shower); 1 twin, en suite (bath).

Price: £32.50 p.p. Single occ. £47.

Breakfast: Flexible.

Meals: Available locally.

Closed: Christmas & New Year.

From Swindon, A419 to Cirencester. At Waitrose roundabout, follow signs to Town Centre until 'Other Directions' sign. Follow this, hugging Park wall on left. When wall ends, road bends to right; Coxwell St is entrance 50 yds on right.

Entry No: 198   Map no: 9

Stephen & Anna Langton
Old Court
Coxwell Street
Cirencester
Gloucestershire GL7 2BQ
Tel: 01285 653164
Fax: 01285 642803
e-mail: langton@cripps.f9.co.uk

Imagine being woken by the aroma of freshly-baked baguettes and croissants — well, here you are. The enterprising and energetic Maurice and Nanette turned the town's bakery into a boulangerie-cum-deli (Nanette will make you a wonderful packed lunch). Behind the 400-year-old frontage is a very simple, toy-strewn family home with an assortment of characterful furniture and bric-a-brac — nothing fancy, but charming, nonetheless. Bedrooms, under the eaves, have rooftop views. It's easy, cheerful, a happy family base and good value. Ideal for the young at heart and the easy-going.

Rooms: 1 double, with additional single bed, and 1 twin, sharing private bathroom (shower).

Price: £17.50 p.p. Single supp. £7.50. Family rate for both rooms £50 (£60 if children aged 10 and over).

Breakfast: Flexible.

Meals: Packed lunch around £5 p.p.

Closed: Never.

Take A361 to Lechlade. Burford St is the main street. The Flour Bag is on the right. During shop hours, look out for a large figure of a fibreglass baker!

Entry No: 199   Map no: 4

Maurice & Nanette Chaplais
The Flour Bag
Burford Street
Lechlade
Gloucestershire GL7 3AP
Tel: 01367 252322
Fax: 01367 253779

In a delightfully unspoilt area of the Cotswolds, this attractive long stone house sits in splendid, peaceful isolation. Lovely high windows in the central part give onto the views and from the soft green-painted conservatory you can admire the garden that the Barrys have so lovingly created. Inside, the décor is fresh — so are the flowers — the furniture and books old, the charming owners happy and proud to have you in their home. Beds are incredibly comfortable with excellent sheets and pillows.

Rooms: 1 double, en suite (bath); 1 twin and 1 double sharing bath and shower.

Price: £30-£34 p.p. Single supp. by arrangement.

Breakfast: 8-9am.

Meals: Excellent pubs nearby.

Closed: Christmas, New Year & Easter.

Steep honey-coloured gables, mullioned windows and weathered stone tiles enclose this lovely 17th-century house on a quiet village lane. It is English to the core — and to the bottom of its lovely garden (the house sits in six acres). Caroline is a competent hostess with a cool, gentle manner and a talent for understated high-class interior décor. The two ample, airy guestrooms are furnished with antiques and the bathrooms are modern. Caroline can organise local bike hire and delivery.

Rooms: 1 twin and 1 double, both en suite (bath & shower).

Price: £25-£35 p.p. Single supp. £10.

Breakfast: Flexible.

Meals: Excellent pub nearby.

Closed: December & January.

From Cirencester A417 towards Lechlade. At Meysey Hampton crossroads left to Sun Hill. After 1 mile left at cottage. House is 400 yards down drive.

Entry No: 200   Map no: 4

Richard & Jill Barry
Hampton Fields
Meysey Hampton
Cirencester
Gloucestershire GL7 5JL
Tel: 01285 850070
Fax: 01285 850993

South through village from A417. Turn right after Masons Arms. House is 200m on left.

Entry No: 201   Map no: 4

Roger & Caroline Carne
The Old Rectory
Meysey Hampton, Nr. Cirencester
Gloucestershire GL7 5JX
Tel: 01285 851200
Fax: 01285 850452
e-mail: caroline.carne@lineone.net
Web: www.sawdays.co.uk

A fine new Georgian house, built in 1990 using reclaimed stone and tiles. The drawing room is elegant with magazines, dogs and Turkish needlepoint cushions strewn about; every downstairs room has an open fire. The bedrooms, in the old farmhouse wing, overlook the garden, tennis court and swimming pool. They are decorated with fine fabrics and have comfortable beds and good linen. Clare loves to paint and cook — she runs painting courses from her studio. The house is secluded and very quiet, yet you can walk across a few fields to visit other great gardens. *Riding, tennis and pool by arrangement.*

Rooms: 1 king-size double, en suite (bath); 1 twin with private bathroom.

Price: £25-£37.50 p.p. Single supp. £15.

Breakfast: Flexible.

Meals: Excellent pub nearby.

Closed: Christmas, New Year & Easter.

The solid walls of this farmhouse have sheltered the King family for 75 years and, for friends, family and neighbours alike, it is a welcoming, bustling meeting place. The son works the arable and dairy farm with his father, and the daughter and son-in-law's nearby farm sends fresh produce for your breakfast — some of it organic. This is an honest value B&B — Sonja knows her stuff and there's no standing on ceremony: come here to enjoy a slice of real working farming life. The famous Westonbirt Arboretum — breathtaking whatever the season — is a stroll away across the field.

Rooms: 1 twin and 1 double, both en suite (shower); 1 twin with en suite (shower & basin) but separate wc.

Price: From £20 p.p.

Breakfast: Flexible.

Meals: Available locally.

Closed: Never.

From Malmesbury B4040 for Easton Grey. Turn right to Shipton Moyne, go through village and at first x-roads take 'no through road' on right. Follow drive for 0.5 miles, bearing left where drive bends to left.

Entry No: 202   Map no: 4

The Inskip Family
Park Farm
Shipton Moyne
Tetbury
Gloucestershire GL8 8PR
Tel: 01666 880464
Fax: 01666 880488
e-mail: clareinskip@hotmail.com

A433 from Tetbury for 5 miles. On entering Knockdown, farm on right before crossroads.

Entry No: 203   Map no: 4

Sonja King
Avenue Farm
Knockdown
Tetbury
Gloucestershire GL8 8QY
Tel: 01454 238207
Fax: 01454 238033
e-mail: sonjames@breathemail.net

A treat: utterly delightful people with wide-ranging interests (ex-British Council and college lecturing; arts, travel, gardening...) in a manor-type house full of beautiful furniture. The house was born of the Arts and Crafts movement and remains fascinating: wood panels painted green and log-fired drawing-room for guests, quarry tiles on windowsills, handsome old furniture, comfortable proportions... elegant but human. The garden's massive clipped hedges and great lawn are impressive, as is the whole place. Refined but easy.

Rooms: 2 twins and 1 double, 1 with private bath/shower & 2 with shared bathroom.

Price: £31.50 p.p. Single supp. £5.

Breakfast: Served until 9.15am.

Meals: Dinner £17.50 p.p. B.Y.O wine.

Closed: December & January.

Boyts is ravishing, a 16th-century stone farmhouse in landscaped gardens. There is a huge fireplace in the sitting room, stone-flagged floors, window seats, wooden mullions, leaded windows around which climb a magnolia. The dining room has a fireplace, oil paintings, mahogany table. The bedrooms are just as lovely. The Italianate-style gardens have a canal and ornamental ponds, crested newts, ha-has and paddocks, and views to open farmland. Sally is lovely and John, ex-Army, has a keen, wry sense of humour.

Rooms: 1 double and 1 twin, both en suite (bath); 1 single with bath.

Price: £35 p.p. Single £25.

Breakfast: Until 9.30am.

Meals: Local pub with restaurant.

Closed: 21 December-2 January.

Take B4060 from Stinchcombe to Wotton-under-Edge. Go up long hill, house is at top on left — the gateway is marked.

Entry No: 204   Map no: 4

Hugh & Crystal St John Mildmay
Drakestone House
Stinchcombe
Dursley
Gloucestershire GL11 6AS
Tel: 01453 542140

From M5 junc. 16, A38 for Gloucester. After 6 miles, take Tytherington turn. From north, leave M5 at exit 14 and south on A38 towards Bristol. Tytherington turning after 3 miles.

Entry No: 205   Map no: 3

Mr & Mrs Eyre
Boyts Farm
Tytherington
Wotton-under-Edge
Gloucestershire GL12 8UG
Tel: 01454 412220
Fax: 01454 412220
Web: www.sawdays.co.uk

Just the thing for the diminutive, agoraphobic vegetarian. This delightful home, which comes with straw bedding and bottled water, is kept strictly under lock and key. There are no comforts at all. Meals, mostly carrots and lettuce, are eaten in the annexe with low-level views. Superb country walks cannot be taken.

Rooms: 1 tiny single en suite.

Price: Freedom.

Breakfast: Multi-seed pellets.

Meals: Taken communally.

Closed: That's the idea.

Through Warren, to end of long dark tunnel. Ignore sign saying 'Freedom', instead take 'Dead End'. Gates will be closed behind you.

Entry No: 206   Map no: 4

Mr MacGreggor's
Dunroamin
Bun Knees End
Gloucestershire GL8 8QY

John organises private and corporate fishing days on the local chalkstreams — why not set off with your rod and get the benefit of his expertise? Anthea is artistic and has cleverly brought together collections of shells, boxes, antique bric-a-brac and papier-mâché in pretty rooms; she's an excellent cook, too. Bedrooms have fretwork shelves, washstands, padded headboards on extra-large beds, and some antique furniture. There's a big welcome. *Kennel provided for dogs.*

Rooms: 1 twin and 1 small double, both en suite.

Price: £25-£27 p.p. Single supp. £10.

Breakfast: Flexible.

Meals: Dinner, from £15 p.p., by arrangement. Packed lunch £5 p.p.

Closed: Christmas & New Year.

Hampshire & Isle of Wight

From A303, Salisbury exit on A343. After approx. 6 miles, right for Grately station. After 1 mile, turn left into unmarked road. House is on left after 300 yards.

Entry No: 207   Map no: 4

John & Anthea Russell
Fair Game House
King Lane
Over Wallop, Stockbridge
Hampshire SO20 8JQ
Tel: 01264 889 884
Fax: 01264 889 883
e-mail: fair.game@lineone.net

Lindy and Tony have transformed their 200-year-old barn into a light and sunny space, kept simple with plain walls and seagrass flooring. Moroccan rugs, antiques, and a woodburning stove add warmth and theatre to the drawing room. Lindy, who speaks French, organises garden tours and the bookshelves reflect her interest in garden design. Visitors can unwind in the peace of the terrace overlooking mixed borders and cornfields beyond, admire the unusual waterfowl on the pond or saunter to the pub past the thatched cottages. *Children over 10 welcome. Golf, fishing and antique shops nearby.*

Rooms: 1 double, en suite (shower); 1 twin with private bathroom.

Price: Double £30 p.p., twin £25 p.p. Single supp. £10.

Breakfast: Flexible.

Meals: Good food available locally.

Closed: Christmas & New Year.

From Salisbury, A354 towards Blandford, through Coombe Bissett. After 1.5 miles, left on bend to Rockbourne. There, 200 yds after 30 mph zone, house drive signed to left. After 50 yds take right fork to house.

Entry No: 208   Map no: 4

Lindy & Tony Ball
Marsh Barn
Rockbourne
Fordingbridge
Hampshire SP6 3NF
Tel: 01725 518768
Fax: 01725 518380

Outdoor types will be utterly at home at Sue's smallholding on the edge of the New Forest; there's plenty of space for wet clothes and muddy boots, and cattle graze within 10 feet of the window. You may hear the call of a nightjar in June and Dartford warblers and Montagu's harriers nest nearby. Sue keeps a few sheep, free-range poultry, a horse and two cats; well-behaved dogs are welcome in the downstairs bedroom. Guests have their own little sitting room, warm, simple bedrooms, a friendly atmosphere and good home cooking.

Rooms: 1 double, en suite (bath/shower); 1 twin/double, en suite (bath).

Price: From £22 p.p. Single supp. £8. Reductions for longer stays.

Breakfast: 7-9am.

Meals: Dinner, from £12 p.p., by prior arrangement. Packed lunch £5 p.p.

Closed: Christmas & New Year.

On A338, 1 mile south of Fordingbridge, left at small x-roads for Hyde and Hungerford. Up hill and right at school on corner for Ogdens. Left at next x-roads for Ogdens North. House is on right at bottom of hill.

Entry No: 209   Map no: 4

Sue Browne
Sandy Corner
Ogdens North
Fordingbridge
Hampshire SP6 2QD
Tel: 01425 657295

The warmth of Carole Hayles's welcome is matched by the lushness of the stunning garden with its weeping willow and rhododendrons. There are two ageing Spaniels, two cats, welcome signs on the door knobs, sherry decanters and pots of china. Comfortable bedrooms are full of little extras, with lots of minute detail. You can walk across a buttercup meadow into 15 miles of unspoilt New Forest. Or you could hire a bike (or stable your horse), play golf on the local course, fish in the lakes, sail on the Solent or relax on the sandy beaches only 15 minutes away.

Rooms: 2 doubles, en suite (shower); 1 double, en suite (bath).

Price: £28-£35 p.p.

Breakfast: 8.30-9.30am.

Meals: Available locally.

Closed: Christmas.

Enjoy a bracing early morning swim in the sea — it's a short sprint away; then back for a full English breakfast round the dining room's exotic glass-topped table, once owned by Gucci. Simon and actor Gary have decorated their 17th-century home — a poorhouse in a previous life — with theatrical flair. Pale yellow bedrooms come with all sorts of unexpected extras like bath oils and sherry. Go for the one with the four-poster piled high with cushions to disguise the fact that the headboard was stolen a century ago.

Rooms: 1 four-poster and 1 family room each with private bathroom; 1 double, en suite (bath/shower).

Price: £25-£30 p.p. Single occ. £50. £15 per child.

Breakfast: Until 9.30am.

Meals: Available locally.

Closed: Never.

From London, M3, then M27 and A31. Burley is signed approx. 5 miles before Ringwood. In centre of Burley take right into Pound Lane. Large sign at top of drive.

Entry No: 210   Map no: 4

Carol Hayles
Burbush Farm
Pound Lane, Burley, nr. Ringwood
Hampshire BH24 4EF
Tel: 01425 403238
Fax: 01425 403238
e-mail: burbush-farm@excite.com
Web: www.sawdays.co.uk

From Lymington, B3058 for Milford-on-Sea. The house is on the left, just past the village green.

Entry No: 211   Map no: 4

Gary Payne & Simon Box
The Bay Trees
8 High Street
Milford-on-Sea
Hampshire SO41 0QD
Tel: 01590 642186
Fax: 01590 645461
Web: www.sawdays.co.uk

A town house — on the main road and by traffic lights, but surprisingly quiet, especially at night. The Jeffcocks are impeccably mannered and they care about their guests. Numerous cafés, restaurants and inns are a stroll away and Josephine and David will direct you to Lymington's myriad charms. Narrow and deep, the Edwardian house has some lovely pieces of furniture, a deep red dining room, lots of books and family portraits. There's a Stannah lift on the main staircase. Bedrooms are traditionally furnished with tallboys, dressing tables and displays of good china. *Children over eight welcome.*

Rooms: 1 twin next to private bathroom; 1 double with private bathroom down the passage.

Price: £25-£27 p.p. Single supp. £8.

Breakfast: Flexible.

Meals: Available nearby.

Closed: Christmas & New Year.

A new house for Anthea, but the same enthusiastic welcome as in her previous *Special Place*. She adores her new acquisition — it dates from the 13th century when a Richard de Ranville sailed here from Normandy and settled his family. Now Grade II* listed, the herringbone brickwork is fascinating. There are five acres of garden and paddock, lovely prints and lots of book and large beds in big rooms that overlook a courtyard of old barns. The dining room — in the palest grey — ha two large decorative carved wall lights. Anthea is a dynamo doing B&B for the fun of it.

Rooms: 1 king-size, 2 large twin/doubles, each en suite (bath/shower).

Price: £25 p.p. Single supp. £10.

Breakfast: Flexible.

Meals: Available locally.

Closed: December 20-January 4.

From Brockenhurst A337 to Lymington. Pass hospital to traffic lights on corner of Southampton Rd and Avenue Rd. Left into Avenue Rd. A short driveway, first right, leads to back of house.

Entry No: 212   Map no: 4

Josephine & David Jeffcock
West Lodge
40 Southampton Road
Lymington
Hampshire SO41 9GG
Tel: 01590 672237
Fax: 01590 673592
Web: www.sawdays.co.uk

Two miles west from Romsey on A3090, 1.5 miles from junc. 2 on the M27. 100 yards past turning marked 'Gardener's Lane' on the right side of the dual carriageway. Drive entrance marked by flagpole.

Entry No: 213   Map no: 4

Anthea Hughes
Ranvilles Farm House
Ower
Romsey
Hampshire SO51 6AA
Tel: 02380 814481
Fax: 012380 814481

The builders were in when we inspected Gill's new house, but the signs were very promising. There are pale oak floors, generous windows, an old oak beam, brick fireplaces and a lightness to this 1860s mews house. One bedroom has views to the east over Winchester and St Catherine's Hill; from the other you can see Christ Church. Breakfast is buffet-style — freshly-squeezed orange juice, fresh fruit, fruit compote, organic yoghurt, home-baked bread and Danish pastries. If it's fine you'll eat under a parasol on the patio. *Children over 11 welcome.*

Rooms: 1 twin, en suite (bath & shower); 1 double with private bathroom.

Price: £30-£35 p.p. Single occ. £55.

Breakfast: Until 9.30am.

Meals: Available locally.

Closed: Occasionally.

From M3, junc. 11, follow signs for Winchester. At 2nd r'bout, take B3335 to St. Cross. After 1.5 miles, turn left after pedestrian crossing into St. James Lane. Alexandra Terrace is 3rd on left.

Entry No: 214   Map no: 4

Gill Dowson
4 Alexandra Terrace
Winchester
Hampshire SO23 9SP
Tel: 01962 863356
Fax: To come.

Lovely people and a charming house, Georgian in look — rather like an old rectory. It is in its own 15-acre grounds, yet just minutes from Winchester; elegantly decorated, full of antiques and ancestral portraits. The bedrooms have chintz, mahogany furniture and beautiful views. Sue modestly calls herself an 'amateur artist' — some of her watercolours decorate the bedrooms. An inspiration to the more energetic or divinely inspired, the house is on the Pilgrim's Way so the walking is ready-made. *Children over 10 welcome.*

Rooms: 1 twin, en suite (bath/shower); 1 twin with private bathroom.

Price: £25-£30 p.p.

Breakfast: Flexible.

Meals: Available locally.

Closed: December-January.

From M3, junc. 9, A272 to Winchester. At next r'bout, straight over. Left at small r'bout signed Morestead, then immediate left. 1 mile after Morestead, right to Owslebury. Through village, then left fork to Whadden Lane. 1st entrance 200 yds down Whadden Lane on left — no name.

Entry No: 215   Map no: 4

Sue & Tim Torrington
Great Hunts Place
Owslebury, Nr. Winchester
Hampshire SO21 1JL
Tel: 01962 777234
Fax: 01962 777242
e-mail: tt@byngs.freeserve.co.uk
Web: www.byngs.freeserve.co.uk

Susie is a natural, easy, courteous host in a house that sent our inspector into mild raptures. A galleried landing joins the newish addition to the old Victorian flint-and-brick schoolhouse and you can't see the join! An instantly welcoming sense of family life greets you. And it gets better. The kitchen is a pure country-life retreat, all old oak and terracotta, the nerve centre of the vivacious Susie's cooking and entertaining — plainly a matter of great pride to her. You have your own delightful sitting room with open fire and piles of books. The garden is expansive.

Rooms: 1 double and 1 twin, each with private bathroom.

Price: £27 p.p. Single supp. £8-£10.

Breakfast: Until 9.30am.

Meals: Dinner, 3 courses, £18 p.p., by arrangement.

Closed: Mid-December-mid-January.

Privacy in a B&B is rare. Here you have it, just 12 minutes walk from the centre of town, Cathedral and water meadow in your own half of a Victorian townhouse beautifully furnished and decorated and immensely welcoming. Fizzy serves sumptuous breakfasts and fresh flowers abound. You are also left with an 'honesty box' so you may help yourselves to drinks. The rooms are small and cosy with lovely big, antique mirrors, bedspreads and furniture and there is a log fire in the sitting room. *Children over seven welcome.*

Rooms: 1 twin and 1 double, both en suite (shower & bath).

Price: £25-£27.50 p.p. Single occ. £40

Breakfast: Flexible.

Meals: Available nearby.

Closed: Christmas.

From M3 exit 9, A272 to Petersfield. After 2 miles, fork right to Warnford and Preshaw, over crossroads. House is 2nd on left after 300 yards.

Entry No: 216   Map no: 4

Susie Church
The Old School House
Lane End
Longwood, nr. Winchester
Hampshire SO21 1JZ
Tel: 01962 777248
Fax: 01962 777744

Leave M3 at junc. 9 and follow signs for Winchester Park & Ride. Under m'way, straight on at r'bout signed to St. Cross. Left at T-junc. St. Faith's Rd about 200m ahead.

Entry No: 217   Map no: 4

Guy & Fizzy Warren
Brymer House
29/30 St. Faith's Road
St. Cross, Winchester
Hampshire SO23 9QD
Tel: 01962 867428
Fax: 01962 868624

Lord Nelson's cloak hung here — he was a friend of Admiral Thomson who created the house. Four generations of Hanbury-Batemans have lived here and beautiful furniture remains from each. Wooden and stone floors reflect the light that floods in; upstairs, all is carpeted. There are intriguing curios, statues and vases and Elisabeth, who is Austrian and an interior designer, brings it all together in elegant harmony. Bedrooms are immaculate; ornate mirrors and antique furniture. Lovely mature gardens, tennis court and croquet lawn. A good area for walking and fishing, too. *Babes in arms and children over 12 welcome.*

Rooms: 1 large twin, en suite; 1 large twin with basin and private bathroom.

Price: £35 p.p. Single supp. £10.

Breakfast: Flexible.

Meals: Dinner, 3 courses, £25 p.p.; 2 courses, £15 p.p., by arrangement.

Closed: Never.

From Andover, on A303, take turning past petrol station for Longparish. From B3048, 1st right for Forton, then 1st left onto private road. Go through gateway and up drive to house.

Entry No: 218   Map no: 4

Bill Hanbury-Bateman
Forton House
Long Parish
Andover
Hampshire SP11 6NN
Tel: 01264 720236
Fax: 01264 720885
e-mail: bandbbest@aol.com

There is one jewel within another: a fine house within seven acres of beautiful garden within 100 acres of private woodland. Breakfast in the chinoiserie dining room is charming, the tennis court is hidden in the gardens, you can fish, glide, ride and, if you book in advance, even go up in a hot-air balloon! But back to those gardens: Japanese and dahlia gardens, fine specimen trees, formal terraces, a croquet lawn, exotica, all done with flair and imagination. Jeremy is an architectural photographer and they are both natural hosts. The perfect English country house. *Children over 12 welcome.*

Rooms: 3 twins: 2 en suite and 1 with private bathroom.

Price: From £30 p.p. Single supp. £7.50.

Breakfast: Flexible.

Meals: Dinner £20 p.p. Available on request.

Closed: Christmas Day.

South on A3 to traffic lights at Hindhead. Go straight across; after 400 yards, turn right onto B3002. Continue for 3 miles. Entrance to house (signed) is on right in a wood.

Entry No: 219   Map no: 5

Jeremy & Philippa Whitaker
Land of Nod
Headley
Bordon
Hampshire GU35 8SJ
Tel: 01428 713609
Fax: 01428 717698
Web: www.sawdays.co.uk

In two acres of beautifully landscaped gardens, Mizzards Farm is a lovely 16th-century farmhouse on a site with a medieval history. It has its own lake, an upstairs conservatory, heated covered pool, outdoor chess, croquet lawn and rare bantams for company. Splendid breakfasts in the spectacular, vaulted dining room, and the general atmosphere is of relaxed elegance. The bedrooms are comfortable and attractive, one with a four-poster and correspondingly grand marble bathroom. Harriet and Julian are keen to advise on walks in this designated AONB. *Children over eight welcome.*

Rooms: 1 twin, 1 double and 1 four-poster, all en suite (bath/shower).

Price: £28-£33 p.p. Single supp. by arrangement.

Breakfast: 8-9am.

Meals: Dinner available locally.

Closed: Christmas.

In the loveliest part of the island, with high ground, great walks on the Downs and in an Area Of Outstanding Natural Beauty. Newtown Nature Reserve is down the road, with all its migrant birds and wild flowers. The house is lovely, too, next to the church. Guests are given a separate flat, which has a mix of modern furniture and some old pieces. Nothing is too much trouble for your hosts. Sheila takes in your delicious breakfast: fresh fruit, free-range eggs, croissants, the full works.

Rooms: 1 separate flat with twin beds; 1 twin in the house, en suite (bath).

Price: £27.50 p.p. Single supp. £5.

Breakfast: Flexible.

Meals: Available locally.

Closed: Christmas Day.

From A272 at Rogate, turn towards Harting/Nyewood. Cross humpback bridge; drive is first turning on the right. Signed.

Entry No: 220   Map no: 5

Harriet & Julian Francis
Mizzards Farm
Rogate
Petersfield
Hampshire GU31 5HS
Tel: 01730 821656
Fax: 01730 821655
e-mail: julian.francis@hemscott.net

From Yarmouth take road to Shalfleet through village. After 0.5 miles turn right for Calbourne. The house is by the church across the green.

Entry No: 221   Map no: 4

Sheila & Oliver Mathews
The Old Rectory
Calbourne
Isle of Wight PO30 4JE
Tel: 01983 531247
Fax: 01983 531253
e-mail: oliver.mathews@virginnet.co.uk
Web: www.sawdays.co.uk

The Harrisons bought this stunning Jacobean pile for its matchless gardens: 15 acres of pathed wilderness, exotic and subtropical flowers. A stroll is an adventure; you come across an old swimming pool cascading with plants, a bench on a lofty vantage point, a crystal clear stream banked with bamboo, a smooth lawn, a walled garden, a sunken rose garden and a grass tennis court. The massive house has lovely rooms and acres of space; it would take a lot more furniture to fill it. In a quiet village in lovely downland. Come to the Isle of Wight if only to see the garden.

Rooms: 3 doubles and 3 twins, en suite (bath/shower).

Price: £22-£27.50 p.p. Single supp. £10.

Breakfast: 8-9.15am.

Meals: Light meals available if ordered in advance. Pub 3 minute's walk through gardens.

Closed: Christmas.

You sleep on a French rosewood bed, and there's a huge cast iron bath IN your room — ideal for wallowing by candlelight with a glass of wine. There's a head-clearing simplicity in this unique 'first-floor' Saxon house — built with living space on the first floor and the windowless ground floor reserved for defence purposes or storage. Limewashed walls, wooden floors and exposed A-frame beams in both the bedrooms and you have a private garden. The self-catering cottage with huge sofa and Shaker style dining furniture is equally stunning. *Children over 12 welcome.*

Rooms: 1 double, en suite (bath) and 1 double, en suite (bath/shower); each room has an extra single bed. Self-catering cottage, sleeps 4+.

Price: £30-£35 p.p. Single occ. by arrangement. From £300-£600 p.w.

Breakfast: Flexible.

Meals: Available locally.

Closed: Never.

0.5 miles south of Chale Green on B3399; after village, turn left at Gotten Lane; house at end of lane.

From Newport, drive into Shorwell, down a steep hill, under a rustic bridge and turn right opposite a thatched cottage. Signed.

Entry No: 222   Map no: 4

John & Christine Harrison
North Court
Shorwell
Isle of Wight PO30 3JG
Tel: 01983 740415
Fax: 01983 740409
Web: www.sawdays.co.uk

Entry No: 223   Map no: 4

Caroline Smith
Gotten Manor
Gotten Lane, Chale
Isle of Wight PO38 2HQ
Tel: 01983 551368
Fax: 01983 551368
e-mail: b&b@gottenmanor.co.uk
Web: www.gottenmanor.co.uk

"Not a whisper of noise," says our inspector of this delightful house, part 17th century and part 19th, in one of the rare, undiscovered corners of rural England. If you enjoy the luxuries of space and tranquillity, this pristine house, full of antiques, old paintings and fine furniture, will bring joy to your heart. Large, airy and comfortable bedrooms with immaculate white linen and carpets that are soft underfoot. Guy not only makes bread but also grows fruit and vegetables which Amanda loves to cook and share, *en famille*, with guests at her elegant dining table. There's tennis, too. *Children over 12 welcome.*

Rooms: 1 twin, en suite (bath); 1 double, en suite (bath/shower).

Price: £34 p.p. Single supp. £10.

Breakfast: Flexible.

Meals: Dinner, 3 courses, £20 p.p. Packed lunch by arrangement.

Closed: Occasionally.

Herefordshire

From Tenbury Wells, to Leysters, on A4112, left at x-roads in village. Ignore sign to Leysters church. House on left, through white gate (after postbox in wall).

Entry No: 224   Map no: 9

Guy & Amanda Griffiths
The Old Vicarage
Leysters, Leominster
Herefordshire HR6 0HS
Tel: 01568 750574
Fax: 01568 750208
e-mail: guy.griffiths@virgin.net
Web: www.sawdays.co.uk

An utterly fascinating place. The 17th-century farmhouse, cider house, dairy, granary and 14-acre private nature reserve are perched at the top of a small valley; the views are tremendous. In the huge dining room is the old cider mill, and dinner may feature the Wiles' home-smoked fish or meat and home-made bread. Much of what they serve is organic — all the wines are. One room is across the courtyard, the other three in the granary annexe; they are all timber-framed, compact and well thought out and have their own sitting rooms. *Children over eight welcome.*

Rooms: 4 suites, each with own bathroom or shower room.

Price: £29.50 p.p. Single occ. £34.50.

Breakfast: Until 9.30am.

Meals: Dinner £15.50-£21.50 p.p.

Closed: Never.

From Leominster, take A49 north but turning right onto A4122, signed Leysters. Lower Bache is then signed after village of Kimbolton.

Entry No: 225   Map no: 9

Rose & Leslie Wiles
Lower Bache House
Kimbolton
Nr. Leominster
Herefordshire HR6 0ER
Tel: 01568 750304

A wonderful place that, after Herculean labours, has been brought back to life by James and Henrietta. It is set in parkland, high above the River Lugg, with views to the Black Mountains. There are comforting features such as a cast-iron bath in an attractive, modern bathroom, huge (and many) windows releasing light into rooms filled with some grand old furniture and interesting prints. It is snug, cosy, grand and without pretence — country house living at its most appealing. They cook a great breakfast, too. *Children over five welcome.*

Rooms: 2 doubles and 1 twin, all en suite.

Price: £25 p.p. Single supp. £10.

Breakfast: Flexible.

Meals: Dinner £17.50 p.p.

Closed: Christmas & Easter.

From Leominster B4361 north. 0.5 miles on, left for Eyton. 1.5 miles on, left for Kingsland. House is 0.5 miles on right.

Entry No: 226   Map no: 9

James & Henrietta Varley
Eyton Old Hall
Eyton
Leominster
Herefordshire HR6 0AQ
Tel: 01568 612551
Fax: 01568 616100
e-mail: varleyeoh@hotmail.com

Wisteria-clad Church House has all the advantages of being in a small town, with a rural atmosphere thrown in. A church on one side, a large garden which disappears into rolling hills on the other. Much of the house is Shaker in style: refreshingly simple bare boards and flat paint. Andrew (a wine merchant; Liz is a concert singer) hires out mountain bikes. The whole family makes super company; you can't fail to relax. Cotton sheets, flowers, home-made jams and a delightfully chubby bath.

Rooms: 1 twin with basin and 1 double sharing bathroom.

Price: From £20 p.p. Single supp. by arrangement.

Breakfast: Until 9.30am.

Meals: Dinner available locally.

Closed: Christmas.

Deep in the middle of nowhere, this is an unpretentious, modernised mill house. Rooms are small and cosy, with exposed beams and slate window sills, and only the old mill itself interrupts the view of the surrounding greenness. Best of all, though, is sinking into downy sleep to the sound of the Arrow River burbling away — a real tonic for frazzled city-dwellers. Grace is chatty and informal and though guests have the run of the cottage the lovely kitchen tends to be the gravitational centre of this home.

Rooms: 1 double, en suite (shower); 1 double sharing bathroom & wc with extra twin.

Price: £18-£22 p.p. No single supp.

Breakfast: Until 9am.

Meals: Dinner, from £12 p.p., by arrangement.

Closed: Christmas.

Take A438 from Hereford. After Winforton & Whitney-on-Wye and after toll bridge on left, sharp right for Brilley. Left fork to Huntington, over x-roads and next right to Huntington. Right into 'No through' road, then 1st right.

Coming into Kington, follow signs for the town centre. Go through middle of town and up long steady hill to St. Mary's church. House is on left opposite.

Entry No: 227   Map no: 9

Entry No: 228   Map no: 9

Andrew & Lis Darwin
Church House
Church Road
Kington
Herefordshire HR5 3AG
Tel: 01544 230534
Fax: 01544 231100

Grace Watson
Hall's Mill House
Huntington
Kington
Herefordshire HR5 3QA
Tel: 01497 831409

House and garden have that impressive Tudor scale — panelling, cavernous fireplaces, flagstones and a huge fireplace in the hall, straight oak staircase and and polished floorboards. A pleached Hornbeam avenue is being created on the house's approach and the decoration on the wrought iron gateway, mentioned in Pevsner, went to America, but has been traced and will be reinstated. The high brass beds have linen sheets and patchwork quilts. Bathrooms are big and comfortable.

Rooms: 2 twins, 1 en suite (bath), 1 with private bathroom.

Price: £25 p.p.

Breakfast: Flexible.

Meals: Dinner, by arrangement, £15 p.p.

Closed: Never.

Quite breathtaking. This Georgian gentleman's residence overlooks one of the finest views in England. Recline on the sofa in your divinely comfortable bedroom and gaze across the Wye Valley to the Malvern Hills and west to the Black Mountains. Rooms are gracious and full of beautiful things The 14th-century barn is now a splendid party hall and the magnificent four acres of garden include terracing, a walled garden with perfumed rose walk and parterres with rills of water. An elegant home — and Stephanie's cooking is worth a detour.

Rooms: 1 double and 1 twin, both with private bathrooms.

Price: From £25 p.p. Single supp. £5.

Breakfast: Flexible.

Meals: Dinner £16 p.p. Packed lunch £3.50 p.p.

Closed: Christmas.

From Leominster, A44 and follow signs for Brecon. After approx. 6 miles, left into Dilwyn. Round 3 sharp bends, and house is set back on right behind stone gate piers and iron gates.

Entry No: 229   Map no: 9

Tom & Jane Hawksley
The Great House
Dilwyn
Hereford
Herefordshire HR4 8HX
Tel: 01544 318007

From A438 Hereford/Brecon road, proceed towards Kington on A4111 through Eardisley village. Bollingham House is 2 miles up hill on left, behind a long line of conifers.

Entry No: 230   Map no: 9

Stephanie & John Grant
Bollingham House
Eardisley
Herefordshire HR5 3LE
Tel: 01544 327326
Fax: 01544 327880
e-mail: bollhouse@bigfoot.com
Web: www.sawdays.co.uk

Such an unusual place, miles from nowhere on the Welsh borders. Built in the 17th century as a grain barn, lovingly renovated with weatherboarding and stone tiling, it has a vast open threshing bay which frames the woods and hills like an old-time idyll of rural England. The cattle byres round the yard, perfect in their ancient curviness, house the conservatory where guests may sit. The bedrooms have simple modern furniture and share a small shower room. Ann makes her own bread and preserves which she serves to guests. Honest value and superb views.

Rooms: 1 family room (double and a single) and 1 twin, sharing shower & wc.

Price: £20 p.p. Children under 12, £16.

Breakfast: About 8.30am.

Meals: Dinner £14 p.p. B.Y.O. wine. Packed lunch also available.

Closed: Never.

The staircase, mentioned in Pevsner's Guide to Historic Houses, is 17th-century. Most of the house was built in 1500 and is breathtaking in its ancient dignity, its undulating floors, two-foot thick walls and great oak beams. Take a book from the small library and settle into a window seat looking over the gardens. There is a guest sitting room, too, festooned with work by local artists. Candles feature all over the house. The two beamed and four-postered bedrooms verge on the luxurious; so does the other one. Gorgeous. If you're celebrating a special occasion, Jackie will spoil you with wine or chocolates.

Rooms: 1 double and 1 king-size four-poster, both en suite; 1 suite with king-size four-poster, en suite (bath).

Price: Double £25 p.p. Four-poster £30 p.p. Suite £34 p.p. Single supp. £15.

Breakfast: Until 10am.

Meals: Available locally.

Closed: Christmas.

From Hay take B4350 to Clifford. Pass Castle & turn right to Bredwardine. Take third left at top of hill, signed Priory Wood. Pass between chapel & small playing field. Castleton Barn is ahead on right.

Entry No: 231   Map no: 9

Ann Tong
Castleton Barn
Priory Wood, Clifford
Nr. Hay-on-Wye
Herefordshire HR3 5HF
Tel: 01497 831690
Fax: 01497 831296

From Hereford, A438 into village. House on left with a large green sign and iron gates.

Entry No: 232   Map no: 9

Jackie Kingdon
Winforton Court
Winforton
Herefordshire HR3 6EA
Tel: 01544 328498
Fax: 01544 328498
e-mail: winfortoncourt@talk21.com
Web: www.sawdays.co.uk

A place of peace and tranquillity set on the edge of the Black Mountains and with magnificent views. There has been a house here since medieval times and this was built around the time of the Civil War. It exudes history. House and owner have an easy relationship — there's a quiet impressiveness about both. Many rooms are book-lined, one bedroom has an African mood, with artefacts brought back by Antony's son. Oils, fireplaces ducks, geese, chickens and a happy Labrador. It's not at all stuffy and Antony makes his own bread and marmalade.

Rooms: 2 doubles and 1 single, sharing bathroom.

Price: £20 p.p. No single supp.

Breakfast: Flexible.

Meals: Available locally.

Closed: Never.

From Abergavenny, take Hereford rd (A465). Left (signed Longtown) after 5 miles. Fork right at entrance to Longtown at sign with no arms. After 2.5 miles, signed on left on low stone wall. House 600 yds up drive.

Entry No: 233   Map no: 9

Antony Egremont-Lee
Middle Trewern
Longtown
Herefordshire HR2 0LN
Tel: 01873 860670

The house is late Victorian and filled with warmth and charm, with a long plank table at which to eat Aga-cooked breakfasts and dinners. There are fine views from both house and garden across the Monnow Valley to the Brecon Beacons and the Black Mountains. Somehow, the tranquillity and assurance of the church have communicated themselves to this house. The Knights Templar, then the Knights of St. John, once owned Garway church; it is a Norman gem. *Children over eight welcome.*

Rooms: 1 four-poster and 1 twin, each with basin, sharing bathroom. Separate shower & wcs.

Price: £20-£25 p.p. Single supp. £5-£10.

Breakfast: Until 9.30am.

Meals: Dinner, £17.50 p.p., by prior arrangement.

Closed: Never.

From Hereford A49 towards Ross. After 5 miles A466 towards Monmouth. After 7 miles B4521 right towards Abergavenny. At Broad Oak right towards Garway. First right past school signposted Garway Hill. Old Rectory is 150 yards on right.

Entry No: 234   Map no: 9

Caroline Ailesbury
The Old Rectory
Garway
Herefordshire HR2 8RH
Tel: 01600 750363
Fax: 01600 750364

The front is Georgian, the back Victorian. Inside, thick, thick walls and stone flags speak of a more ancient history. Valerie and Carol are clearly content in their uncontrived home. The pretty, traditional bedrooms have marvellous views of the richly-wooded countryside. Their grandchildren are regular visitors: your children may share toys in the house and garden, and you also have your own large piece of the two and a half acre garden and use of the tennis court. There's a small library; music appreciation is high on the agenda.

Rooms: 1 twin with private bath, shower & wc; 2 doubles sharing bathroom, shower & wc.

Price: £25 p.p. Under 5s, £5; 5-12s, £15.

Breakfast: Flexible.

Meals: Packed lunch on request.

Closed: Never.

Wisteria wraps itself around the warm brick walls, sheep bleat behind the stable, a pond shimmers... and you play tennis, swim in the neighbour's outdoor pool or walk the Malvern Hills. The guests' drawing room is elegant; there are books by the fire and plump armchairs and sofas to sink into. Half-timbered bedrooms with window-seats, ornately-carved canopied beds, Jacobean panelling, and an upstairs drawing room all seem like icing on the cake. Michael is an excellent cook and dinner is a special occasion, so do eat in.

Rooms: 3 doubles, 2 four-posters and twin/double, all en suite.

Price: £34.50 p.p. Single supp. £15. Small children free.

Breakfast: Flexible.

Meals: Dinner £22 p.p.

Closed: Christmas & New Year.

From Ross-on-Wye east on A40 towards Gloucester. Turn right to Hope Mansell. Take 3rd lane on left opposite Gallery. After 1 mile, house is on left between lane sign-posted 'village hall' and the church.

Entry No: 235   Map no: 9

Mrs Carol Ouvry/Mrs Valerie Godson
The Old Rectory, Hope Mansell,
Ross-on-Wye, Herefordshire HR9 5TL
Tel: 01989 750382
Fax: 01989 750382
e-mail: rectory@mansell.wyenet.co.uk
Web: www.sawdays.co.uk

Leave M50 at junc. 2, towards Ledbury. Take first left to Bromsberrow Heath. Right by post office in village and go up hill. House is on right.

Entry No: 236   Map no: 9

Michael & Ellen Ross
The Grove House
Bromsberrow Heath
Ledbury
Herefordshire HR8 1PE
Tel: 01531 650584

The 1612 barn behind the Georgian façade is a soaring tangle of timbers, a paean to carpentry. The hall, open to the roof, is beautiful, with a graceful staircase. Heavy oak beams are on bold display, and part of the timber cruck can be seen. Guests have a sitting room and breakfast is served in the beamed dining room. The bedrooms are pleasantly comfortable, in some Judi provides towelling robes for the quick flit to the antique bath. A delightfully unexpected house with a charming hostess, and there is a lovely garden to enjoy too... all this in the centre of luscious Ledbury.

Rooms: 1 double, en suite (shower); 1 double and 1 twin, both with basin, sharing bathroom.

Price: £28 p.p. Single occ. £48.

Breakfast: Until 9.30am.

Meals: Dinner & packed lunch sometimes available by request — otherwise, lots of places in town.

Closed: Christmas Day & Boxing Day.

From Ledbury bypass, take A449 signed Worcester/town centre. Barn House on left just past Somerfields but before central town crossroads.

Entry No: 237   Map no: 9

Judi Holland
The Barn House
New Street
Ledbury
Herefordshire HR8 2DX
Tel: 01531 632825

Moor Court is an active, traditional livestock and hop farm which still dries its own hops — you can watch their oast house at work. You will eat well — home-produced meat, preserves and vegetables; Elizabeth is an excellent cook. The buildings, about 500 years old, ramble and enfold both gardens and guests in a homely, traditional way. Elizabeth makes her own soft furnishings and has chosen dainty fabrics and furniture appropriate for timber-framed rooms of antiquity.

Rooms: 1 twin, en suite (bath/shower); 1 twin and 1 double, en suite (bath).

Price: £18.50 p.p. Single occ. £25.

Breakfast: Flexible.

Meals: Dinner, 3 courses, £14 p.p.

Closed: Never.

From Hereford, east on A438. A417 into Stretton Grandison. First right past village sign, through Holmend Park. Veer left past phone box. Moor Court is on left, 1 mile from Stretton turnoff.

Entry No: 238   Map no: 9

Elizabeth & Peter Godsall
Moor Court Farm
Stretton Grandison
Nr. Ledbury
Herefordshire HR8 2TP
Tel: 01531 670408

Super people with humour and most hospitable instincts, the Daltons call their house "rambling, romantic, ancient, silent". A big old manor with gardens and croquet lawn just beside the lovely 12th-century church. You may breakfast beside the great log fire in the Tudor dining room on chilly mornings or under the spreading chestnut tree on warmer days; relax after dinner in the cosy, little oak-panelled sitting room. Rooms are big, family-style, with books, flowers and garden views. Easy, unstuffy — wonderful value. Two excellent pubs within walking distance, too.

Rooms: 2 twins/doubles, 1 en suite (bath) and 1 private bathroom.

Price: £20-£23.50 p.p. Single supp. £5.

Breakfast: Flexible.

Meals: Dinner £18 p.p., and packed lunch, available on request.

Closed: Never.

Just walk into that barn and look up. Wow! The roof is breathtaking, a copse of beams and timbers. Few conversions are as successful as this one, but Judy is an artist, a painter, and impossibly resourceful — so no wonder. It is fresh, new, bright and clean; it is comfortable, too, and as they have just moved from Prior's Court (in previous editions of our book) they will bring cohorts of loyal fans — so come soon. It is a generous place — they will ferry you to the pub in the evening. Lovely people.

Rooms: 1 double, en suite (bath & shower); 1 twin with private bathroom (bath & shower).

Price: £25 p.p. Single supp. £5.

Breakfast: Flexible.

Meals: Available locally.

Closed: Never.

From A417 travelling south, left to Ullingswick at x-roads. Continue through village. Turn left then right at signs to Ullingswick church. Drive is on right before church lychgate.

Entry No: 239   Map no: 9

Christopher & Susan Dalton
Upper Court
Ullingswick
Herefordshire HR1 3JQ
Tel: 01432 820295
Fax: 01432 820174
e-mail: ucbb@hotmail.com

At Burley Gate roundabout on A417, take A465 towards Bromyard. At Stoke Lacy church, on right, turn right then 2nd right to entrance.

Entry No: 240   Map no: 9

Roger & Judy Young
Dovecote Barn
Stoke Lacy
Herefordshire HR7 4HJ
Tel: 01432 820968
Fax: 01432 820969
e-mail: dovecotebarn@mail.com

The whole place is peppered with antiques and has an undeniable charm, but you don't have to tiptoe for fear of spoiling a contrived tidiness — Julia is easy-going and natural. Bedrooms are beamy and snug — the en-suite room is under the thatch with garden views, the other two look onto an avenue of horse chestnuts that were planted on the village green to commemorate the jubilee of George V. There's a duck pond and an excellent village pub. Hard to believe that this 15th-century cottage is only five minutes drive from Stansted; no noise here, though — the flight path is in the opposite direction.

Rooms: 1 double, en suite; 1 double with basin and 1 twin with wc & basin, sharing downstairs bathroom.

Price: £22-£28 p.p.

Breakfast: Flexible.

Meals: Packed lunch on request.

Closed: Never.

From Stansted Mountfitchet take B1051 for approx. 5 miles, through Elseham. Left for Henham (signed) and right at War Memorial. Woodend Green is on right with avenue of large trees. Cottage is on far right corner opposite.

Entry No: 241   Map no: 11

George & Julia Griffiths
Pleasant Cottage
Wood End Green, Henham
Bishops Stortford
Hertfordshire CM22 6AZ
Tel: 01279 850792

Hertfordshire, Bucks & Beds

Lutyens built this wonderful house in 1901 for his mother-in-law, the Dowager Lady Lytton. Set down a long drive in six acres of beautiful gardens and fields, each elevation of the house is different. Architectural peculiarities — such as internal, octagonal windows — abound and Samantha has applied her considerable artistic skills to the interior. Unusual colour schemes offset magnificent antiques, tapestries and chinoiserie. The family is happy to share its home and can converse in a clutch of languages.

Rooms: 1 double, en suite (shower); 1 family suite with bathroom; 1 double with private shower sometimes available.

Price: Double £35 p.p. Single occ. £45. Family suite £70 per couple and £15 per extra person.

Breakfast: Flexible.

Meals: Dinner, £25 p.p.; wine, £5 p.p; by arrangement.

Closed: 20 December-3 January.

Into Knebworth on B197, turn into Station Rd which becomes Park Lane. 300 yards after crossing m'way bridge, left into public footpath. After 300 yards, bear left through lodge gates. House is at end.

Entry No: 242   Map no: 11

Samantha Pollock-Hill
Homewood
Knebworth
Hertfordshire SG3 6PP
Tel: 01438 812105

A mere 30 minutes by train from central London and 10 minutes from Luton Airport, this is an oasis. Surrounded by cornfields, woods and lovely views, the house is large and old, yet wonderfully cosy. The kitchen is bright and informal and we can imagine Claire cooking brilliantly for dinner served in the pretty dining room. There are antiques, Limoges porcelain, lovely soft furnishings and informal bedrooms with comfortable beds. Claire, friendly and chatty, sweeps visitors of all ages into her easy-going welcome. There's a large quiet garden.

Rooms: 1 twin, en suite (bath); 1 twin with private bathroom and shower.

Price: £27.50 p.p. Single occ. £35.

Breakfast: Flexible.

Meals: Dinner, £20 p.p., by arrangement.

Closed: 20 December-3 January.

From A1 junc. 4, B653 towards Wheathampstead. After Brocket Hall, follow signs to Kimpton. After 2nd r'bout, follow signs to Kimpton and take 2nd left to Porters End. First house on left after 0.5 miles.

Entry No: 243   Map no: 11

Alex & Claire van Straubenzee
Paddock Lodge
Porters End
Kimpton
Hertfordshire SG4 8ER
Tel: 01438 832423

Tucked beneath the Chilterns in 20 acres of grounds (and lakes) this 16th-century water-mill, a mile from the village, has a very pretty room in the 'Hay-loft'. Most of the chintz-and-antique bedrooms are in a converted stable-block — hotel privacy in a B&B — and you may stay all day, gazing at the lake from the conservatory and victualling yourself from the little kitchen. Rachael is an easy no-rules hostess and can lend you a bike... or offer fly-fishing, tennis, pool table and 'Ping-Pong'. Self-catering in the mill, with features in situ, too.

Rooms: 2 twins and 5 doubles, all en suite.

Price: £32.50 p.p. Children £7.50. Single supp. £5-£15. Self-catering, from £250 per week. Weekends sometimes available.

Breakfast: 7-9am Mon-Fri; 8.30-10am Sat-Sun.

Meals: Occasionally dinner, by arrangement, £15 p.p.

Closed: Never.

From Dunstable, SW on B489. Right at r'bout by Plough pub. Bellows Mill in 3rd road on left.

Entry No: 244   Map no: 10

Rachael Hodge
Bellows Mill
Eaton Bray, Dunstable
Bedfordshire LU6 1QZ
Tel: 01525 220548
Fax: 01525 222536
e-mail: rachael@bellowsmill.co.uk
Web: www.bellowsmill.co.uk

Come to the Old Vicarage and be welcomed into the heart of this charming family. With a church across the way and gracious, comfortable rooms, it is a lovely house, built by the Rothschilds in 1865 when they bought the village of Mentmore. Guests can use the large drawing room and enjoy Susie's delicious recipes in the dining room or *al fresco* in the lovingly-tended gardens with spectacular views over unspoilt countryside. Bedrooms are peaceful and airy (one overlooks the swimming pool). Waddeson Manor is nearby; London is less than an hour away, by car or train.

Rooms: 1 twin, en suite (bath); 1 double, en suite (shower).

Price: £27.50 p.p. Single supp. £5. Children under 12, £10 when sharing.

Breakfast: 7.30-9am.

Meals: Dinner £15 p.p. Available on request.

Closed: Occasionally.

At Cheddington roundabout, left for Mentmore. Pass gates to Mentmore Towers. Old Vicarage is on right opposite church.

Entry No: 245   Map no: 10

Charles & Susie Kirchner
The Old Vicarage
Mentmore
Buckinghamshire LU7 0QG
Tel: 01296 661243
Fax: 01296 661243
e-mail: susie.kirchner@tesco.net
Web: www.sawdays.co.uk

Sarah's conversion, architectural rather than religious, has turned a fascinating church into a fascinating home, complete with tower and spiral staircase, original stained glass and stone-mullioned windows. Yet with stealth and a sure touch, the comforts have crept in. Any austerity has been exorcised. Each of the bedrooms has its own church window; one has a Winnie the Pooh mural; and a bathroom has painted fish swimming round the walls. Sarah is ease personified and cooks a delicious breakfast in the magnificent kitchen/schoolroom. This is a one-off.

Rooms: 1 twin, 1 double and 1 single, sharing 1 bathroom and 1 shower room.

Price: £22.50 p.p. Single, £25.

Breakfast: Flexible.

Meals: Excellent restaurants & pubs nearby.

Closed: Never.

From Aylesbury, A413 towards Buckingham. On reaching Winslow centre, turn left into Horn St between The Bell Hotel and The George. Church on left.

Entry No: 246   Map no: 10

Sarah Hood
The Congregational Church
15 Horn Street
Winslow
Buckinghamshire MK18 3AP
Tel: 01296 715717
Fax: 01296 715717
Web: www.sawdays.co.uk

Come if you're interested in gardens —
Sue designs them and will enjoy
showing you around her developing
plot; it merges with the surrounding
fields and you can see the medieval
ridges and furrows that she has cleverly
worked around. You are only 22 miles
from the bustle of London, yet are
immersed in much of historical,
geological and architectural interest.
Bedrooms are bright, towels soft and
colours restful; the bedrooms that share
the bathroom have a lovely view. A
good sense of space and light
throughout, and Sue will spoil you with
some home-made treats.

Rooms: 1 twin & 1 double with basins
(shared bathroom); 1 twin with private
bathroom.

Price: £25 p.p. Single supp. £10.

Breakfast: 7am-9am. Can be flexible.

Meals: Good selection of places in
Westerham.

Closed: 22-29 December.

Kent

*M25, junction 6, follow signs to
Westerham (A25). After Westerham
town sign and 30mph sign, take first left
into Farley Lane. After approx. 200m,
turn left at top, then left again.*

Entry No: 247   Map no: 5

Sue & Alastair Marr
Worples Field
Farley Common
Westerham
Kent TN16 1UB
Tel: 01959 562869
e-mail: marr@worplesfield.com
Web: www.worplesfield.com

In May the scent from the azaleas and rhododendrons is intoxicating. But even the glories of the garden cannot diminish the impact of this part-Edwardian, part-Tudor house. The Streatfeilds have been in Chiddingstone for centuries — the castle was their seat — but carry their history lightly. They are well-mannered, intelligent, easy folk. Some furniture is well-worn and faded but everything feels authentic. Bedrooms are huge, with views over the gardens, grazing sheep and hills. You can settle into the fireside chairs in the library. Everything for children, too. It's worth every penny.

Rooms: Main house: 1 twin and 1 double with shared bathroom. Annexe: 1 double, en suite (bath).

Price: £25 p.p.; single occ. £25-£35. Minimum 2 nights' stay at weekends.

Breakfast: Until 9am.

Meals: Light suppers and dinners £9-£16 p.p.

Closed: Christmas & New Year.

From A21, Hildenborough exit. Follow signs to Penshurst Place, then to vineyard. Pass it, then right at T-junc. towards Edenbridge. Through village, bear left (following signs to Edenbridge). House is 0.5 miles on left.

Entry No: 248   Map no: 5

Mr & Mrs Mervyn Streatfeild
Hoath House
Chiddingstone Hoath
Nr. Edenbridge
Kent TN8 7DB
Tel: 01342 850362
Fax: 01342 841066
e-mail: jstreatfeild@hoath_house.freeserve.co.uk

Frank and Judith are so full of life that it's little surprise that the guest sitting room remains largely unused. You'll find guests in the kitchen with them. Cluttered bookshelves, home-made bread (Judith's) and marmalade (Frank's), good conversation, a charming three-legged dog and ducks and geese on the pond all add up to something special. The bedrooms are stylishly simple and one en suite bathroom is entered through the modern-day equivalent of a priest hole. This is peaceful, so don't worry about the nearby road.

Rooms: 1 double, en suite (shower); 1 twin with private shower.

Price: £23-£25 p.p.

Breakfast: Until 9am.

Meals: Available locally.

Closed: Never.

Leave A21 at Hildenborough & Chiddingstone. Take exit to Weald. There, left into Scabharbour Rd at Forge garage. After about 3 miles, right at T-junc. onto B2027 towards Edenbridge. Jessops is 0.5 miles on left.

Entry No: 249   Map no: 5

Judith & Frank Stark
Jessops
Tonbridge Road
Bough Beech
Kent TN8 7AU
Tel: 01892 870428
Web:
www.webspear.co.uk/Jessopsbedandbreakfast

Nicholas is known to the family as Marco Pierre Morris — an enthusiastic cook, he loves to prepare breakfasts of home-made breads, jams, yoghurt, eggs and, maybe, hash browns or kippers. On arrival, you may try his home-made cakes and drop scones. Guests have their own beamed sitting room in the old Bake House and bedrooms are simple, but fresh. The house dates from about 1750 and, curiously, manages to be in two places at once — the parish boundary runs straight through the middle with one half in Leigh, the other in Chiddingstone.

Rooms: 2 twins, each en suite (1 shower & 1 bath); 1 twin with private bathroom.

Price: £22.50 p.p. Single supp. £7.50.

Breakfast: Flexible.

Meals: Available locally.

Closed: Never.

Carolyn is experienced and easy-going about looking after guests; you will settle in quickly. Her Grade II-listed, 16th-century and heavily beamed house was begun in 1545. A small flock of sheep and two horses peacefully graze the 20 acres; dogs, cats and chickens (own eggs for breakfast) roam freely. Both the Carrells' children were raised and married from here and happy family vibes remain. The bed heads in the twin were made from old Horsmonden church pews; all rooms are light and airy with pastel colours, floral curtains and green views. Guests can use the drawing room and there's a terrace for tea. *Children over 10 welcome.*

Rooms: 1 twin with private bathroom; 2 singles, each with basins, sharing bathroom and separate wc.

Price: £24-£27 p.p.

Breakfast: Flexible.

Meals: Available locally.

Closed: 1 November-1 April.

B2027 0.5 miles north of Chiddingstone Causeway. Equidistant between Tonbridge, Sevenoaks & Edenbridge.

Entry No: 250   Map no: 5

Nicholas & Ginny Morris
Charcott Farmhouse
Charcott
Leigh, Tonbridge
Kent TN11 8LG
Tel: 01892 870024
Fax: 01892 870158
e-mail: nicholasmorris@charcott.freeserve.co.uk

4 miles south of Tunbridge Wells on the A267. 1 mile south of Frant Village, on the left. Name on fence at bottom of drive.

Entry No: 251   Map no: 6

Mrs Carolyn Carrell
Rowden House Farm
Frant
Tunbridge Wells
Kent TN3 9HS
Tel: 01892 750259

Matfield's oldest house, just off the village green where Siegfried Sassoon played cricket, and others still do. Debbie's talents as a garden designer and her easy, open manner, make staying in this listed 16th-century farmhouse a great treat. Furnishings are traditional, there are tiled floors, exposed beams and huge and elegant fireplaces. Low-beamed double bedrooms with stripped oak floors are Elizabethan in style; the twin is more Edwardian, with rose chintz and white fabrics. The wildlife-friendly garden (David is interested in conservation) has ponds, a potager and a small plant nursery specialising in unusual perennials.

Rooms: 2 doubles with basins and private/shared bathroom; 1 twin with private shower room.

Price: From £30 p.p. Single supp. £10.

Breakfast: Until 9am.

Meals: Available locally.

Closed: Christmas.

The Parkers were so taken with the drawing room that they bought the house. Once the house library, the room is huge, with ribbon-and-wreath cornicing and a panelled ceiling. Breakfast is served here — maybe home made yoghurt with Kentish cherries? One of the bedrooms has French doors to the terrace, both are light and inviting with fluffy towels and treats on the tea tray. Your hosts are great garden lovers, as you will see from theirs, and very knowledgeable about the ones you can visit locally, too. *Children over five welcome.*

Rooms: 1 double with private bathroom; 1 twin, en suite.

Price: £25-£35 p.p. Single supp. £10.

Breakfast: Flexible.

Meals: Available locally.

Closed: Christmas & New Year.

From A21, 1 mile south of Pembury, turn north onto B2160. Turn left at x-roads in Matfield and first left at Five Wents into Maycotts Lane.

Entry No: 252   Map no: 6

A262 to Goudhurst. In centre of village, B2079 to Marden. West Winchet is two miles from village, on left.

Entry No: 253   Map no: 6

David & Debbie Jolley
Maycotts, The Green
Matfield
Tonbridge
Kent TN12 7JU
Tel: 01892 723983
Fax: 01892 723222
e-mail: debbie.jolley@dial.pipex.com

Annie Parker
West Winchet
Winchet Hill
Goudhurst, Cranbrook
Kent TN17 1JX
Tel: 01580 212024
Fax: 01580 212250
Web: www.sawdays.co.uk

A small manor house built in the 1600s by a wealthy wool merchant to store and display his wares. Its ancient character and architectural details have survived intact. It's a delightfully artistic, beamed, home. Mr Wetton, charming and friendly, does most of the looking after; Anne is a picture framer. Bedrooms are charming and lack nothing. Grand piano in the drawing room, a conservatory for breakfast and an English country garden to explore. Basil and Bertie, the resident alpacas, are an enchanting improvement on mechanical mowers.

Rooms: 1 twin, en suite (bath), 1 twin, en suite (bath/shower) and 1 double, en suite (shower).

Price: £28 p.p. No single supp.

Breakfast: Until 9am.

Meals: Not available.

Closed: Christmas & New Year.

This beautiful, porticoed, brick house has a gorgeous drawing room, some fabulous antiques and family portraits. There's a secret garden within the grounds and an arbour and a pond. The front bedroom is large with good furniture, fine views and an open fire in winter — a rare treat. Bathrooms all have towelling robes, gels, tissues, shower caps, etc. John is calm and unflappable, with a touch of mischief; Gillian welcomes you into their home with a great sense of ease. *Pets by arrangement. Children over 12 welcome.*

Rooms: 3 doubles, 1 en suite (bath), 2 with private bathrooms.

Price: From £35 p.p. Single supp. £5.

Breakfast: Until noon!

Meals: Dinner £25 p.p.

Closed: Christmas & New Year.

From Maidstone/Hastings A229. At lights at Linton x-roads, turn off for Coxheath & through village. Take 1st left down Hunton Hill. Pass church, park & school, then right into Grove Lane.

Entry No: 254   Map no: 6

Gavin & Anne Wetton
The Woolhouse
Grove Lane
Hunton
Kent ME15 0SE
Tel: 01622 820778
Fax: 01622 820645

From Dover, M2 to Medway Services. Drive into station, continue on road past pumps. Ignore exit signs. Left at T-junc., first left & continue for 200m. Left at next T-junc. House is third on left.

Entry No: 255   Map no: 6

Gillian & John Yerburgh
Hartlip Place
Place Lane
Nr. Sittingbourne
Kent ME9 7TR
Tel: 01795 842583
Fax: 01795 842673

Chubby is a real eccentric — gregarious and full of stories of her travels as a guide in India, Africa and the Mediterranean. This converted Kent barn is her bolthole and she shares it enthusiastically with her guests. You have your own entrance — the bed is luxuriously big and so is the bathroom — and you breakfast in the conservatory on sunny mornings. Chubby is also passionate about her garden — look for the Italian influences and ask about her unusual plants. The love and time she puts into it all is very obvious. The pond, which probably dates from medieval times, now has a collection of ornamental waterfowl and two black swans.

Rooms: 1 twin/double, en suite (bath).

Price: £25 p.p. Single supp. £5.

Breakfast: Flexible.

Meals: Supper (in kitchen) by arrangement.

Closed: Occasionally.

There has been a house here since the Domesday Book. The old part, built of Kentish ragstone, has massive white-painted (medieval?) beams; the 19th-century extension continued the low ceilings. Two inviting bedrooms have white broderie duvet covers and fresh flowers. Meals are eaten in the elegant dining room while kingfishers and herons find their dinner in the spring-fed pond outside. Denise is quietly welcoming, generous and loves children, gardening, her two ginger cats and a West Highland terrier. Superb for ferry and tunnel.

Rooms: 2 twins, sharing bathroom.

Price: From £25 p.p. Single occ. from £30.

Breakfast: Flexible.

Meals: Dinner, 3 courses, £17.50 p.p., by arrangement. Packed lunch £7.50 p.p.

Closed: Christmas.

From Ashford A28 towards Tenterden. In High Halden, turn into Church Hill and take first left. Entrance 100 yards on right.

Entry No: 256   Map no: 6

Mrs Chubby Carnegie
Rectory Barn, Church House
Church Hill
High Halden, Nr Ashford
Kent TN26 3JB
Tel: 01233 850287
e-mail: chubbycarnegie@tesco.net

Exit at M20 junc. 9. At second r'bout take A20 to Charing. After 1 mile, left at Godinton Lane. After 2 miles, pass cottages on left. Worten House is 2nd turning on right. Red postbox by gate. House at end of drive.

Entry No: 257   Map no: 6

Charles & Denise Wilkinson
Worten House
Great Chart
Ashford
Kent TN23 3BU
Tel: 01233 622944
Fax: 01233 662249
Web: www.sawdays.co.uk

Fascinatingly, a few bricks, a cellar and a well remain from the 10th century and subsequent centuries all added their bit. The rewards are great if you love old buildings: a sitting room canopied with beams, a fireplace for logs three-feet long, an oak table running the length of the room and some hunting trophies. But it is easy-going and old-fashioned, not grand, with a slightly worn feel, floral loose covers on chairs, a mix of old furniture and some modest bedrooms. One of them is beamed to the apex of the roof and has fine views over the farmland. *Children by arrangement.*

Rooms: 1 double with private bathroom, 1 twin, en suite (bath).

Price: £28 p.p. Single supp. £7.

Breakfast: Flexible.

Meals: Dinner, by arrangement, £5-£20 p.p.

Closed: Never.

The six acres of gardens with a pond, obelisk and orchards are immaculate; the views in this AONB are magnificent. Susan and Markham clearly love meeting new people. This is a large, traditional country house — strong colours contrast well with dark, antique furniture and Liberty prints; the hall is hung with Chinese silk carpet, Thai pictures and Indian pictures. The music room houses an organ that Markham plays, occasionally giving concerts for charity — guests are welcome to attend. There is a luxurious indoor swimming pool for guests.

Rooms: 1 four-poster, 1 double and 1 twin, all en suite (shower).

Price: £29-£32 p.p. Single supp. £3.

Breakfast: Until 9.15am.

Meals: Dinner, 2 courses, £17 p.p. (incl. coffee).

Closed: Christmas.

From A28 Ashford-Tenterden road, into Great Chart. Turn into Ninn Lane and continue until Manor sign at end of drive on left.

Entry No: 258   Map no: 6

Mr & Mrs P. Wynn-Green
Goldwell Manor
Great Chart, Ninn Lane
Ashford
Kent TN23 3BY
Tel: 01233 631495
Fax: 01233 631495
e-mail: gillian@rootes-alliott.co.uk

From A2 at Faversham, take Brogdale Road to Eastling. 1.5 miles past Carpenters Arms pub, turn right (by postbox). House is 0.5 miles on right.

Entry No: 259   Map no: 6

Susan & Markham Chesterfield
Frith Farm House
Otterden
Faversham
Kent ME13 0DD
Tel: 01795 890701
Fax: 01795 890009
e-mail: markham@frith.force9.co.uk

Jac cheerfully deals with everyone's needs — she'll drive you into Canterbury, babysit and prepare family meals or special suppers. Chris cooks a great breakfast. You have the run of the house with its two inglenooks and complete privacy in your own wing, with a sitting room. Bedrooms are spotless and fresh, with ribbon-trimmed duvet covers and floral borders. Bathrooms are modern and the garden is great for children. The Brays' two grown-up boys are county cricket players; the county ground is a 10-minute walk away.

Rooms: 1 double, en suite (shower); 1 double with adjoining twin, en suite (bath); 1 twin/double with private bathroom.

Price: From £20 p.p. Children £5-£15, according to age.

Breakfast: Flexible.

Meals: Lunch £5 p.p. Dinner £10 p.p., by arrangement.

Closed: Never.

If you enter by the back door you will miss the dazzling effect of the hall on first sight. It beckons you into the rest of the house. When house and garden are gorgeous, hosts enchanting and the area hums with history, what more can one ask? Fine bedrooms, good furniture, a big, cast-iron bath that will diminish you. Katie arranges flowers beautifully and is generous with them amid the Georgian elegance; both she and Neil, who runs an Audio Book Library from the converted stables, are very present to enjoy your company. *Children by arrangement.*

Rooms: 2 twins/doubles, 1 en suite (bath) and 1 with private shower room.

Price: £30-£35 p.p. Single supp. £10.

Breakfast: Until 9.30am. Weekends by arrangement.

Meals: Dinner, £25 p.p., by arrangement. Light suppers can be organised.

Closed: Christmas & New Year.

From M20 exit 11, take B2068 for Canterbury. After crossing A2, house is about 100 yards on right and is white with post box in wall. (Head for county cricket ground and phone if lost).

Entry No: 260   Map no: 6

Chris & Jac Bray
Sylvan Cottage
Nackington Road
Canterbury, Kent CT4 7AY
Tel: 01227 765307/769
Fax: 01227 478411
e-mail: jac@sylvan5.fsnet.co.uk
Web: www.sawdays.co.uk

From Canterbury take A257. Go through Wingham. Continue on Ash bypass. Take 4th turn left on bypass signposted Weddington. House 200 yds on left.

Entry No: 261   Map no: 6

Katie & Neil Gunn
Great Weddington
Ash, Nr. Canterbury
Kent CT3 2AR
Tel: 01304 813407
Fax: 01304 812531
e-mail: traveltale@aol.com
Web: www.sawdays.co.uk

Deep in woodland and with views across a small valley, this Victorian vicarage has been lovingly renovated. Upstairs has been decorated and finely furnished with great attention to detail and the large, blue drawing room is full of curios. The dining room has a huge mahogany table and seascapes on the walls. Bedrooms are large, light and comfortable, with crisp cotton sheets; Judy puts out fresh flowers. You will be well looked after here — "Beautiful house, wonderful hosts" said one of our readers.

Rooms: 1 double, en suite (shower); 1 twin/double with private shower and separate wc; 1 family with private bathroom.

Price: £32.50-£40 p.p.

Breakfast: Flexible.

Meals: Dinner, £25 p.p., by arrangement.

Closed: Christmas.

Deep in the countryside and near the coast, but only 15 minutes from Canterbury, Woodmans was originally two 17th-century cottages and has been a pub and private hotel. Rendered, with a Kent peg-tiled roof, it's a comfortable warren of a place, full of books and flowers, relaxing and peaceful. There's a private entrance to the bedroom which has sloping beams, packed bookshelves, potted plants and a big bathroom. Breakfast will be brought on a tray to your room if you don't feel like emerging, or to the garden on sunny mornings. *Babies welcome.*

Rooms: 1 double, en suite.

Price: £25 p.p. No single supp.

Breakfast: Until 9.30am.

Meals: Dinner, 3 courses, £15 p.p. Packed lunch £5 p.p.

Closed: Never.

From Dover, B2011 Folkestone Rd. Pass train station, right into Elms Vale Rd, signposted Hougham. After 1 mile, keep right and house is on right after 300 yards.

Entry No: 262   Map no: 6

Bryan & Judy Evison
The Old Vicarage
Chilverton Elms, Hougham, Dover
Kent CT15 7AS
Tel: 01304 210668
Fax: 01304 225118
e-mail: vicarage@csi.com
Web: www.sawdays.co.uk

From A2, 2nd exit to Canterbury. Follow ring road & B2068 for Hythe. Over A2, on for 2 miles, through Lower Hardres, past Granville pub. Right for Petham & Waltham. 1.5 miles after Waltham, right into Hassell St. House 4th on left.

Entry No: 263   Map no: 6

Sarah Rainbird
Woodmans
Hassell Street
Hastingleigh
Kent TN25 5JE
Tel: 01233 750250

The Lathams are well-travelled, friendly and active. The house is a mixture of styles: Tudor, Georgian and modern coexist in harmony. High ceilings and a conservatory with terracotta-tiled floor brimming with greenery conjure up images of the decadent '20s. It is gloriously homely with comfortable bedrooms and green and yellow baths. Guests have their own log-fired drawing room with wonderful views. All this only 10 minutes from the Chunnel. *Children over 10 welcome.*

Rooms: 3 twins, 2 en suite (bath) and 1 let only to members of same party willing to share bathroom.

Price: £25-£27.50 p.p. Single occ. £32.50.

Breakfast: Until 9.30am.

Meals: Dinner, £18-£20 p.p., by arrangement.

Closed: Christmas & New Year.

From M20 junc. 11, take B2068 north. After 4.6 miles, left opposite B.P. garage. House is at bottom of hill on left, after 1.7 miles. Turn left into drive.

Entry No: 264   Map no: 6

Richard & Virginia Latham
Stowting Hill House
Stowting
Nr. Ashford
Kent TN25 6BE
Tel: 01303 862881
Fax: 01303 863433

So robust is the wisteria-clad 15th-century timber-framed Hall that it survived intact when it slid 50 feet down the hill in a dramatic subsidence in 1726. Noel Coward, who stayed here, would have admired its obduracy, as will you. A striking entrance leads straight to the huge sitting room, with massive fireplace and a panelled oak staircase. Everywhere 18th- and 19th-century paintings gaze down — some are for sale. Bedrooms are suitably simple and all have 40-gallon iron bathtubs and panoramic views. Fun people — it's hard to leave.

Rooms: 2 doubles, both en suite, 1 with adjoining twin for children.

Price: £27.50 p.p. Single occ. £35.

Breakfast: Until 9.30am.

Meals: Available locally.

Closed: Christmas & New Year.

From M20 at junc. 11, A20 south, then B2068 (Stone St), to Lympne. Approx. 0.25 miles on is County Members pub, and school sign on right. Left opposite convex mirror. House at end of lane.

Entry No: 265   Map no: 6

Peter & Matty Gaston
The French House
Lympne, Nr. Hythe
Kent CT21 4PA
Tel: 01303 265974
Fax: 01303 262545
e-mail: gastons@frenchouse.freeserve.co.uk
Web: www.frenchouse.freeserve.co.uk

Gabled windows look over open countryside, and roses and climbers decorate the pretty pink and blue brickwork. Such a handsome house. In the garden there are all sorts of things for your comfort — huge, cotton parasol, wooden tables and chairs and cushioned loungers. You are right on Romney Marsh which begs to be explored. Jack cooks a great breakfast and in the stable twin you have complete privacy. They have an easy humour and know well how to look after guests. *Children over 10 welcome.*

Rooms: 1 twin in stable with sitting room and bathroom; 1 double, en suite (bath); 1 twin with private bathroom.

Price: From £22-£30 p.p. Single occ. from £25.

Breakfast: Flexible.

Meals: Excellent pub 1.5 miles away.

Closed: Christmas.

In a unique English village on the Isle of Oxney, this is a house with a history. King Canute gave a house on the present site to the Church in 1032. The charming, friendly Watsons have years of experience entertaining and cosseting guests. There are big, thick towels on heated towel rails, superb white linen on the beds plus super goodies in the bathrooms. Electric blankets and log fires if needed, maps etc in the bedrooms... and a sense of English comfort in this lovely home. Breakfast can be eaten in the garden in summer; candlelit dinner, in the main dining room, is a special treat.

Rooms: 1 twin with private bathroom; 1 double, en suite (shower).

Price: From £37.50 p.p. Single supp. £15.

Breakfast: Until 9am.

Meals: Dinner, £25 p.p., by arrangement.

Closed: Christmas & New Year.

M20, exit 10 for Brenzett. A2070 for approx. 6 miles. Right for Hamstreet, & immed. left. In Hamstreet, right onto B2067, then left for Warehorne church. Through Warehorne to level crossing. House is 1 mile on, on right.

Entry No: 266   Map no: 6

Jack & Adele Sherston
Terry House
Warehorne
Ashford
Kent TN26 2LS
Tel: 01233 732443
Fax: 01233 732466
e-mail: jsherston@ukonline.co.uk

From Tenterden take B2082, signed Wittersham. Turn right at War Memorial, go for 275 yards, entrance on left just past school warning sign on brick wall & before church.

Entry No: 267   Map no: 6

Ian & Mim Watson
Wittersham Court
Wittersham
Tenterden
Kent TN30 7EA
Tel: 01797 270425
Fax: 01797 270425
e-mail: watsoni5@aol.com

A working farm and in the family since 900, with views that glue you to the spot; not a road or railway line in sight. Comfort and elegance go hand-in-hand: large rooms, high ceilings, beautiful mahogany furniture and an enormous dining table. Rosemary looks after her guests well and enjoys cooking with local produce. Guests always comment on the peace and quiet. Bedrooms are huge and light, never fussy, have superb bathrooms... and those views! *Children over 12 welcome.*

Rooms: 2 twins, 1 en suite and 1 with private bathroom; 1 double with private bathroom.

Price: £25-£30 p.p. Single occ. variable.

Breakfast: Until 8.45am.

Meals: Evening meal, from £11 p.p., by arrangement.

Closed: 1 December-31 January.

At traffic lights in centre of Hawkhurst, A268 towards Rye. 1.5 miles after lights, at Four Throws post office, immediately right into Conghurst Lane. Driveway is signed on left after 1.25 miles on left.

Entry No: 268　　　　　Map no: 6

Rosemary Piper
Conghurst Farm
Hawkhurst
Kent TN18 4RW
Tel: 01580 753331
Fax: 01580 754579
e-mail: rosa@conghurst.co.uk
Web: www.sawdays.co.uk

Step from the front door, rod in hand, and see if you can catch supper; this detached farmhouse is on the edge of a trout lake. You self-cater here and have the whole place to yourself — sitting room, breakfast room, two bedrooms and a lovely conservatory where you can take in the watery magic outside and watch visiting wildlife. You'll find a bottle of wine in the fridge and enough food to see you through breakfast the next day. There are log fires for winter and a tennis court and large, lawned, fenced garden (safe for children) for warmer days. Best of all, you can use the owners' beach hut at nearby Sandilands.

Rooms: 1 double and 1 twin, sharing bathroom.

Price: Lowest — 2 nights, winter weekend, £212; highest — one week, high season, £699.

Breakfast: Welcome hamper provided.

Meals: Self-catering.

Closed: Never.

Lincolnshire & Rutland

You will receive an information pack, including directions, when you book.

Entry No: 269   Map no: 16

Valley Cottage
Swaby
Lincolnshire
Tel: 01386 701177
Fax: 01386 701178
e-mail: info@ruralretreats.co.uk
Web: www.ruralretreats.co.uk/2000

The rolling wolds and flat fens of unsung Lincolnshire go on for ever. The Grange sits beautifully among it all, artistically old-furnished, oak-doored and beamed and with floral curtains. Original tiles and shutters, claw-footed baths and fireplaces create an atmosphere that can only unwind you. The kitchen is the sort of place where you want to chat to Anthony while he cooks your Lincolnshire sausages. Frances is a furniture historian. *Children over seven welcome.*

Rooms: 1 double, en suite (bath & shower); 1 twin/double with private bath & shower and, occasionally, 1 extra single.

Price: £25 p.p. for single night; £20 p.p. for longer stays. Single supp. by arrangement.

Breakfast: Flexible.

Meals: Available locally.

Closed: Christmas & New Year.

This '30s home built on the Stamps' family farm has been extended with flair to Anne's own design giving it lots of interest in the long, low roof line. There are tall windows with views over rolling fields and French doors from the bedrooms. It is a warm, generous and bright house. Anne and Richard love doing B&B — they have even won an award for it and have attracted a loyal following. They offer you space and light, beautiful rooms and delicious food and are committed to conservation. You can walk along the farm trail (also award-winning!) and discover a trout lake. *Children over eight welcome.*

Rooms: 1 twin and 1 double, both with bath and shower.

Price: £25 p.p. Single occ. £30.

Breakfast: Flexible.

Meals: Light suppers available on request. Short walk to good pub.

Closed: Christmas & New Year.

From Spilsby take A16 north for 1 mile. In Partney bear left at church, signed A16 Grimsby. Drive is 60 yards on left, down a grassy track.

Entry No: 270   Map no: 16

Frances & Anthony Collard
The Grange
Partney
Spilsby
Lincolnshire PE23 4PQ
Tel: 01790 753151
Fax: 01790 753151

Turn off A157 in East Barkwith at War Memorial into Torrington Lane. Bodkin Lodge is last property on the right on edge of village.

Entry No: 271   Map no: 16

Anne & Richard Stamp
Bodkin Lodge
Torrington Lane
East Barkwith
Lincolnshire LN8 5RY
Tel: 01673 858249

Utter stillness here at the base of the Lincolnshire Wolds and the view of the lake from the bedrooms is dreamy. Ann is new to B&B and thoroughly spoils her guests. Lincolnshire sausages and her own jams and marmalades at breakfast, tea on arrival and home-made cake. Guests have the run of downstairs; the traditional, neat sitting room and the dining room have views of the large, formal gardens. A lovely one-mile walk along the line of the old railway starts from the door. Ann will help you plan trips further afield, too. *Children over 12 welcome.*

Rooms: 1 twin, en suite (shower); 1 double, en suite (bath).

Price: £24 p.p. Single supp. by arrangement.

Breakfast: Flexible.

Meals: Dinner, £10-£15 p.p., by arrangement. B.Y.O wine.

Closed: Christmas.

The farmhouse is 200 years old, the farm is down the road from the house, there is a large lake nearby and Christine Ramsay is one of the most welcoming and helpful people we have met — she also bakes a delicious cake. Guests have their own cosy sitting room with open fire and the dining room is where you'll eat *en famille*. The flower-filled garden is lush, the bedrooms are light, airy and peaceful. Guests keep coming back. *Children over five welcome.*

Rooms: 1 twin/double, en suite (shower); 1 double with private bath, shower & wc next door.

Price: £22.50 p.p. Single supp. by arrangement.

Breakfast: Flexible.

Meals: By arrangement. Good local pubs.

Closed: Christmas & New Year.

From Wragby take A157 for Louth. After approx. 2 miles, at triple road sign, take right turn. Red postbox at drive entrance, past graveyard.

Entry No: 272   Map no: 16

Ann Hobbins
The Manor House
West Barkwith
Lincolnshire LN8 5LF
Tel: 01673 858253
Fax: 01673 858253

From Lincoln, A15 north. Second left after Scampton RAF station signed Fillingham. First right onto B1398. Second left to Fillingham. First house at bottom of hill on right.

Entry No: 273   Map no: 16

Christine & Bill Ramsay
Church Farm
Fillingham
Gainsborough
Lincolnshire DN21 5BS
Tel: 01427 668279
Fax: 01427 668025

Lincoln is so close, yet you feel entirely cut off from any bustle; rabbits and squirrels may play for you on the croquet lawn while you breakfast. The fine, unusually asymmetrical, 18th-century manor is enclosed in the most magnificent walled garden. Jill looks after you well — home-made cake when you arrive and huge breakfasts to set you up for the day. The rooms are of generous proportions with garden views, pale paint and floral curtains. *Children over 10 welcome.*

Rooms: 2 twins, 1 en suite (bath/shower), 1 with private bath/shower; 1 double, en suite (shower).

Price: From £24 p.p. Single supp. £5.

Breakfast: Flexible.

Meals: Ploughman's supper on request.

Closed: Christmas & New Year.

"More character than many period homes" says our inspector and it's hard to believe this single-storey house was built in the '60s. Bridget's an interior decorator and her talent is evident. There's a conservatory feel to the light-filled, stone-floored dining room with French doors onto the extremely pretty garden. Chintz, checked curtains, matching, padded headboards and a gilt-trimmed Edwardian copy of a Louis XIV chair in the bedroom — the beds are extremely comfortable. A full-height mirror in the bathroom with deep, cast iron bath. Bridget has an easy humour and huge warmth.

Rooms: 1 twin with private bathroom across the hall.

Price: £19.50 p.p. Single supp. £5.

Breakfast: Flexible.

Meals: Dinner, 2 courses, £10 p.p., by arrangement.

Closed: Christmas & New Year.

From Lincoln, A15 south. In Bracebridge Heath, house is last on left hidden among trees with walled garden.

Entry No: 274   Map no: 10

A607 Grantham to Lincoln road. On reaching Carlton Scroop take first left for Hough Lane. Last house on left.

Entry No: 275   Map no: 10

Jill & Michael Scoley
The Manor House
Sleaford Road
Bracebridge Heath
Lincolnshire LN4 2HW
Tel: 01522 520825
Fax: 01522 542418

Mrs Bridget Hankinson
Churchfield House
Carlton Scroop
Grantham
Lincolnshire NG32 3BA
Tel: 01400 250387
Fax: 01400 250241

Built with local handmade bricks which have mellowed gloriously, this impressive, listed Queen Anne vicarage is in a dream-like village setting. The sitting room is panelled throughout, the typical square Lincolnshire hall with stone flags leads to a red pine staircase with more panelling. Michael, ex-Navy, ex-MP, and Julia both love cooking and have a huge fruit and vegetable garden. Bedrooms and bathrooms are as comfortable as you could wish.

Rooms: 1 twin and 1 double, both with private bathroom.

Price: £25 p.p. Single supp. £7.50.

Breakfast: Until 9am.

Meals: Dinner, £18.50 p.p. (inc. wine), on request. Packed lunch available.

Closed: Christmas & Boxing Day.

Anne and Chris have worked hard restoring their 18th-century Barnack stone farmhouse and it matters to them that you enjoy the old beams and shutters, the floral and freshly-decorated bedrooms and the lovely farmscape views. Anne is a good Aga cook and you'll savour the local bacon and sausages and home-made preserves. Chris is funny and something of a poet; he can be persuaded to recite some of his verses. There's B&B here for horses, too and bridleways, cycle trails and George the potbellied pig.

Rooms: 1 double, en suite; 1 twin with private bathroom.

Price: £25-£30 p.p. Single supp. £10.

Breakfast: Flexible.

Meals: Many local pubs and restaurants.

Closed: Christmas & New Year.

Wrangle is 9 miles north of Boston on A52. In village follow signs to Angel Inn. House opposite church by War Memorial.

Entry No: 276   Map no: 11

Michael & Julia Brotherton
The Old Vicarage
Wrangle
Boston
Lincolnshire PE22 9EP
Tel: 01205 870688
Fax: 01205 871857
e-mail: jb141@aol.com

Leave A1 at Wansford, travelling towards Peterborough on A47 for 0.75 miles. Turn left to Southorpe; through village, house is 100yds after phone box on right.

Entry No: 277   Map no: 11

Anne Harrison-Smith
Midstone House
Southorpe
Stamford
Lincolnshire PE9 3BX
Tel: 01780 740136
Fax: 01780 740136

The Domesday-mentioned mill operated until 1910, milling corn for local villages. Today many of the old features are intact and rooms ingeniously organised around them. It's a beautiful, watery place: a footbridge leads over the River Welland to a mill pond and meadow, ducks splash around and one bedroom has its own patio by the waterside. Pretty bedrooms all have river views, printed floral bedspreads and curtains and, often, fresh flowers. There are good bathrooms and wooden floors everywhere. No cooked breakfast, but cereal, yoghurt, fruit, ham, cheese and eggs.

Rooms: 4 twins/doubles, all en suite.

Price: £24-£30 p.p. Single occ. £30-£45.

Breakfast: Flexible.

Meals: Good local pubs.

Closed: Never.

Drift off to sleep on a cloud of rose scent: Ozric makes the only genuine English rose oil and water, distilled here in an outbuilding. Outside your bedroom lies a bed of roses, three and a half acres of them: magical. The house is full of intriguing features: two boat-shaped windows that open onto the garden; a vast studio/sitting room built in the 1900s by Gardner of the R.A. and filled with paintings and African carvings. There are some fearsome fish on the Portuguese tiles round the claw-footed bath, but Ozric and Chantal are extremely warm and welcoming.

Rooms: 1 twin with adjoining shower; 1 double, en suite (bath); 1 twin and 1 single with adjoining shower.

Price: £30 p.p.

Breakfast: Flexible.

Meals: Dinner available locally.

Closed: Christmas & New Year.

From Stamford, A16 to Spalding. At Tallington, Mill Lane is 2nd turning on right before the old village school.

Entry No: 278   Map no: 11

John & Susan Olver
The Mill
Mill Lane
Tallington
Lincolnshire PE9 4RR
Tel: 01780 740815
Fax: 01780 740280
e-mail: johnolver@compuserve.com

From Bourne, A15 north towards Sleaford, first hamlet on left signed to Cawthorpe. The house is last on right before road becomes a track.

Entry No: 279   Map no: 11

Ozric & Chantal Armstrong
Cawthorpe Hall
Bourne
Lincolnshire PE10 0AB
Tel: 01778 423830
Fax: 01778 426620
Web: www.sawdays.co.uk

Come in April, if you can; the surrounding fields are a sea of yellow with acres upon acres of daffodils. The peace, the marshes, the solitude, though, are here year-round. Follow the model steam train round the garden, ride the bikes, watch the birds. Pipwell is lovingly decorated in rich blues and greens, each room with its own character. An attractive country-house clutter of old pine tables, fresh flowers, the smell of home-made cakes (for you), things suspended and perched, makes the house feel human and warm; so does Lesley's friendly welcome.

Rooms: 1 double, en suite (bath/shower); 1 double with private shower room and 1 twin, en suite (shower).

Price: Double £22 p.p. Single occ. £30-£35.

Breakfast: 7-9am.

Meals: Packed lunch, £3-£4 p.p.

Closed: Christmas & New Year.

Go for the room with the view across Rutland Water. The village provides boats for sailing or fishing, or horses or bikes. This solid stone building was a Victorian coach house and the yard at the back has alcoves of hanging roses with garden furniture for lazy summer afternoons; croquet on the lawn, too. Inside, it has high ceilings, stone archways, antique furniture and lots of space. The beds are spread with lacey linen and Cecilie is a delightful hostess and a brilliant cook.

Rooms: 1 twin and 1 double, both with private bathroom.

Price: £32 p.p. Single supp. £10.

Breakfast: Flexible by arrangement.

Meals: Dinner, £20 p.p., on request.

Closed: Occasionally.

Turn off A17, 1.5 miles north-east of Holbeach, into Washway Rd. Go past phone box, pub and garage and house is on left.

Entry No: 280   Map no: 11

Lesley Honnor
Pipwell Manor
Washway Road
Saracen's Head, Holbeach
Lincolnshire PE12 8AL
Tel: 01406 423119
Fax: 01406 423119

From A1 Stamford by-pass A606 towards Oakham for 3 miles. Fork left for Edith Weston. Pass village sign take first right, Church Lane. Past church right again down hill. House is on right on sharp left bend.

Entry No: 281   Map no: 10

Tony & Cecilie Ingoldby
Old Hall Coach House
Edith Weston
Oakham
Rutland LE15 8HQ
Tel: 01780 721504
Fax: 01780 721311

The flavour of country living in Primrose Hill: the big, colourful, kitchen, complete with Aga, hanging pots and pans, wooden floor and table, is where you take a delicious breakfast and Carole's advice on what's on in London. The gorgeous bedrooms are a mix of brass, sisal flooring, crisp linen, bathrobes, wood and contemporary décor. They are bright and comfortable, grand but not imposing. Carole is experienced at looking after guests and thoroughly professional. *Near to: Regent's Park, Camden Lock and market*

Rooms: 1 twin, en suite (bath); 1 double with private bathroom.

Price: From £45 p.p. Single supp. £25.

Breakfast: Extensive Continental served 8-9am Mon-Fri; 8.30-9.30am Sat-Sun. Negotiable!

Meals: Available locally.

Closed: Never.

Five minutes walk from Chalk Farm tube (Northern Line): cross Adelaide Rd, right for 20 steps, then left into Bridge Approach. Cross bridge, turn right. No. 30 is on right. Free parking weekends, ticket parking nearby.

Entry No: 282   Map no: 5

London

Andrew & Carole Ingram
30 King Henry's Road
Primrose Hill
London NW3 3RP
Tel: 020 7483 2871
Fax: 020 7483 4587
e-mail: ingram@30kinghenrysroad.co.uk
Web: www.30 kinghenrysroad.co.uk

In the heart of vibrant Camden Town, well set back in a quiet, wide, tree-lined street, moments from Regent's Park — what a superb central London base! The stunningly spacious kitchen was designed by Peter (an architect and lighting specialist) and every room in the modernist house has had the best brought out of it. All is distinctive and understated, with luxurious carpets, cool colours and fresh flowers in the bedrooms. Friendly and welcoming, Peter and Joanna will happily share their knowledge of London. *Near to: Camden Lock and market.*

Rooms: 1 twin with bunks, 1 twin/double sharing bathroom & 1 small double, en suite (shower & private wc).

Price: £40 p.p. Single night supp. £5 p.p. Single supp. £10.

Breakfast: 7-10am.

Meals: Many restaurants within walking distance.

Closed: Never.

This is special indeed, and remarkable value for London, so close to Regent's Park. A very modern Japanese-style house built round a courtyard with a peaked glass roof so that it fills with light and air. Wood and glass take pride of place, colours and shapes are subtle and pure, bedrooms have low platform beds, the minimalist-decor living quarters are open-plan, green-planted and ethnic-ornamented with treasures from far-flung holidays. Rodger and Sue are a delightful, articulate couple; Peckham the parrot completes the picture.

Rooms: 1 double and 1 single, sharing bathroom (single room only let to member of same party willing to share bathroom).

Price: £40 p.p.

Breakfast: Extensive Continental, 7.30-10am.

Meals: Available locally.

Closed: Never.

From Camden Town tube station, up Parkway. Albert St is the second on the left. House is on the left. Parking meters outside house. Public transport: Camden Town tube (Northern Line).

Entry No: 283   Map no: 5

Joanna & Peter Bell
Albert Street
London NW1 7NR
Tel: 020 7387 6813
Fax: 020 7387 1704

From Camden Town tube station, take Camden Rd towards Holloway. Pass Camden Rd BR station and 4th right into Murray St. House is on corner of Murray St and Camden Mews.

Entry No: 284   Map no: 5

Sue & Rodger Davis
66 Camden Square
London NW1 9XD
Tel: 020 7485 4622
Fax: 020 4785 4622
e-mail: rodgerdavis@btinternet.com

There's a dramatic vibrancy to Valerie's home. Just off Upper Street, with its numerous restaurants, and right by the Almeida and Sadler's Wells, she has many artists and actors to stay and has a theatre background herself. The Victorian house is stuffed with oriental, French and Italian pieces. The basement bedroom is filled with light and character, with an iron bedstead and an Indian patchwork tapestry. Walls, doors and much of the furniture are ragged, sponged and stencilled in the colourful style of the Bloomsbury Set. The theatrical mood continues in the conservatory, crammed with tropical plants, ferns, seashells and candles. An inspiring place to stay.

Rooms: 1 double with private shower room.

Price: £40 p.p. £15 single supp.

Breakfast: 8-9am. Continental only.

Meals: Available locally.

Closed: Occasionally.

This part of London is full of sky, trees and wildlife; Pissarro captured on canvas the view up the hill in 1870 and the original painting can be seen in the National Gallery. There's good stuff everywhere — things hang off walls and peep over the tops of dressers; bedrooms are stunning, with antiques, textiles, paintings and big, firm, new beds. Sue, a graduate from Chelsea Art College, employs humour and intelligence to put guests at ease and has created a very spec garden, too.

Rooms: 1 twin/double, en suite; 1 twir and 1 single sharing shower room.

Price: From £40 p.p.

Breakfast: Until 10am.

Meals: 2-course dinner, £15 p.p. 3 courses, £20 p.p, both by arrangement.

Closed: Never.

From Highbury & Islington tube, turn right out of station and down Upper Street, past Town Hall on left. Left immediately before Shell garage.

Entry No: 285   Map no: 5

Valerie Rossmore
Florence Street
Islington
London N1 2DT
Tel: 020 7359 5293
Fax: 020 7359 5293

Main line trains from Victoria or London Bridge — 20 mins to Crystal Palace, then 7 mins walk. Sue will give you directions or collect you. Good buses to West End and Westminster.

Entry No: 286   Map no: 5

Sue & Tim Haigh
24 Fox Hill
Crystal Palace
London SE19 2XE
Tel: 020 8768 0059
Fax: 020 8768 0063
e-mail: timhaigh@compuserve.com
Web: www.sawdays.co.uk

This is fun! A house-cum-gallery in a conservation area where each room exhibits original, modern art. The bedroom has all the useful things that you don't want to lug around town with you — radio, hairdryer and alarm clock. Bold colours, wooden floors, huge curtain-less windows and indoor trees give an exotic feel. Breakfasts are cooked on the Aga and eaten in the vast and stylish kitchen with deck views over the subtropical garden (full of intriguing spaces, wooden pathways and unusual plants). Biddy, kind and easy-going, has brought a breath of fresh air to the world of B&B. *Near to: Greenwich and Blackheath Village.*

Rooms: 1 twin, en suite (shower).

Price: From £30 p.p.

Breakfast: Flexible.

Meals: Dinner by arrangement. Good restaurants and pubs nearby.

Closed: Never.

From Brockley station, cross Brockley Rd & walk up Cranfield Rd. Pass church and Breakspears Rd meets it almost opposite. Free on-street parking. Public transport: mainline trains, Brockley to London Bridge. Best buses, 171 & 36 to centre.

Entry No: 287   Map no: 5

Biddy Bunzl
57 Breakspears Road
London SE4 1XR
Tel: 020 8469 3162
Fax: 020 8469 3162
e-mail: bunzl@btinternet.com
Web: www.sawdays.co.uk

All the personality, charm and individual attention of a private house — right in the heart of London, too. But also a huge canopied four-poster bed, telephone, fax and laundry facilities, your own sitting room and a great bathroom. Continental breakfast with newspaper is equally inspired.
Everything is prepared on site by Jenny (full-time housekeeper). This means the orange is freshly squeezed and the jams are home-made. You will not find better comfort or facilities in Central London at these prices. *Near to: Westminster Abbey, Tate Gallery, Buckingham Palace, Thames.*

Rooms: 1 king-size four-poster with own sitting room and bathroom.

Price: £47.50 p.p. Single occ. £85.

Breakfast: 8-9am. Continental included. Full English £7 p.p.

Meals: Many excellent local restaurants nearby.

Closed: Christmas.

Public transport: 1 minute walk from Pimlico tube (Rampayne St exit), or 5 minute walk from Victoria. Best bus, 24 to Trafalgar Sq. Parking: NCP or 2 hour meters.

Entry No: 288   Map no: 5

Mrs Helen Douglas
Number Ninety-Six
96 Tachbrook Street
London SW1V 2NB
Tel: 020 7932 0969
Fax: 020 7821 5454
e-mail: helen@numberninety-six.co.uk
Web: www.numberninety-six.co.uk

Just off the King's Road, this quiet, yet perfectly central house, is Georgian and strewn with wisteria. It is set back from the road, with its own off-street parking. Inside, it's a real family home. Jane serves continental breakfasts in the stunning kitchen-cum-conservatory; a cool, friendly space looking onto a lovely London garden. High up, top-floor bedrooms are pretty and atticky and have unique views of, on one side, one of London's most magnificent buildings — Sir Christopher Wren's Royal Hospital — and on the other side of the Avenue of Gardens. Jane loves cooking, so do eat in if you wish. *Near: the Thames, Sloane Square and Harrods.*

Rooms: 1 twin and 1 room with futon and an extra single, sharing 1 bathroom.

Price: £40-£50 p.p. Single supp. £10.

Breakfast: Continental only, 8-10am.

Meals: Dinner, £20 p.p., by arrangement. B.Y.O. wine.

Closed: Never.

Parallel with King's Road between Smith Street and Royal Avenue.

Entry No: 289   Map no: 5

Jane Barran
17 St. Leonard's Terrace
London SW3 4QG
Tel: 020 7730 2801
Fax: 020 7730 2801

This is a sophisticated London base; your hostess is delightful and adept at putting guests at their ease. The yellow walled drawing room has masses of interest and the dining room is charming, with blue damask-patterned walls, pink napkins, pink flowers and a tall gilt candlestick that is lit for breakfast. Bedrooms are cool, cream and clutter-free, with glazed chintz curtains and gilt mirrors and picture frames; the en suite bathroom has yellow-painted woodwork and the other is crimson. Sally is very well-travelled; she organises heritage tours of London and the rest of Britain, so is full of ideas for you.

Rooms: 1 double, en suite (bath); 1 double with private bathroom downstairs.

Price: £30 p.p. Single occ. £40.

Breakfast: Flexible.

Meals: Many restaurants nearby.

Closed: Never.

Leave Fulham Broadway tube station and walk directly ahead down Harwood Road. At T-junc. right into New Kings Rd, then 2nd left into Wandsworth Bridge Rd. Number 34 is a few houses along on the right. (5 minutes walk.)

Entry No: 290   Map no: 5

Sally Usher
34 Wandsworth Bridge Road
London SW6 2TH
Tel: 020 7731 2805
Fax: 020 7731 2805

Caroline mixes the sophistication of the city with the human warmth of the countryside and her lovely big kitchen is clearly the engine-room of the house. It leads through to a light breakfast room on seagrass matting, with doors onto a pretty brick garden with its chairs and table — hope for fine days. The house is long and thin — Fulham style — and reaches up to the guestroom in the eaves, which needs no more explanation than the picture above. A really warm place to stay in a very accessible part of the Metropolis. *Near to: Kings Road antique shops.*

Rooms: 1 twin/double with en suite shower and private bathroom.

Price: £40-£45 p.p. Single supp. £25. Price negotiable for longer stays.

Breakfast: Continental only, 8.30-9.30am Mon-Fri; 8.30-10am Sat-Sun.

Meals: Available locally.

Closed: Never.

India's fine art and fabrics decorate Amanda's pretty Fulham house. You breakfast in the coral rag-rolled family kitchen; French windows open onto a small garden where you can eat in summer. The lower-ground bedroom and bathroom, in blue and white, are bright and breezy; the upstairs double has elephant wallpaper. There's also Huggy the dog — a sometime star of the screen. The restaurants and antiques shops of the New Kings Road are less than a minute by foot and across the road is Parsons Green for a bit of summery London sunbathing. *Children over 12 welcome.*

Rooms: 1 twin/double, en suite (bath); 1 twin/double and 1 single room, each with private bath.

Price: £35 p.p. Single supp. £10-£15.

Breakfast: Continental only. Until 9.30am.

Meals: Available locally.

Closed: Rarely.

Three mins from Parsons Green tube (District Line, Wimbledon branch). Straight over green, keeping White Horse pub on left and Bradbourne St is over the King's Road, ahead of you. House on left.

Public transport: Four minutes walk to Parsons Green tube. Parking £4.80 per day in street.

Entry No: 291   Map no: 5

Caroline Docker
Parthenia Road
Fulham
London SW6 3BD
Tel: 020 7384 1165
Fax: 020 7610 6015
e-mail: geodocker@btinternet.com

Entry No: 292   Map no: 5

Mrs Amanda Turner
3 Bradbourne Street
Fulham
London SW6 3TF
Tel: 020 7736 7284
e-mail: abt@cwcom.net
Web: www.luxuryinlondon.co.uk

This is a bright, cheerful Fulham home where life gravitates to the back of the house. The kitchen is home to dachshunds and cats who may need to be moved from the sofa. Guests eat breakfast and delicious home-made suppers here. The walls are bright yellow, the tablecloth gingham, the carpets matting... and everything throughout the house feels freshly painted and cosy. The groovy colours continue upstairs with electric greens and cloudy sky blues. Rooms are very comfortable with thick duvets on beds, and the large bathrooms is white and immaculate. There's a plethora of great restaurants nearby. Be well looked after in central London. *Children over 10 welcome.*

Rooms: 1 double, en suite; 2 singles sharing 1 bathroom.

Price: £30 p.p. Single £40.

Breakfast: Until 9.30am.

Meals: Dinner, £20 p.p., by arrangement. B.Y.O. wine.

Closed: Never.

You enter Joan's homely kitchen conversion directly from a peaceful mews. Continental breakfasts on the central wooden table mean home-made marmalade, toast, croissants etc. Bedrooms upstairs are pretty with antique furniture and brand new beds – and your bath resides in a gleaming white room. This is a real home in a very central position and Joan herself is a keen traveller who enjoys meeting people from all over the world. She put mineral water in the rooms and there's quiet, sunny patio and lovely roses in the garden. *Children over 12 welcome.*

Rooms: 1 double and 1 single sharing bathroom.

Price: Double £30 p.p. Single £40. Single occ. of double £45.

Breakfast: 8.30-9.30am.

Meals: Available locally.

Closed: Occasionally.

Public transport: 2 minutes from Parson's Green tube (District Line, Wimbledon branch). No.14 bus to Knightsbridge. Parking in street all day.

Entry No: 293   Map no: 5

Rachel Wilson
Winchenden Road
London SW6 5DH
Tel: 020 7731 3901
e-mail: rachel.k.wilson@talk21.com

Public transport: 4 minute walk to Fulham Broadway tube (District Line, Zone 2), and several buses. Parking: ticket parking, £4.80 per day, in street.

Entry No: 294   Map no: 5

Joan Lee
5 Hartismere Road
London SW6 7TS
Tel: 020 7385 0337
Fax: 020 7385 0337

A soothing, restful retreat from London's hustle and bustle — it's villagey here and you could happily while away an afternoon browsing in smart shops or walking along the Thames. Helen and Nigel have created 'Chelsea chic' in leafy Barnes — throughout their taste is impeccable. There's an Edwardian bergère sofa in the large cream double and a Victorian roll-top in the next door bathroom; the other guestroom is at the top of the house with river views from its bathroom in the winter. The Smiths are an engaging, well-travelled couple, interested in art, gardening and fly-fishing — they have a lovely retriever, too. *Children over 12 welcome.*

Rooms: 1 king-size, en suite (bath) and 1 queen-size with private bathroom.

Price: From £30 p.p. Single supp. £10.

Breakfast: Until 9.30am.

Meals: Available locally.

Closed: Christmas & New Year.

From Great West Rd, take Hammersmith Bridge to Barnes. At lights by Browns Restaurant, right along Lonsdale Rd for just over 1 mile. Left into Gerard Rd and 1st left into Charlotte Rd. House is 1st on left.

Entry No: 295   Map no: 5

Helen & Nigel Smith
1 Charlotte Road
Barnes
London SW13 9QJ
Tel: 020 8741 5504
Fax: 020 8741 5504

Foragers and hunter-gathers will feel especially at home and you can do as the moo takes you. No running water, but the river is close; no electricity, but fuel a fire from storm-felled oak. Superbly tasty fungi grow in the kitchen — feel free to help yourself. Walks start from the very airy bedroom, where rustic straw matting ensures a full night's weep. Early birds and night owls particularly welcome. Tractors essential in bad weather.

Rooms: One, open-plan.

Price: £25 p.p. (cost of post-stay Chiropractor).

Breakfast: Mooosli.

Meals: Forager's supper, free.

Closed: At night.

Follow your nose.

Entry No: 296   **Map Ref No: 5**

WC Fields
Comfort's End
Barnes
London 0LD 5POT

This unusual, relaxed and very English set-up in a Norman Shaw listed house is a monument to Elisabeth's creative inspirations. She is a sculptor and caster, so classical busts and reliefs in stone, marble and plaster peer at you from surprising places. The bedroom is a lovely large space with table and armchairs. You have your own galley kitchen where a fridge is well stocked for you, complete with home-made bread. Elisabeth is a warm hostess; she loves music in the house and also lets the charming music room, with Steinway A grand, to musicians. *Near to: Kew Gardens.*

Rooms: 1 twin with en suite bathroom and own kitchen.

Price: £25 p.p. Single supp. £15. Music room £30 extra. Minimum two nights.

Breakfast: Flexible — help yourself.

Meals: On nearby Chiswick High Road.

Closed: Never.

Public transport: Turnham Green tube, 4 minutes walk. Visitors' parking outside, plus one off-road space.

Entry No: 297   Map no: 5

Elisabeth Whittaker
Queen Anne's Grove
Bedford Park
London W4 1HW
Tel: 020 8995 9255
e-mail: elisabeth.whittaker@virgin.net
Web: www.sawdays.co.uk

Take in the village atmosphere of Portobello Market, or cruise the tempting shops of Notting Hill. This grand mid-Victorian town house has tall sash windows and wrought iron balconies. The French flavour of the elegant drawing room, with pictures, gilt mirrors, ormolu and bronze candlesticks, fine china and Louis XIV furniture under crystal chandeliers, contrasts with the minimalist state-of-the-art kitchen. The Turnbulls are flexible, easy hosts and you can borrow the key to nearby Ladbroke Square Gardens. *Children over 12 welcome.*

Rooms: 1 double, en suite (bath) and twin, with private bathroom. Single also available.

Price: £40 p.p.

Breakfast: Flexible.

Meals: Available locally.

Closed: Never.

Exit Notting Hill Gate tube on north side towards Portobello Market. At lights by Devonshire pub, right and cross road. Kensington Park Rd is 50 yds on left. House is 200 yds on left with red door.

Entry No: 298   Map no: 5

Ben & Bev Turnbull
9 Kensington Park Road
London W11 3BY
Tel: 020 7229 0231
Fax: 020 7792 1266
e-mail: bevturnbull@hotmail.com

Wonderful accommodation in a Kensington 1860s Victorian town house. The newly-decorated bedrooms are on the ground floor and you have your own key and entrance. The rest of the house is still the family home. The mood is of elegance — pale yellows, light flooding in through the big windows — and easy formality, with mahogany table, dresser with dry flowers and silver, antique chairs and floral fabrics. Breakfast is served in the dining room overlooking the charming, secluded garden. Nanette really enjoys people. *Near to: Kensington Gardens, Holland Park, High St Kensington. Children over 12 welcome.*

Rooms: 2 twins, en suite (bath & shower); 1 double, en suite (shower).

Price: £40-£45 p.p. Single supp. £25.

Breakfast: 8.30-9am Mon-Fri; 9-9.30am Sat-Sun.

Meals: Available locally.

Closed: Never.

Left out of Earls Court Rd station, over Cromwell Rd, then left into Pembroke Rd. Warwick Gardens is 3rd on right. Parking £6 per day next door. Public transport: 8 mins walk to High St Kensington/Earl's Court tube.

Entry No: 299   Map no: 5

Nanette Stylianou
Warwick Gardens
London W14 8PL
Tel: 020 7603 7614
Fax: 020 7602 5473
Web: www.sawdays.co.uk

Sunny's gorgeous family home is right opposite Holland Park and well-placed for High Street Kensington and Notting Hill. The whole top floor is generally given over to guests, complete with fridge. Both rooms have been beautifully decorated in gentle yellows and greens with pale green carpets, soft white duvets, pelmeted windows and a lovely, curved chest of drawers in the double. The bathroom is marble-tiled and skylit. Great comfort is guaranteed. Breakfast is taken Continental-style. This whole house is bright and sunny. *Near to: Kensington Gardens, Albert Hall. Off-street parking sometimes available. Children over 10 welcome.*

Rooms: 1 double and 1 single, sharing bathroom.

Price: From £40 p.p. Single occ. £55.

Breakfast: 8-10am.

Meals: Available locally.

Closed: Christmas, New Year & occasional holidays.

Public transport: nearest tube Holland Park, 7 mins walk, or High St Kensington. Best buses, 9 & 10 to Knightsbridge.

Entry No: 300   Map no: 5

Sunny & Al Murray
101 Abbotsbury Road
London W14 8EP
Tel: 020 7602 0179
Fax: 020 7602 1036
e-mail: al.sunny@101abb.freeserve.co.uk

It's amazing how many owners in this book have lived all over the world (the Andrews have returned from Brunei and the Middle East) and how many have experience in catering — Margaret cooks. This is a large Richmond home (1930s leaded bay windows) with a big lawny garden at the back. The bedroom is of a good size and decorated in pale blue. Everything is new-feeling and fresh. There is a road passing the front door which should be mentioned, but double glazing sorts out most of the noise. There will be no half measures here and delicious dinners can be arranged in advance. *Near to: Richmond Park; sightseeing tours can be arranged.*

Rooms: 1 twin with private bathroom.

Price: £30 p.p. Single supp. £10.

Breakfast: Until 10.30am.

Meals: Dinner, £30 p.p., by arrangement.

Closed: Christmas.

Public transport: best bus, 33 to Hammersmith. 10-minute walk to Richmond tube. Free parking opposite.

Entry No: 301   Map no: 5

Margaret Andrew
131 Queen's Road
Richmond
London TW10 6HF
Tel: 020 8948 6893
Fax: 020 8948 6893

A perfectly shaped 18th-century house — its setting is utterly rural and the large grounds deserve exploration. You can play tennis, swim in the heated outdoor pool, shelter under an arbour or cross the bridged pond to an enchanting island. This is a very traditional house with displays of china, an oak, oval dining table that seats 12 and antique furniture; bedrooms are coolly elegant and there are good views all around. This is a place of peace — close to Sandringham, good sailing, golf courses and walking and beaches.

Rooms: 1 twin/double, en suite (bath).

Price: £35 p.p.

Breakfast: Flexible.

Meals: Dinner, 3 courses, £22.50 p.p.; 2 courses, £19.50 p.p.

Closed: Christmas.

Norfolk

From Kings Lynn A47 towards Swaffham. After 4 miles, left at Middleton by church and left again into Hill Road. Turn right into drive (opp. Paul Drive).

Entry No: 302   Map no: 11

Mrs C. Knight
The Old Hall
Middleton
Kings Lynn
Norfolk PE32 1RW
Tel: 01553 840490
Fax: 01553 840708
e-mail: emidas@talk21.com

A delectable house that has featured in glossy magazines. Allan, an interior designer, has decorated and furnished with a confident hand — soft yellows and blues in the bedrooms, deep, fabric pelmets, shining wooden floors, rugs, chaises and armchairs. The dining room is a bold terracotta and everywhere there are interesting curios and well-framed prints; you may play the grand piano. Originally the Dower House to Docking Hall, the 1755s house is Grade II* listed with an immaculate, lush garden to the rear. Kippers and smoked salmon for breakfast, if you wish.

Rooms: 1 twin, 1 four-poster and 1 double, each with private bathroom.

Price: From £30-£35 p.p. Children over 10, £20 p.p. Single supp. £10.

Breakfast: From 7.30-9.30am.

Meals: Dinner, on request, £17.50 p.p. B.Y.O wine. Packed lunch, from £9.50 p.p.

Closed: Occasionally.

From Kings Lynn, take A148 towards Cromer. After Hillington, take the B1153 to Docking. Right at x-roads into Docking Village. House is on left, after church.

Entry No: 303   Map no: 11

Allan Urquhart
Holland House
Chequers Street
Docking
Norfolk PE31 8LH
Tel: 01485 518295
Fax: 01485 518295

Mary runs a bustling household with good humour; "clean, but not always tidy", which is fine by us. The atmosphere is as welcoming and down-to-earth as it is laid-back and 'family'; children are part of the scene. There is bold design sense, too; everything wooden has been painted in bright, unusual colours, everything draped in brightly-coloured coverings. Upstairs, faded carpets, fresh flowers, good sheet a lovely bathroom with sequinned Indian wall-hanging and wooden floor. In the sitting room there are deep sofas a log-burner, wooden floor and low-beamed ceilings.

Rooms: 1 double, en suite (bath); 1 double with private shower. Cot and fold-up bed available.

Price: £20-£25 p.p. Single supp. £2.50 Discounts for longer stays by arrangement.

Breakfast: Flexible.

Meals: Available locally.

Closed: Christmas.

From Burnham Market, follow signs to Fakenham for 2 miles — next village is North Creake. Over bridge, sharp left, house 0.25 miles on right.

Entry No: 304   Map no: 11

Mary & Jeremy Brettingham
Glebe Farmhouse
Wells Road
North Creake, Fakenham
Norfolk NR21 9LG
Tel: 01328 730133
Fax: 01328 730444
e-mail: jezzab@globalnet.co.uk

Big rooms, high ceilings, roaring fires, long views and low bedroom windows. The friendly Elizabeth has a good sense of humour and cooks an excellent lemon cake — it will probably be taken fresh from the oven when you arrive. The working farm (arable and hens) has dogs and geese, chicks in spring and a lovely, lived-in feel. Your breakfast eggs are organic and farm fresh — it's only 200 yards from henhouse to plate. Guests have their own sitting room and dining rooms; the large bedrooms are simple and elegant. City-dwellers will feel that they have escaped from it all. *Children over 12 welcome.*

Rooms: 1 twin en suite (bath) and 1 twin and 1 double sharing bathroom.

Price: £21-£25 p.p. Single supp. in season, £5.

Breakfast: 8.30am-9am Mon-Fri, 8.30-10am Sat-Sun.

Meals: Dinner, by arrangement, £15 p.p.

Closed: Christmas & New Year.

From Fakenham B1146 towards East Dereham. After 2 miles turn left to Gt. Ryburgh. In village, 2nd left up Highfield Lane opposite pink cottage and on for 0.5 miles — house on right.

Entry No: 305   Map no: 11

Elizabeth Savory
Highfield Farm
Great Ryburgh
Fakenham
Norfolk NR21 7AL
Tel: 01328 829249
Fax: 01328 829422

Vegetables and fruit are home-grown organic and Jane is an imaginative, Aga-abetted, cook. Meanwhile, Michael pours the drinks and they both love having guests. Their converted barn is eminently comfortable and life here easily spills into the greenhouse, with farmland views, and the wildflower garden, where you can have fresh juice before breakfast in the kitchen. One of the bedrooms is softly carpeted and the other is more rustic with sea-grass matting. Jane says people often don't realise how close they are to the coast. Holkham, Wells and Walsingham are nearby.

Rooms: 1 twin/double next to private bathroom; 1 twin/double with large private shower room.

Price: £22 p.p. No single supp.

Breakfast: Until 9am, or by arrangement.

Meals: Dinner, 3 courses, £14 p.p. B.Y.O wine.

Closed: Christmas.

From Fakenham, A148 towards Kings Lynn. After 4 miles, left opposite garage to Tatterford. At white gates, turn left, right and then left. The barn is set back on the right.

Entry No: 306   Map no: 11

Michael & Jane Davidson-Houston
Manor Farm Barn
Tatterford
Nr. Fakenham
Norfolk NR21 7AZ
Tel: 01485 528393

Two of the bedrooms are huge and high-ceilinged, with chairs where you can enjoy the view through the fine long windows. They are generous with towels, bathrobes and other extras, such as a fridge and sofa. This is a large family farm with plenty of dogs and horses (stabling is available) and delightful hosts — real farmers, their walls bearing the proofs of their successes at point-to-pointing and showing. It is a lived-in, easy-going house, with comfortable touches of elegance such as grand piano, gilt cornicing, etc. *Children over 12 by arrangement.*

Rooms: 2 doubles,1 en suite (shower) and 1 (bath/shower); 1 twin with private bathroom & wc.

Price: £18-£25 p.p. Single supp. £5.

Breakfast: Flexible.

Meals: Pub within walking distance.

Closed: Christmas week.

A conservation award-winning farm tucked away in the heart of rural Norfolk; you are next door to a tiny 13th-century church and are surrounded by lovely gardens (the coast is only 20 minutes away). The two guestrooms, with large sitting room and small kitchen, are in the beautifully converted stables. Antiques, lovely rugs, cushions and artefacts add to the luxury. Breakfast is delicious, with home eggs, bacon and sausages and is served in the dining room of the main house. Libby and Robin have created something special. Kennel and stable available. *Children over 10 welcome.*

Rooms: 1 double and 1 twin in the stable annexe.

Price: £25 p.p. Single supp. £5.

Breakfast: Until 9.30am.

Meals: Available locally.

Closed: Never.

Take A148 north-east and second of two turnings right to Harpley (no signpost) opp. Houghton Hall sign. After 200 yds x-roads, straight over. House 400 yds on left, white with copper beeches.

Entry No: 307   Map no: 11

Amanda Case
Lower Farm
Harpley
Nr. Kings Lynn
Norfolk PE31 6TU
Tel: 01485 520240

A1065 Swaffham/Fakenham road. 6 miles on, go through Weasenham. After 1 mile, right for Wellingham. There, house is on left, next to church.

Entry No: 308   Map no: 11

Mrs Elisabeth Ellis
Manor House Farm
Wellingham
Fakenham, Kings Lynn
Norfolk PE32 2TH
Tel: 01328 838227
Fax: 01328 838348
Web: www.sawdays.co.uk

Another lovely Norfolk Georgian house, red-brick and with those gateposts that mark a boundary so stylishly. This is the English home at its best, the house that everyone would like to live in. It has the elegant proportions of the late 18th-century country house; the hall, drawing room and dining room are gracious and beautifully furnished. The big-windowed bedrooms look onto the lovely garden and your hostess — sweet, friendly and most helpful — speaks French. *Children by arrangement; dogs and pool similarly.*

Rooms: 2 twins, each with private bathroom. Sitting room available. Extra room available occasionally.

Price: £25-£30 p.p. Please book in advance.

Breakfast: Flexible.

Meals: Dinner, £15-£20 p.p., on request.

Closed: Christmas.

It is fun to meet people of such character as Mrs Garnier. She calls a spade a spade and tells colourful stories of her amazing house and her family's long local history. From 1349 until the Dissolution of the Monasteries, it was a college of priests, conveniently sited near to the church. Later, it was saved from ruin and brought back to life. It has a superb panelled dining room, big bedrooms and great views. The two en suite bathrooms are ingeniously converted from large cupboards. *Children over seven welcome.*

Rooms: 1 twin and 1 twin/double, both en suite (bath); 1 double next to private bathroom. Also extra shower and wc.

Price: From £20 p.p.

Breakfast: Flexible.

Meals: Afternoon tea served free of charge. Lunch & evening meal available in local pub.

Closed: Never.

From Swaffham take A1065; turn right to Litcham after 5 miles. House is on left as you come into village. Georgian red brick with stone balls on gatepost.

Entry No: 309   Map no: 11

John & Hermione Birkbeck
Litcham Hall
Litcham
Nr. Kings Lynn
Norfolk PE32 2QQ
Tel: 01328 701389
Fax: 01328 701164

From Thetford take A1075 north towards Watton. After 9 miles, left to Thompson. After 0.5 miles take second left at red postbox on corner. Left again, house is at dead end.

Entry No: 310   Map no: 11

Mrs Garnier
College Farm
Thompson
Thetford
Norfolk IP24 1QG
Tel: 01953 483318
Fax: 01953 483318
Web: www.sawdays.co.uk

Lying on the outskirts of the rural village of Hingringham, this Georgian vicarage is a very relaxed family home. The views over unspoilt countryside are lovely. The elegant staircase, under a glass pyramid, leads to two lovely bedrooms. Breakfast and dinners are served in the dining room — lots of home produce and local fare at each. Just five miles from the coast and Blakeney and its seals. Walks, birds and several lovely National Trust properties all around. *Use of grass tennis court by arrangement.*

Rooms: 1 twin/double, en suite (bath); 1 double with private bathroom.

Price: From £23 p.p. Please ask about single supp.

Breakfast: Usually 9am or by arrangement.

Meals: Dinner, 3 courses, £15 p.p., by arrangement.

Closed: Christmas.

An 18th-century windmill with the river lapping the wall. A magnificent sitting room overlooks the marshes; some bedrooms look over the endless seascape — one has a walk-around balcony. Everything is special here, from the obvious thrill of staying in a windmill to the great welcome and good coffee at breakfast. Jeremy took it over in '98, a guest who fell in love with the place. He upped sticks from his Battersea restaurant and now does wonders with local ingredients: caught-that-day fish or the delicious seamarsh samphire. Bring your binoculars.

Rooms: 2 twins, 1 en suite and 1 with shared bathroom; 3 doubles, 1 en suite and 2 with private bathrooms; 1 single with shared bathroom.

Price: £30-40 p.p. Singles usually pay double occ. rate.

Breakfast: 8.30-9am.

Meals: Dinner £17.50 p.p.

Closed: Never.

From Fakenham, follow road signed Cromer for 6 miles. Left at Crawfish pub into Hindringham, down hill and left, before church, into Blacksmith's Lane. Follow up hill, house on left at top with flinted entrances.

Entry No: 311   Map no: 12

Rosie & Robin Waters
The Old Vicarage
Blacksmith's Lane
Hindringham
Norfolk NR21 0QA
Tel: 01328 878223

From Holt take Cley Road — through the narrow — and only — street in Cley. Mill is signed on the left. Drive over the bridge to the car park.

Entry No: 312   Map no: 12

Jeremy Bolam
Cley Mill
Cley-next-the-Sea
Holt
Norfolk NR25 7RP
Tel: 01263 740209
Fax: 01263 740209

A big, easy-going family home on the edge of a rural Norfolk village, it is a 17th-century rectory with Victorian additions. The huge drawing/dining room, the wonderful double room with great canopied brass bedstead, the west-facing garden with croquet lawn... enjoy them all. The Winter children are growing up and moving out, but yours are more than welcome. It may seem untidy but the atmosphere is just utterly relaxed and the family are fun. Jo is an enthusiastic local and architectural historian. The coast is very close for swimming, sailing and seal-watching. *All-weather tennis court available by arrangement.*

Rooms: 1 twin with private bath, shower & wc; 1 double, en suite (bath).

Price: £22.50 p.p. Discount for children.

Breakfast: Flexible.

Meals: Dinner £12.50 p.p. Available on request. B.Y.O. wine.

Closed: Christmas & New Year.

From Fakenham A1067 towards Norwich. At Guist clock tower turn left; second turning to Wood Norton. House is on right after 100 yards, through overgrown entrance, over 2 cattle grids.

Entry No: 313   Map no: 12

Jo & Giles Winter
The Old Rectory
Wood Norton
Norfolk NR20 5AZ
Tel: 01362 683785
Web: www.sawdays.co.uk

A splendid 18th-century flint and brick house for family holidays in North Norfolk, half a mile from that much loved piece of coastline with its swimming, sailing, bird- and seal-watching trips. The Lacostes have young children of their own, so cots and high chairs are available and children's needs easily dealt with; you can hire bikes, too. The bedrooms are sumptuously comfortable, the furniture traditional, the paintings by local artists. Pauline is a trained chef and the food is excellent. There's an outdoor, heated pool.

Rooms: 1 twin and 1 double, en suite (shower); 1 family room, en suite (bath & shower); 1 double, en suite (bath).

Price: From £27.50 p.p. Single supp. £10-£15.

Breakfast: 8.30-9.15am.

Meals: Dinner, £12-£16.50 p.p. High teas by arrangement.

Closed: Never.

From Fakenham, A148 for Cromer. At Holt, left through town centre. Pass B.P. garage, left after corner following sign to Weybourne. Down hill to Weybourne, right at T-junc.; entrance opp. church and coast rd junc. 20 yds on, right into car park.

Entry No: 314   Map no: 12

Charles & Pauline Lacoste
Rosedale Farm
Holt Road
Weybourne, Holt
Norfolk NR25 7ST
Tel: 01263 588778
e-mail: rosedale.lacostes@tinyworld.co.uk

Heydon is one of Norfolk's finest Grade I Elizabethan houses. Sarah has opened up the Georgian Old Laundry beside the house and has kept many original features — white walls, scrubbed tables, stone flags. Everything else, beds, carpets, etc are new and of high quality. Bedrooms are fresh and light; one has a bathroom with a fireplace and a free-standing bath. With your own courtyard, you feel pretty well self-contained, but great breakfasts are served in the open-plan dining/sitting room downstairs. Visitors can walk in the front park and the swimming pool can be used if you ask beforehand. A rare treat.

Rooms: 2 twins/doubles, 1 en suite (bath) and 1 with private bathroom.

Price: £30 p.p. Single supp. in high season, £5.

Breakfast: Flexible.

Meals: Dinner by arrangement. Good pub nearby.

Closed: Self-catering only at Christmas.

From Norwich, B1149 for 10 miles. 2nd left after bridge, signed Heydon. After 1.5 miles, right into village, straight into park, over cattle grid, past Hall to left and follow signs.

Entry No: 315   Map no: 12

Sarah Bulwer-Long
The Old Laundry
Heydon Hall
Heydon
Norfolk NR11 6RE
Tel: 01263 587343
Fax: 01263 587805
Web: www.sawdays.co.uk

Old, and beautiful, a large tapestry hangs in the stairwell and foot-square stone slabs make up the ground floor. The rugs are old, too, from Persia and the East. The grand piano in the smaller sitting room is played by your hostess's husband — he is also a cellist. This is the sort of house we love to include, for we value the well-worn dignity, furniture and style of such unassuming good taste. The bedrooms have colourful bedcovers, and are modern enough to be comfortable rather than hedonistic. They overlook the mature garden, a place for croquet and badminton. The twins can be a self-contained flat. Marvellous value.

Rooms: 3 twins: 1 en suite, 1 with private bathroom, 1 with private shower room. Two of the rooms can be used as private flat with sitting room & kitchen.

Price: £20-£25 p.p.

Breakfast: Flexible.

Meals: Dinner, 2 courses, £12 p.p.

Closed: Never.

From Norwich 10-15 minute drive. Bramerton is signposted from A146 (Norwich-Lowestoft road). House is opposite church in centre of village, with white 5-bar gate.

Entry No: 316   Map no: 12

Mrs J. Perowne
The White House
Bramerton
Norfolk NR14 7DW
Tel: 01508 538673

Not only former rectory, but former bishop's residence too. Elegant but not over-grand, big but not overbearing and quite beautifully decorated and furnished with many antiques and old paintings. This immaculate house is owned by a thoroughly human and friendly couple who keep horses (stable room for yours too), a cat and two very large, much-loved lurchers. They open their arms to their guests, feed them finely and sleep them in extreme comfort. *Children over five welcome.*

Rooms: 1 double, en suite (shower) and 1 twin with private shower & bath.

Price: £30 p.p. Single supp. £8.

Breakfast: Flexible.

Meals: Dinner, £18 p.p, and packed lunch, available on request.

Closed: Occasionally.

Flemish flax weavers used to wash the flax in the moat and dry it in the magnificent barn. Grade II*, red-brick and mellow, the house has a grand scale; soaring ceilings, handsome fireplaces, huge sash windows, cast iron baths, good, large, beds. It's full of light, and parquet floors, chandelier, balustrade and frescos add grandeur. Guests have their own sitting room. Evenings here are heavenly — a drink on the terrace, dinner, then a wander through the rose walk and the ancient trees. The garden is two and a half acres, with a tennis court. Richard and Teena are super.

Rooms: 1 large double with private bathroom; 1 large twin, en suite (bath).

Price: £35 p.p. Single supp. £10.

Breakfast: Until 10am.

Meals: Dinner from £25 p.p., by arrangement.

Closed: Occasionally.

1 mile S of Norwich on roundabout at junction of A47 & A140 to Ipswich, take exit for Caistor St. Edmund. After a mile, left at crossroads and house is on immediate right.

Entry No: 317   Map no: 12

Kassy & Jonathan Pusey
The Old Rectory
Caistor St. Edmund
Norwich
Norfolk NR14 8QS
Tel: 01508 492490
Fax: 01508 495172
e-mail: pusey@paston.co.uk

Take A143 Yarmouth/Beccles road. In Toft Monks take Post Office Rd (opposite Toft Lion pub) for 0.4 miles to T-junc. Right down Aldeby Rd for 0.1 mile, fork right and house is on right, 0.2 miles on.

Entry No: 318   Map no: 12

Richard & Teena Freeland
The Elms
Toft Monks, Beccles
Norfolk NR34 0EJ
Tel: 01502 677380
Fax: 01502 677362
e-mail: richardfreeland@btconnect.com
Web: www.sawdays.co.uk

The lawns cascade down Conifer Hill, wisteria perfumes the garden and you look out over hill and farmland. Don't forget your costumes — there's a heated swimming pool. Richard and Patricia are utterly charming and so easy to talk to; their respective passions are fishing and gardening. They'll bring you sherry in the drawing room and light a fire for you. The big bedrooms have thick carpets and the scent of wisteria fills our favourite room — it looks over lawns and a daffodil-covered hill.

Rooms: 1 twin/double, en suite (bath), 1 twin with private bathroom plus 1 double let to same party willing to share bathroom. Extra wc and basin available.

Price: £25 p.p. No single supp.

Breakfast: Flexible.

Meals: Good pubs and restaurants nearby.

Closed: Never.

A143 Diss/Yarmouth road for 9 miles. At r'bout left towards Harleston, then immediately left to Starston. Over x-roads, into village, over bridge, immediately right. After 0.5 miles, drive on left by white railing.

Entry No: 319   Map no: 12

Mrs Patricia Lombe Taylor
Conifer Hill
Low Road
Starston, Harleston
Norfolk IP20 9NT
Tel: 01379 852393
Fax: 01379 852393

An Elizabethan manor house — the deeds from 1601 hang in the hall — and a near-perfect traditional interior. High ceilings, heavy drapes, Louis XV chairs are set off by original oak floors and colour-washed walls. The enthusiastic Swiss-born Mrs Baxter is an interior designer and runs paint courses; her son offers an organic menu. Bedrooms are uncluttered but luxurious with decanter of sherry and Molton Brown toiletries; the dining room is opulent and candlelit. The moat is the star of the garden — you can row out to a little pontoon to have a drink. *Children over 12 welcome.*

Rooms: Main house: 2 doubles, both en suite (1 shower, 1 bath). Barn: 1 twin with private shower room and sitting room.

Price: £35 p.p. Single supp. £15.

Breakfast: Flexible.

Meals: Dinner, 4 courses, £20 p.p; lunch, £12.50 p.p.; by arrangement.

Closed: Christmas & New Year.

From centre of Starston (by the bridge), north along Church Hill (alongside church), which becomes Hardwick Rd. Entrance to house is 1.2 miles from junc. by church. Follow farm track to house.

Entry No: 320   Map no: 12

Christina Baxter
Starston Hall
Starston
Norfolk IP20 9PU
Tel: 01379 854252
Fax: 01379 852966
e-mail: starstonh@aol.com

The sleep of the gods awaits at this strikingly symmetrical Grade-I listed country mansion. Inside, long, sweeping corridors lead absolutely nowhere, while grand, ancient furniture remains utterly unused. Wander through the maze of rooms (you'll have time on your hands here) and come across hilarious booby traps, or climb to the top for glorious views. Superb beds if you can find them, though you may discover they are already taken. Many arrive and never leave.

Rooms: 257.

Price: Daylight robbery.

Breakfast: Flexible.

Meals: Feasts for the eyes, only.

Closed: Firmly.

Symbols: Lots, but I don't know what they mean.

Entry No: 321   Map no: 12

Cleo Patra
1 Fair Row
Shroud
Nofolk

"God made the country and man made the town," said William Cowper. In this God-given corner of England you're immersed in a restorative peace. The Church and the ironstone listed Vicarage have sat side by side since the 18th century. Birdsong and the sound of tennis being played on the grass court add to the Englishness of it all; you will effortlessly sink into the country house pace. The cream twin and the pale green double are extremely comfortable. Lots of choice for breakfast and your favourite newspaper can be waiting on the table. *Children over seven welcome.*

Rooms: 1 double, en suite (shower); 1 twin with private bathroom.

Price: From £27.50 p.p. Single supp. £5.

Breakfast: Flexible.

Meals: Packed lunch and dinner by arrangement.

Closed: Christmas.

From M40 junc. 11, dual carriageway for Northampton. 0.75 miles on, left at r'bout for Northampton, & left again 2 miles on. Follow brown signs for Canons Ashby to Moreton Pinkney. There, fork right across green on tarmac track. Gates beside church.

Entry No: 322   Map no: 10

Northamptonshire

Colonel & Mrs T.J.S. Eastwood
The Old Vicarage
Moreton Pinkney
Daventry
Northamptonshire NN11 3SQ
Tel: 01295 760057
Fax: 01295 760057
e-mail: tim@tandjeastwood.fsnet.co.uk

The house is a 300-year-old thatched cottage. The gardens and the beautiful things in it are a treat. And then there's Liz — a charming and gracious hostess. There's something special at every turn: a Bechstein piano in the cottage sitting room, a Jacobean trunk in the single room, Gothic headboards in the twin, a beautiful bureau in the bathroom. Guests have said that "staying here is like staying with a good friend". You'll understand what they mean. Log fires, beautiful, *Cordon Bleu* dinners and the lovely conservation village of Staverton complete the idyll. *Children over eight and babes in arms welcome.*

Rooms: 2 doubles and 1 twin all en suite (bath/shower); 1 single, en suite (bath).

Price: £36 p.p. Single supp. £10.

Breakfast: Flexible.

Meals: Dinner, 3-course *Cordon Bleu*, £24.50 p.p.

Closed: Christmas & New Year.

From Daventry, A425 to Leamington Spa. 100 yds past Staverton Park Conference Centre, turn right into village, then first right. Keep left, and at 'Give Way' sign, sharp left. House immediately on right.

Entry No: 323   Map no: 10

Mrs Elizabeth J. Jarrett
Colledges House
Oakham Lane
Staverton, Daventry
Northamptonshire NN11 6JQ
Tel: 01327 702737
Fax: 01327 300851

Part of the Althorp estate, this former 1840s farmhouse is a family home at the end of a grand avenue of lime trees; in the garden you'll see traces of medieval ridge and furrow farming methods. Valerie and Ian are great company; they are very knowledgeable and enthusiastic about the area and pull off the trick of giving you both comfort and privacy. Their daughter runs a livery from the stable yard and extensive paddocks — the riding is superb and your horse is welcome, too. The large bedrooms have sofas and armchairs and great beds and views. The cockerel is friendly but can't tell the time — nonetheless, guests cheer him on.

Rooms: 1 twin with private bathroom; 1 double, en suite (bath), plus extra twin, let only to members of same party.

Price: £25 p.p. Single supp. £5.

Breakfast: Flexible.

Meals: Dinner £15 p.p. B.Y.O wine.

Closed: Never.

From Northampton, A45 towards Daventry. After approx 1.5 miles, take 3rd exit at r'bout (signed Althorp). After 1 mile, take first exit at r'bout (signed Nobottle). In 2 miles, house is just beyond Nobottle on left, on brow of hill.

Entry No: 324   Map no: 10

Valerie K. Cocks
Nobottle Grange
Nobottle
Northampton
Northamptonshire NN7 4HJ
Tel: 01604 759494
Fax: 01604 590799
e-mail: nobottlegrange@hotmail.com

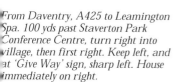

Traditional Scottish griddle-scones on arrival plus, perhaps, home-made marmalade, bread, fruit cake and shortbread, a log fire and comfy sofas make this a nourishing haven for pilgrims on St. Cuthbert's Way or en route for Holy Island, five miles away. Built from local stone, the Grade II-listed manse adjoins the southernmost Church of Scotland, whose stained glass windows can be admired from the garden. The two bedrooms are elegant and restrained in style, with good period furniture. Mrs Huddart, locally born and bred, has a good sense of humour.

Rooms: 1 double and 1 twin, both en suite (bath).

Price: £25 p.p. Single supp. £7.50.

Breakfast: Until 9am.

Meals: Dinner, £17.50 p.p., by arrangement. Packed lunch from £4 p.

Closed: 20 December-5 January.

From Newcastle A1 north, then B6353 left to Lowick. In town, left at Post Office, then 1st right, signed.

Entry No: 325   Map no: 20

Mrs Barbara Huddart
The Old Manse
Lowick
Berwick Upon Tweed
Northumberland TD15 2TY
Tel: 01289 388264
Web: www.sawdays.co.uk

Northumberland

A totally surprising one-storey house, full of beautiful things. It is an Aladdin's cave, larger than you could imagine. The sitting room is bright and elegant, with fine views to Bamburgh Castle; the dining room has deep red rugs and a mahogany oval table. The garden/breakfast room, the hub of the house, has a country cottage feel to it. In summer the table can be moved outside to the sun-trapping courtyard for breakfast. The bedrooms have fresh flowers and very good books. Mary is welcoming, has a good sense of humour and stacks of local knowledge.

Rooms: 1 twin and 1 double, sharing private bath & shower.

Price: £25 p.p. Single supp. £5.

Breakfast: 8.30-9am.

Meals: Dinner, £17.50 p.p., by arrangement.

Closed: Christmas & occasionally in winter.

Sylvia is a doyenne of farmhouse B&B, with 25 years experience under her belt. Sylvia recently received an MBE for her 'Household and Farming Museum' — she is justly proud of her gong. She has a wonderful sense of community and Charlie, even if he's been up since dawn with his sheep, will come and have a chat as you have breakfast. Large bedrooms, long views, handmade quilts, family furniture, generous breakfasts. True farmhouse B&B. *Children over 10 welcome.* They also have 2 self-catering houses that stand in 1.5 acres of gardens.

Rooms: 2 doubles, en suite (bath); 1 twin, private bathroom. Self-catering in Middleton Hall: Firwood Bungalow sleeps 10; Humphrey's House sleeps 6.

Price: £28 p.p. Single supp. £10. Self-catering £100-£200 p.w.

Breakfast: Flexible.

Meals: Available locally.

Closed: Christmas & New Year.

From Newcastle north on A1, then right signed Bamburgh on B1341. Continue to village, pass 30mph sign and hotel, then 1st right. House is 400 yards on right.

Entry No: 326   Map no: 20

Mary Dixon
Broome
22 Ingram Road
Bamburgh
Northumberland NE69 7BT
Tel: 01668 214287
e-mail: mdixon4394@aol.com

North past Alnwick for about 6 miles. On left when reach dual carriageway. Chillingham road then 300 yds on left past farm buildings.

Entry No: 327   Map no: 20

Charles & Sylvia Armstrong
North Charlton Farm
Chathill
Alnwick
Northumberland NE67 5HP
Tel: 01665 579443
Fax: 01665 579443
e-mail: glenc99@aol.com

Sophisticated, gracious living in an immaculately elegant Georgian villa perched on a rocky promontory — the sea views are magnificent. The Athertons are avid antique collectors, charming and friendly. Food is bought locally, whatever is best and freshest; you breakfast at a polished table with real silver, on fresh fruit and organic yoghurt, locally smoked Craster kippers, smoked salmon, or a full breakfast. The superb bedrooms have beautiful curtains, huge French mahogany beds and luxurious linen and towels. There is a sumptuous drawing room with grand piano and well-stocked library, too. Perfect.

Rooms: 3 doubles: 2 en suite (bath) and 1 with private bathroom.

Price: £37.50 p.p. Single occ. £45.

Breakfast: Until 9am.

Meals: Available locally.

Closed: Christmas & New Year.

This honest farm lies in 400 acres of mixed arable land that sweep down to the coast. The Jacksons are hardworking but still find time to greet and know their guests. The bedrooms are large, bright and well-furnished; there is a conservatory at the back in which to have tea on arrival, and the croquet lawn, with its splendid views to the sea, will draw even the most hapless beginner out to its uneven folds. Breakfast is a feast, but it is the Jacksons and their genuine warmth that make this place so enjoyable.

Rooms: 2 doubles & 1 twin, all en suite (shower). Bathroom also available.

Price: £25 p.p. Ask about single supp.

Breakfast: Until 9am.

Meals: Dinner, £14 p.p., by prior arrangement. Packed lunches from £3.50 p.p.

Closed: Christmas & New Year.

Take A1068 Warkworth/Alnmouth. On entering High Buston, the Hall is first building on the right.

Entry No: 328   Map no: 20

Ian & Therese Atherton
High Buston Hall
High Buston, Alnmouth
Northumberland NE66 3QH
Tel: 01665 830606
Fax: 01665 830707
e-mail: highbuston@aol.com
members.aol.com/highbuston

From Alnwick, A1068 to Alnmouth. At Hipsburn r'bout follow signs to station and cross bridge. Straight on to Bilton Barns down first left-hand lane, about 0.5 miles from road.

Entry No: 329   Map no: 20

Brian & Dorothy Jackson
Bilton Barns
Alnmouth
Alnwick
Northumberland NE66 2TB
Tel: 01665 830427
Fax: 01665 830063
Web: www.biltonbarns.co.uk

Tucked behind trees you will find this stone-built farmhouse overlooking the most fantastic views. Kris will greet you with home-made scones if you arrive around teatime and provides a lavish array of breakfast goodies as well as the 'full works'. Newly equipped and country-fresh bedrooms have ravishing views over the garden or the hills. You can use the large sitting room which is flooded with the evening sunlight and opens onto a terrace where you can sit. A perfect place from which to explore numberless local stately homes and castles and the fabulous countryside of the Northumberland National Park.

Rooms: 1 twin with private bathroom; 2 doubles, both en suite.

Price: £23 p.p. Single occ. £28.

Breakfast: 8.30am, or other times by request.

Meals: Light evening meal, approx. £8.50 p.p.

Closed: Occasionally.

Thropton is 2.5 miles west of Rothbury on the B6341. The farmhouse is on the left at the far end of the village.

Entry No: 330   Map no: 20

Kris Rogerson
Thropton Demesne Farmhouse
Thropton
Rothbury
Northumberland NE66 7LT
Tel: 01669 620196

Once home to Capability Brown's family — even he couldn't improve upon the rolling Northumberland landscape — 18th-century Shieldhall and its later outbuildings have been lovingly restored by Celia and Stephen. Each guest suite has a different style (Stephen is a cabinet-maker of great artistry) and has its own private stone entrance arch off a central rose-clad courtyard. Walk in the surrounding hills or play croquet on the lawn before dinner in the oak-beamed, inglenooked dining room, replete with antiques and curios. Celia is a friendly and attentive hostess who adores cooking for her guests.

Rooms: 1 family suite and 2 doubles, all en suite (shower); 1 family suite, en suite (bath).

Price: £23.50-£28 p.p. Single supp. £8.50.

Breakfast: Flexible.

Meals: Dinner £16.50 p.p.

Closed: 1 November-1 March.

From Newcastle take A696 (signed Jedburgh). On B6342 take right 5 miles north of Belsay and house is on left after 300 yards.

Entry No: 331   Map no: 20

Celia & Stephen Gay
Shieldhall
Wallington
Morpeth
Northumberland NE61 4AQ
Tel: 01830 540387
Fax: 01830 540490
e-mail: robinson.gay@btinternet.com

Just two miles from Hadrian's Wall, it is at the end of a long sweeping drive with woodland on one side, pasture on the other, birdsong and the sound of horses' hooves, and the occasional roe deer ambling into view. The house is well lived-in, elegant and comfortable, with old family paintings and some splendid antiques. The bedrooms are crisp, pretty and beautifully furnished. There is a walled garden and breakfast can be taken on the terrace. After many years abroad the Stewarts have returned to Katie's roots; she grew up in this lovely house. *Children over 10 welcome.*

Rooms: 1 double & 1 twin, both en suite (bath); 1 twin with private bathroom.

Price: £25-£30 p.p. No single supp.

Breakfast: Until 9am.

Meals: Available locally.

Closed: October-February.

Simplicity at its pure best. Lizzie has done to this 'gentleman's residence' of about 1800 what many of us would like to do with our lives: it is uncluttered, clean, focused, and pays attention to inherent — rather than added — detail. So there are no frills or flounces, no serried ranks of objects to impress you; the eye is drawn to the Georgian details the doors, windows, waxed floorboards, proportions. Fresh flowers, rugs, comfortable beds and wonderful views enhance this stylish place. Lizzie is a notable cook, too and runs classes.

Rooms: 2 doubles, en suite (1 bath, 1 shower); 1 single, en suite (shower).

Price: £22.50 p.p. Single £25.

Breakfast: Flexible.

Meals: Dinner, 2 courses, £12.50 p.p.; 3 courses, £15 p.p, by arrangement.

Closed: Never.

Go 7 miles north of Corbridge on A68. Turn left on A6079 and after 1 mile, turn right through Lodge gates with arch. House 0.5 miles down drive.

Entry No: 332   Map no: 20

Simon & Katie Stewart
The Hermitage
Swinburne
Nr. Hexham
Northumberland NE48 4DG
Tel: 01434 681248
Fax: 01434 681110
e-mail: stewart@thehermitagenow.freeserve.co.uk

A69 signed Ovington, on left if travelling to Hexham. Through Ovington village, passing 2 pubs. House signposted on the left, after sharp corner.

Entry No: 333   Map no: 20

Liz Pelly
Ovington House
Ovington
Prudhoe
Northumberland NE42 6DH
Tel: 01661 832442
Fax: 01661 832442
e-mail: ovhouse@talk21.com

Jillie's grandmother studied at the Slade and her paintings line the walls; glass and china ornaments fill every surface. This wisteria-clad Victorian vicarage next to the 12th-century church was falling down when the Steeles bought it, but now it is an elegant, traditional country home. Long windows are generously draped and pelmeted, there are tall-backed dining chairs, silver and crystal and lovely oils dotted around. Bedrooms are on the expected large scale and the baths have claw feet. You can play tennis or croquet while Jillie prepares a traditional supper using fresh vegetables from the kitchen garden. *Children over 12 welcome.*

Rooms: 1 large double, en suite (bath & shower), 1 small double, en suite (shower) and 1 twin, en suite (bath & shower).

Price: £33-£36 p.p. Single supp. £10.

Breakfast: Flexible.

Meals: Dinner £18.50 p.p.

Closed: Occasionally.

From A1, A46 to Lincoln and left onto A1133 for Gainsborough. Drive through Langford, 1 mile on, and turn left for Holme. House 100 yds on, on right, by church.

Entry No: 334   Map no: 16

Nottinghamshire & Leicestershire

Jerry & Jillie Steele
The Old Vicarage
Langford
Newark
Nottinghamshire NG23 7RT
Tel: 01636 705031
Fax: 01636 708728

Built in 1920 for the manager of the local coal mine, here's a well-proportioned house with a big, open hall filled with flowers and with numerous rooms off it. Guests have two sitting rooms with sofas and log fires. Colin and Erica are amusing and have given lots for you to do: golf (six holes), snooker, darts, croquet, tennis and swimming. If the weather's dreary, there are lots of board games to play by the fire. All bedrooms have ample lounging-around space and fireplaces. Bathrooms are big and one has black and cream Edwardian tiles; it is now decorated as a 'print room'. *Pets by arrangement.*

Rooms: 2 doubles, 1 with private bathroom, 1 en suite (shower); 1 twin, en suite (bath).

Price: £23-£28 p.p. For 3 nights or more, £23 p.p. Single supp. £5.

Breakfast: Flexible.

Meals: Dinner, for 4 people or more, £22 p.p., or light supper, by arrangement. Meals available locally.

Closed: Christmas.

From A617 Newark-on-Trent to Mansfield, 0.25 miles west of Kirklington, right at two small white bollards, just before turn to Eakring.

Entry No: 335　　　　Map no: 10

Erica McGarrigle
Archway House
Kirklington, Newark
Nottinghamshire NG22 8NX
Tel: 01636 812070
Fax: 01636 812200
e-mail: mcgarrigle@archway-house.co.uk
Web: www.sawdays.co.uk

Southwell's Minster is 'the most rural Cathedral in England' and can be seen, floodlit every night, from some of the Old Forge's bedrooms. Hilary has lived in Southwell for 38 years and feels strongly about it; you can walk to the shops and pubs from this house. Pink in front and very pretty, it has a cottagey feel, though it is bigger than it looks. Filled with antiques and interesting things, rooms are small but pretty (pastels) and Hilary's breakfasts are famous. You may eat them in the plant-filled conservatory or, in summer, by the pond.

Rooms: 1 twin and 2 doubles, all en suite; 1 twin with private bathroom.

Price: £28-£32 p.p. Single occ. £35-£42.

Breakfast: 8-9am; earlier by arrangement.

Meals: Plenty of pubs & restaurants within walking distance.

Closed: Never.

From Nottingham, A612 to Southwell. Right into Westgate & pass the Minster. Approx. 100 yds on, fork right at the library and almost immediate right down alley beside Old Forge.

Entry No: 336　　　　Map no: 10

Hilary Marston
The Old Forge
Burgage Lane
Southwell
Nottinghamshire NG25 0ER
Tel: 01636 812809
Fax: 01636 816302
Web: www.sawdays.co.uk

Di Shouls' huge enthusiasm for organic food has caught on; most of us now agree with her. This is an organic smallholding. She's a staunch supporter of the village shop and makes her own marmalade and jams; she nearly won the prize for the Best Breakfast in Nottinghamshire. The house is simple and delightful, with much warmth. Sheets are cotton, with warm duvets, electric blankets and heaters. Breakfast is served on Royal Minton china. There are log fires and a huge welcome for children and young people. Pine furniture, dried flowers, soothing colours and long views over the Trent Valley.

Rooms: 2 twins and 1 family room (double, 2 singles & cot), sharing 2 bathrooms. Baby & child equipment available.

Price: £17.50 p.p. No single supp.

Breakfast: 7-9am.

Meals: Pubs nearby.

Closed: Never.

From A46 towards Newark to East Bridgford. At village crossroads right into Kneeton Road. 20 yards after Reindeer pub, left up farm track.

Entry No: 337   Map no: 10

Mrs Di Shouls
Barn Farm Cottage
Kneeton Road
East Bridgford
Nottinghamshire NG13 8PJ
Tel: 01949 20196

You'll be bowled over by the view. From the generous windows of the majestic red drawing-room, beyond the manicured gardens, the Vale of Belvoir is at your feet. The house has been in the family for generations and has an eclectic feel. Gilt-framed portraits, a grandfather clock and a majestic dining room recall a grander age. Plastic chairs on the terrace and fake flowers speak of a no-nonsense approach to contemporary life. Definitely ask for one of the front bedrooms. Beyond the lawns and cherished roses you are blessed with that view.

Rooms: 2 doubles and 1 twin, all with private baths; 1 twin, en suite (shower) .

Price: £22.50-£25 p.p. Single supp. £2.50-£5.

Breakfast: Flexible.

Meals: Good pubs nearby.

Closed: Christmas.

From Nottingham, take A606 to Upper Broughton. Drive to top of hill, then sharp left into Colonel's Lane. Signed.

Entry No: 338   Map no: 10

Hilary Dowson
Sulney Fields, Colonel's Lane
Upper Broughton, Melton Mowbray
Nottinghamshire LE14 3BD
Tel: 01664 822204
Fax: 01664 823976
e-mail: acollinson@compuserve.com
Web: www.sawdays.co.uk

Passing traffic is less frequent than passing horses — why not bring your own? The lasting impression of this cottage (17th-century and added to) is of an uplifting lightness and brightness; the house is filled with laughter and the Cowdells are terrific hosts. There's a fine collection of paintings and furniture, which has been amassed over the years. Double oak doors lead from the dining room to the guest sitting room and there are fresh flowers everywhere. Bedrooms are restful and fresh — one has three-way views and the garden was designed by Bunny Guinness from Gardeners' Question Time. *Children over 12 welcome.*

Rooms: 2 twins/doubles, 1 en suite (bath) with extra single bed and 1 en suite (shower).

Price: From £22.50 p.p. Single supp. £5.

Breakfast: Flexible.

Meals: Packed lunch £3 p.p.

Closed: Occasionally.

From A46 Newark-Leicester road, turn onto B676, signed Melton. At staggered x-road, straight over signed Grimston. 1 mile on, right to Grimston. There, up hill, past church. House on left, just after right-hand bend at top.

Entry No: 339   Map no: 10

Mr & Mrs RL & ME Cowdell
The Gorse House
Grimston
Melton Mowbray
Leicestershire LE14 3BZ
Tel: 01664 813537
Fax: 01664 813537
e-mail: cowdell@gorsehouse.co.uk

The ruggedly handsome 1607 manor house with wildly high dormers, grand framework of gnarled timbers and the warmth of distinctive local 'gingerbread' ironstone is a stalwart piece of Old England in a time-locked village. Today it is a bustling family home where seasoned logs burn in the drawing room fireplace. For lovers, the Crow's Nest bedroom with its raised beam across the floor is perfect... trip on the obstacle and tumble into bed. The light, fresh Winter Room's next door bathroom has walls adorned with corn husks and dragonflies painted by a friend of Vicki's.

Rooms: 2 king-size: 1 en suite (bath) and 1 with wc and private bath (this room can also have 2 extra singles).

Price: £37.50 p.p. Single occ. £45.

Breakfast: Flexible.

Meals: Dinner, 3 courses, £27.50 p.p.

Closed: Never.

Oxfordshire

M40, exit 11 to Banbury. Take A422 for Stratford-upon-Avon, through Wroxton village, right to Hornton. House is first on right at Round Green, opposite school.

Entry No: 340   Map no: 10

Malcolm & Vicki Patrick
The Manor House
Hornton
Nr. Banbury
Oxfordshire OX15 6BZ
Tel: 01295 670386
Fax: 01295 678247
e-mail: vicki@horntonmanor.demon.co.uk

There's a marvellous glow to this lovingly restored house. A rare, original and fine example of a large 1650s Yeoman farmhouse, it has more than its fair share of oak beams, stone mullioned windows, big fireplaces and bread ovens. What's more, there are fine antiques, paintings and, in the attic, a games room with a full-size billiards table. Beamed bedrooms are large, light and airy, with views to the valley or to the church; this is an exceptionally pretty village with a proper green. The Hainsworths' two dogs are lovely — 'weird-haired' pointers, apparently!

Rooms: 1 double and 1 twin, en suite (bath).

Price: £32.50 p.p. Single supp. £12.50.

Breakfast: Flexible.

Meals: Available in excellent village pub/restaurant.

Closed: Never.

From A422, 7 miles north-west of Banbury, turn left down hill through Alkerton, then up hill. First left by church. Mill House is on right.

Entry No: 341   Map no: 10

Keith & Maggie Hainsworth
Mill House
Shenington
Banbury
Oxfordshire OX15 6NH
Tel: 01295 670642
Fax: 01295 678170

This is a new home for the Wills — the were in Fulford House, also a *Special Place* — and they have given it their special charm and individuality. The s levels of the Hornton stone house and the garden add interest and the view over the thatched roofs of the village cottages is lovely. Morning tea and breakfast can be brought to you on th sunny terrace; on colder days you eat a a Georgian dining table. The bedroom and bed are large, with a sitting area a sofa-bed, so it will easily sleep a child two. It's chintzy and light, with antiques. Marypen and Stephen are ea company.

Rooms: 1 double/family room, en su (shower), plus 1 small room which ca be let to members of same family.

Price: £30 p.p. £15 per child. Single supp. £10.

Breakfast: 7.30-9am for Full English. Flexible for Continental.

Meals: Not available.

Closed: Christmas.

A422 Banbury to Stratford. Through Wroxton and third left, signed Balscote. Through Balscote, house is on left at T-junc., opposite Butchers Arms.

Entry No: 342   Map no: 1

Stephen & Marypen Wills
Swallows Barn
Balscote
Nr. Banbury
Oxfordshire OX15 6JJ
Tel: 01295 738325
Fax: 01295 738314

The deep comfort of this 1770 farmhouse bears witness to Sara's profession — interior design. Cushions, curtains and sofas are adorned with beautiful fabrics — orange and yellow checks here, Colefax and Fowler florals there. The kitchen glows with sunshine yellow and cupboards are hand-stencilled. Stephen and Sara have been here for 28 years and happily share their books, piano, tennis court, gardens, lake and local knowledge. The beds are memorably comfortable and have goosedown pillows and linen sheets.

Rooms: 3 twins/doubles, all en suite (1 shower, 1 bath and 1 bath & shower).

Price: £28 p.p. Single supp. £8.

Breakfast: Flexible.

Meals: Dinner, 4 courses, £17 p.p., by arrangement.

Closed: Never.

Low ceilings, exposed beams and stone fireplaces — and the bedrooms, perched above their own staircases like crows' nests, are delightful. The barn room has its own entrance. All rooms are unusual and full of character, old and luxurious; the family's history and travels are evident all over. Your hosts will occasionally dine with guests. They are good listeners, amusing and utterly friendly, as is Ulysses, their large soppy golden retriever. It's all so easy that you may not want to leave.

Rooms: 1 double, en suite (bath); 1 twin/double, en suite (bath/shower); 1 twin/double with private bathroom.

Price: £31 p.p. Single supp. £10.

Breakfast: 8-9am.

Meals: Dinner £21 p.p.

Closed: Christmas.

In Kings Sutton follow signs to Charlton but, before leaving Kings Sutton, take last turning right, off Astrop Road, opposite a tree with a seat around it. Farmhouse is at the bottom of the lane.

Entry No: 343   Map no: 10

Sara & Stephen Allday
College Farmhouse
Kings Sutton
Banbury
Oxfordshire OX17 3PS
Tel: 01295 811473
Fax: 01295 812505
e-mail: sallday@compuserve.com

From M40, junc.10 and take A43 towards Northampton. After 5 miles, left to Charlton. There, left and house is on left, 100 yds past the Rose & Crown.

Entry No: 344   Map no: 10

Col & Mrs Nigel &
Rosemary Grove-White
Home Farmhouse, Charlton,
Nr. Banbury, Oxfordshire OX17 3DR
Tel: 01295 811683
Fax: 01295 811683
e-mail: grovewhite@lineone.net
Web: www.sawdays.co.uk

All the nooks, crannies and beams you would expect in such an ancient thatched cottage in a Cotswold village, but much more than that: lots of music, fun and laughter, too, not to mention a wealth of inside information about gardens to visit. Judith is a keen gardener who writes books on the subject; her passion for plants is palpable in her own wonderful cottage garden. Her style and intelligence are reflected in the lived-in, elegant house. Charming, bright pastel bedrooms, thoroughly relaxed atmosphere — and fresh everything...

Rooms: 1 double and 1 twin, both en suite (bath).

Price: £32 p.p. Single occ. £42.

Breakfast: Until 9.30am.

Meals: Dinner, 4 courses, £22 p.p., by arrangement.

Closed: Christmas & New Year.

Andrew has done a fine job of masterminding the conversion of this Cotswold stone barn and cowshed; Susie's background as a professional cook will be brought to bear here, too. Their home is in seven acres of newly landscaped gardens with not another house in sight. Breakfast is served around a large walnut table in the upstairs section of a two-storey flagstoned hall with floor-to-ceiling windows. Wide steps lead to the drawing room; all around there are things of interest — fine furniture, prints, pill boxes, family portraits. The bedrooms are extremely light and airy and have new everything. *Children over 10 welcome.*

Rooms: 3 doubles, all en suite.

Price: £25-£30 p.p. Single supp. £5.

Breakfast: Flexible.

Meals: Available locally.

Closed: Christmas & New Year.

Sibford Gower is 0.5 miles south off B4035 which runs between Banbury and Chipping Campden. House is on main street on same side as church and school.

Entry No: 345   Map no: 10

Judith Hitching
Gower's Close
Sibford Gower
Nr. Banbury
Oxfordshire OX15 5RW
Tel: 01295 780348
e-mail: j.hitching@virginnet.co.uk

From Chipping Norton, take A361 to Banbury and approx. 4 miles on, take first sign for Swerford (single track road). Follow road under railway bridge and up hill. House first on left by telegraph pole.

Entry No: 346   Map no: 10

Andrew & Susie Little
Badger Farm
Swerford
Nr. Chipping Norton
Oxfordshire OX7 4AU
Tel: 01608 730785

Deep in the heart of beautifully maintained Ditchley Park, Newbarn Farm is a walkers' — and riders' — paradise. You can stroll straight out across the lawns and into 6,000 acres of grounds and woodland. The Dents themselves have nine acres of fields and lawn, with a small spring-fed lake which further softens the scene. The house (1740 plus discreet extension) is comfort itself and piloted by an easy-going Rosie. There's a large drawing room where the space and lack of clutter lets the mind unfurl. Bedrooms are large, not over-adorned, pretty with fruit and flowers, and comfortable. It's profoundly rural and very friendly.

Rooms: 1 double, en suite (bath); 1 twin with private bath.

Price: From £35 p.p. No single supp.

Breakfast: Flexible.

Meals: Excellent pubs nearby.

Closed: Christmas.

Helen has a real interest in birds — you'll see evidence of it in the house and the garden. This is a charming, easy-going 1720 farmhouse home where the two well-furnished bedrooms share a bright, big shower room — perfect for families or friends travelling together. Separate access to the twin room overlooking the cobbled courtyard is up a daunting iron spiral staircase. The double bedroom featured in a Laura Ashley catalogue. The affectionate sheepdog Chloe is so beloved by children that one American girl sends her a Valentine annually.

Rooms: 1 double and 1 twin, sharing shower room.

Price: From £23 p.p. Single occ. from £30.

Breakfast: Flexible.

Meals: Available locally.

Closed: Christmas.

From Oxford, A44 north for Woodstock/Evesham. Through Woodstock and 1 mile on, at Shell garage, left signed Charlbury (B4437). House is 2.5 miles on, on left at end of wood, down track and over cattle grids.

Entry No: 347   Map no: 10

Take A44 north from Oxford's ring road. At r'bout, 1 mile before Woodstock, left onto A4095 into Bladon. Take last left in the village. House is on second bend in road, with iron railings.

Entry No: 348   Map no: 10

Rosanagh & Andrew Dent
Newbarn Farm
Ditchley Park
Oxfordshire OX7 4EX
Tel: 01993 898398
Fax: 01993 891100
e-mail: rdent@waitrose.com

Helen Stevenson
Manor Farmhouse
Manor Road
Bladon, nr. Woodstock
Oxfordshire OX20 1RU
Tel: 01993 812168
Fax: 01993 812168
Web: www.sawdays.co.uk

Bridget confides "I used to be solicitous, then realised guests didn't want that". Bridget, gracious and elegant, the house and the setting are intoxicating. Our inspector calls it "a Sawday idyll". This is country elegance with no concession to modernity: furniture and rugs fit beautifully, the kitchen is stone-flagged and wood-boarded. The Garden House has a bedroom, kitchen and sitting room for B&B or self-catering. The River Windrush trickles through the garden, the church and the ruins of Minster Lovell Hall sit beside it.

Rooms: 1 twin with private bathroom; 1 double in Garden House with bath and shower.

Price: £37.50 p.p. Single supp. £10.

Breakfast: Until 9.30am.

Meals: Dinner £20 p.p.

Closed: Never.

This beautiful farmhouse was once owned by St. John's College, Oxford, and the date stone above the entrance reads 1629, although parts of the house are even older. There's the happy buzz of family life here — it's relaxed and informal and you settle in easily, welcomed with tea and home-made shortbread. Bedrooms are light and airy, with small stone-arched and mullioned windows; there are Tudor fireplaces, timbered and exposed walls. The huge, twin bedroom has ornate plasterwork and views of the garden and church; the green and peach double is cosier, again with lovely views.

Rooms: 1 double and 1 twin, en suite (shower).

Price: £25 p.p. Single supp. £10. Reductions for stays of 3 nights or more.

Breakfast: Until 9am.

Meals: Good restaurants nearby.

Closed: Mid-December-mid-January.

From Burford, A40 towards Oxford. At next r'bout, left for Minster Lovell. Head for Minster Lovell Hall across bridge. House on right before church, in cul-de-sac marked 'Unsuitable for motor vehicles'.

Entry No: 349   Map no: 10

From Oxford, A420 towards Swindon for 8 miles and right at r'bout, signed Witney (A415). Over 2 bridges, immediately right by pub car park. Right at T-junc.; drive on right, past church.

Entry No: 350   Map no: 4

Ms Bridget Geddes
The Old Vicarage
Minster Lovell
Oxfordshire OX8 5RR
Tel: 01993 775630
Fax: 01993 772534
e-mail: ageddes@lix.compulink.co.uk
Web: www.sawdays.co.uk

Mary Anne & Robert Florey
Rectory Farm
Northmoor
Nr. Witney
Oxfordshire OX8 1SX
Tel: 01865 300207
Fax: 01865 300559
e-mail: pj.florey@farmline.com

Roses and clematis cover this pretty 17th-century thatched cottage where breakfast is served around the huge pine table in the farmhouse kitchen. The beamed bedrooms have lovely views and are all individual; one has a 17th-century four-poster bed with cabbage rose chintz drapes and, as with all bedrooms, hand-embroidered sheets and pillow slips. Sip tea or wine around a winter day's log fire. Daughter Katie makes prize-winning food using as much local produce as possible. Glorious walks from the doorstep and a shaggy old English sheepdog.

Rooms: 1 four-poster, en suite (bath) and 1 twin, en suite (bath). In barn annexe: 1 half-tester, en suite (shower).

Price: £25-£37.50 p.p. Single supp. by arrangement.

Breakfast: Until 9am.

Meals: Dinner, 3 courses, £19.50 p.p. (including coffee).

Closed: Never.

From M4, junc. 14, north on A338. Left onto B4001. Through Lambourn & 1 mile north of village, fork left. Drive 3 miles to Kingston Lisle, left to Uffington. Through village, right after church. House is 0.75 miles out, on left.

Entry No: 351   Map no: 4

Carol Wadsworth
The Craven
Fernham Road
Uffington
Oxfordshire SN7 7RD
Tel: 01367 820449/820351
e-mail: Carol@thecraven.co.uk
e-mail: thecraven.hypermart.net

Refreshingly original (viz the large projected clock on the drawing room wall) as well as ravishingly beautiful — and Anthea and Stephen are fun, too. Clocks are their main business now, with a workshop in the outhouse. They are as laid back as they are efficient... unusual for owners of houses like this. The décor is oak floors, white walls, wood, antique and contemporary simplicity (no chintz), with the odd dash of exotica from extensive long-haul travel. The drawing room has a vast fireplace for winter.

Rooms: 1 twin/double, en suite (shower); 1 double, en suite (bath); 1 double with private bathroom.

Price: £ 40 p.p. Single supp. by arrangement.

Breakfast: 9am Mon-Fri, 10am Sat-Sun.

Meals: Dinner available locally.

Closed: Christmas & New Year.

From M40, A329 towards Wallingford. In Stadhampton take lane immediately after mini-roundabout, left across village green. House straight ahead.

Entry No: 352   Map no: 4

Anthea & Stephen Savage
The Manor
Stadhampton
Oxfordshire OX44 7UL
Tel: 01865 891999
Fax: 01865 891640
e-mail: action@timebeam.com

Horse-loving Joanna will teach you to ride, by arrangement, and even offers B&B to itinerant horses and their riders. Her husband, who is passionate about roses, may be able to organise rough shooting for field sports enthusiasts, complete with gun dog. Simple comfort in peaceful surroundings is the watchword at this extended, semi-detached old workers' cottage with its clean, functional, no-frills, lemon-yellow rooms in a separate garden flat overlooking a courtyard. If roses, wine, shooting, hunting and stud farms are your thing, you could do no better. Probably not for Guardian readers.

Rooms: 2 twins in separate garden flat, sharing private bathroom.

Price: £20 p.p. More than 3 nights, £15 p.p. Single occ. £25.

Breakfast: 7.15-9.30am. Flexible by arrangement.

Meals: Not available.

Closed: Never.

Junc. 8/9 M4 to Henley. A4130 to Oxford. Crowmarsh Gifford r'bout, turn left onto Wallingford bypass. Right at next r'bout, over river, left at 1st of double r'bouts to Moulsford. A mile on, turn right into Caps Lane. Cottage is 1st on left.

Entry No: 353   Map no: 4

Mrs Joanna Alexander
The Well Cottage
Caps Lane
Cholsey
Oxfordshire OX10 9HQ
Tel: 01491 651959
Web: www.sawdays.co.uk

A place to remind yourself of the wonders of English country life. So perfectly peaceful; birds make the biggest noise. In the evening, more music to the ears: the crackle of the fire and the sound of easy chatter. It is a lovely house with a sitting room full of Persian rugs and with a baby grand that beckons those who can play. Bedrooms are unmistakably 'country' and low ceilings and uneven floors reveal their 16th- and 17th-century roots. There are eight acres of grounds with all-round views and free-range hens.

Rooms: 2 twins/doubles, both en suite (bath & shower).

Price: £27.50 p.p. Single occ. £35.

Breakfast: 7.30-9am.

Meals: Good choice of places locally.

Closed: January-April & September-December.

From Henley go NW on Peppard Rd for 3 miles, then right for Shepherds Green. House is on right after 0.3 miles. Phone to advise time of arrival, and no bookings after noon on day of stay, please.

Entry No: 354   Map no: 5

Sue Fulford-Dobson
Shepherds
Shepherds Green
Rotherfield Greys, Henley-on-Thames
Oxfordshire RG9 4QL
Tel: 01491 628413
Fax: 01491 628413
Web: www.sawdays.co.uk

A very English, and lived-in, cosy Georgian house with natural charm and elegance. You can breakfast on a small 18th-century table beneath the painted gaze of Inigo Jones, a forebear of Mr Wallace, or settle by a log fire in the guests' panelled drawing room in the evening. In good weather, breakfast can be served in the garden, under the vines and in a lovely welcoming atmosphere; the Wallaces genuinely enjoy people. There are mature trees and shrubs, old roses and herbs, an acre of garden and superb countryside (AONB).

Rooms: 2 twins/doubles, en suite (1 bath, 1 shower), 1 single next to private bathroom.

Price: £28 p.p. £26 p.p. for two or more nights.

Breakfast: 7.30-9am.

Meals: Many good pubs nearby.

Closed: Never.

Holmwood is a large Georgian country house set in beautiful grounds. The interior is immaculate and exactly right for its period. In the galleried hall a staircase sweeps you regally up to the very large rooms: all except one look onto the garden and far beyond. There's a stately drawing room, woodland to explore, tennis and croquet to play. The real French doors of the dining room and drawing room open onto the grounds. Brian and Wendy are irreproachably efficient and genuinely friendly. *Children over 12 welcome.*

Rooms: 2 twins, 2 doubles and 1 single, all en suite (bath).

Price: Twins/doubles £30 p.p. Single £40. Single occ. of double £50.

Breakfast: 7.45-9.45am.

Meals: Available locally.

Closed: Christmas.

Close to M40 junc. 4 & 5, and M4 junc.8/9. Once in Frieth, follow road through village & on towards Hambleden & Henley. House is 0.75 miles along on right.

Entry No: 355   Map no: 5

Wynyard & Julia Wallace
Little Parmoor
Frieth
Henley-on-Thames
Oxfordshire RG9 6NL
Tel: 01494 881447
Fax: 01494 883012

From Henley-on-Thames, A4155 towards Reading. After 2.5 miles, College on left & pub on right. Before pub turn into Plough Lane. House is up hill on left.

Entry No: 356   Map no: 5

Brian & Wendy Talfourd-Cook
Holmwood
Shiplake Row
Binfield Heath, Henley
Oxfordshire RG9 4DP
Tel: 0118 947 8747
Fax: 0118 947 8637

An enthralling house that twists and turns through the ages — an Elizabethan landing, a Georgian panelled hall, a Victorian cast-iron bath. The same family has lived here for five generations. From the spectacular panelled hall with its piano and fireplace, you ramble into the heart of the house. The huge bedrooms are romantic (especially the four-poster) and have lovingly-equipped bathrooms. This is a house where tradition is treated with respect and if you stay over the weekend you'll share one — a Sunday breakfast of boiled eggs and kedgeree.

Rooms: 1 four-poster, en suite (bath); 1 double (queen boat bed) with private bathroom; 1 twin, en suite (shower).

Price: From £40 p.p. Single occ. £60. Single night supp. £20.

Breakfast: Until 9am Mon-Sat; 8.30am Sun.

Meals: Good pub & restaurants within a mile.

Closed: December-mid-January.

In Henley centre, take Duke St. After 170m, right into Greys Rd. After almost 2 miles (as you leave 30mph zone) take second drive on right, signed 'Hernes Estate. Private Drive'.

Entry No: 357   Map no: 5

Richard & Gillian Ovey
Hernes
Henley-on-Thames
Oxfordshire RG9 4NT
Tel: 01491 573245
Fax: 01491 574645
e-mail: oveyhernes@aol.com
Web: www.sawdays.co.uk

David's family has farmed here for four generations — he tends a 200-head Friesian herd. In season you may have venison sausages from a locally-managed deer herd with your farm eggs for breakfast. The Breidden hills and views of the Severn dominate the setting and the simple garden, sensibly, does not try to compete with the views. There are three bedrooms in this 1740s border farmhouse — one with flowery curtains and borders, a half-tester bed with chunky rope twist columns and a twin with Victorian wrought iron bedsteads. A smashing place — simple and excellent value.

Rooms: 1 double, 1 twin, both small en suite (shower); 1 double, sharing bathroom with family, but en suite from Jan 2001.

Price: From £20 p.p.

Breakfast: Flexible.

Meals: Available locally. Packed lunch £3 p.p., by arrangement.

Closed: Never.

From Shrewsbury A458 Welshpool road. After Ford, right onto B4393. At Crew Green, left for Criggion. House is first on left after Admiral Rodney pub.

Entry No: 358   Map no: 9

Liz Dawson
Brimford House
Criggion
Nr. Shrewsbury
Shropshire SY5 9AU
Tel: 01938 570235
e-mail: brimford.house@virginnet.co.uk

Shropshire

Pam — theatrical, laughing, genuine — is just lovely. The house is ancient, magpie-gabled and the church and pound are 800 years old. Beams criss-cross the rooms and vertical framing has been exposed to great effect. There's a grand piano in the drawing room and, on the rambling first floor, bedrooms are pretty and double glazed. Pam's breakfasts are as generous as her spirit. There's an atmosphere of life, warmth, elegance and good taste and guests return time after time. *Children over 11 welcome.*

Rooms: 1 twin and 1 double, en suite (shower); 1 family room with 1 double and 2 single beds, en suite (bath/shower).

Price: £22-£25 p.p. Single occ. from £25.

Breakfast: 7.30-9.30am.

Meals: Packed lunch, by arrangement. Good pub within walking distance.

Closed: Never.

In this handsome William & Mary house, Jane goes to great lengths to ensure your comfort. She puts goodies in the bathroom and you're free to come and go anytime (unusual for a B&B). Large bedrooms are bright and sunny, with rich fabrics, deep mattresses, fat duvets and good linen. This is not 'shabby chic'. Gentle music is played at breakfast and Molly, their flat-coat retriever, will lead you to the trout pool, where you can fish from bank or boat. Jane can organise on-road cycling tours, silk painting and fly-fishing tuition. *Children over 12 welcome.*

Rooms: 1 double and 1 twin/double with single, both en suite (bath/shower).

Price: From £35 p.p. Single supp. £10.

Breakfast: Until 9am.

Meals: Excellent pubs & restaurants nearby.

Closed: Christmas.

From Shrewsbury, take A5 north. Through Nesscliffe and after 2 miles, left to Knockin. Through Knockin, past Bradford Arms. House is 150 yards on left.

Entry No: 359   Map no: 9

Pam Morrissey
Top Farmhouse
Knockin
Nr. Oswestry
Shropshire SY10 8HN
Tel: 01691 682582
e-mail: p.a.m@knockin.freeserve.co.uk

From Whitchurch bypass, take B5476 signed Tilstock and Wem. Dearnford Hall is 0.5 miles from r'bout on left. Park at the front door.

Entry No: 360   Map no: 9

Charles & Jane Bebbington
Dearnford Hall
Whitchurch
Shropshire SY13 3JJ
Tel: 01948 662319
Fax: 01948 666670
e-mail: dearnford_hall@yahoo.com
Web: www.sawdays.co.uk

From the double room, with hand-printed wallpaper and oak chests, you look to Acton Burnell hill — England's first parliament was held here. The yellow room has lovely views of a lake, the garden and the Welsh Hills; sunsets can be spectacular. Wooden doors, floors, carved settle and chests sit well with elegant furniture and lovely prints and photographs. A two-acre garden hugs the house, there's a pool and a croquet lawn. Parts of the house were built in 1660; the site is mentioned in the Domesday book. Very special. *Children by arrangement.*

Rooms: 1 double and 1 double/twin, each en suite (bath) and 1 double/twin, en suite (shower).

Price: £25 p.p. Single occ. £30.

Breakfast: Flexible.

Meals: Available locally.

Closed: Christmas.

The handsome Georgian farmhouse — which has a lovely courtyard with period outbuildings — is splendidly decorated. Rooms are English to the core: florals and chintz, soft carpets and (deliciously comfortable) four-posters. Vivacious Christine cannot do enough to spoil her guests — bedrooms are beautified with extras like fresh carnations, fluffy bathrobes and cafetieres, while Gareth their chef creates 'food adventures'... George runs the 350-acre farm with equal enthusiasm. A bountiful place.

Rooms: 3 doubles, 1 king-size and 1 family/twin, all en suite.

Price: £35-£50 p.p. Single supp. by arrangement.

Breakfast: Flexible.

Meals: Dinner, £25 p.p. 5-course gourmet, £35 p.p. Packed lunch £5 p.p.

Closed: Christmas & New Year.

From A5 & Shrewsbury, turn onto A458 towards Bridgnorth. Approx. 200 yds on, right to Acton Burnell. On for 6 miles and, entering Acton Burnell, left to Kenley. 0.5 miles on, left to Acton Pigot. House first on left, over cattle grid between 2 pillars.

Entry No: 361   Map no: 9

Mrs Hildegard Owen
Acton Pigot
Acton Burnell, Nr. Shrewsbury
Shropshire SY5 7PH
Tel: 01694 731209
Fax: 01694 731399
e-mail: acton@farmline.com
Web: www.actonpigot.co.uk

4 miles south of Shrewsbury on A458. In Cross Houses, left after petrol station, signed Atcham. Down lane and right to Brompton; follow to farm.

Entry No: 362   Map no: 9

Christine Yates-Roberts
Upper Brompton Farm
Cross Houses, Shrewsbury
Shropshire SY5 6LE
Tel: 01743 761629
Fax: 01743 761679
e-mail: upper.brompton.farm@dial.pipex.com
Web: www.upperbromptonfarm.com

One feels immersed in beauty in Shropshire; the greenness revives the spirit. Built in 1901, this imposing Victorian house was positioned on the lower slopes of north Long Mynd to take in the panorama. The Scarratts restored it from dereliction and added a stunning, proper glass conservatory facing Lawley and the Stretton Hills. William Morris fabrics, big furniture and lots of books give a traditional feel and there's a sense of privacy, too — you have your own staircase. Super garden. *Children over 12 welcome.*

Rooms: 1 double with private bath; 1 twin/double, en suite (bath).

Price: £25-£30 p.p. Single supp. £5. Special breaks also available.

Breakfast: Flexible.

Meals: Good pubs and restaurants nearby. Packed lunch from £2.50 p.p.

Closed: Christmas-New Year.

Since 1869 this Methodist chapel has stood among a tumble of rock, gorse, twisting streams, woodland and pasture all crowned by the mysterious Devil's Chair ridge. The dining and sitting room, with its choir gallery, is open right to the roof. There is old pine furniture and patterned rugs on an original wooden floor and a woodburning stove on local stone flags. The twin has views over the streamed valley and the single (with an extra pull out bed) looks up the steep Stiperstones Range. This is a walker's paradise and Jean will transport luggage to your next stop. Simple and good value.

Rooms: 1 twin and 1 single (with pull-out addition), sharing private shower, wc and basin.

Price: From £18 p.p.

Breakfast: Flexible.

Meals: Packed lunch by arrangement. Dinner available locally.

Closed: Occasionally.

From Shrewsbury, south on A49. In Dorrington, right to Smethcott. After 3 miles, left at crossroads (signed Smethcott). House is 0.5 miles on.

Entry No: 363   Map no: 9

Jackie & Jim Scarratt
Lawley House
Smethcott, Church Stretton
Shropshire SY6 6NX
Tel: 01694 751236
Fax: 01694 751396
e-mail: lawleyhouse@easicom.com
Web: www.sawdays.co.uk

From Shrewsbury A488 for Bishop's Castle. Left on edge of Plox Green for Snailbeach and Stiperstones. In village, turn left before pub up Perkinsbeach Dingle. Chapel on right.

Entry No: 364   Map no: 9

Jean Lees
The Old Chapel
Perkinsbeach Dingle
Stiperstones, Shrewsbury
Shropshire SY5 0PE
Tel: 01743 791449
e-mail: jean@a-lees.freeserve.co.uk

Best of all must be the beds — 17th-century French wedding, Gothic brass, 1940s Italian boudoir, and more — but the whole converted crofter's cottage has lovely fabrics, beams, antiques and attention to detail. Run by mother and daughter, Jinlye sits, old, luxurious and sheltered, at 1,400ft surrounded by ancient hills, rare birds, wild ponies and windswept ridges. The skies are infinite; humanity was here 12,000 years ago and you can walk deep in ancient wilderness before returning to superb home comforts. *Children over 12 welcome.*

Rooms: 3 doubles, 2 twins/doubles and 2 twins, all en suite; 1 double with private bath. Self-catering also available.

Price: £27-£40 p.p. Single occ. £42-£57.

Breakfast: 8-9am.

Meals: Packed lunch by arrangement. Excellent pubs and restaurants nearby.

Closed: Never.

You get absolute privacy and peace in the converted dairy across the flower-filled yard. The twin beds are plumply made up and you can make yourself herbal and fruit teas and fresh coffee. From the large window you can watch the light changing over the rolling hills and beyond. A mile away from the hurly burly of the main road, it is delightfully peaceful and tranquil. Fiona, charming and utterly natural, serves you breakfast in the main house in a room with a woodburner and French windows leading to the garden.

Rooms: 1 twin, en suite (bath).

Price: £21 p.p. Single occ. £42.

Breakfast: Flexible.

Meals: Available locally.

Closed: Never.

From Shrewsbury, A49 to Church Stretton, past the Little Chef and right towards All Stretton. Turn right immediately past the phone box and up the hill to Jinlye.

Entry No: 365   Map no: 9

Mrs Janet Tory
Jinlye, Castle Hill
All Stretton, Church Stretton
Shropshire SY6 6JP
Tel: 01694 723243
Fax: 01694 723243
e-mail: info@jinlye.co.uk
Web: www.jinlye.co.uk

From Bridgnorth, take A458 to Shrewsbury. 0.5 miles after Morville, turn right into a stone road and follow signs to Hannigans Farm.

Entry No: 366   Map no: 9

Mrs Fiona Thompson
Hannigans Farm
Morville
Bridgnorth
Shropshire WV16 4RN
Tel: 01746 714332
Fax: 01746 714332

Found in a land of fat sheep and ancient hill forts, this 17th-century mill ended Gill and Andrew's search for a refuge from the city. With an absence of fussiness in the house, total seclusion and surrounding natural beauty, this feels like a retreat — just what your hosts (a designer and an illustrator) want. Rooms are comfortable and decorated with taste: the en suite double has a Victorian brass bed and newly restored original roll-top bath. A sympathetic stone and oak extension has become a large en suite twin room. The River Unk flows through the mill's three acres of meadowland and gardens. *Children over eight welcome.*

Rooms: 2 doubles: 1 en suite (bath); 1 with private bathroom. 1 twin, en suite (bath with shower attachment).

Price: £25-£29 p.p. Single supp. £10.

Breakfast: Until 9.30am.

Meals: Dinner, £17 p.p., by arrangement.

Closed: Occasionally.

"One of the most beautiful houses I've ever been in!" said our inspector. Roger owns a restaurant in Ludlow and two in Chelsea, but this is his *home*. Come to discover the sophisticated comfort and elegance hiding behind the grey stone exterior: stone-flagged floors, woodburning stoves, polished tables, antiques, vast and luxurious bathrooms, pure cotton sheets and amazing electronics in each bedroom to delight musicians and baffle the over-50s. An unstinting welcome and unequalled value. There's a huge, luxury cottage, too — a romantic retreat for two.

Rooms: 1 twin/double, with sitting room and en suite (bath); 1 double, en suite (bath). Self-catering cottage for 2.

Price: Twin/double £44 p.p.; double £35 p.p. Single supp. £12. Cottage from £160-£200 for 3 nights

Breakfast: Until 9.30am.

Meals: By arrangement.

Closed: Never.

From Clun take A488 towards Bishops Castle. First left, signed Bicton. There, 2nd left signed Mainstone. House is first right after Llananhedric Farm.

Entry No: 367   Map no: 9

Gill Della Casa & Andrew Farmer
The Birches Mill
Clun
Nr. Craven Arms
Shropshire SY7 8NL
Tel: 01588 640409
Fax: 01588 640409

Take B4368 W to Clun. Left at fork towards Knighton on A488. Over bridge. Cockford is 1 mile from bridge, signed on left. House on right up drive.

Entry No: 368   Map no: 9

Roger Wren
Cockford Hall
Clun
Shropshire SY7 8LR
Tel: 01588 640327
Fax: 01588 640881
Web: www.sawdays.co.uk

Standing in lush gardens that slope down to a millstream and across meadows to the River Teme, this is a gracious house with fine Georgian windows and valley roof. It has a millstream and a weir, a motte and a heronry, a point-to-point course and a ha-ha. Yvonne is a qualified cook and walkers who want to stretch their muscles in the surrounding Welsh border country will do so knowing they can tuck into a first-rate dinner when they return. Good-sized bedrooms with fine furniture, luxurious beds and cotton sheets.

Rooms: 1 double, en suite (shower); 2 twins/doubles with private bath.

Price: £25-£30 p.p. Single supp. £10.

Breakfast: Until 9am.

Meals: Dinner £18 p.p. Book in advance.

Closed: Never.

From Ludlow, A49 to Shrewsbury. At Bromfield take A4113. Right in Walford for Buckton, continue to second farm on left. Look for large sign on building.

Entry No: 369   Map no: 9

Hayden & Yvonne Lloyd
Upper Buckton
Leintwardine, Craven Arms
Ludlow
Shropshire SY7 0JU
Tel: 01547 540634
Fax: 01547 540634

A tiny lane leads you to Cleeton Court, a part 14th-century attractively renovated farmhouse. With views over sheep meadows and heathland, you feel immersed in countryside. Ros greets you with fresh coffee and home-made cake — she is genuinely enthusiastic about B&B and likes to allow you to settle into your own pace. You have your own entrance and use of the drawing room — prettily striped in yellow and cream, with comfortable sofas and log fire. Bedrooms are full of character with beams, a four-poster with chintzy drapes and good pieces of furniture. An easy place to relax. *Children over five welcome.*

Rooms: 1 four-poster and 1 twin, both en suite (bath).

Price: £25-£35 p.p. Single occ. £35.

Breakfast: Flexible.

Meals: Many excellent restaurants in Ludlow & good local pubs.

Closed: Christmas & New Year.

From Ludlow, A4117 towards Kidderminster for 1 mile. Left on B4364, signed Cleobury North. On for 5 miles. In Wheathill, right for Cleeton St. Mary and on for 1.5 miles. House is on left, opposite a farmyard.

Entry No: 370   Map no: 9

Rosamund Woodward
Cleeton Court
Cleeton St. Mary
Shropshire DY14 0QZ
Tel: 01584 823379
Fax: 01584 823379

Your every need is anticipated. The bathrooms are packed with goodies, there's stacks of information to browse through, and books to share. The brass beds have crisp, flowery, fresh linen and it's all warm, quiet and very comfortable. Number Twenty Eight is on a beautiful Georgian street of listed and restored buildings, just outside the town walls and only 85 metres from the river (the ducks take their morning stroll past the house). The house is a gem and your hosts are generous, genuine and welcoming.

Rooms: 1 twin, en suite (bath/shower); 1 double, en suite (shower). Cottage: 1 twin and 1 double, both en suite (bath/shower). Westview House: 2 doubles both en suite (bath/shower).

Price: From £37.50 p.p. Single supp. £20.

Breakfast: Flexible.

Meals: Not available. Michelin-starred restaurants within walking distance.

Closed: Never.

The stupendous site and generous size of this early Georgian house reflect the status of the ancestor who built it in 1740. The present-day Salweys are farmers and Hermione's scrumptious food is based on home-reared beef and lamb and garden vegetables. The large softly-furnished bedrooms have antique chairs and modern bedding and one has a Louis XV bed. The Salweys are lovely interesting people and the estate even has a Georgian bath house near the trout lake.

Rooms: 1 twin and 1 double, en suite (bath); 1 double with private bathroom.

Price: £40 p.p. Single supp. £5.

Breakfast: Flexible.

Meals: Dinner £20 p.p.

Closed: 31 October-1 April.

House at bottom of Lower Broad Street, between Broadgate and Ludford Bridge.

Entry No: 371   Map no: 9

Patricia & Philip Ross
Number Twenty Eight
28 Lower Broad Street
Ludlow, Shropshire SY8 1PQ
Tel: 01584 876996
Fax: 01584 876860
e-mail: ross.no28@btinternet.com
Web: www.sawdays.co.uk

From Ludlow, over River Teme by traffic lights, 2nd right to Presteigne & Richard's Castle on B4361. After about 100 yards, drive is first right.

Entry No: 372   Map no: 9

Humphrey & Hermione Salwey
The Lodge
Ludlow
Shropshire SY8 4DU
Tel: 01584 872103
Fax: 01584 876126
Web: www.sawdays.co.uk

Leintwardine was once a Roman garrison; it is still in one of England's best defended, last unspoilt areas. This handsome former farmhouse is part 17th century, off a country lane so quiet that buzzards and deer are often seen close by. Log fires and beams, a sparkling communal dining table, a large garden bursting with colour, an orchard, welcoming hosts, modern comforts plus a certain elegance... all this amid a rare plethora of castles and historic towns. *Children over 10 welcome.*

Rooms: 1 double and 2 twins, en suite (shower); 1 double with private bathroom.

Price: £26-£29 p.p. Children 10-12, £13-£15. No single supp.

Breakfast: Flexible.

Meals: Dinner £17.50 p.p.

Closed: Christmas.

From Leintwardine, cross river and first right for Knighton. First left for Hereford and first right up narrow unmarked lane. House 300 yards on left.

Entry No: 373   Map no: 9

Hildegard & Graham Cutler
Lower House, Adforton
Leintwardine, Craven Arms
Shropshire SY7 0NF
Tel: 01568 770223
Fax: 01568 770592
e-mail: lowerhouse@sy7.com
Web: www.sy7.com/lowerhouse

The 14th-century French-style castle casts its spells over the house — you can see it from one of the guest bedrooms and the house's huge stone fireplace probably came from there. In the 16th century the house was a row of weaver cottages, today it is one thoroughly English home — interesting furniture, comfortable sofas, beautiful bits and pieces and paintings with stories to tell. From the drawing room you walk into garden where birdsong fills the scented air. Jane, charming and flexible, will look after you well. *Cot and highchair available for babies.*

Rooms: 1 double and 1 twin, sharing connecting bathroom (separate entrances). Possible extra double sharing bathroom with owner.

Price: £20 p.p. No single supp.

Breakfast: Flexible.

Meals: Good pub food a few yards away.

Closed: Christmas.

On A361 Frome/Shepton Mallet road, right to Nunney. Down hill to market square, left over humpback bridge and immediately left. House is first on right (2 Horn St).

Entry No: 374   Map no: 4

Jane Stagg
The Bell House
Nunney
Nr. Frome
Somerset BA11 4NP
Tel: 01373 836309
Fax: 01373 836309

Somerset

Rosalind, cheerful and chatty, is a geologist and a walking enthusiast, she knows a lot about the area. Animal lovers are especially welcome — there are sheep, goats, chickens, ducks and cats. The large Garden Suite has been adapted for wheelchair users. Accessible from its own private garden and with inglenook fireplace, the suite retains its 17th-century charm; the other rooms have a more modern feel. Wells Cathedral can be seen in a fold in the hills and you can walk there to hear evensong.

Rooms: Garden Suite (twin/double + extra single and adapted en suite shower); 2 doubles, en suite (1 bath, 1 shower); 1 en suite; 1 single & 1 twin/double sharing bathroom & separate wc.

Price: From £22 p.p.

Breakfast: Until 9am.

Meals: Available locally. Packed lunches & light snacks by arrangement.

Closed: Occasionally.

From Wells, A371 towards Shepton Mallet for 1 mile, then left onto B3139. In Dulcote, left at stone fountain. Farmhouse clearly marked, 4th on right.

Entry No: 375   Map no: 3

Rosalind Bufton
Manor Farm
Dulcote, Wells
Somerset BA5 3PZ
Tel: 01749 672125
Fax: 01749 672125
e-mail: rosalind.bufton@ntlworld.com
Web: www.wells-accommodation.co.uk

A more exquisite house would be hard to find. Phoebe, a shepherd, sought the perfect home for her flock and her (now grown) children: she found it. Terracotta walls, rugs, flagstones and brick — stunning. The antique beds have handmade mattresses, good linen and fat pillows and in the barn you have utter, luxurious, privacy. The indoor swimming pool gives on to the view, through a Gothic, arched window, and the house has featured in many magazines. It's magnificent. *Babies and children over 12 welcome.*

Rooms: Suite: double with drawing & dining room, plus 3 single rooms usually let to one party. Barn: huge double suite, with dressing room and kitchen/living area. Cider Cellar double, en suite.

Price: £130 per suite per night. Cider Cellar double £90 per room. Singles by arrangement.

Breakfast: Flexible.

Meals: Dinner, 3 courses, £25 p.p., by arrangement.

Closed: Never.

From Wells, A39 to Glastonbury. Left at North Wootton sign. Follow signs for West Pennard. At T-junc., right onto A361. After 500 yds, first left. Through tunnel of trees, house on left.

Entry No: 376   Map no: 3

Ms Phoebe Judah
Pennard Hill Farm, Stickleball Hill
East Pennard, Shepton Mallet
Somerset BA4 6UG
Tel: 01749 890221
Fax: 01749 890665
e-mail: phebejudah@aol.com
Web: www.sawdays.co.uk

The endearing intimacy of this 17th-century cottage puts you instantly at ease. The bedrooms are cosy and light; some look onto the busy village street, all have old family books. You eat well — local organic produce and home-made bread. Naturalists and walkers especially will love it, given the hosts' passion for local natural history. Malcolm has written a guide on walks from the garden gate, leading out onto the Mendip Hills and to the Somerset Levels. He will give you route notes and map, and transport luggage to your next stop.

Rooms: 1 twin, en suite (shower), 1 double, en suite (bath/shower); 1 double with private bathroom.

Price: £20 p.p. No single supp.

Breakfast: Until 9.30am.

Meals: Good food in pub opposite.

Closed: Christmas.

Wandering among the medieval outbuildings, you might almost imagin that you'd stumbled upon a museum: there's an ancient forge, bellows, a cide press, a pony trap and a threshing floor — not to mention Tony's collection of classic cars. The 18th-century farmhouse, with flagstone floors, old beams, pine panelling, country antique furniture and examples of Wendy's embroidery, is sunny and delightful. O the southern slopes of the Mendips, it i the perfect base for walks — if, that is, you're not lying in the garden, dozing under the old apple tree. *Children over 10 welcome.*

Rooms: 1 double, en suite (shower); 1 twin/double, en suite (bath); 1 double with private bath.

Price: £24-£28 p.p. Single supp. £10.

Breakfast: 8-9am.

Meals: Available nearby.

Closed: Christmas.

The house is in the village, on the A371 (Wells to Cheddar road), directly opposite the Westbury Inn.

Entry No: 377   Map no: 3

Malcolm & Linda Mogford
The Old Stores
Westbury-sub-Mendip
Wells, Somerset BA5 1HA
Tel: 01749 870817
Fax: 01749 870980
e-mail: MOGLIN980@aol.com
Web: www.sawdays.co.uk

From Wells towards Cheddar on A371. At Westbury-sub-Mendip pass Westbury Inn & Post Office Stores on right. House is 200 yards on, after lay-by on left.

Entry No: 378   Map no: 3

Tony & Wendy Thompson
Stoneleigh House
Westbury-sub-Mendip
Nr. Wells, Somerset BA5 1HF
Tel: 01749 870668
Fax: 01749 870668
e-mail: stoneleigh@dial.pipex.com
Web: www.sawdays.co.uk

Catherine is a Guide at Wells Cathedral and always delighted to take guests on a tour. Engaging and interested, she will give you fresh coffee in the cottagey kitchen, with pine table, a dresser hung with huge cups and saucers, dried flowers and views of fields. Guests have their own pretty sitting room. Upstairs, the bedroom is reached through your bathroom and has French-feel blue-stained bedheads and wardrobe, antique patchwork quilts and books. It's all exquisitely pretty and excellent value. Set in eight acres and in superb walking country. *Dogs welcome, grass tennis and croquet available.*

Rooms: 1 twin/double, en suite (bath/shower). Further twin available for members of same party.

Price: £22.50 p.p. Single supp. £5.

Breakfast: Flexible.

Meals: Available locally.

Closed: Christmas & New Year.

One of the grandest houses in this book, Pennard has been in Susie's family since the 17th century — the cellars date from then, the superstructure is stately, lofty Georgian — but the Deardens are delightfully unstuffy and welcoming. Guests have the run of the library, formal drawing room, billiards room and six acres of garden with a spring-fed pool to swim in. Or walk in 300 acres of cider orchards, meadows and woods. Susie was born and brought up here, and knows a lot about the area; multilingual Martin deals in antiques. It is warm, civilised with plain, properly unhotelly bedrooms.

Rooms: 1 double, en suite (shower), 1 twin, en suite (bath) and 1 twin/double with private bathroom.

Price: From £30 p.p. Single supp. by arrangement.

Breakfast: Flexible.

Meals: Good pubs and restaurants nearby.

Closed: Christmas.

A371 to middle of Croscombe. Right at red phone box and then immediately right into lane. House is up hill on left after 0.25 miles. Drive straight ahead into signed field.

Michael & Catherine Hay
Hillview Cottage
Paradise Lane
Croscombe, nr. Wells
Somerset BA5 3RL
Tel: 01749 343526
Fax: 01749 676134
e-mail: wells@alderking.co.uk

From Shepton Mallet south on A37, through Pylle, over the hill and next right to East Pennard. Pass church to T-junction at very top. House on left.

Martin & Susie Dearden
Pennard House
East Pennard, Shepton Mallet
Somerset BA4 6TP
Tel: 01749 860266
Fax: 01749 860266
e-mail: m.dearden@ukonline.co.uk
Web: www.sawdays.co.uk

The Good Life in the depths of Somerset: organic vegetables, home-made bread and marmalade, milk and eggs from the farm nearby. The Dowdings have returned to England from France — they ran a *Special Place* there, too — and have converted their farm's old stone barn into a super self-contained apartment. There's a continental feel to it all — you can do your own thing or have Susie cook breakfast for you in the main house. In the centre of the oak-floored sitting room is a woodburning stove and flower-filled bedrooms have oak floors and doors and exposed beams, treated with linseed to give a golden glow.

Rooms: 1 double, en suite (bath); 1 twin with private bathroom, let to one party at a time.

Price: £22-£25 p.p. Single supp. £5.

Breakfast: Until 9.30am or you can cook your own.

Meals: Available locally or you can cook your own.

Closed: Never.

From A303 to Wincanton. Turn onto A371 towards Castle Cary. Right to Shepton Montague. Right at x-roads by Montague Inn towards Redlynch. House first on right after church.

Entry No: 381   Map no: 3

Charles & Susie Dowding
Lower Farm
Shepton Montague
Wincanton
Somerset BA9 8JG
Tel: 01749 812253
e-mail: susiedowding@netscapeonline.co.uk

English to the core, this listed and charming Regency house has the feel of a small country hotel with flagged hall, high ceilings and long windows. The five bedrooms are decorated with good period furniture, fine bedspreads and elaborate drapes. First floor rooms feel grand, the second floor rooms, cosier. Roy is chatty and excellent company; ask him to show you the views from the Observatory at the top of the house. He's a jazz musician (clarinet), too, and a wildlife enthusiast: the grounds have recently been planted with thousands of trees and the lake stocked with exotic ducks and black swans.

Rooms: 1 four-poster, 1 twin, 1 double and 1 family room, all en suite (bath); 1 family room with private bath.

Price: £24.50-£37.50 p.p. Single occ. £45-£53.

Breakfast: Until 9am.

Meals: Available locally.

Closed: Christmas.

From London, M3 junc. 8, take A303. At Podimore roundabout take A372 to Somerton. Lynch is at junction of North Street and Behind Berry.

Entry No: 382   Map no: 3

Mr Roy Copeland
The Lynch Country House
Somerton
Somerset TA11 7PD
Tel: 01458 272316
Fax: 01458 272590
e-mail: the_lynch@talk21.com
Web: www.thelynchcountryhouse.co.uk

With huge flair the Burnhams have married old with new and sumptuousness with simplicity. Coir matting sits happily with dark, antique furniture; wrought-iron real candle chandelier and high-backed chairs give the dining room a sense of warm, pre-Raphaelite Gothic. Bedrooms are not flowery or fussy but uncluttered; linen is crisp, cotton robes soft. Jane is a keen cook; the garden yields herbs and vegetables, and breakfast includes Heal Farm sausages and bacon. You may not want to leave the deep comfort of the 300-year-old thatched cottage. *Children by arrangement.*

Rooms: 1 twin with private bath; 1 double, en suite (shower).

Price: £25 p.p. Single occ. £35.

Breakfast: Until 9am.

Meals: Dinner, £19 p.p.

Closed: Christmas.

The dining room with its crystal decanters, fine china and wooden window seat overlooks the flower-adorned stable. This is deeply rural, yet elegant. Philip and Susan are palpably happy here on the Somerset Levels, a rare natural wetlands habitat of unique tranquillity. One bedroom has pale yellow striped wallpaper and fine mahogany pieces and another is cream and rose with a cotton-covered sofa; both have garden views. The drawing room with a fine, stone hearth and grand piano has French windows to the gorgeous garden. *Babies and children over 12 welcome.*

Rooms: 1 twin and 1 double, both with private bathrooms.

Price: £30 p.p. Single supp. £5.

Breakfast: Flexible.

Meals: Dinner, £16-£20 p.p., by prior arrangement.

Closed: Christmas & New Year.

From Somerton Lake take B3153 for Langport. Turn right 2 miles on for Pitney just before Halfway Inn. Go through Pitney. House is last but one on right, with dark green railings.

Entry No: 383   Map no: 3

Peter & Jane Burnham
Estate Farmhouse
Pitney
Langport
Somerset TA10 9AL
Tel: 01458 250210
Fax: 01458 253227

From Langport, A372 through Aller and right at left-hand bend signed Beer. Pass Bere Farm on right and take first lane on left at stone barn.

Entry No: 384   Map no: 3

Philip & Susan Morlock
Beer Farm
Bere Aller
Langport
Somerset TA10 0QX
Tel: 01458 250285
Fax: 01458 250285

It was a happy landing here for Jane and Iain after 23 moves in 25 years. Their roots are now firmly planted and they love their local hamstone house; built in 1690 and surrounded by two acres of garden and paddock. Mullioned windows, National Trust paint colours and mahogany antiques; it's traditional with every comfort. French country feel bedrooms with carved headboards and handsome furniture; from the twin under the eaves you can glimpse the stream which marks the boundary. The most friendly hosts; keen gardeners will find a kindred spirit in Jane. *Children over 10 welcome.*

Rooms: 1 double, en suite (shower); 1 twin with private bathroom.

Price: £28 p.p. No single supp.

Breakfast: Flexible.

Meals: Dinner, £15-18 p.p., by prior arrangement. B.Y.O.

Closed: Christmas & New Year.

The village is a stone-and-thatch delight Courtfield, Grade II-listed, deep in the village but hidden in a fine, walled, two acre garden, is very much a family home Richard, a keen entomologist and painter, has filled the house with art, both his and his daughter's. There is a tennis court and a stunning conservatory; perfect for breakfast or for a candlelit dinner with views of the floodlit church. Valerie, whose Russian father was an hotelier in Cairo, has inherited his flair for cooking and entertaining. The bedrooms are large and delightful. One of our favourites. *Children over eight welcome.*

Rooms: 1 twin and 1 double, both with private bathroom.

Price: £28 p.p. Single supp. £10

Breakfast: Flexible.

Meals: Dinner £17.50 p.p. B.Y.O. wine

Closed: Christmas & New Year.

From A303 take A37 to Yeovil, up hill to big r'bout and follow signs to Thorne. Right at r'bout and straight across at next two crossroads. Take first right to village, house is first on right.

Entry No: 385   Map no: 3

Jane & Iain Galloway
Brooke House
Thorne Coffin, Yeovil
Somerset BA21 3PZ
Tel: 01935 433396
Fax: 01935 475556
e-mail: jane@logspt.demon.co.uk
Web: www.sawdays.co.uk

From A303, A356 south towards Crewkerne. Second left to Norton-sub-Hamdon. House in centre of village at foot of Church Lane.

Entry No: 386   Map no: 3

Richard & Valerie Constable
Courtfield
Norton-sub-Hamdon
Stoke-sub-Hamdon
Somerset TA14 6SG
Tel: 01935 881246
e-mail: val@courtfield.fsnet.co.uk
Web: www.sawdays.co.uk

Extremely pretty with its thatched roof and Strawberry Hill Gothic windows, this house will instantly cast its spell on you. Your hosts have created immense comfort; soft, large sofas in the guest sitting room, thick carpeting, easy chairs in the bedrooms and excellent meals using garden produce at house-party dinners. Carved Tudor oak beams in the sitting room and panelled passages speak of the house's history, and there are French doors from the dining room onto the sweeping lawns. In a tiny conservation hamlet surrounded by farmland, the peace is deep.

Rooms: 5 twins/doubles, all en suite bath/shower.

Price: From £37.50 p.p. Single supp. £10.50.

Breakfast: Flexible.

Meals: Dinner, 4 courses, £17.50 p.p., by prior arrangement.

Closed: Never.

The Parrys describe their cosy, comfortable, cottage as 'happy' and they take genuine pleasure in sharing it. Surrounded by beautifully kept (National Gardens Scheme) gardens and a cleverly-planted arboretum, within the folds of the Blackdown Hills (an AONB), this is a magical and peaceful place. Both your hosts are unpretentiously friendly and cheery people and Pam dishes up generous portions of fresh, delicious, country fare, either in the snug dining room or the airy conservatory. Simple décor and wonderful value.

Rooms: 1 family suite, en suite (bath); 1 double and 1 single (let only to members of same party) with private bath & separate wc.

Price: Per room: family suite, £50; double, £30; single, £24.

Breakfast: Until 9.30am.

Meals: Dinner, 2 courses, £10 p.p.; 3 courses, £12 p.p.

Closed: Perhaps Christmas Day.

At Horton Cross r'bout at junction of A303 and A358, take A358 towards Chard. After Donyatt, left signed Ilminster. After 1 mile, lane to right signed Cricket Malherbie. House on left after a mile, 200 yards past church.

Entry No: 387   Map no: 3

From Taunton, south on B3170, or from A30/A303, north on B3170. Turn west for Churchinford. Follow finger posts for Stapley.

Entry No: 388   Map no: 3

Michael Fry-Foley
The Old Rectory
Cricket Malherbie
Ilminster, Somerset TA19 0PW
Tel: 01460 54364
Fax: 01460 57374
e-mail: theoldrectory@malherbie.freeserve.co.uk
Web: www.malherbie.freeserve.co.uk

Pam Parry
Pear Tree Cottage
Stapley
Churchstanton, Taunton
Somerset TA3 7QA
Tel: 01823 601224
Fax: 01823 601224
e-mail: colvin.parry@virgin.net

If you have been to Johannesburg you may know their old Bay Tree Restaurant. Robert is a South African and as easy and interesting as they so often are. Lesley now cooks wonderful meals at the cottage and runs cookery courses, too. It is a delicious place; a perfect Somerset cottage with an apple orchard and views across fields to the lofty church. The interior is utterly in keeping; pine, coir carpets, straw table mats, wooden beams on the ceilings and a warm sense of fun. All this, and with such easy access to the M5. *Children over 10 welcome.*

Rooms: 1 twin, en suite (bath); 1 double, en suite (shower).

Price: £25-£28 p.p. Single supp. by arrangement.

Breakfast: Until 9am.

Meals: Supper or dinner available on request.

Closed: Christmas.

In 1992 the Ritchies fled London and headed for Somerset's lovely Quantock Hills to renovate this exquisite 17th-century farmhouse. Their philosophy is simple — why should visitors be any less comfortable on holiday than they are at home? Thus, their place is deliciously welcoming, with very pretty, fresh and large rooms looking over the cobbled courtyard or open fields. Breakfast will include home-baked bread and home-made jams. Try to stay for dinner which Charles and Jane prepare using fresh local ingredients.

Rooms: 1 twin with private bathroom, 1 double with private shower and 1 double, en suite (shower).

Price: £22.50-£25 p.p. Single supp. £5

Breakfast: Until 9am.

Meals: Dinner £22.50 p.p., supper £15 p.p., by arrangement.

Closed: Never.

Exit M5 at junc. 26 and take West Buckland road for 0.75 miles. First left just before Stone garage. Bear right; 3rd house at end of lane, below church.

Entry No: 389   Map no: 3

Lesley & Robert Orr
Causeway Cottage, West Buckland,
Wellington, Somerset TA21 9JZ
Tel: 01823 663458
Fax: 01823 663458
e-mail: orrs@westbuckland.freeserve.co.uk
members.tripod.com/~causeway_cottage/cause
way.htm

Leave M5 at junc. 25. A358 towards Minehead. Leave A358 at West Bagborough turning. Follow through village for 1.5 miles. Farmhouse third on left past pub.

Entry No: 390   Map no: 3

Charles & Jane Ritchie
Bashfords Farmhouse
West Bagborough
Taunton, Somerset TA4 3EF
Tel: 01823 432015
Fax: 01823 432520
e-mail: charlieritchie@netscapeonline.co.uk
members.netscapeonline.co.uk/charlieritchie

1,000 feet up on the Quantocks — glorious hills known, it seems, to few outside the South West. The views are long and the position beautiful, in 20 acres of fields, birdsong and woodland. The farmhouse has had 300 years to form its character: wooden panelling in the little guest sitting room, flagstone floors, beams, inglenook fireplace with woodburner and open fires. The house is kept meticulously by the very friendly Pamela who also makes all her own jams, marmalade and bread. The bedrooms are as comfortable as they are attractive. *Children over 10 welcome.*

Rooms: 2 doubles and 1 twin, en suite (1 bath, 2 showers).

Price: £23-£25 p.p. Single occ. £30.

Breakfast: Until 9.30am.

Meals: Pubs nearby.

Closed: Never.

Familiar with garderobes, piscinas and solars? If not, visit this remarkable Grade I-listed 15th-century farmhouse and be enlightened. Explore the West Bedroom with massive-timbered walls, a ceiling open to the beamed roof and a four-poster bed, and don't miss the oak panelled Gallery Bedroom with recently uncovered secret stairway. Feel baronial while seated for breakfast beside the Great hall's massive fireplace at the 16-ft oak table. Minimum disturbance to fabric and flavour and maximum atmosphere.

Rooms: 1 family room and 3 doubles, all en suite (shower &/or bath).

Price: £21-£28 p.p. Single occ. £32.

Breakfast: Until 9.30am.

Meals: Dinner available locally.

Closed: Never.

From Taunton, A358 north towards Williton/Minehead. Approx. 7 miles on, right for West Bagborough. Through village, up hill for 0.5 miles. Farm is on left.

Entry No: 391   Map no: 3

Mrs Pamela Smith
Tilbury Farm
Cothelstone
Taunton
Somerset TA4 3DY
Tel: 01823 432391

From Bridgwater, A39 west around Cannington. After second roundabout, follow signs to Minehead. Take first left after Yeo Valley creamery. Farm is first house on the right.

Entry No: 392   Map no: 3

Ann Dyer
Blackmore Farm
Cannington, Bridgwater
Somerset TA5 2NE
Tel: 01278 653442
Fax: 01278 653427
e-mail: dyerfarm@aol.com
Web: www.sawdays.co.uk

An unusual-looking house... so no surprise to discover that it was the romantic fantasy of a love-struck local man, George Carew; he built it for his mistress in 1830. The interior is as striking as the Italianate terracotta, triple-gabled exterior. Rosie and Luke — young and enthusiastic — have used 'Heritage' colours throughout the house and matched them well with lovely pieces of furniture, polished wood floors and rugs. The bedrooms are well proportioned with lovely views through leaded windows over the garden; they have luckily been left in their original shape, so all the rooms have a basin and share bathroom facilities.

Rooms: 2 doubles; 1 twin, sharing bathroom and extra wc.

Price: £22.50 p.p. Single supp. £2.50.

Breakfast: Until 9am.

Meals: Dinner, £15 p.p., by arrangement. Packed lunch £5 p.p.

Closed: Christmas & New Year.

A358 from Taunton for Minehead, for 9.5 miles (passing Flaxpool garage on left). Next right at brow of hill for Crowcombe, past church. House (with five-bar gate) 500 yds past pub on right.

Entry No: 393   Map no: 3

Rosie & Luke Macdonald
Hooks House
Crowcombe
Taunton
Somerset
Tel: 01984 618691
e-mail: lukemacdd@hookhouse.fsbusiness.co.uk

At the neck of the Brendons and at the foot of the Quantocks, Richard and Kate have set their cap at doing a professional job. At their 300-year-old corn mill, they like guests to gather for a drink before dinner at a formally-set table — breakfasts and suppers are ambitiously varied and all home-made. There are two bedrooms in the house — one pink and floral and a cooler, cream twin — and a three-bedroomed apartment. Our favourite is the Garden Suite, with a double bed and a wooden-floored sitting room with cream damask sofa bed. A steam railway and darting wildlife complete the idyll.

Rooms: 1 double and 1 twin in the house, each en suite (bath); 3-bed apartment and a Garden Suite for 2/4.

Price: £25.50-£37.50 p.p. Single supp. £10.

Breakfast: Flexible.

Meals: Dinner, 5 courses, £18.50 p.p. Packed lunch, £5-£8 p.p.

Closed: Never.

A358 Taunton to Minehead, left at sign to Stogumber & Bee World. Take 2nd left, then 1st right, down hill and over ford. House on left.

Entry No: 394   Map no: 3

R.D.J. Spicer & Mrs K.M. Butler
Northam Mill
Water Lane, Stogumber, Taunton
Somerset TA4 3TT
Tel: 01984 656916
Fax: 01984 656144
e-mail: bmsspicer@aol.com
Web: www.northam-mill.co.uk

The Quantocks are a treat and from here you have at least 38 square miles of great walking. Wildlife bounds, flits and creeps through the garden, woods and heathland: wild deer, hill ponies, badgers and almost 50 species of birds. Laze on the terrace or by the ornamental pond in the rambling garden and soak in the views to the Mendips and Glastonbury Tor. The rooms are comfortable (old and antique furniture, china and flowers); breakfast al fresco and dine by candlelight. Michael and Penny take only one party at a time and guests have their own sitting room.

Rooms: 1 twin/double, en suite (bath) and 1 double with private bathroom.

Price: From £25 p.p.

Breakfast: Flexible.

Meals: Supper from £7 p.p., or will drive to and from local pub. Packed lunch, £4 p.p. All by arrangement.

Closed: Never.

From Bridgwater, A39 through Cannington. Main road forks right (at Cottage Inn); straight on and over x-roads to Over Stowey. Left signed Ramscombe Forestry Trail. Keep to tarmac by turning right up hill. Cottage in front. Left through gates.

Michael & Penny Taylor-Young
Friarn Cottage
Over Stowey
Bridgwater
Somerset TA5 1HW
Tel: 01278 732870
Fax: 01278 732870
Web: www.sawdays.co.uk

The Vincents have made the house 'smile' again; handsome and Georgian, overlooking Watchet harbour and marina, this was once home to the land agent of the Wyndham estate. Both bedrooms are pleasing — the double has duck-egg blue walls and pretty floral curtains and looks down onto a Mediterranean courtyard; the twin, with blue chintz valances and matching curtains, has a sea view. Expect home-made cakes and biscuits and generous breakfasts; Susan holds cookery demonstrations. Within sight and sound of sea and steam railway, the garden is a lovely place to relax — among palm trees, ponds and burgeoning borders. *Children by arrangement.*

Rooms: 1 double with private bathroom and 1 twin, en suite (shower).

Price: From £22 p.p.

Breakfast: Flexible.

Meals: Available locally.

Closed: Christmas.

From railway station and footbridge in Watchet, follow up South Road (towards Doniford). After 50 yds, left into Beverly Drive. Wyndham House is 50 yds on left.

Susan & Roger Vincent
Wyndham House
4 Sea View Terrace
Watchet
Somerset TA23 0DF
Tel: 01984 631881
Fax: 01984 631881
e-mail: rhy@dialstart.net

The angular Gothic-ness of the 1860s house is a counterpoint to Janet's softness. A lane that winds to the centre of Dunster; Exmoor footpaths start behind the house. Janet loves people to explore by bike or foot and can help with luggage and transport. Bedrooms are quiet and simple — the double has a view to Blue Anchor Bay, the castle and church. Stripped pine, cream curtains, fresh flowers — it's homely. Garden fruit for breakfast and home-laid eggs. *Children by arrangement.*

Rooms: 1 double and 1 twin/double, both en suite (shower); 1 twin, en suite (bath).

Price: £20-£25 p.p. 10% discount for 3 nights or more. Single occ. £25.

Breakfast: Flexible.

Meals: Packed lunch from £3.50 p.p.

Closed: Christmas.

The picture-book Priory — 'Old' it is, 12th century old — leans against its church, has a rustic gate, a walled garden, flowers everywhere. Indoors, the old oak tables, flagstones, panelled doors, books and higgledy-piggledy corridors sing "there'll always be an England". But a perfect English house in a sweet Somerset village needs a touch of pepper. Cosmopolitan Jane has a red sitting room and some Mexican-style hand-painted wardrobes. House and hostess are at once friendly, elegant and homely.

Rooms: 1 ground-floor twin with private shower; 1 twin and 1 four-poster, both en suite (bath); 1 double with private shower.

Price: From £22.50-£32.50 p.p. Single supp. by arrangement.

Breakfast: Flexible.

Meals: Available locally.

Closed: Christmas.

From Willtion, A39 for Minehead for 8 miles. Left to Dunster. There, right fork into 'The Ball'. At T-junc. at end of road, right. House 75 yds on right.

Entry No: 397   Map no: 3

Mrs Janet Lamacraft
Higher Orchard
30 St. George's Street
Dunster
Somerset TA24 6RS
Tel: 01643 821915

Turn off A39 into village of Dunster, right at blue sign 'unsuitable for goods vehicles'. Follow until church. House is adjoined.

Entry No: 398   Map no: 3

Jane Forshaw
The Old Priory
Dunster
Somerset TA24 6RY
Tel: 01643 821540

A rambling, old, characterful (even down to the towel rails), pink house, garden-sheltered and tree-protected, Edgcott is a haven on the expansive heath. George Oakes painted those striking Strawberry Hill Gothic murals the full length of the sitting/dining room. Two bedrooms are on the small side and furniture tends towards basic style. Mrs Lamble is an easy-going gentle hostess, a dedicated gourmet who cooks with her own garden vegetables. She's also an Exmoor enthusiast; rides, walks, village visits galore will be suggested. You may also play the family piano.

Hugo owns the Rising Sun Hotel in Lynmouth and wife Pam's new venture must be the most luxurious B&B on Exmoor. Dark wood Heals beds have embroidered linen, fat pillows and sumptuous cushions; beside them are big bedside lamps and a tray with bottles of mineral water. Deep luxury. Downstairs — part 14th, part 18th century — there are real fires everywhere and fine prints and oils. Breakfast is a feast of freshly-squeezed orange juice, fresh fruit salad, butcher's sausages and bacon. The Jeunes have stables and a dressage arena — you can bring your horse — and a lovely garden.

Rooms: 1 twin and 1 double, each en suite (shower).

Price: £25-£30 p.p. No single supp.

Breakfast: Flexible.

Meals: Available locally.

Closed: Never.

Rooms: 1 twin and 1 double, both with private bathroom; 1 twin/double, en suite (bath/shower).

Price: £20-£23 p.p. No single supp.

Breakfast: Flexible.

Meals: Dinner, 4 courses, £15 p.p., by arrangement. B.Y.O. Also, excellent pubs in village.

Closed: Never.

From Dulverton, passing post office on left, take B3223 (signed Exford). Follow wooded road up hill for 2.5 miles. After sharp left bend, House signed on right.

Entry No: 399   Map no: 3

From Taunton take A358, then left on B3224 to Exford. There, take Porlock Lane. House is 0.25 miles from village.

Entry No: 400   Map no: 3

Pam & Hugo Jeune
Highercombe
Nr. Dulverton
Somerset TA22 9PT
Tel: 01398 323451
e-mail: 21pjuk@yahoo.com
Web: www.highercombe.co.uk

Gillian Lamble
Edgcott House
Exford
Somerset TA24 7QG
Tel: 01643 831495
Fax: 01643 831495

You can breakfast on the Walkerdine's narrow boat if it's fine and in the evening they will serve you dinner on board and take you for a gentle chug up the canal. The cottage takes its name from the nearby bridge on the Shropshire Union Canal (one of England's prettiest). Diana, who has just received an MBE for her work with deaf children, makes her own soup, bread and jam; David grows the vegetables. Bedrooms have floral curtains and covers — all is spotless and cosy with open fire, oak furniture and fresh flowers.

Rooms: 2 doubles, each with private bathrooms (1 bath & 1 shower).

Price: £25-£27.50 p.p. Single supp. £5

Breakfast: Flexible.

Meals: Dinner £15 p.p. Packed lunch £ p.p.

Closed: Christmas & New Year.

From Stafford, A518 signed Newport. 4 miles on, left at Haughton opp. church signed Church Eaton. There, right along main street. At end of village, left along Little Onn road. Over canal bridge and left after 300 yds. Cottage on left.

Entry No: 401   Map no: 9

Diana Walkerdine
Slab Bridge Cottage
Little Onn
Church Eaton
Staffordshire ST20 0AY
Tel: 01785 840220
Fax: 01785 840220
e-mail: dwalkerdine@allcomm.co.uk

Staffordshire

Copies of the National Geographic jostle with Lloyd George's war memoirs in this cosy listed Georgian town house full of books. Tomes on diversional therapies can be found in the shared bathroom, intimating Cindy's interests. Robin is an extrovert retired pottery artist who still loves to paint. Guests love them both. Breakfast is eaten on upholstered bench seats in a square bay window overlooking a garden with ginkgo, copper beech, chestnut, elm and oak trees; the sun streams in. An upright piano stands ready to be played. Bedrooms are warm with candlewick or damask covers.

Rooms: 1 double, en suite; 1 double and 1 twin, sharing bathroom.

Price: £16-£19 p.p. Single supp. £6-£8.

Breakfast: Flexible.

Meals: Variety of excellent restaurants within 2 minutes walk.

Closed: Christmas.

A lively, 15th-century, family home opposite Chartley Castle. Once through the Elizabethan black, studded oak door you see panelled walls and heavily-beamed ceilings. In the hall there is a warm, higgledy-piggledy feeling with umbrellas, walking sticks, wellies, riding boots and family pictures. The rooms are large, airy and flower-filled; in the four-poster bedroom the bathroom is hidden behind a secret panelled door. The floors are uneven, the bedrooms are excellent, the breakfasts hearty and your hosts delightful. *Children over 12 welcome.*

Rooms: 1 four-poster and 1 twin, both en suite (shower).

Price: From £25 p.p. Single supp. £5.

Breakfast: Until 9.30am.

Meals: Good food available locally.

Closed: Christmas & New Year.

From junc. 14 of M6, onto A34 for Stone. 5 miles on, at r'bout with Shell station, take 3rd exit to town centre and turn immediately right into Stafford Road. House is 150 yards on right.

Entry No: 402   Map no: 9

Cindy & Robin Busfield
Field House
Stafford Road
Stone
Staffordshire ST15 0HE
Tel: 01785 605712
Fax: 01785 605322

Halfway between Stafford & Uttoxeter on A518, just past Chartley Castle ruin on left and at top of the hill, on right.

Entry No: 403   Map no: 9

Sarah Allen
Chartley Manor Farm
Chartley
Nr. Stafford
Staffordshire ST18 0LN
Tel: 01889 270891
Web: www.sawdays.co.uk

Guardhouse, moat, turrets: a pink crenellated castle c.1270 awaits you. The interior is Jacobean with vast, oak-panelled drawing and dining rooms, all with massive carved fireplaces. Upstairs, billiards and pool in an immense room; everything here is on a superlative scale. Bedrooms are panelled and romantic, bathrooms excellent. Despite the suit of armour, weapons, art and delicate carved pieces from the East, this is very much a home rather than a museum. A remarkable place; relax into it and let osmosis do its work. Two restored stone turrets for self-catering also available.

Rooms: 3 four-posters, all en suite (1 bath/shower, 2 bath & shower); 2 self-catering turrets, each for 2/4 with living room, dining area, bathroom and kitchenette.

Price: £38-£44 p.p. Singles charged at room rate. Turrets from £60 per night.

Breakfast: Until 9.30am.

Meals: Available locally.

Closed: 1 November-February. Self-catering always available.

Caverswall is signed, near Blythe Bridge, just off A50. Take M1 junc. 23A, or M6 junc. 14 & 15. Entrance to Castle between two churches in village.

Entry No: 404   Map no: 9

Yvonne Sargent
Caverswall Castle
Caverswall
Staffordshire ST11 9EA
Tel: 01782 393239
Fax: 01782 394590
e-mail: yasargent@hotmail.com
Web: www.sawdays.co.uk

An oak-panelled, four-postered Tudor retreat only two miles from Alton Towers. This is an enchanting, rambling, farmhouse, the kind of time capsule you can't simulate: oak timber, stone, tapestry drapes, curios, pewter and books galore. There are gorgeous, almost grand, lawned grounds, full of birdsong, and a summerhouse, tennis and croquet. Rare breed cattle graze peacefully. Rooms have majestic four-poster beds (with good mattresses) and great views. Chris and Margaret are busy, informal people and the attitude here is very much 'stay as friends'.

Rooms: 3 doubles, all en suite (1 with shower and 2 with baths).

Price: £23-£26 p.p. Single supp. £3-£

Breakfast: Until 9.30am.

Meals: Available locally.

Closed: Christmas Eve/Day.

From Uttoxeter, B5030 for Rocester & Alton Towers. By JCB factory, left onto B5031. At T-junc. after church, right onto B5032 & over bridge. First left signed Prestwood. Farm is 0.75 miles on right.

Entry No: 405   Map no: 9

Chris & Margaret Ball
Manor House
Prestwood
Nr. Denstone, Uttoxeter
Staffordshire ST14 5DD
Tel: 01889 590415
Fax: 01335 342198
Web: www.sawdays.co.uk

Our first inspector was so impressed that she popped back for a riding lesson. "Utterly charming people," wrote the second. They are devoted to all things horsey and love eventing and dressage. It is gorgeous riding country, with vast views. The place is full of bird-life, dogs, cats and the ubiquitous horses. It is all you might dream of from a B&B: a 'working' home, dining room with Welsh dresser and grandfather clock, a kitchen with Aga and pine table, fruit from the garden and home-made jam. You pass through the Denstone school grounds to get here.

Rooms: 1 twin, en suite (bath); 2 doubles sharing private bathroom.

Price: £25 p.p.

Breakfast: Until 9am.

Meals: Pubs and restaurants available locally.

Closed: Christmas.

In village, follow signs to Denstone College and enter grounds. Left in front of College buildings. Continue for 300 yards to stud.

Entry No: 406   Map no: 9

Phyl Price
Denstone Stud and Riding Centre
Hall Riddings
Denstone
Staffordshire ST14 5HW
Tel: 01889 591472
Fax: 01889 591472

A classic of its kind, just what you expect from an old vicarage in Suffolk, run by Jane, who adores her house and garden. There's a fine Pembroke table in the flagstoned hall, a large open log fire in the sitting/dining room, a long refectory table covered in magazines like County Life and The Field, a comfortable sofa, a piano and family photos and hunting scenes. Bedrooms are large, chintzy and handsomely furnished. It is an elegant, pretty, traditional country-house England. Jane grows her vegetables and keeps hens and house with equal talent. *Children over seven welcome.*

Rooms: 2 twins, each with private bathroom; 1 single room off one of the twins.

Price: From £27 p.p. Single £28. Single occ. £35.

Breakfast: Flexible.

Meals: Dinner £15 p.p. BYO wine. Packed lunch £3 p.p.

Closed: Christmas Day.

From Cambridge, take A1307 towards Haverhill. Left to Withersfield. At T-junction, left. Almost 3 miles on, high yew hedge and at 'Concealed Entrance' sign on left, sharp turn into drive.

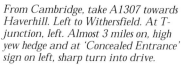

Entry No: 407   Map no: 11

Ms Jane Sheppard
The Old Vicarage
Great Thurlow
Newmarket
Suffolk CB9 7LE
Tel: 01440 783209
Fax: 01638 667270

Suffolk

The Cromwellian General Fairfax owned the fireplace; it is in the dining room — splendid, with carved stone pillars and faces, sumptuous oak panelling and massive moulded beams. The hall has panelling dated 1617 and a fine fireplace. It is a beautiful house, rich in interest, delicate, but lived in, and with lots of family photos. The bedroom has an ornate Tudor four-poster, sagging beams and good views. The twin room is in the attic, with uneven oak floors, great views and a romantic garret mood. Diana is exceptionally charming, and so is her lovely garden.

Rooms: 1 four-poster and 1 twin, each with private bathroom.

Price: Four-poster, £32 p.p., twin £27 p.p.

Breakfast: Until 9.30am.

Meals: Available locally.

Closed: Christmas.

Leave Long Melford on the Clare road, turn right to Stansted (signed) and right again at village pub. After 0.5 miles, house is set back on right.

Entry No: 408   Map no: 11

Diana Banks
Bretteston Hall
Stanstead
Sudbury
Suffolk CO10 9AT
Tel: 01787 280504
Fax: 01787 280504

You may help yourself to the sherry on the oak dresser (17th century, no less), a hint of the generosity of the house. It is 15th century, timber-framed, thatched, as pretty as can be and immaculate inside with fine antique furniture and fresh flowers. Guests have their own sitting rooms: shelves of books and open log fires. Home-laid eggs for breakfast, local bacon and home-made bread. The impeccable bedrooms have plain walls, good furniture, goose down duvets, a decanter of Madeira, fresh fruit, sweets and Penhaligons toiletries. Delightful people, too.

Rooms: 1 twin/double, en suite (bath & shower); 1 double with small sitting-room and en suite bathroom.

Price: £28-£32.50 p.p. Single occ. £35-£45.

Breakfast: Flexible.

Meals: Dinner, £22.50 p.p., occasionally available. Excellent local pubs & restaurants.

Closed: Occasionally.

From Bury St. Edmunds, A413 towards Haverhill, then B1066 towards Glemsford for 6 miles to Hartest. After 30mph signs continue for approx. 0.25 miles, lane is on left (signed Cross Green) on sharp double bend.

Entry No: 409   Map no: 11

Bridget & Robin Oaten
The Hatch
Pilgrims Lane
Cross Green, Hartest
Suffolk IP29 4ED
Tel: 01284 830226
Fax: 01284 830226

A paean to architecture — Tudor, Queen Anne, Georgian and Edwardian — this is a perfectly-preserved and recently restored Grade I-listed house. Ionic and Corinthian columns on fireplaces, Jacobean and Georgian panelling, shuttered windows. All of the large bedrooms have bathrooms with original fittings. The delicious breakfasts are as splendid as the beautiful walled garden and two majestic plane trees — possibly the oldest and tallest in East Anglia. The house was previously owned by the novelist Norah Lofts who was inspired to write many of her books from here. The whole place is stunning.

Rooms: 1 double, 1 four-poster, 1 twin/double, all en suite.

Price: £45 p.p. Single occ. £55.

Breakfast: Flexible.

Meals: By arrangement or available locally.

Closed: Never.

Don't be fooled by the plain exterior. Diana was once a stage manager in the London theatre and it shows; she is outgoing, fun, brilliant with people and has a marvellous sense of taste. The bedrooms are perfect, with attractive duvets and curtains, pale walls and lots of nice touches. The terracotta of the sitting room walls is stunning. The garden is surprisingly large, with a terrace, fishpond, lawn and herbaceous borders — very pretty; sit and enjoy it. To cap all this Diana will cook you mouth-watering dinners.

Rooms: 1 twin and 2 doubles, all en suite (shower or bath).

Price: From £25 p.p. Single occ. from £40.

Breakfast: Flexible.

Meals: Dinner £15 p.p. B.Y.O. wine.

Closed: Christmas & January, but open New Year.

From A14, take Bury Central exit and follow brown signs towards Historic City Centre. At r'bout, 1st left into Northgate St. House on right, shortly after traffic lights. Courtyard parking at far end of house.

Entry No: 410   Map no: 11

Joy Fiennes
Northgate House
Northgate Street
Bury St. Edmunds
Suffolk IP33 1HQ
Tel: 01284 760469
Fax: 01284 724008
e-mail: northgate_hse@hotmail.com

From Sudbury, take B1115 to Lavenham. Pass Swan Hotel on right, take next right into Market Lane, cross Market Place, turn right, then left. Red House is on right next to school.

Entry No: 411   Map no: 11

Diana Schofield
The Red House
29 Bolton Street
Lavenham
Suffolk CO10 9RG
Tel: 01787 248074

An impressive, beautifully decorated and furnished Grade I-listed house dating from the 13th century. The hub of this beamed, oak-floored, high-ceilinged family home is the huge stone-flagged Great Hall where you relax among huge sofas and cushions to gaze into the enormous inglenook fireplace. The bright, many-windowed, beam-vaulted bedrooms have handmade mattresses and beds, pure cotton sheets and flowers everywhere; each has its own character. Wonderful details including intriguing Elizabethan wall paintings. *Children over 10 welcome.*

Rooms: 1 double and 1 twin/double, both en suite (bath/shower); 3 four-poster, en suite (bath & showers).

Price: £39-£54 p.p. Single occ. £59-£69.

Breakfast: Until 9am Mon-Fri; 9.30am Sat-Sun.

Meals: Packed lunch and dinner, £25 p.p., by arrangement.

Closed: Christmas & New Year.

Turn at The Swan onto Water St then right after 50 yards into private drive to the Priory car park.

Entry No: 412   Map no: 11

Tim & Gilli Pitt
Lavenham Priory
Water Street, Lavenham, Sudbury
Suffolk CO10 9RW
Tel: 01787 247404
Fax: 01787 248472
e-mail: mail@lavenhampriory.co.uk
Web: www.lavenhampriory.co.uk

This little pink cottage was once a pub, but has been tenderly restored to create a pretty, family house; your room, in the converted barn, will appeal to the romantic in you. Sue welcomes you with a glass of Madeira by the enormous inglenook fire, then takes you through the neat little garden full of honeysuckle, aqualegia and Canterbury bells to the barn. A stable door opens into the primrose yellow bedroom with exposed beams and soaring rafters. The chintz-headed king size bed is covered in cushions, there are fresh flowers on the table and watercolours of Mauritius on the walls. Stunning!

Rooms: 1 double, en suite (shower).

Price: £27.50 p.p. Single supp. £7.50.

Breakfast: Flexible.

Meals: Packed lunch, £3 p.p. Other meals available in Lavenham.

Closed: Never.

From Sudbury, take B1115 to Lavenham. Pass Swan Hotel on right, take next right into Market Lane. Straight across Market Place into Prentice Street. House is last on right at bottom of hill.

Entry No: 413   Map no: 11

Mrs Sue Wade
Anchor House
Prentice Street
Lavenham
Suffolk CO10 9RD
Tel: 01787 249018
Fax: 01787 249018
e-mail: suewade@tinyworld.co.uk

Keen conservationists and historians, Juliet and Christopher manage the farm, the wildlife habitats and archaeological sites and serve their own produce for supper in the main hall and a feast of bantam eggs and home-grown bacon and sausages for breakfast. In a relaxed family atmosphere, there's plenty to do: nature trails, planned local walks etc... and the Hawkins have a flexibility that will appeal to all. A glorious place, unspoiled 16th century and lived in by the family for 300 years. Period furniture, lovely bedrooms overlooking a wildflower meadow and beautiful walled garden, and Juliet, a bundle of energy and enthusiasm.

Rooms: 1 double/family room with basin, 1 twin and 1 single/twin, all sharing private bathroom.

Price: £25-£30 p.p. Reduction for longer stays.

Breakfast: Until 9.30am.

Meals: Dinner, £12-£15 p.p., available on request. B.Y.O. wine.

Closed: Christmas.

From Lavenham, A1141 towards Monks Eleigh. After 2 miles, right to Milden. At crossroads, right to Sudbury on B1115. The Hall's long drive is 0.25 miles on left.

Entry No: 414   Map no: 11

Juliet & Christopher Hawkins
The Hall
Milden, Nr. Lavenham
Suffolk CO10 9NY
Tel: 01787 247235
Fax: 01787 247235
e-mail: gjb53@dial.pipex.com
Web: www.sawdays.co.uk

Janus-like, it looks both ways, Georgian to the front and richly-beamed 1485 Tudor behind. One of the arched Tudor fireplaces in the house was found with the help of Alfred Munnings R.A., a frequent visitor. The house has high ceilings and long windows, so is filled with light. The bedrooms are elegant, formal and very English: flower-patterned wallpaper, padded bedheads, thick curtains, armchairs, standard lamps, lots of books... pretty and full of thoughtful touches. There is a walled garden with a vine-filled greenhouse.

Rooms: 1 twin with bathroom & separate wc; 1 double, en suite (shower).

Price: £26 p.p. Single occ. £30.

Breakfast: Until 9.30 am.

Meals: Available nearby.

Closed: Christmas.

Take B1115 from Sudbury towards Lavenham for 3.5 miles. Turn right to Lt. Waldingfield. House is on left, 200 yards beyond The Swan.

Entry No: 415   Map no: 11

Mrs Susan T del C Nisbett
Wood Hall
Little Waldingfield, Nr. Lavenham
Suffolk CO10 0SY
Tel: 01787 247362
Fax: 01787 248326
e-mail: nisbett@nisbett.enta.net
Web: www.sawdays.co.uk

Rachel Thomas has thought of everything and the result is an idyllic home in an exquisite setting. Guests have the run of this gorgeous 15th-century house: a warm, light drawing room with a grand piano, oak beams, open fireplace; a sun room to catch the evening light; cosy dining room with Suffolk tiles and inglenook fireplace. The guest bedroom area is self-contained, with a king-size bed and many thoughtful touches. Low, leaded windows overlook the peaceful gardens which include a grass tennis court. Bicycles are available. Rachel is a delight — and a great cook.

Rooms: 1 king-size with private bath, shower & wc.

Price: From £25-£27 p.p. Single occ. £30.

Breakfast: Until 9.30am.

Meals: Dinner, £15 p.p., by arrangement. B.Y.O. wine. Also excellent local pubs.

Closed: Christmas-New Year.

Romantically decorated, oak-beamed bedrooms, one with its own ground-floor entrance. A charming sitting room with inglenook fireplace is available to 'long stayers'. The house itself, dating from the 16th century, is lovely with a walled garden, 400-year-old pond, beautiful lawns and — best of all — the River Box meandering through the grounds. Kiftsgate roses cascade over the huge and very splendid adjacent 17th-century barn. A fairytale house in a fairytale setting. Your hosts are attentive and friendly and your privacy is respected. Hard tennis court available.

Rooms: 1 ground floor twin/double and 1 double, all en suite (bath); 1 single with private bathroom.

Price: £30 p.p.

Breakfast: Until 9.30am.

Meals: Available at excellent local pubs.

Closed: Christmas-New Year.

Approx. 4 miles between Hadleigh & A12 on country road, 2 miles from Shelley & 1 mile from Polstead. Ring for details as many approaches possible!

Entry No: 416   Map no: 12

Rachel & Richard Thomas
Sparrows
Shelley
Ipswich
Suffolk IP7 5RQ
Tel: 01206 337381
e-mail: thomas@sparrows.freeserve.co.uk
Web: www.sawdays.co.uk

3 miles from the A12, on the B1068 between Higham and Stoke-by-Nayland. House on south side of road, 300 yards east of Thorington Street.

Entry No: 417   Map no: 12

Patrick & Jennie Jackson
Nether Hall
Thorington Street
Stoke-by-Nayland
Suffolk CO6 4ST
Tel: 01206 337373
Fax: 01206 337496
e-mail: patrick.jackson@talk21.com

This Elizabethan jewel is snug beside the equally lovely church. The beautiful drawing room with carved pine mantelpiece and marble hearth faces south over the water meadow. There, cattle graze contentedly; beyond, lazily flow the Rivers Brett and Stour. Blue and white Spode china, silver cutlery, embroidered sheets and fresh fruit and flowers add to the architectural elegance, yet this is a welcoming house. Meg Parker really enjoys guests of all ages; she will lend you a rowing boat, canoe or punt. Or you may fish, play tennis or swim in the pool.

Rooms: 1 double, en suite; 1 twin/double plus single with private bathroom; 1 large twin with bathroom nearby.

Price: £25-£29 p.p. Single occ. £28-£35.

Breakfast: Flexible.

Meals: Excellent places nearby.

Closed: Never.

West off A12 at Stratford St. Mary. House is on left, opposite church sign, 1 mile down Higham road. The house has pink timbers & a sign on the wall.

Entry No: 418   Map no: 12

Meg Parker
The Old Vicarage
Higham
Nr. Colchester
Suffolk CO7 6JY
Tel: 01206 337248

A beautifully-proportioned house in 7.5 acres of gardens, meadows and woodland. The meadow is a County Wildlife site with orchids and a carpet of wild flowers. Cindy is young and energetic, with enough enthusiasm for her family and her guests. Flagstoned hall, a large oak table in a striking burgundy dining room and a stunning sitting room with French windows. The bedrooms are well furnished and have maps, books, radio, fresh flowers and garden views; one has a wrought-iron four-poster with beautiful embroidered linen. Bathe by candlelight in excellent bathrooms.

Rooms: 1 double room, and 1 single (with basin) sharing adjacent bathroom 1 double, en suite (bath).

Price: Double £27-£29 p.p.; Single £20. Fri & Sat £2 p.p. extra.

Breakfast: Flexible.

Meals: Dinner, 2 courses, £14 p.p., or 3 courses, £21 p.p., by arrangement. B.Y.O. wine. Lunch & packed lunch by request.

Closed: Never.

From A12 Woodbridge bypass, exit at roundabout signed Orford and Melton. Follow for 1 mile to lights; there, turn right and house is immediately on right.

Entry No: 419   Map no: 12

Mrs Lucinda de la Rue
Melton Hall
Woodbridge
Suffolk IP12 1PF
Tel: 01394 388138
Fax: 01394 388982
e-mail: delarue@meltonh.fsnet.co.uk
Web: www.sawdays.co.uk

This is deeply special, the remains of an Augustinian monastery often visited by Mary Tudor, breathtaking, a tour-de-force by a gifted designer who loves the old stones of the place. Decorative stonework clasps the windows, the dining room soars with vaulting and is filled with light. A stripped oak floor, stone pillars and fireplace for the dining room — cloister-like, and fabulous. 47 steps lead up to cascades of damask, huge stone-arched windows, sea-grass matting... the highest standards but fun, too. Frances, artist and musician, is delightful; the area is silent but for the call of the birds. Come.

Rooms: 1 large twin with private bathroom (down small staircase); 1 large double, en suite (shower); 1 small double, en suite (bath & shower).

Price: £30-£37.50 p.p. Single supp. £15. Brochure on request.

Breakfast: Flexible.

Meals: Dinner by arrangement. Several restaurants nearby.

Closed: Occasionally.

From A12 at Woodbridge, take B1084 towards Orford. In Butley village at the Oyster Inn, take Hollesley road for 1 mile to x-roads. Private entrance to Priory on immediate right after x-roads.

Entry No: 420   Map no: 12

Frances Cavendish
Butley Priory
Butley, Nr. Woodbridge
Suffolk IP12 3NR
Tel: 01394 450046
Fax: 01394 450482
e-mail: headoffice@bella-figura.co.uk
Web: www.name.is/butley.priory

Wrap-around sea-views — you are almost on the beach and the setting is out of *Orlando and the Marmalade Cat*. Phil (from Zimbabwe) and Juliet are easy-going hosts, and enjoy sharing this very special place. The furniture is Victorian, some mahogany, some walnut, the colours soft, the bedlinen the sort you always meant to buy at home. The white cotton crocheted bedspreads come from the market at Victoria Falls. There are old things, good taste, books and magazines galore, fresh milk on the morning tea tray, home-made biscuits, rugs on wooden floors and a special light from every window. You can borrow bikes, play table tennis in the cellar, sail. Perfect.

Rooms: 1 double and 1 twin, both en suite.

Price: £29.50-£32.50 p.p. Single occ. £49-£55.

Breakfast: Until 9.30am.

Meals: Packed lunch available. Dinner by arrangment.

Closed: Never.

From Ipswich take A12 north. Turn right onto A1094 after 20 miles. Ocean House is in the centre of Aldeburgh seafront with parking outside.

Entry No: 421   Map no: 12

Juliet & Phil Brereton
Ocean House
25 Crag Path
Aldeburgh
Suffolk IP15 5BS
Tel: 01728 452094
Fax: 01728 453909
e-mail: jbreroh@aol.com

Off to a flying start, just five minutes from the Snape Maltings and the Aldeburgh Festival, but a house worth including anywhere. It is a beamy old farmhouse, with a good 16th-century slope to the floors and two lovely bedrooms with armchairs, attractive furniture, books and fresh flowers. There are views over the four acres of garden and woodland, with spectacular snowdrops and daffodils in early spring. The entrance is most attractive too, the hall opening into the dining room, with fresh flowers on the large old dining table and a fine open fireplace, lit on winter mornings.

Rooms: 1 twin, with private bathroom; 1 double, en suite (bath).

Price: £25 p.p.

Breakfast: 8-10 am or by arrangement.

Meals: Available locally.

Closed: Christmas & New Year.

With enthusiasm and good taste, Jane is restoring her 16th-century Tudor farmhouse in deepest, softest Suffolk. Partly moated, and with a thatched summerhouse, it has 17th-century additions, an abundance of beams, fleur de lys mouldings and, on the bressaumer beam above the fireplace, intriguing 'witch' markings. Fresh flowers everywhere and the decoration is restrained and stylish. The house has mostly seagrass flooring and splashes of chintzy colour. Rooms are let only to one party. Jane was a professional cook; stay in for dinner.

Rooms: 1 double and 1 twin, sharing private bathroom & shower.

Price: £25 p.p. No single supp.

Breakfast: Flexible.

Meals: Dinner, £15-£20 p.p., by prior arrangement.

Closed: Christmas & New Year.

From A12 south of Saxmundham, take B1121 signed to Benhall. First left at crossroads into Grays Lane. House is 45m on left.

Entry No: 422　　　　　Map no: 12

Virginia Reed
Benhall Cottage
Grays Lane
Benhall, Saxmundham
Suffolk IP17 1HZ
Tel: 01728 602359
Fax: 01728 602359

From A1120 at Earl Soham, take Kenton road and follow signs to Monk Soham for approx. 2 miles. Take right fork at top of hill and house is second entrance on right.

Entry No: 423　　　　　Map no: 12

Jane & Peter Cazalet
Monk Soham Hall
Monk Soham
Nr. Woodbridge
Suffolk IP13 7EN
Tel: 01728 685178
Fax: 01728 685944

You can see the wooden runners for the early window shutters, and the 12th-century moat is listed. It is a gorgeous old house, 13th century in parts, with sloping floors and unstained beams. The dining room, for the candlelit dinners at the large table, was once the dairy. The family room has a billiard table and toy cupboard, and the sitting room a baby grand, open fire and lots of books. There's a tennis court in the large garden. Elizabeth is both delightful and generous: home-made cake on arrival, local honey, home-made bread and marmalade for breakfast.

Rooms: 2 twins and 1 double, sharing bathroom. Extra wc available.

Price: £20 p.p. No single supp. Children 10-15, £10-£15.

Breakfast: Flexible.

Meals: Dinner and supper available on request (24 hrs notice preferred). B.Y.O. wine.

Closed: 13 December-13 January.

Michael's natural flair for interior design is reflected throughout the house, from the dramatic window treatments to the ingenious, concealed bathrooms. Hope House is a Grade II-listed 17th-century gentleman's residence, with 15th-century timber-framed origins. The bedrooms, with large armchairs and crisp, cotton sheets, are deeply comfortable. The elegant, panelled drawing room is decorated in yellows and blues and has lovely plump sofas. In summer, the scent of garden flowers fills the room and there's a lovely sunny terrace, too. Michael loves house-parties, so why not come with friends?

Rooms: 2 doubles and 1 twin, all en suite (shower).

Price: £35-£65 p.p.

Breakfast: Flexible.

Meals: Dinner, for 6 or more (you can invite friends), and packed lunch, by arrangement.

Closed: Never.

Take A1120 (Yoxford to Stowmarket) to Dennington. B1116 north for approx. 3 miles. Farm on right 0.9 miles north of Bell pub.

Entry No: 424   Map no: 12

Elizabeth Hickson
Grange Farm
Dennington
Woodbridge
Suffolk IP13 8BT
Tel: 01986 798388
Web: www.sawdays.co.uk

From A12 in Yoxford, A1120 towards Peasenhall. House is 0.5 miles on the left, set back from road.

Entry No: 425   Map no: 12

Michael Block
Hope House
High Street
Yoxford
Suffolk IP17 3HP
Tel: 01728 668281
e-mail: hopehouseyoxforduk@compuserve.com

It is the sort of place whose address, if you are in the village for the day, you scrawl hopefully on a scrap of paper. Walberswick is enchanting, and Ferry House is, too: built in the 1930s for a playwright, using a butterfly design to catch the light, it has Art Deco touches, hand-painted tiles, simple but pretty rooms, fresh flowers everywhere, lots of books and a sense of fun. Make your own toast at breakfast (a nice touch). There's a warm cloakroom for wet birdwatchers' clothes and a welcoming glass of sherry. Your hostess is as nice as her village. *Children over 10 welcome.*

Rooms: 1 double with en suite wc & basin and 2 singles sharing wc & basin and a guest bathroom.

Price: From £18 p.p.

Breakfast: Until 9.30am.

Meals: Dinner available locally. Packed lunch available on request.

Closed: Christmas week.

From A12 take B1387 to Walberswick. Ferry House is on the left at far end of village, near the river.

Entry No: 426   Map no: 12

Cathryn Simpson
Ferry House
Walberswick
Southwold
Suffolk IP18 6TH
Tel: 01502 723384
Fax: 01502 723384

Irresistible: a listed Jacobean farmhouse with Georgian additions, meticulously restored, oozing with character, both ancient and modern and in a very quiet hamlet with a 12th-century thatched church. Sarah, well-travelled and entertaining, has created a relaxed atmosphere in which you feel entirely at home. Let her cook for you — she does this excellently from her Aga-warm kitchen — using local ingredients. The bedrooms have gorgeous fabrics, fresh flowers and linen sheets. One has a medieval bedstead, with carved head- and foot-boards; all are peaceful. Plans are afoot for two en suite bathrooms.

Rooms: 1 double, 1 single and 1 twin, sharing one bathroom (bath & shower).

Price: From £24-£35 p.p.

Breakfast: Flexible.

Meals: Dinner by arrangement.

Closed: Christmas.

Take A12 towards Wangford. Turn left signed Stoven/Uggeshall. Farmhouse is first on left before church.

Entry No: 427   Map no: 12

Sarah Jupp
Church Farmhouse
Uggeshall
Southwold
Suffolk NR34 8BD
Tel: 01502 578532
Fax: 01953 888306
e-mail: sarahjupp@compuserve.com

This lovely old farm — 400 acres of mixed arable and dairy — is Suffolk at its rural best. At the end of a half-mile drive, the house is 16th century and as comfortable as it is unpretentious. The rooms are generous, with plenty of books and pictures, armchairs, beams... deliciously cosy. Guests have their own sitting room with an open fire, overlooking the patio and garden (home-grown vegetables and fruits are often served at dinner in the beamed dining room). You can walk to the pub, and Southwold and the sea are eight miles away. Pat is delightful and loves having people to stay.

Rooms: 1 double, en suite (bath); 1 twin, en suite (shower) and 1 twin/double with private bathroom.

Price: £18-£24 p.p. Single supp. £4.

Breakfast: 8.30-9am.

Meals: Dinner & packed lunch available on request.

Closed: Never.

These old Suffolk farmhouses combine bricks and beams in the softest way. This one, 16th century, is no exception; stay to enjoy it all day if you wish. It is old-fashioned yet friendly, warm and cottagey, with lots of beams and antique furniture and William Morris-type floral sofas and chairs. The dining room is a treat, once a cheese-room. You can wander in and out of the large kitchen for a chat with Rosemary, the kindest of women, but you have your own wing, so can be private. Four miles away is Wingfield Old College and gardens, home of the arts summer festival and, seven miles away, Bressingham gardens.

Rooms: 2 doubles and 1 twin, each with private adjacent bathroom.

Price: From £23.50 p.p. Single occ. from £26.

Breakfast: Flexible.

Meals: Dinner available locally.

Closed: Christmas week.

From A12, take A144 Halesworth road. In Bramfield turn off by Queen's Head on Walpole road. Farm is 0.75 miles on right.

Entry No: 428   Map no: 12

Patricia Kemsley
Broad Oak Farm
Bramfield
Halesworth
Suffolk IP19 9AB
Tel: 01986 784232
Web: www.sawdays.co.uk

From Scole/A140, right onto A143 towards Great Yarmouth. After 7 miles, right at Harleston onto B1116 to Fressingfield. Pass church and Fox & Goose on left. At top of hill, right, then left into Priory Road.

Entry No: 429   Map no: 12

Stephen & Rosemary Willis
Priory House
Priory Road
Fressingfield, Eye
Suffolk IP21 5PH
Tel: 01379 586254
Fax: 01379 586254

A real sense of history here — this unusual house contains part of a 13th-century Bishop's Palace and still has wall paintings from that period in the Rose Garden room. The house stands within a four-acre moated enclosure complete with ruined gatehouse. Pure magic! Part of a 450-acre working farm, it has a deep emphasis on wildlife and countryside conservation; there are hens, too, and five circular walks to try on the estate. The house itself is eccentric and charming, the bedrooms are very individual and have lovely views. *Children over 10 welcome.*

Rooms: 2 doubles, en suite (bath/shower); 1 twin, en suite (shower).

Price: From £25 p.p. Single supp. from £10.

Breakfast: 8.30-9.15am.

Meals: 3 pubs/restaurants within 3 miles.

Closed: January-April.

A remote and ancient famhouse, an aesthetic treat. It is charmingly scruffy, flagstoned, filled with beautiful and interesting things, surprising, uplifting, fun, exquisitely unmodernised… yet comfortable. The library is crammed with books, the kitchen is a beachcomber's haven. This is an estuarine corner of rare loveliness; the views are wide and clean, you can stroll to the river to be among the gulls, avocets and duck. Solitary, winter-bleak splendour with an engagingly relaxed, interesting, artistic and cultured architect. Come if you are easy and open, and do what you want.

Rooms: 1 double with private bathroom.

Price: £30 p.p. Single supp. £10.

Breakfast: Flexible.

Meals: Good pubs & restaurants nearby.

Closed: Sometimes.

From A143, right turn (B1062) to Homersfield. After 500 yds, take 3rd right signed 'South Elmham Hall'. Follow signs for 2 miles.

Entry No: 430   Map no: 12

Mrs Jo Sanderson
South Elmham Hall
St. Cross, Harleston
Suffolk IP20 0PZ
Tel: 01986 782526
Fax: 01986 782203
e-mail: jo.sanderson@btinternet.com
Web: www.southelmham.co.uk

From Orford Market Square, take lane towards castle, and 1st right past castle, marked 'Gedgrave Only, No through Road'. House is on left after 0.5 miles.

Entry No: 430a   Map no: 12

Mr Hugh Pilkington
Richmond House
Gedgrave
Nr Orford
Suffolk IP12 2BU
Tel: 01394 450102
Fax: 01394 450102

To be friendly and flexible but not intrusive — that was the aim of the Careys when they started B&B four years ago. They have succeeded. Theirs is a converted stables and squash court originally belonging to the adjacent manor house, and it has a mature charm. There are many trees in the garden, a paddock and a pool. Surprisingly, amid a hushed tranquillity, you are close to the M25 and the airports. Bedrooms are not large but one opens onto the garden, one has a balcony and the Applestore room is self-contained. *Children over eight welcome.*

Rooms: 1 twin with private shower room; 1 double, en suite (bath) with sitting room; Applestore twin, en suite (shower).

Price: £32 p.p. (£35 p.p. from May 2001). Single supp. £7.50.

Breakfast: 7-9am.

Meals: Available locally.

Closed: Never.

From M25, exit 11, take A319 into Chobham. Left at T-junc., left at mini-r'bout by Total garage onto A3046. After 0.7 miles, right between street light and postbox. House is 2nd on left.

Entry No: 431   Map no: 5

Joan Carey
Swallow Barn
Milford Green
Chobham, Nr. Woking
Surrey GU24 8AU
Tel: 01276 856030
Fax: 01276 856030
e-mail: swallowbarn@compuserve.com

Surrey & Berkshire

This late-Georgian parsonage, in a pretty village setting, has all the warmth and cosy comfort of a traditional English home plus warm colours, light streaming in through French windows, the wrap-around snugness of plump sofas, and those deft touches that make all the difference — like the dark green bathrobes in your room (the en suite shower rooms are small). There is sherry by the log fire, home-cooked food using free-range meats and local produce, and chats over dinner with your well-travelled, articulate and relaxed hosts.

The Italianate garden of this large, handsome 1780s manor is magnificent. You can play tennis and pretend you play croquet; it's the perfect spot to lose track of time and is so English you can almost smell the cucumber sandwiches. It's also so rural that you feel a world away from Woking. Guestrooms have good antique furniture, pretty bedspreads and garden views. There are six acres of garden in 100 acres of vineyards, plus home-laid eggs and garden fruit for breakfast. *Children over eight welcome.*

Rooms: 2 twins/doubles and 1 double, each with small en suite shower; 1 double with private bathroom. All available as singles.

Rooms: 3 doubles, all en suite (bath & shower).

Price: £25-£50 p.p.

Price: From £37.50 p.p. Single supp. £12.50.

Breakfast: 7-8.30am Mon-Fri; 8-9am Sat-Sun.

Breakfast: Until 9.30am.

Meals: Dinner, 4 courses, from £15 p.p. Light supper £10 p.p.

Meals: Available locally.

Closed: Never.

Closed: Christmas & Easter.

At M25 junc. 13, take A30 towards Egham. At next r'bout, A30 to Basingstoke. Uphill to lights. Turn right, take 3rd right, at T-junc. turn left. House is immediately on right. Parking is tight, but the Clarks can help you.

Go west on A319 through Chobham (church on left). Continue towards Knaphill and turn left into Carthouse Lane. Manor signed on right.

Entry No: 432   Map no: 5

Entry No: 433   Map no: 5

Sandi & Peter Clark
The Old Parsonage
Parsonage Road
Englefield Green, Surrey TW20 0JW
Tel: 01784 436706
Fax: 01784 436706
e-mail: the.old.parsonage@talk21.com
Web: www.sawdays.co.uk

Teresa & Kevin Leeper
Knaphill Manor
Carthouse Lane
Woking
Surrey GU21 4XT
Tel: 01276 857962
Fax: 01276 855503

So near London and Guildford, it is a surprise to bump along Littlefield's farm track and find this lovely old house, isolated in 400 acres of farmland. A very easy-going John clearly enjoys the higgle and piggle of his 1550s house — wooden floors, big open fires, worn carpets and rugs, window seats, beamed ceilings, church panel doors, original wattle and daub, big deep baths, lovely rooms with views, weird and wonderful timbered walls. Outside, a traditional English rose garden is walled in with red-brick — and beyond, two acres of super-kempt lawn (his son is a green keeper!).

Rooms: 1 twin with private bathroom; 2 doubles, both en suite (bath).

Price: £30 p.p. Single supp. £10.

Breakfast: Until 9.30am.

Meals: Supper, with wine, £25 p.p., by arrangement.

Closed: Never.

From A3 at Guildford, A323 for Aldershot. Continue to black and white r'bout, go beyond it for 400m & Littlefields is signed on left. From M3, follow signs to Guildford. In Worplesden, right at White Lyon pub, on to r'bout and right. House 400m on left.

Entry No: 434   Map no: 5

John & Pooh Tangye
Littlefield Manor
Littlefield Common
Guildford
Surrey GU3 3HJ
Tel: 01483 233068
Fax: 01483 233686
Web: www.sawdays.co.uk

Gillian welcomes guests from all over the world (she's an English language teacher), yet she and David will make you feel like their first ever; their conversation is lively and informed. The house is just as delightful: part 16th, 18th and 19th century, it has exposed timber frames and bold colours — like the dining room's red. The guest sitting room, with its log fireplace and piano, is hung with a collection of hats and ethnic treasures. In the walled garden the distant rumble of the A3 reminds you how well placed you are for Gatwick and Heathrow. This beats even the best airport hotel.

Rooms: 1 twin/double, en suite (bath/shower); 1 twin/double with private shower; 2 singles (1 with basin) sharing shower room.

Price: £27.50-£32.50 p.p.

Breakfast: Until 9am.

Meals: Available locally.

Closed: Christmas & New Year.

A3 south. 5 miles after Guildford, Eashing is signed left before service station. House 150 yds on left behind white fence.

Entry No: 435   Map no: 5

David & Gillian Swinburn
Lower Easing Farmhouse
Eashing, Nr. Godalming
Surrey GU7 2QF
Tel: 01483 421436
Fax: 01483 421436
e-mail: davidswinburn@hotmail.com
Web: www.sawdays.co.uk

You will fall under Greenaway's spell the moment you enter. In a vast sitting room, low-slung beams and striking colours jostle for your attention. A sturdy, turning oak staircase leads you to the bedrooms; a peek at them all will only confuse you — they are all gorgeous. There's an ornate bedstead in the Chinese room and, in another, an oak bedstead and beams. A further room has a hint of French decadence: golds, magentas and silks. All this and a glorious garden — no wonder so many return time and again.

Rooms: 1 twin and 1 single sharing bathroom; 1 double, en suite (bath).

Price: £32.50-£40 p.p. Single occ. £45.

Breakfast: Until 9am.

Meals: Available locally.

Closed: Never.

High it is, looking across two and a half acres of smooth lawns to the village and the Surrey hills. The 1532 rambling farmhouse has the sort of family clutter that makes you feel immediately at home. You have the big, log-fired living room, stone-flagged dining room and snug study for yourselves, while the three prettily furnished bedrooms share a bathroom upstairs. Unlike many houses with masses of beams, low ceilings and dark furniture, this is light and inviting. Patrick is quiet and gently courteous; Carol is kind and loves children. There are cots and Z-beds aplenty.

Rooms: 1 double, en suite; 1 double and 1 twin, sharing bathroom.

Price: £25-£27.50 p.p. Single occ. £2.

Breakfast: 6.30-9.30am.

Meals: Available locally.

Closed: Christmas.

A3 to Milford, then A283 for Petworth. At Chiddingfold, Pickhurst Road is off the green. House is third on left, with a large black dovecote.

From A3, 1st exit after M25 (signed Ripley/Ockham). Through Ripley & West Clandon, over dual carriageway (A246) onto A25. 3rd right to Shere. There, right to Cranleigh. House is 5 miles on left, 1 mile past Windmill pub.

Entry No: 436   Map no: 5

Entry No: 437   Map no: 5

Sheila Marsh
Greenaway
Pickhurst Road
Chiddingfold, Surrey GU8 4TS
Tel: 01428 682920
Fax: 01428 685078
e-mail: jfvmarsh@nildram.co.uk.
Web: www.sawdays.co.uk

Patrick & Carol Franklin Adams
High Edser
Shere Rd
Ewhurst/Cranleigh
Surrey GU6 7PQ
Tel: 01483 278214
Fax: 01483 278200

Originally a 16th-century inn, the farm is now a haven of peace. The pond is part of what used to be a moat; a bridge takes you to a small island. Classical music drifts across the garden from the conservatory while you swim or play tennis. Inside, low beams, wattle-and-daub walls, log fires, rugs and, in the dining room, heavy oak Jacobean-style furniture. One bedroom has a king-size brass bedstead, another a brass four-poster; the attic bathroom has a whirlpool. Ann and David are relaxed, unpretentious, easy hosts.

Rooms: 1 double & 1 four-poster, both en suite (bath). 1 twin, en suite (shower), sometimes available.

Price: £30 p.p. Single occ. £45-£55.

Breakfast: Until 9.30am.

Meals: Available locally.

Closed: Never.

A lesser-spotted woodpecker lives in the apple tree just outside your bedroom — a room with sloping ceiling, wooden floors and ethnic rugs. The bathroom is half-panelled and creamy yellow. You can breakfast formally in the dining room or with Anne in the kitchen. Explore the garden — it has had 30 years of love poured into it — or the nearby Kennet Canal that is alive with watery activity. Pat and Anne are new to B&B, so she has unbounded enthusiasm for sharing her exquisite 350-year-old cottage and there are very few house rules.

Rooms: 1 double with private bathroom.

Price: £25 p.p. Single occ. £32.

Breakfast: Flexible.

Meals: Available locally.

Closed: 22-28 December.

At crossroads in Leigh, south towards Norwood Hill. After 1 mile, take first right after sign to Mynthurst, then continue up drive for 0.5 miles. House on right.

Entry No: 438   Map no: 5

Ms Ann Dale
Herons Head Farm
Mynthurst
Leigh
Surrey RH2 8QD
Tel: 01293 862475
Fax: 01293 863350

Junc. 12 off M4, A4 towards Newbury. 3 miles on, left immediately before Mulligans fish restaurant. On for 1 mile and farm is 100 yards past 2nd left hand turning, just before 30mph sign.

Entry No: 439   Map no: 5

Pat & Anne Froom
Field Farm
Sulhamstead
Reading
Berkshire RG7 4DA
Tel: 0118 930 2735

The welcome is the same, the house is new — and what a place! The Welfares moved here from another Special Place and Pevsner has described this as "The most ambitious house in Hungerford". A classic town house with a Queen Anne façade and, inside, wood panelling and beams, wonky floors, period furniture and family portraits. Bedrooms are just right, and so is breakfast in the 18th-century dining room. Antique shops to the front and a walled garden with cordon-trained fruit trees to the rear. *Children over eight welcome.*

Rooms: 2 doubles, both en suite.

Price: £28 p.p. Single supp. £10.

Breakfast: Until 9am Mon-Fri; flexible Sat-Sun.

Meals: Dinner available locally. Packed lunch £5 p.p.

Closed: Christmas.

Junc. 14 from M4. Turn off A4 at Bear Hotel onto Salisbury Road (A338). Over canal bridge into High St. Wilton House 200 yds past Town Hall on right.

Entry No: 440   Map no: 4

Deborah & Jonathan Welfare
Wilton House
33 High Street
Hungerford
Berkshire RG17 0NF
Tel: 01488 684228
Fax: 01488 685037
e-mail: welfares@hotmail.com

Parts date back to the 16th century; today it's a working farmhouse and a home to which Mary welcomes her guests in a natural and instantly likeable way. The house is surrounded by a two-acre garden and rolling fields. Her delicious meals are largely home-grown — lamb and veg particularly — and you eat in the beamed kitchen. The bedrooms, simply and attractively decorated, are bright and airy and look out onto the garden, traditional barns and fields. One of the most modern bathrooms has a 16th-century beam. The sitting room has a large open fire and there is a huge selection of books.

Rooms: 3 twins/doubles, 2 en suite (bath/shower) and 1 next to private bath/shower.

Price: £26-£28 p.p. Single occ. £35-£45.

Breakfast: Usually until 9am.

Meals: Dinner, £18 p.p., by arrangement.

Closed: Never.

From M4 junction 14, A338 north towards Wantage. After 0.5 miles, first left (B4000). House is on first farm road on right after Pheasant Inn.

Entry No: 441   Map no: 4

Mary & Henry Wilson
Fishers Farm
Shefford Woodlands
Hungerford, Berkshire RG17 7AB
Tel: 01488 648466
Fax: 01488 648706
e-mail: mail@fishersfarm.co.uk
Web: www.fishersfarm.co.uk

A wooded track leads to this beautiful, mellow 17th-century farmhouse, with tall chimneys and a cluster of overgrown outbuildings surrounding a pond. Wood-panelled walls and timber beams, a vast open brick fireplace, an Aga, mullioned leaded windows and welcoming sofas create an atmosphere of relaxed, country-house charm. The large, and comfortable, timbered bedrooms (one canopied bed incorporates original oak panelling) overlook fields and rolling lawns, where guests may relax in complete peace, accompanied only by birdsong and the occasional grazing sheep. *Children by arrangement.*

Rooms: 1 double with private bathroom; 1 twin/double/family, en suite (bath). 1 small single.

Price: £25-£30 p.p. No single supp. Advance booking only.

Breakfast: Flexible.

Meals: Good pubs nearby.

Closed: Never.

Sussex

Directions given on booking.

Entry No: 442   Map no: 5

Maggie Paterson
Fitzlea Farmhouse
Selham
Nr. Petworth
Sussex GU28 0PS
Tel: 01798 861429

A secret hideaway in the woods, Amberfold isn't just a B&B but a tranquil retreat, perfect for a pair of independent nature-lovers. You have your own lavishly-stocked fridge (replenished daily) — there's enough for a copious breakfast with plenty to spare for a picnic lunch as well. The rooms are pristine and decorated in a simple country style, you have your own front door and terrace, and there are miles of beautiful, unspoilt woodlands to explore right on the doorstep. Don't jump out of your skin if a deer comes to your window to investigate!

Rooms: 2 studios, both doubles with shower and wc.

Price: From £25 p.p. Single supp. £10.

Breakfast: Self-service, so any time!

Meals: Local pubs within walking distance.

Closed: Never.

Olde Worlde charm at its most authentic. The Lodge was built in pure Neo-Gothic style as the gatehouse to the local manor and has kept its other-world, other-age atmosphere (delicious church windows). It sits in a large, rambling garden, is totally secluded and instantly wraps you in peace. There is a woodburning stove in the garden room for chilly days, a plant-filled conservatory to introduce the garden, two warm, elegant bedrooms and a delightful hostess.

Rooms: 2 doubles, en suite (1 bath, 1 shower).

Price: £25 p.p. Single occ. £35.

Breakfast: Flexible.

Meals: Dinner available locally.

Closed: Never.

From Midhurst, A286 towards Chichester. After Royal Oak pub on left, Greyhound on right, go 0.5 miles, left to Heyshott. On for 2 miles, do not turn off, look for white posts and house sign on left.

Entry No: 443   Map no: 5

Alex & Annabelle Costaras
Amberfold
Heyshott
Midhurst
Sussex GU29 0DA
Tel: 01730 812385
Web: www.sawdays.co.uk

Village is 3 miles west of Chichester on the B2178. The lodge is 170 yds on the left after Salthill Road. Look for the sign for Oakwood School.

Entry No: 444   Map no: 5

Jeanette Dridge
Chichester Lodge
Oakwood School Drive
East Ashling, Chichester
Sussex PO18 9AL
Tel: 01243 786560
Web: www.sawdays.co.uk

Lots of beams, charming bedrooms, a cosily cluttered drawing room full of a Bechstein piano and comfortable armchairs: this is a haven for musicians — and cat-lovers. It has the feel of a well-loved and lived-in family home, and indeed Mary has lived here for 30 years. The house looks out over Chidham harbour "five minutes walk from the water's edge" and is surrounded by great walking and bird-watching country. A lovely setting for a delightful house.

Rooms: 1 twin and 1 double with shared bathroom; 1 double with private bathroom.

Price: From £21 p.p.

Breakfast: Flexible.

Meals: Excellent pub in village.

Closed: Christmas.

From Chichester, head for Portsmouth. Pass Tesco on right. 3rd exit off r'bout, to Bosham/Fishbourne. Follow A259 for 4 miles, pass Saab garage on right. Next left into Chidham Lane. House last on left, 1 mile down.

Entry No: 445   Map no: 5

Mary Hartley
Easton House
Chidham Lane
Chidham, Chichester
Sussex PO18 8TF
Tel: 01243 572514
Fax: 01243 573084
e-mail: eastonhouse@chidhamfsnet.co.uk

This was a hotel for years, but Janetta took away the modern extensions and, after 17 years of the right sort of improvements, the Queen Anne architecture of the original house sings once more. Bedrooms — one with its own veranda — overlook the huge fruit garden. Breakfast in summer on a bowl of freshly-picked soft fruit and, after the last, juicy mouthful, you'll be brought sizzling, hot Chichester Elffick sausages. The scent of sweet peas fills the house and, outside, the nearby sailing harbour bustles with nautical life. *Children over eight welcome.*

Rooms: 1 double, en suite; 1 twin/double, en suite (shower); 1 four-poster (separate from house), en suite (bath).

Price: £28-£35 p.p. Single supp. £12. No single night bookings at weekends.

Breakfast: Until 9am Mon-Fri; 9.30am Sat-Sun.

Meals: Available locally.

Closed: November-February.

From Chichester, A259 towards Portsmouth. 3 miles on, left at r'bout for Bosham. Right at Berkeley Arms pub, on right. House on left, past garage.

Entry No: 446   Map no: 5

Janetta Field
Critchfield House
Bosham Lane
Old Bosham, Chichester
Sussex PO18 8HG
Tel: 01243 572370
Fax: 01243 572370
e-mail: janetta@critchfield.demon.co.uk

Bees buzz contentedly, water bubbles in the fountain and you may swim in the pool . The Sedgwicks — Nigel is studying History of Art and Juliet has a framing business — have created a much-loved secure haven. The bedrooms are large with good lighting and generous tea trays; there's a Waring & Gillows bed from which you can gaze across the coastal plain to the distant slopes of the South Downs and the sun streams in. This is an officially sunny place, hence the many local market gardeners. Juliet frequently travels to London for exhibitions via the excellent rail connection but the three-acre garden and double-glazing shield you from train noise.

Rooms: 1 king-size, en suite (bath); 1 double and 1 twin, sharing bathroom.

Price: £30-£35 p.p. Single supp. £5.

Breakfast: Flexible.

Meals: Dinner and packed lunch by arrangement.

Closed: Christmas.

From Chichester A27 east (or west from Arundel). South on B2132 for Yapton. Turn right on Lake Lane just before level crossing. House 0.5 miles on right.

Entry No: 447   Map no: 5

Nigel & Juliet Sedgwick
Todhurst Farm
Lake Lane, Barnham
Arundel
Sussex PO22 0AL
Tel: 01243 551959
e-mail: nigelsedg@aol.com

Kippers and porridge for breakfast, home-made cakes for tea — Vivien spoils her guests while husband Tim manages a local racehorse stud. The Flint House was built by Napoleonic prisoners of war and was once part of the Goodwood estate. Bedrooms are in the old cattle byres — originally converted for the Reads' growing family — and are good-sized with attractive furniture and décor, fresh flowers and a pretty yellow kitchen for making (real) coffee and tea. Lovely views from the garden and there's a tennis court.

Rooms: 2 twins/doubles, both en suite (bath & shower).

Price: £27.50-£35 p.p. Single occ. £30-£35.

Breakfast: Flexible.

Meals: Available locally.

Closed: Christmas.

A272 to Midhurst, then A286 to Singleton. Left turn signed Goodwood: up over Downs, pass racecourse, take next right signed Lavant. House is first on right after 0.5 miles.

Entry No: 448   Map no: 5

Tim & Vivien Read
The Flint House
East Lavant
Chichester
Sussex PO18 0AS
Tel: 01243 773482

Built for the miller in 1767, Duncton Mill, with its walled gardens and charming ensemble of farm buildings, is now the domain of Tom and Sheila, who put heart and soul into their home and B&B. The 70-acre estate is a dream for country-lovers and anglers are in their element here, too, with several spring-fed trout lakes in which to dangle their lines. The rolling South Downs spread out before you, there is an outdoor heated pool and good, local pubs. Breakfasts might include home-grown figs in late Summer. *Children over eight welcome. Self-catering available.*

Rooms: 1 twin/double, and 1 double, both en suite.

Price: £25-£30 p.p. Single occ. £40.

Breakfast: Until 9.30am.

Meals: Available locally.

Closed: Christmas.

Built as an open hall in the Middle Ages... lots of history in one gorgeous spot. This is the quintessential picture-book B&B: patchwork quilts, exposed timber walls, books at every turn and clematis, honeysuckle and roses rioting all over the place. Alan and Caroline have put a lot of care and love into restoring and furnishing this house as it deserves and quirky, traditional and imaginative touches work well together. Fresh, country-style bedrooms and natural materials complement the rural setting where cows graze and farmers work the land.

Rooms: 2 doubles, 1 with adjoining single room, both en suite (1 shower and 1 bath & shower).

Price: From £25 p.p. Single occ. £38. Single £23.

Breakfast: Flexible.

Meals: Packed lunch available.

Closed: Christmas-New Year.

From A23 take Henfield exit. In Sayers Common, right into Reeds Lane. At T-junc. left into Twineham Lane and immediately fork right towards Henfield. 2nd left up Blackstone Lane. House is in centre of hamlet.

300 yds off A285 Petworth to Chichester road. Look for brown and white tourist signs just south of Duncton village.

Entry No: 449   Map no: 5

Sheila & Tom Bishop
Duncton Mill House
Duncton, Nr. Petworth
Sussex GU28 0LF
Tel: 01798 342294
Fax: 01798 344122
e-mail: sheila@dunctonmill.com
Web: www.dunctonmill.com

Entry No: 450   Map no: 5

Alan & Caroline Kerridge
Yeoman's Hall
Blackstone
Nr. Henfield
Sussex BN5 9TB
Tel: 01273 494224
Fax: 01273 494224
e-mail: stay@yeomanshall.fsnet.co.uk

First a farm, then an ale house; what seems small from the outside opens out into a rambling, higgledy-piggledy 16th-century period piece inside, with quirky angles and exposed timbers. Frances, with skill and dedication, did the renovation herself. And she landscaped the gardens — complete with a 1,000-year-old box hedge — where nightingales and owls enjoy the woodland. Bedrooms are beamed and neat with the best linen. Living and dining rooms are oak-beamed, uncluttered and cheerful. Your host is an independent character but always happy to share a drink and a chat in front of the inglenook fire.

Rooms: 1 double and 1 twin, both en suite (shower); 1 single, en suite (bath).

Price: £25-£27.50 p.p. Single £30.

Breakfast: Flexible.

Meals: Dinner, 2 courses, £15 p.p. Packed lunch by arrangement.

Closed: Never.

Rarely have we met such dedicated hosts, Jennifer organising behind the scenes, Graham proving that nothing is too much trouble. He makes preserves, too, and will book a table at the village pub for you. Visitors from 54 nations have enjoyed the comforts of this unspoilt, wisteria-clad 1930s bastion of old-Englishness set to the gentle music of fantails. It is surrounded by peaceful views over lovely gardens, has a huge fruit and veg plot that could feed an army, and log fires in winter. *Children over 10 welcome.*

Rooms: 1 double with private bath & wc; 2 twins sharing 1 bathroom and 2 wcs.

Price: From £30 p.p. Single supp. £10.

Breakfast: Flexible.

Meals: Available locally.

Closed: Never.

From Gatwick, take M23 south and follow signs to Cuckfield. There, right at 1st mini-r'bout, left at 2nd and right at 3rd. Left at T-junc. Copyhold Lane is 1st on right, after entrance to Borde Hill Gardens.

Entry No: 451   Map no: 5

Frances Druce
Copyhold Hollow
Copyhold Lane
Borde Hill, Haywards Heath
Sussex RH16 1XU
Tel: 01444 413265
e-mail: 10@copyholdhollow.freeserve.co.uk
Web: www.copyholdhollow.freeserve.co.uk

From M25, A22 to Maresfield. At mini-r'bout in centre of village, under stone arch opposite church and pub, and over 5 speed bumps. House first on left.

Entry No: 452   Map no: 5

Major Graham & Jennifer Allt
South Paddock
Maresfield Park
Nr. Uckfield
Sussex TN22 2HA
Tel: 01825 762335

Celia's enthusiasm for this beamy house is delightful. She used to sell antiques, but probably not very profitably as she admits to keeping "the ones I liked and didn't want to sell" — and it is easy to see why. This is a typical 15th-century Sussex farmhouse with bags of character. The beautiful garden has been lovingly restored to its original layout and there are two bridged wildlife ponds. The two single rooms are full of charm and style with some interesting pieces of furniture (of course). The double is light and airy and overlooks the garden — you'll covet the apothecary chest. *Children over 14 welcome*

Rooms: 1 double with private bathroom; 2 singles with shared bathroom.

Price: £26 p.p.

Breakfast: Until 9am.

Meals: Available locally.

Closed: Christmas & New Year.

There's been a house here since the 12th century, though the present building dates from the 17th. The house and garden are traditional English country house style. The food is wonderful. Paris-trained Sarah conjures up an adventurous, but always beautifully-judged, menu; sea-bass or octopus, for example. She will also prepare you a hamper for Glyndebourne (10 minutes away) and the orange juice for breakfast is freshly squeezed. A perfect escape for cultured sybarites and there's a heated pool and a tennis court.

Rooms: 3 twins, 2 en suite (1 bath, 1 shower) and 1 with private bathroom.

Price: £45 p.p. Single supp. by arrangement.

Breakfast: Until 9.30am.

Meals: Dinner, 3 courses, £22 p.p. B.Y.O. wine. Lunch and hampers available on request.

Closed: Never.

From Uckfield, A26 Lewes road. Right for Isfield and on for 1 mile. Right over level crossing and house is on steep left bend with high fence and gate, approx. 0.5 miles on.

Entry No: 453   Map no: 5

Celia Rigby
The Faulkners
Isfield
Sussex TN22 5XG
Tel: 01825 750344
Fax: 01825 750577

0.5 miles past Halland on A22, south from Uckfield, first left off Shaw r'bout towards East Hoathly, on for 0.5 miles. Drive on left with post box. Where drive divides into 3, take central gravel drive.

Entry No: 454   Map no: 5

Sarah Burgoyne
Old Whyly
East Hoathly
Sussex BN8 6EL
Tel: 01825 840216
Fax: 01825 840738

A listed 17th-century house beside the church in the heart of a tiny village, just 10 minutes from Glyndebourne. Alison was chef to the Beatles and will not only give you a delicious hamper, but tables and chairs, too. Willie is a former world rackets champion who gives tennis coaching, and, in the large, pretty garden, there is a tennis court and a swimming pool. You can relax by the inglenook fire in the drawing room after a walk on the Cuckoo Trail or the South Downs walk, then settle down for a great supper — maybe home-grown vegetables with local fish. This is an easy-going, fun and informal household.

Rooms: 1 double plus 1 single sharing bathroom (single room let only to member of same party).

Price: Double, £22.50 p.p. Single, £28.`

Breakfast: Flexible.

Meals: Dinner, £18 p.p. B.Y.O. wine.

Closed: Christmas & Easter.

Horses were the previous inhabitants. Set about by architect Edmund to make the most of light and natural materials, the farm is a wonderful conversion. Anne, relaxed and informative, was housing editor of *Ideal Home* magazine and there's an easy stylishness here. Nothing over-smart; simple bedrooms with an interesting mixture of furniture and art, good books, rugs, terracotta tiling, polished and gnarled wood. Sit in the conservatory and you feel practically in the garden. The countryside — Kipling country — is beautiful, and breakfasts a feast with home- and locally-made food.

Rooms: 1 double, en suite (shower); 1 double with private bathroom shared with 1 single, let only to members of same party.

Price: £23-£24 p.p. 10% discount for 3 or more nights.

Breakfast: Until 9.30am.

Meals: Dinner available nearby.

Closed: Christmas & New Year.

From Boship roundabout on A22, take A267. First right to Horsebridge and immediately left to Hellingly. Globe Place is next to church, in Mill Lane.

Entry No: 455   Map no: 6

Alison & Willie Boone
Globe Place
Hellingly
Sussex BN27 4EY
Tel: 01323 844276
Fax: 01323 844276
e-mail: aliboone@talk21.com
Web: www.sawdays.co.uk

From A21 take A265 at Hurst Green for Lewes. Drive through Etchingham and over level crossing. House is on left (sign on right) 2.5 miles on, down a drive which dips.

Entry No: 456   Map no: 6

Anne Lucey
Glebe Farm
Burwash
Etchingham
Sussex TN19 7BG
Tel: 01435 882240
e-mail: glebarn@aol.com

A rural haven with chickens and geese and 40 acres of grazing surrounded by ,000 of woodland; this is just the place or walkers and bird-watchers woodpeckers and hobbys, for example). 'rom the garden room you can see "the pot where Harold camped before he got it in the eye in 1066". The Collins re good, knowledgeable company and heir home is peaceful and relaxing. With xposed beams, a woodburning stove in he sitting room and an inglenook ireplace in the dining room, there's tacks of woody character and cosy edrooms with unspoilt views through ead latticed windows. *Children over 10 velcome*

Rooms: 3 doubles, all en suite (bath).

Price: From £24.50 p.p. Single occ. rom £29.

Breakfast: 8-10am.

Meals: Supper, by arrangement.

Closed: January.

People swoop back like swallows for the garden. The trimmed lawn hugs a huge ornamental pond and there is a heated pool kept at 88° in the walled garden. By another tiny pond you can breakfast in summer if you are not in the sun-drenched dining room, with its long wooden table and starched napkins. The house is full of beautiful things and, though there is no sitting room for guests, one is made to feel totally at home... so much so that you may stay here all day in the garden. Bathrooms are superb, and one of the bedrooms overlooks both garden and sea.

Rooms: 1 twin, en suite (shower); 1 double with private bathroom.

Price: £32.50 p.p. Single supp. £12.50.

Breakfast: 8-9.30am. Earlier by arrangement.

Meals: Pub nearby.

Closed: Christmas.

From Battle on A271, first right to Heathfield. After 0.75 miles, right into drive.

Entry No: 457   Map no: 6

Paul & Pauline Collins
Fox Hole Farm
Kane Hythe Road
Battle
Sussex TN33 9QU
Tel: 01424 772053
Fax: 01424 773771

From Rye, A259 to Winchelsea; after Bridge Inn, sharp left up steep hill signed Winchelsea. After medieval arch, 1st left, house 200 yards, 1st on left.

Entry No: 458   Map no: 6

Mrs Sarah Jempson
Cleveland House
Winchelsea
Sussex TN36 4EE
Tel: 01797 226256
Fax: 01797 226256
e-mail: sarah.jempson@virgin.net
Web: www.clevelandhouse-garden.co.uk

Julia lived in Paris for 12 years, loves to cook and is an effervescent presence in this gorgeous 15th-century farmhouse with its hipped roof and asymmetric beams. It was renovated in the '30s and of the three bedrooms the double is the most striking, decorated in pale colours and with a beautiful view down the Tillingham valley. The twin rooms are more simply furnished; one is predominantly rose floral, the other muted green and white. It's peaceful here — there are three acres of mature gardens — and only five miles from Rye. *Children over five welcome.*

Rooms: 1 double, en suite (shower); 2 twins/doubles with basins and private bathrooms.

Price: £30-£34 p.p. Single supp. £5.

Breakfast: Flexible.

Meals: Dinner, 3 courses, £18 p.p., by arrangement.

Closed: Christmas.

A grand house where both Wellington and Nelson are said to have stayed. The 'best' and biggest four-poster bedroom is full of Victorian and Georgian furniture; there's another four-poster and a simpler, though comfortable, twin room with monogrammed counterpanes. The Princess is a dog-lover — she has five — and an engaging host (she will regale you with her family's history). The dining room and guest drawing room are classically smart. All this just a few minutes walk from the centre of Rye.

Rooms: 1 twin and 2 four-posters, all en suite (shower).

Price: £38-£55 p.p. No single supp.

Breakfast: Flexible.

Meals: Not available.

Closed: Christmas.

From A21, left onto B2089 for Rye and on for 4 miles. Leaving Broad Oak, left for Peasmarsh. Downhill, then first right into Hayes Lane. House on left, just past oast house.

Entry No: 459   Map no: 6

Julia & Thierry Sebline
Hayes Farm House
Hayes Lane, Peasmarsh, Rye
Sussex TN31 6XR
Tel: 01424 882345
Fax: 01424 882876
e-mail: julia.sebline@virgin.net
business.virgin.net/hayes.farmhouse

From A21, left after Robert Bridge r'bout for Rye (B2089). On reaching one-way system, first left and over mini-r'bout. Next left onto A268, and house on immediate left after small bridge.

Entry No: 460   Map no: 6

Princess Tia Romanoff
Mountsfield
Rye Hill
Rye
Sussex TN31 7NH
Tel: 01797 227105
Fax: 01797 227106

Teddy bears inside, hedgehogs outside and a really excellent cat". This most welcoming, rule-free townhouse in lovely history-laden Rye also has fine antiques, masses of books and paintings, occasional groups of amateur dramatists in the big and otherwise quiet garden, a smugglers' Watchtower and a small library for rainy days. Sara is lively, attentive and fun and will give you big organic/free-range breakfasts, as well as information about what to do and see.

Rooms: 2 four-posters, both en suite (1 bath and 1 shower).

Price: £32-£42 p.p. Single occ. £45-£65.

Breakfast: 8-9.30am Mon-Sat; 8-10am Sun.

Meals: Dinner available nearby.

Closed: Never.

In Rye, follow signs to town centre and enter Old Town through Landgate Arch into High Street. West Street is third on left. House is halfway up on left.

Entry No: 461   Map no: 6

Sara Brinkhurst
Little Orchard House
West Street
Rye
Sussex TN31 7ES
Tel: 01797 223831
Fax: 01797 223831

Rigorous care and effort have transformed this perfectly square Victorian hunting lodge. The entire house has been furnished and newly decorated for great comfort with thick carpets and big bedrooms and bathrooms — many seasoned travellers say that this is one of the most comfortable house they've stayed in. The French double and twin rooms ha hand-embroidered linen, antique furniture and Designers' Guild curtains both are light and airy. The two-acre garden has a thriving kitchen garden an you breakfast on organic local produce

Rooms: 1 twin en suite (shower); 1 double and 1 single, both en suite (bath).

Price: £35 p.p. No single supp.

Breakfast: Flexible.

Meals: Dinner £25 p.p. (not Sun).

Closed: Christmas & New Year

Warwickshire

From Oxford, A3400 towards Stratford upon-Avon. Through Long Compton. On for 3 miles and take 1st right to Burmington. At top of hill, straight over x-roads. Entrance 30 yards on left.

Entry No: 462　　　　　Map no: 10

Mary & Dorian Manville-Hales
Burmington Leys
Burmington
Shipston-on-Stour
Warwickshire CV36 5AR
Tel: 01608 661523
Fax: 01608 664492
e-mail: dorian.manville-hales@virgin.net

Flagstoned floors, beamed ceilings, deep fireplaces, deep-set mullioned windows — pure Cotswold charm. Your sitting room has old books and polished furniture and the bedrooms, with low ceilings, are uncluttered. Zip-and-link beds in all the rooms; one ground-floor en suite room is suitable for guests with disabilities. Broad paths and billowing plants and flowers that spill out between the courtyard paving stones. Your hostess is a keen gardener and has some spectacular hostas. *Children over 12 welcome.*

Rooms: 3 twins/doubles, en suite (bath & shower); 1 single, en suite (shower).

Price: From £30 p.p. Single supp. £3.

Breakfast: Until 9.30am.

Meals: Supper, 2 courses, £14.50 p.p., dinner, 3 courses, from £18.50 p.p., by arrangement. B.Y.O. wine.

Closed: Never.

From Stratford-upon-Avon, A3400 towards Oxford. After 5 miles, right by church in Newbold-on-Stour & follow signs to Blackwell. Fork right on entering Blackwell. Entrance is just beyond thatched barn.

Entry No: 463   Map no: 10

Liz Vernon Miller
Blackwell Grange
Blackwell, Shipston-on-Stour
Warwickshire CV36 4PF
Tel: 01608 682357
Fax: 01608 682856
e-mail: blackwell.grange@saqnet.co.uk
Web: www.sawdays.co.uk

There's a *chaise longue* in the bathroom, there are old beams to gaze up at as you rest in your bed and a swimming pool (complete with its own jet-stream to swim against) in the garden. Sarah, who grew up in the Big House next door, gives you a welcome worthy of her illustrious past. She claims to know every inch of Warwickshire and proclaims this the prettiest bit. You are likely to agree. She likes guests to have breakfast in the farmhouse kitchen — the surest sign of a relaxed host — and she serves up a real feast with panache and humour. Spectacular walks from the doorstep.

Rooms: 1 double, en suite (bath); 1 double and 1 twin, with shared bathroom.

Price: £28 p.p. No single supp.

Breakfast: Flexible.

Meals: Dinner, 2 courses, £14 p.p.; 3 courses, £20 p.p., excluding wine.

Closed: Never.

From Ilmington, either off A429 or A3400, take Charingworth rd up Foxcote Hill. After approx. 1 mile, right down drive with gates & stone pillars. Right at yew hedge, follow hedge down the hill. House at top of hill on right.

Entry No: 464   Map no: 10

Sarah Holman
Foxcote Farmhouse
Shipston-on-Stour
Warwickshire CV36 4JG
Tel: 01608 682066
Fax: 01608 682852

An 1856 Victorian farmhouse, with log fires to warm your enthusiasm for a good walk on the Heart of England Way. The views stretch on to folklore-sodden Meon Hill and if the stories of local witchcraft and other spookery fail to spark your imagination, there is every chance your bed will inspire you. The Angel Room has a pine box bed and a medieval frieze of flying angels. The two other rooms have romantic four-posters with handmade quilts. Healthy and delicious breakfast menus — 'Winton House Specials' — change daily and make imaginative use of organic fruit from the orchard.

Rooms: 2 four-posters, en suite (shower); 1 twin/family room with private bath.

Price: From £27.50 p.p. No single supp.

Breakfast: Until 9am.

Meals: Excellent local pubs and restaurant.

Closed: Christmas Day.

You'll be in your element if you fish or play tennis, for you can do both from the beautiful, landscaped gardens that slope gently down to the River Stour. Jane, a *Cordon Bleu* cook, runs her 16th- and 17th-century house with huge energy and friendliness. A pretty, blue twin bedroom and a single room are in a self-contained wing with its own large, elegant drawing and dining room; it's seductively easy to relax here. The L-shaped double, with ancient beams and oak furniture, is in the main part of the house; it has a lovely bathroom and shares the drawing and dining rooms.

Rooms: 1 twin and 1 single with shared private bathroom (single let only to members of the same party); 1 double with private bathroom.

Price: From £27 p.p. Single supp. £5.

Breakfast: Until 9am Mon-Sat; 10am Sun.

Meals: Available by arrangement, or locally.

Closed: Christmas.

From Stratford take A3400 south. As you leave the town take B4632 (signposted Broadway and Mickleton) for 6 miles. Turn left for Upper Quinton. House is 400 yds on left.

Entry No: 465   Map no: 10

From Stratford, follow A422 for 4 miles towards Banbury. After 4 miles, right at r'bout onto A429 for Halford. There, take first right. House with black and white timbers straight ahead.

Entry No: 466   Map no: 10

Mrs Gail Lyon
Winton House
The Green
Upper Quinton, Stratford-upon-Avon
Warwickshire CV37 8SX
Tel: 01789 720500
e-mail: gail@wintonhouse.com
Web: www.wintonhouse.com

Jane & William Pusey
The Old Manor House
Halford, Shipston on Stour
Warwickshire CV36 5BT
Tel: 01789 740264
Fax: 01789 740609
e-mail: wpusey@st-philips.co.uk
Web: www.sawdays.co.uk

Spiky plants and driftwood in the garden — a welcome relief from the more familiar herbaceous borders and it would be hard to find a more secluded, peaceful retreat. Carolyn and John could not be nicer and every room feels right; seashell stencils and star-painted ceilings go perfectly with colour-washed walls. Bedrooms have wooden-latched doors to sunny, skylit bathrooms. The annexe room has its own entrance and a four-poster iron bedstead. They keep sheep, horses and poultry, so there are plenty of fresh eggs for breakfast. *Children over eight welcome.*

Rooms: 1 double/twin/family, en suite (bath/shower); 2 doubles, en suite (1 shower and 1 bath/shower).

Price: £19.50-£24 p.p. Single occ. from £28.

Breakfast: Flexible.

Meals: Available locally.

Closed: Christmas.

The garden reaches out to the River Stour with its waterside willows. If you can't stir yourself to make a close inspection, sit on the terrace and watch the sun set over the North Cotswolds. Angie and Chris have an easy-going manner that is infectious. Angie decorates with strong colours; Chris, an interiors photographer, has an eye for arranging things. He also bakes bread most mornings. Flagstones and wooden floors downstairs; upstairs, one Art Deco-ish bedroom and the other decorated in warm shades of terracotta and cream, with cream sofa and canopied bed.

Rooms: 1 double and 1 triple (double and single), both en suite (bath & shower).

Price: £30 p.p. Single supp. £15.

Breakfast: 8.30am.

Meals: Available locally.

Closed: Christmas.

From Stratford-upon-Avon, A422 to Pillerton Priors, then follow sign to Pillerton Hersey. There, turn down Oxhill Bridle Rd, opp. phone box. House is at the end. Or M40 junc. 12, 6 miles on B4451.

Entry No: 467   Map no: 10

Carolyn & John Howard
Dockers Barn Farm
Oxhill Bridle Road
Pillerton Hersey, Warwick
Warwickshire CV35 0QB
Tel: 01926 640475
Fax: 01926 641747

From Stratford, south on A3400 towards Shipston. After 3 miles, signed on right.

Entry No: 468   Map no: 10

Angela & Chris Wright
Alderminster Farm, Alderminster
Nr. Stratford-upon-Avon
Warwickshire CV37 8BP
Tel: 01789 450774
Fax: 01789 450774
e-mail: chriswright72@hotmail.com
Web: www.tpointmc.demon.co.uk/alderminster/

From the bath to your seat in the Stratford theatre could be done in 10 minutes, if you are in a hurry. Perfect. Each suite is magnificently accoutred, with its own sitting room and kitchenette, so you can peacefully enjoy a glass of wine post-performance. Breakfast — taken in the main house — is the time to be sociable here. This is a Grade II listed thatched house, of 1501, a house of great and many beams. Even the barn where you sleep is 17th century, also thatched and listed Grade II. Luxurious, beautiful, authentic and slap in the middle of a huge chunk of the best of England.

Rooms: 2 doubles, en suite.

Price: £30-£33 p.p. Single supp. £10.

Breakfast: Until 9am.

Meals: Pub within 3 mins walk.

Closed: 1 December-7 January.

Here's a big, old house in the country, minus the expected creaks and draught and with every mod con. Carpets are thick, beds four-poster and sumptuous. This feels like a small hotel (there's a helipad for those wanting to make a big entrance), yet it's very much the McGoverns' home. Plush green sofas si by the stone inglenook and you can have drinks here before eating in the candlelit conservatory. (Mark is a Mast of Cheese and once ran a restaurant.) The garden is lush and landscaped and there are fields all around — look out for the fat Hebridean sheep. This is a fully organic, Soil Association registere farm.

Rooms: 2 doubles, both en suite (shower) and 1 four-poster, en suite (bath).

Price: From £42.50 p.p. Single supp. £27.

Breakfast: Flexible.

Meals: Dinner, 3 courses, £25 p.p.

Closed: Never.

From Stratford, take A422 Banbury road for 4 miles and turn off for Loxley. Through village and left at bottom of hill. 3rd house on right.

Entry No: 469   Map no: 10

Mrs Anne Horton
Loxley Farm
Loxley
Warwick
Warwickshire CV35 9JN
Tel: 01789 840265
Fax: 01789 840645

From Stratford, A4200, over Clopton bridge and immediately left onto Tiddington Road. First right onto Loxley Rd. Last house on left with white gates.

Entry No: 470   Map no: 10

Ms Kate McGovern
Glebe Farm House
Loxley, Stratford-upon-Avon
Warwickshire CV35 9JW
Tel: 01789 842501
Fax: 01789 842501
e-mail: scorpiolimited@msn.com
Web: www.glebefarmhouse.com

Drink in the views. The greenness of the surrounding countryside will revive flagging spirits, the peace will soothe the frazzled. David and Julia are a well-travelled and unassuming couple devoted to their ancient house and garden. Mallards glide over the pond and a stream runs by the 400-year-old yew. Inside, Cotswold stone walls, comfortable sofas, beamed dining and drawing room and huge inglenooks complete the peaceful scene while uneven floors enhance the character of this 300-year-old house.

Rooms: 1 twin and 1 double, sharing bathroom.

Price: £25 p.p. No single supp.

Breakfast: Flexible.

Meals: Excellent local pubs & restaurants nearby.

Closed: Christmas & New Year.

Kim has the sort of kitchen city dwellers dream of: big, old and welcoming. It's the hub of the house. She fizzes with good humour and energy and takes pride in those times when family and guests feel easy together. You will be offered tea on arrival, or even a walk round the village. Hers is a large 1900s country house with tennis court, terrace, fine garden, croquet lawn and home-made jams. The rooms are large, soft and supremely comfortable. A special place.

Rooms: 1 twin and 1 double, both with private bathroom.

Price: £22-£28 p.p. Single supp. £8.

Breakfast: Flexible.

Meals: Dinner, for four only, £18.50 p.p., by arrangement.

Closed: Never.

From A423, turn off to Priors Hardwick. After 1.8 miles, left for Priors Hardwick. First hard left on S-bend (No Exit sign). House on right on concrete road behind farm buildings.

Entry No: 471   Map no: 10

Julia & David Gaunt
Hollow Meadow House
Priors Hardwick
Southam
Warwickshire CV47 7SP
Tel: 01327 261540
Fax: 01327 261540
Web: www.sawdays.co.uk

From Banbury, A361 north. At Byfield village sign, left into Twistle Lane, straight on to Priors Marston. House is white, 5th on left with cattle grid, after s-bend.

Entry No: 472   Map no: 10

Kim & John Mahon
Marston House
Priors Marston, Southam
Warwickshire CV47 7RP
Tel: 01327 260297
Fax: 01327 262846
e-mail: john.mahon@coltel.co.uk
Web: www.ivabestbandb.co.uk

With what imagination Prue conjures up a breakfast feast and, best of all, almost all of it will be organic. Expect vegetarian and vegan dishes, home-made bread, smoked salmon and scrambled egg, smoothies and fruit platter with lime and honey dressing. Committed to the environment though she may be, Prue hasn't compromised on comfort and smartness. All bedrooms and bathrooms are large, colourful and warm with biscuits by the bed and excellent smellies in the bathroom. This substantial blue stone 1850s town house is right opposite Warwick's park — it's a 1.5 mile walk to the castle.

Rooms: 2 doubles, both en suite (bath & shower).

Price: £32 p.p. Single supp. £8.

Breakfast: Flexible.

Meals: Supper, by arrangement.

Closed: Occasionally.

Cathy's sense of humour carries her through each gloriously eventful day. This is a paradise for families — there's so much room to play and so much to see: cows, turkeys, geese and Saddleback pigs. The farmhouse, built in 1640, was extended 25 years ago using old bricks and beams. Tiny timbered corridors lead to large bedrooms with wooden floors and leaded windows (the family room has everything needed for a baby). Next door is the magnificent lake, Shrewley Pools, and private fishing is available.

Rooms: 1 king-size with single and cot, 1 twin, both en suite (bath).

Price: From £22.50 p.p. Single supp. £7.50.

Breakfast: Flexible.

Meals: Dinner with home-reared meat, packed lunch & children's high tea, all by arrangement.

Closed: Christmas & New Year.

From Warwick, A4177 towards Solihull. At Five Ways roundabout, 1st left, follow for 0.75 miles; signed down track on left.

On the main Warwick to Leamington road, opposite entrance to St Nicholas' Park.

Entry No: 473　　　　Map no: 10

Prue Hardwick
The Hare on the Park
3 Emscote Road
Warwick
Warwickshire CV34 4PH
Tel: 01926 491366
e-mail: pruespost@tesco.net
Web: www.thehareonthepark.com

Entry No: 474　　　　Map no: 10

Cathy Dodd
Shrewley Pools Farm
Haseley
Warwick
Warwickshire CV35 7HB
Tel: 01926 484315

We challenge you to find anything else of such good value so close to Birmingham. Built in 1737, well-and-truly done-up in 1988, everything about this place is HUGE! The kitchen, with Aga and stone floors, gives onto a stunning patio and conservatory where you can eat breakfast. Drawing room, bedrooms and bathrooms are plush, big and comfortable. Denise, quiet at first, has an infectious laugh and runs her B&B with careful attention to detail. *Prior booking essential. Children over 12 welcome.*

Rooms: 2 doubles and 1 twin, all en suite (bath).

Price: £30 p.p. Single occ. £35.

Breakfast: Until 8.30am.

Meals: Available locally.

Closed: Never.

At M6 junc. 4, A446 for Lichfield. At sign to Coleshill South, get in right lane and turn off. From High St, turn into Maxstoke Lane. After 4 miles, take 4th right. House is 1st on left.

Entry No: 475   Map no: 10

Mrs Denise Owen
Hardingwood House
Hardingwood Lane
Fillongley, nr. Coventry
Warwickshire CV7 8EL
Tel: 01676 542579
Fax: 01676 541336

In one hundred acres of farmland (mixed arable, suckler Jerseys and hay) the house is solid and traditional in a style familiar to farmhouse B&B habitués. There is an open fire in the dining room, a white cloth on the table a baby chandelier and patterned curtains. The sitting room (yours) has two vast floral sofas and matching armchairs, pelmeted curtains, a piano, fire, and a grandfather clock. The comfort upstairs is of the same kind: big soft beds with white covers, fitted carpets, walls with dados and prints, and floral curtains. It is quiet, friendly and authentic.

Rooms: 1 double, en suite (shower); 1 double/triple, en suite (bath/shower).

Price: £30 p.p. Single supp. £10.

Breakfast: Flexible.

Meals: Evening meal £20-£25 p.p.

Closed: Occasionally.

Wiltshire

From Swindon or Cirencester, take A419 to Cricklade. From Cricklade, B4040 for Malmesbury. 3 miles on, there is a sign on left. Go to end of drive (0.5 miles).

Entry No: 476   Map no: 4

Claire Read
Leighfield Lodge Farm
Malmesbury Road, Leigh
Swindon
Wiltshire SN6 6RH
Tel: 01666 860241
Fax: 01666 860241
e-mail: claireread@leighfieldlodge.fsnet.co.uk

Valerie is a talented interior designer and student of fashion history — both passions are apparent as soon as you see the Threlfalls' half of the 16th-century manor house. Dotted around the house you find fashion prints, photographs, a collection of hatboxes and dressmakers' dummies. Valerie is huge fun. In the ballroom, with its wooden floor, grand piano and window seats, you can imagine the elegant ribaldry of the days when it hosted 'coming-out' balls. The dining room is red and hung with William Morris fabrics and paper.

Rooms: 1 double, en suite (bath); 1 twin with private shower.

Price: £25-£30 p.p. Single supp. £6.

Breakfast: Until 9.50am.

Meals: Available locally.

Closed: Christmas & New Year.

The original granary for Malmesbury Abbey was here; now there is this lovely, honey-coloured country farmhouse, with Cotswold stone roof with moss and lichen, traditional walled garden (veg, fruit and flowers), flagstone floors and views through old doors and windows. And it is right next to a fine church in a classically pretty village. The views from the surprisingly modern bathroom are inspiring — cattle peacefully grazing in the paddock; the church can be seen from another, and there are little window seats to sit on. It is all delightful, and comfortable, too. Helen is lovely.

Rooms: 2 doubles, 1 en suite and 1 with private bathroom.

Price: £25-£30 p.p. Single occ. £30.

Breakfast: Until 10am.

Meals: Dinner, 3 courses, £17.50 p.p. Packed lunch also available, both with notice.

Closed: Christmas & New Year.

In the centre of the village is the White Hart pub. 100m due east is a tall Cotswold stone wall with stone pillars. Turn in and the house is on the right.

Entry No: 477   Map no: 4

A429 Malmesbury to Cirencester road. In Crudwell, at Plough, right signed Minety/Oaksey. Straight on, then left between church and tithe barn pillars.

Entry No: 478   Map no: 4

Valerie & Roger Threlfall
1 Cove House
Ashton Keynes
Wiltshire SN6 6NS
Tel: 01285 861226
Fax: 01285 861226
e-mail: roger@covehouse.co.uk

Helen & Philip Carter
Manor Farmhouse
Crudwell, Malmesbury
Wiltshire SN16 9ER
Tel: 01666 577375
Fax: 01666 823523
e-mail: user785566@aol.com
Web: www.sawdays.co.uk

The quiet seclusion of the Legges' home is delightful whatever the season; in winter, large comfy sofas envelop you and fires warm you; in summer, eat on the lawn in the cool shade of the arbour. The bright conservatory with its huge oak table is the sort most of us can only dream of. The cottage garden supplies the fresh vegetables and herbs (mostly organic) which are used to magnificent effect. Liz and Colin are marvellously easy and flexible. Perfect.

Rooms: 1 twin, en suite (bath); 1 twin with private bathroom.

Price: £27.50-£30 p.p. Single supp. £5 by arrangement.

Breakfast: Flexible.

Meals: Dinner, 3 courses, £18 p.p., by arrangement.

Closed: Christmas & Easter.

From the front it is a characteristic townhouse in sight of the Benedictine Abbey; from the back it is a country house with views over the Avon river and Wiltshire. Inside, there is a sense of sunlit space, the foyer/dining room has a gallery, there are old, rare, well-loved possessions, books (they used to run a book shop here) and a fine conservatory. There is also a meditation room. Your hostess is great fun; both she and Dick enjoy having guests in this, the oldest borough in England.

Rooms: 1 twin, en suite (bath), with single attic room for overflow. Separate shower also available.

Price: £22.50 p.p. Attic overflow £20. No single supp.

Breakfast: Flexible.

Meals: Dinner available locally.

Closed: Never.

From A429, B4040 through Charlton, past Horse & Groom pub. 0.5 miles on, left signed 'Bullocks Horn — No Through Road'. Continue to end of lane. Turn right. House is first on left.

Entry No: 479   Map no: 4

Colin & Liz Legge
Bullocks Horn Cottage
Charlton, Malmesbury
Wiltshire SN16 9DZ
Tel: 01666 577600
Fax: 01666 577905
e-mail: legge@bullockshorn.clara.co.uk
Web: www.sawdays.co.uk

From top of High Street, left at Market Cross. House 100m on left next to large traffic mirror.

Entry No: 480   Map no: 4

Dick & M.E. Batstone
St. Aldhelms
14 Gloucester Street
Malmesbury
Wiltshire SN16 0AA
Tel: 01666 822145

Doi is relaxed and friendly: she does B&B because she loves it. Breakfast is cooked just as you want it, when you want it. In summer, you can while away warm evenings in the vine-hung, thyme-carpeted arbour in the garden. Cotswold stone is star here: house, yard, flower beds, delicious walled garden are all softly golden. Gently-decorated bedrooms have space, views, flowers and old photographs; one has a half-tester bed. The dining room has dark blue walls, wooden floors and a solid oak table with tapestry chairs.

Rooms: 2 doubles, 1 en suite (bath), 1 with private bath & shower.

Price: £25 p.p. Single supp. £5.

Breakfast: Flexible.

Meals: Dinner, £15 p.p., by arrangement. B.Y.O. wine. Pubs nearby.

Closed: Christmas.

A comfortable early 19th-century Cotswold stone farmhouse, set in beautiful open countryside on the Roman Fosseway. John is a cabinet-maker, specialising in gilding restoration; Heather collects books and is a writer. The walled garden is full of roses and in the shady courtyard there's a splendid Acacia Hillierii. With a croquet lawn, bike rides, facilities for riding and paths where you can walk where the Romans walked, it's a surprise that Bath is just six miles away.

Rooms: 1 twin with private bathroom and 1 double, en suite (bath & shower).

Price: £25 p.p.

Breakfast: Flexible.

Meals: Dinner available locally. Packed lunch available on request.

Closed: Christmas.

From Malmesbury take B4042 towards Wootton Bassett. Left to Lea & Charlton. In Lea, right opposite school. House is along drive through fields.

From Chippenham A420 towards Bristol to The Shoe hamlet, ignoring signs to North Wraxall. Just past garage on left, before pub, sharp right at x-roads, signed to Grittleton. Over first x-roads. House first on left with gates.

Entry No: 481   Map no: 4

Entry No: 482   Map no: 4

Tony & Doi Newman
Winkworth Farm
Lea
Nr. Malmesbury
Wiltshire SN16 9NH
Tel: 01666 823267
Web: www.sawdays.co.uk

John & Heather Owen
Halls Barn Farm
North Wraxall
Nr. Bath
Wiltshire SN14 7AQ
Tel: 01225 891542
Fax: 01225 892112
e-mail: john-owen@lineone.net

Big, generous beds, and the house is within eight acres of parkland and garden, in an ancient hamlet. This is the sort of impeccably-managed home that appeals particularly to American visitors and to those who love their comforts: huge main rooms with big windows looking over the perfectly-manicured garden, with chintz-covered chairs and lots of big flower arrangements. Bedrooms are smaller, with skylights and sloping beamed ceilings. Helga can tempt you with croquet, tennis and meals on the lawn in summer.

Rooms: 1 twin, 1 double and 1 single. Private or shared bathroom available.

Price: £25-£35 p.p.

Breakfast: Flexible.

Meals: Dinner, £15 p.p., available on request. Also excellent local pubs.

Closed: Never.

A medieval manor house and all that goes with it, plus modern touches when they matter. It looks imposing outside — arched, mullioned windows, jutting gables, tall chimneys — while the interior is, quite breathtakingly, manorial. The vast Tudor fireplace (complete with Elizabethan graffiti), a whole gallery of ancestral oil paintings and the most fascinating historic furniture and artefacts — it's all intriguing. Bedrooms are sunny, luxurious and charming with big beds and views over the grounds. *Children over nine welcome.*

Rooms: 2 doubles and 1 twin, all en suite (bath/shower).

Price: £40-£45 p.p. Single occ. £75.

Breakfast: Until 9.30am.

Meals: For groups only.

Closed: Christmas & New Year.

From M4 junction 17, west along A420. Turn right to Upper Wraxall. Take first left in village opposite village green. House is at end of private drive.

Entry No: 483   Map no: 4

Helga & David Venables
The Coach House
Upper Wraxall, Nr. Bath
Wiltshire SN14 7AG
Tel: 01225 891026
Fax: 01225 892355
e-mail: venables@compuserve.com
Web: www.sawdays.co.uk

From Bath take A36 Warminster road for 5 miles, left onto B3108, under r'wa bridge and up hill. First right, turn off Winsley bypass into old village, then 1st left, into lane marked 'except for access'.

Entry No: 484   Map no: 4

John & Elizabeth Denning
Burghope Manor
Winsley, Bradford-on-Avon
Wiltshire BA15 2LA
Tel: 01225 723557
Fax: 01225 723113
e-mail: burghope.manor@virgin.net
Web: www.sawdays.co.uk

It was built by a local baker in 1807, on a steep hillside with spectacular southern views over the lovely old Cotswold-stone town. The oak sail gallery has been meticulously restored, as well as the Victorian spiral staircase and pointed Gothic windows. The curves of the main part of the mill have created womb-like rooms, decorated in pale pinks and greens with vibrant Tahitian fabrics and hand-woven South American rugs. The beds — king-size circular, water, and Gothic iron — add a touch of fun. Dinners, too, are exotic, with recipes collected during their travels.

Rooms: 2 doubles and 1 suite, both en suite (bath), 1 double, en suite (shower).

Price: £34.50-£49.50 p.p. Single occ. £69-£89.

Breakfast: 8-9am.

Meals: Dinner (vegetarian only), £20 p.p. Mon, Thurs & Sat, by prior arrangement. B.Y.O. wine.

Closed: January & February.

From A363, mini-roundabout at Castle pub, go downhill towards town centre. After 50m, left into private drive, immediately before first house on pavement.

Entry No: 485   Map no: 4

Peter & Priscilla Roberts
Bradford Old Windmill
Masons Lane
Bradford-on-Avon
Wiltshire BA15 1QN
Tel: 01225 866842
Fax: 01225 866648
e-mail: oldwindmill@netscapeonline.com

Renovated with imagination and care, this handsome Bath stone Georgian farmhouse feels almost new. The large double with duck-egg blue walls and flowered frieze has a walnut wardrobe and a mahogany chest-on-chest. The other guestroom, on the ground floor is in the converted dairy, has an iron bedstead, exposed beams to the roof, flintwork walls and a kitchenette; both guestrooms have garden views, and there are teddies and silk flowers. The large, sunny kitchen/breakfast room with pretty striped walls and a flagged floor looks onto the fountain.

Rooms: 2 doubles, both en suite (shower).

Price: £30 p.p. Single supp. £9.

Breakfast: Until 9am.

Meals: Available locally.

Closed: Christmas & New Year.

From A36, Cley Hill r'bout, take turning signed Warminster. Pass two cottages on right. Bugley is first right after bend, by 30mph and 'Cattle Crossing' sign.

Entry No: 486   Map no: 4

Mrs Julie Hocken
Bugley Barton
Victoria Road
Warminster
Wiltshire BA12 7RB
Tel: 01985 213389
Fax: 01985 300450
e-mail: bugleybarton@aol.com

It is a rare treat to have your milk fresh from the cow. This rather grand Victorian Gothic farmhouse is a working, tenanted, arable and dairy farm owned by the Earl of Pembroke. There are very large, pretty bedrooms with crisp, white linen, furnished in the period of the house, impressive garden views, a baby grand and a billiard room. In the summer, the terrace doors are thrown open for an *al fresco* breakfast. Everything is grand but cosy and the Helyers are very friendly. The whole estate is 1,400 acres and a Site of Special Scientific Interest, treasured for its wild flowers and butterflies. *Children by arrangement.*

Rooms: 1 twin/double, en suite (shower) and 1 twin and 1 double/family, each with private bathroom.

Price: £24-£26 p.p. Single occ. £35-£40.

Breakfast: Flexible.

Meals: Dinner available locally.

Closed: Christmas and New Year.

What could be more seductive than the smell of home-baked bread wafting out of the kitchen? It sets the scene for this fine George I farmhouse in a quiet spot off the main road, on the edge of the New Forest. The rooms are full of character, ample and charming, with patchwork quilts, brass beds, stencils. Sue Barry is equally characterful and, as a Blue Badge Guide, is well qualified to tell you about the area. Home-made jams, honey and elderflower cordial, and several black Labradors snuffling about.

Rooms: 1 twin/family and 2 doubles, each en suite (shower); 1 single with private bathroom.

Price: £21-£25 p.p. Single supp. £10.

Breakfast: Until 9am.

Meals: Available locally.

Closed: Christmas & New Year.

From Salisbury, A36 towards Warminster/Bath. Left at Stoford into Great Wishford. Pass church and turn right at Royal Oak pub. House signed on right after 2 miles.

Entry No: 487   Map no: 4

Patricia Helyer
Little Langford Farmhouse
Little Langford, Salisbury
Wiltshire SP3 4NR
Tel: 01722 790205
Fax: 01722 790086
e-mail: bandb@littlelangford.co.uk
Web: www.sawdays.co.uk

From Salisbury, A36 towards Southampton. Approx. 5 miles on, look for Brickworth Lane on left, 200 yds before lights at junction A36/A27. Farmhouse at top of lane on right.

Entry No: 488   Map no: 4

Sue Barry
Brickworth Farmhouse
Brickworth Lane
Whiteparish, Salisbury
Wiltshire SP5 2QE
Tel: 01794 884663
Fax: 01794 884186
Web: www.sawdays.co.uk

A magical garden embraces this enchanting Queen Anne farmhouse. Watercolours, rich oils, polished antiques and the charm of your hosts fill the family home. You could wallow for hours in the roll-topped bath in the splendid oak-panelled bathroom. All the bedrooms are filled with light; one has three glorious views, another, smaller one has a delightful intimacy, as does the sitting room just down the book-lined hall. Meander down to the swans on the river, stride out across the meadows or fish on the farm's lakes. Glorious. *Children over 12 welcome.*

Rooms: 1 twin/double, en suite (bath & shower); 1 double, en suite (shower) and 1 twin with private bathroom.

Price: £25-£30 p.p. Single supp. £10 in high season.

Breakfast: Flexible.

Meals: Good pub/restaurant nearby.

Closed: Christmas.

Its origins lie way back in 1189, other bits were added in the 16th century. If you cherish a yearning to be close to the land and its ancient rhythms, this dynamic, hardworking farmhouse, full of character, people and pets, is for you. You come not to be feted, but to join in with it all. Meals are taken around a 400-year-old monastery refectory table; the food oozes country freshness and its nutritional values are satisfyingly 'old-world'. Downstairs is homely — slightly chaotic, even — but bedrooms are ordered and two have been freshly-decorated. Janet — robust and hardworking — is devoted to hunting and dressage.

Rooms: 1 king-size, en suite (shower); 1 twin, en suite (bath); 2 singles with either private bath or shower.

Price: £22-£26 p.p.

Breakfast: 7.30-9am.

Meals: Dinner, 4 courses inc. wine, £20 p.p. by arrangement. Reduction for 2 courses.

Closed: 23-31 December.

From Salisbury on A36 towards Southampton, right immediately at the dual carriageway (no signs). Then right at signs to Downton/Standlynch. Farm on right after 2 miles.

Entry No: 489   Map no: 4

Ian & Annette Fergie-Woods
Witherington Farm
Nr. Downton
Salisbury
Wiltshire SP5 3QT
Tel: 01722 710222
Fax: 01722 710405

From Devizes, A360 to Salisbury or A342 to Andover. After 4 miles turn right on B3098. Manor is 1 mile west of Urchfont.

Entry No: 490   Map no: 4

Mrs Janet Firth
Eastcott Manor
Easterton
Devizes
Wiltshire SN10 4PL
Tel: 01380 813313
Web: www.sawdays.co.uk

The garden overlooks wheat fields and an ancient hill fort — within it are lavender, roses, hostas and clematis. Carol moved from a larger house in Scotland, where she bred racehorses; here she enjoys being close to the races at Newbury, Wincanton and Bath. Her fine furniture looks good in a drawing room filled with flowers, paintings and family photos, comfortable sofas, scatter cushions and many horsey prints and books. The cosy bedrooms under the eaves have Jane Churchill and Colefax and Fowler fabrics (Carol's other love is interior design). *Children over 12 welcome. Outside kennel available for dogs.*

Rooms: 1 double and 1 twin, each with private bathroom.

Price: £22 p.p. Single supp. £8.

Breakfast: Flexible.

Meals: Dinner from £12.50 p.p. Packed lunch £3 p.p.

Closed: Christmas & New Year.

The vibes are good — and not just because this is crop circle and Stonehenge country. Val and David moved here from London in search of peace; and here they've found it. Val is an enthusiastic gardener and specialist decorator. Her style isn't to over-design anything but there are subtle touches everywhere. Each room has lovely fabrics and bed linen, and bathrooms are bright and fun; the twin has hand-painted wallpaper. You have a cosy sitting room with an open fireplace, and a more formal dining room for Aga-cooked breakfasts.

Rooms: 1 double, en suite; 1 twin and 1 single sharing private bathroom.

Price: From £30 p.p.

Breakfast: Flexible.

Meals: By arrangement.

Closed: Occasionally.

From Devizes, take A342 for approx. 1.5 miles, then turn right signed Stert. House is 6th on right.

Entry No: 491   Map no: 4

Mrs Carol Mitchell
Hill House
Stert
Devizes
Wiltshire SN10 3JB
Tel: 01380 722356
Fax: 01380 722356
e-mail: caminteriors@yahoo.co.uk

From Pewsey, A345 west for Devizes. Turn right for Hilcott at large r'bout by Woodbridge Inn. House is second on left (signed), over cattle grid.

Entry No: 492   Map no: 4

Val & David Maclay
Hilcott Farm House
Hilcott
Pewsey
Wiltshire SN9 6LE
Tel: 01672 851372
Web: www.sawdays.co.uk

On the Down behind the house was fought the Battle of Roundway in 1643. Today you are left in peace to take in the horizon-sweeping views, cosseted by two charming, easy-going hosts; Richard is a wine enthusiast and Pippa a skilled cook who works wonders with fresh ingredients to produce imaginative food. You have the run of the house and its gardens. Chickens range free in the stable yard and there's a grass tennis court. The bedrooms are large and luxurious, the whole house is elegantly furnished and decorated. *Children over 13 welcome.*

Rooms: 2 large twins/doubles, both en suite (bath).

Price: £35-£40 p.p. Single supp. £20.

Breakfast: Flexible.

Meals: Dinner, for not less than 4 people, £22 p.p., by arrangement.

Closed: Christmas & Easter.

Flagstone floors lead you into book-lined, red-bricked rooms scattered with family photographs and fresh flowers. Stylishly cluttered, cosy and with an adoring family retriever and pug, it's a seductively easy place to settle into. Clarissa is a professional cook and looks after you with bundles of energy and enthusiasm. Bedrooms are bright and simply decorated: walls and 'throws' are cream, beds are wooden. Outside, there are five acres of gardens, a tennis court, a swimming pool, and chickens that provide fresh eggs for your breakfast.

Rooms: 1 twin, en suite (shower); 1 twin/double, en suite (bath); 1 double with private bathroom.

Price: From £24-£28 p.p. Single occ. from £30.

Breakfast: Flexible.

Meals: Dinner, 4 courses, £20 p.p.

Closed: Never.

West along A4. Left just before Calne for Heddington. 2 miles to Ivy Inn and left at T-junc. House on left opposite church, 50 yards on.

Entry No: 493   Map no: 4

Richard & Pippa Novis
Heddington Manor
Heddington
Nr. Calne
Wiltshire SN11 0PN
Tel: 01380 850240
Fax: 01380 859176
e-mail: richardnovis@c ompuserve.com

From Marlborough, take A346 for 3 miles. Right to Wootton Rivers. In village, turn right (opp. Royal Oak pub) and drive for 0.7 miles. Drive is on right after sign for Clench Common.

Entry No: 494   Map no: 4

Clarissa Roe
Clench Farmhouse
Clench, Nr. Marlborough
Wiltshire SN8 4NT
Tel: 01672 810264
Fax: 01672 811458
e-mail: clarissaroe@btinternet.com
Web: www.sawdays.co.uk

Bill has applied his considerable artistic flair — he paints in oils and watercolours — to the renovation of this 17th-century thatched cottage. The A-frame sitting room has bold Chinese yellow walls, three plump sofas, light wooden floor and books — it is unintimidatingly stylish. The bedrooms are in similar vein and Bill and Felicity are easy, cultured hosts. There's a heated swimming pool, which you can use, and a sunken Italianate garden whose borders are edged with clouds of lavender. On sunny days or summer evenings you can shelter, colonial style, under a tiled loggia with rattan furniture. Perfect.

Rooms: 1 double, en suite; 1 double and 1 twin, sharing private bathroom.

Price: £21-£25 p.p. Single supp. £5.

Breakfast: 7am-9am.

Meals: Dinner, by arrangement, £15 p.p.

Closed: Never.

A more beautiful setting would be hard to find. In the valley of the Kennet River — which flows briskly past the foot of an immaculate lawn — is a house that deserves to be in a glossy magazine. It looks every inch a dolls' house, but Jeremy and Heather add a deft human touch. The elegance of breakfast taken in the conservatory is balanced by the comforting hubbub emanating from the family kitchen. Upstairs, the cleverly converted bedrooms are ingeniously clustered around the chimney breast. Time here slips by effortlessly; many people come to visit the mysterious crop circles.

Rooms: 1 double, en suite (bath); 1 twin and 1 single with shared bathroom.

Price: £25-£30 p.p. Single £30.

Breakfast: Flexible.

Meals: Available locally. Lunch/packed lunch available on request.

Closed: Christmas.

From Marlborough, take A346 Salisbury Rd south. At r'bout ending Burbage bypass, take B3087 Pewsey Rd. Right at x-roads 0.3 miles on. First house on right.

Entry No: 495   Map no: 4

Felicity & Bill Mather
Westcourt Bottom
165 Westcourt
Burbage
Wiltshire SN8 3BW
Tel: 01672 810924
Fax: 01672 810924
e-mail: westcourt.b-and-b@virgin.net

From Hungerford, A4 towards Marlborough. After 7 miles, right towards Stitchcombe, down hill (bear left at barn) and left at T-junc. On entering village, house is on left.

Entry No: 496   Map no: 4

Jeremy & Heather Coulter
Fisherman's House
Mildenhall
Nr. Marlborough
Wiltshire SN8 2LZ
Tel: 01672 515390

Undeniably beautiful within, and solidly handsome without. Jane is a gifted interior decorator; the colours are splendid and nothing seems to be out of place. However, Jane and Richard are easy and open; Jane was a ballet dancer and is refreshingly new to this B&B thing. Richard has green fingers and grows the fruit that will appear in pretty bowls on your breakfast table. The kitchen is engagingly beamed and straight out of a smart magazine. There are some fine pieces of furniture, sofas to sink into and enough comfort to satisfy a pharaoh.

Rooms: 1 double, en suite (shower/bath); 1 double/twin, en suite (shower).

Price: £30 p.p. Single occ. by arrangement.

Breakfast: Flexible.

Meals: Dinner £15-£20 p.p.

Closed: Christmas & New Year.

Worcestershire

A46 from Evesham or Stratford-upon-Avon, then exit signed Salford Priors. On entering village, turn right opp. church, signed Dunnington. House is on right, approx. 1 mile on, after 2nd sign on right for Dunnington.

Entry No: 497   Map no: 9

Mrs Jane Gibson & Mr Richard Beach
Salford Farm House
Salford Priors, nr. Evesham
Worcestershire WR11 5SG
Tel: 01386 870000
Fax: 01386 870300
e-mail: salford@wside.globalnet.co.uk

Good food, good wines (80 on the list) and a warm welcome await your arrival. You'll be singing the praises of your accommodating hosts — capable, friendly Ann, who does the cooking, and Tony, who imports wines — when their combined knowledge and palpable enjoyment are on show at meal times. When they held occasional 'Wine Weekends' they discovered that they loved entertaining so much that they threw open the doors of their home full-time. Bedrooms are spic-and-span, large, too, and overlook the long garden with views of the Malvern Hills.

Rooms: 1 twin/double and 1 double, both en suite (bath); 1 double with private bathroom.

Price: £24.50-£27.50 p.p. Single occ. £31. Discounts for longer stays; winter breaks available.

Breakfast: 8-9am.

Meals: Dinner, 4 courses, £16.90 p.p.

Closed: Christmas & New Year.

At the foot of the majestic Malvern Hills, so there are fine views all around A fine 15th-century house that was subsequently Georgianised, Welland Court is surrounded by 23 acres and a two-acre trout-stocked lake (guests ma fish here). Inside, you are bound to enjoy the dazzling black-and-white floored hall, antique-filled dining and drawing rooms and large bedrooms (where the house Scotch awaits you). *Cordon Bleu* dinners at the beautifully-set mahogany dining table.

Rooms: 1 twin, en suite (shower); 1 twin and 1 twin/double, en suite (bath/shower).

Price: £37.50 p.p. Single supp. £10.

Breakfast: Until 9.30am.

Meals: Dinner, inc. aperitif & wine, £35 p.p., available on request.

Closed: Never.

From M50 junc. 1, onto A38 for Worcester. After 1.5 miles, left for Upton-on-Severn and cross River Severn. At T-junc., right onto B4211. Left onto B4209 for Malvern Wells. Farm 3rd on right.

Entry No: 498   Map no: 9

Ann & Tony Addison
Old Parsonage Farm
Hanley Castle
Worcester
Worcestershire WR8 0BU
Tel: 01684 310124
Fax: 01684 310124
e-mail: opwines@aol.com

West on A4104 to Upton-upon-Severn. Once there, cross river, turn left up main street, continue for 3 miles until phone box on left. Turn left at sign and take left fork.

Entry No: 499   Map no: 9

Philip & Elizabeth Archer
Welland Court
Upton-upon-Severn
Worcestershire WR8 0ST
Tel: 01684 594426
Fax: 01684 594426
e-mail: archer@wellandcourt.demon.co.uk
Web: www.sawdays.co.uk

There has been a watermill on this site since the 14th Century. Today the spectacular, beamed Granary is a 40-foot long kitchen-cum-dining-cum-sitting area; it's such a sociable space and Ann can chat to guests while preparing an all-organic breakfast with fruit from the garden. The huge curved beams in the bedrooms are ancient ship's timbers from Gloucester Docks. You are just 10-minutes' walk from Broadway, yet mercifully feel miles from the masses. Large bedrooms, two grand pianos and kind hosts — Ann, a professional musician, and Hugh a war veteran.

Rooms: 2 doubles, each with extra single, both en suite (shower).

Price: £37.50 p.p. Single £45.50.

Breakfast: Until 9am.

Meals: Available locally.

Closed: Never.

From Oxford, A44 to Broadway. Take Snowshill Road out of Broadway & after 0.75 miles, Mill is signed on right.

Entry No: 500   Map no: 9

Hugh & Ann Verney
The Mill
Snowshill Road
Broadway
Worcestershire WR12 7JS
Tel: 01386 858298

"Guests staying here have everything my friends would have — biscuits by the bed, magazines, books, bath essences," says Christina. Here, in her listed limestone farmhouse that dates from 1820, she pampers guests without being overly solicitous. The house is deceptively big, with a cottagey drawing room and a modern open kitchen with sofa. The bedroom is a suite separated from the house by a latch door. There are windows to the south and the west, with panoramic views over rolling countryside. Newsham is in an AONB so do explore the waterfalls, moorland, castles and exquisite villages. A handy stopover en route to Scotland.

Rooms: 1 twin, en suite (bath & shower). Extra twin available for members of same family, sharing bathroom.

Price: £25 p.p.

Breakfast: Flexible.

Meals: Available locally.

Closed: Christmas & New Year.

Yorkshire

From Scotch Corner west on A66. Approx. 7 miles on, down hill turning left to Newsham. Through village and 2nd left for Helwith. House on right at top of hill, name on gate.

Entry No: 501   Map no: 15

Christina Farmer
Hill Top
Newsham
Richmond
Yorkshire DL11 7QX
Tel: 01833 621513
e-mail: cdfarmer@lineone.net

What an entrance! A Virginia creeper covers the outside, lilies fill the oak hall with a lingering fragrance and Richard's ancestors look down from the stone stairs. The house was once bigger and what remains is the Victorian section of a Georgian mansion. Now a manageable size, the house is in tiptop condition. A sense of space remains, with high, plaster-worked ceilings and pale bedrooms. Fireplaces everywhere, big baths, high beds, large windows onto the beautiful grounds and a terraced lawn that runs down to the Tees. You can fish, play tennis or croquet.

Rooms: 2 twins, both with private bathroom.

Price: £30 p.p. No single supp.

Breakfast: Flexible, with notice.

Meals: Dinner, 2-3 courses, by arrangement.

Closed: 10 December-1 February.

Prepare to be amazed. In every room and in every corner of the *breathtaking* garden, the marriage of natural beauty and sophistication exists in a state of bliss. The four Doric columns at the entrance draw you through the hall into the dining room and to views of the Swale Valley. Beds from Heals, period furniture, cast-iron baths, myriad prints and paintings and one double bed so high you wonder how to get onto it. Tim and Austin, both ex-English teachers, have created something unique and very special.

Rooms: 1 double and 1 twin, each en suite (bath & shower). 1 double with private bathroom and sitting room.

Price: From £28 p.p. Single supp. £10.

Breakfast: Until 10am.

Meals: Available in Richmond.

Closed: Never.

From A1, exit onto B6275. North for 4.2 miles. Turn into drive (on left before Piercebridge) and take 1st right fork.

From Richmond Market Place, house is at bottom of the hill opposite Barclays Bank. Look for a green door with 'Millgate House' sign.

Entry No: 502   Map no: 15

Entry No: 503   Map no: 15

Caroline & Richard Wilson
Cliffe Hall
Piercebridge, Darlington
Yorkshire DL2 3SR
Tel: 01325 374322
Fax: 01325 374947
e-mail: petal@cliffehall.freeserve.co.uk
Web: www.sawdays.co.uk

Austin Lynch & Tim Culkin
Millgate House
Richmond
Yorkshire DL10 4JN
Tel: 01748 823571
Fax: 01748 850701
e-mail: oztim@millgatehouse.demon.co.uk
Web: www.sawdays.co.uk

A short stroll from the centre of this pretty, old market town with its castle ramparts, theatre, pubs and Saturday market, step off the cobbled street and you find yourself in a country garden on the edge of stunning views of the Swale Valley. The owners of this elegant listed Georgian house have changed, but we are sure that you will get the same friendly welcome. There is *trompe l'oeil* everywhere. Guests have excellent rooms on the ground floor with pure cotton sheets on the beds. The conservatory has a fine view — Turner painted Easby Abbey; you could do the same from the garden here.

Rooms: 1 twin with private bathroom and 1 double, en suite (shower).

Price: From £24 p.p. Single supp. £6.

Breakfast: Flexible.

Meals: Available locally.

Closed: Open Easter 2001 onwards.

From Scotch Corner (A1 30 miles north of Wetherby), follow signs to Richmond. In Richmond, turn left at library and left into Frenchgate. House is at top on right with black railings.

Entry No: 504   Map no: 15

Elizabeth & Ken Parham
58 Frenchgate
Richmond
Yorkshire DL10 7AG
Tel: 01748 823227
Fax: 01748 823227
e-mail: liz@parhamengland.co.uk
Web: www.parhamengland.co.uk

The Harrops professionally and discreetly cosset you — for example, they'll leave tea and coffee on a tallboy outside your bedroom door each morning and place dressing gowns in the guestrooms. There's a pale green striped double and a twin with a delicate rose-print paper; both are elegantly furnished. Breakfast is eaten in the open kitchen. Dinner is an occasion and the polished mahogany dining table — laid with fine china, crystal and silver — lends the touch of formality that the excellent food deserves. Pasture land and ancient trees are all around.

Rooms: 1 double and 1 twin, each with private bathroom.

Price: £35 p.p. Single supp. £10.

Breakfast: Flexible.

Meals: Dinner, £23 p.p., by arrangement.

Closed: Occasionally.

At Scotch Corner leave A1/M or A66 and turn east, through Middleton Tyas, onto road toward Croft. After 1 mile, at sharp left bend, turn right into lane. House is 500 yds on.

Entry No: 505   Map no: 15

Mr & Mrs J.A. Harrop
Brook House
Middleton Tyas
Richmond
Yorkshire DL10 6RP
Tel: 01325 377713
Fax: 01325 377713

In the heart of the Yorkshire Dales National Park, this is a superb base for walkers. If you're arriving by car, take the 'over the top' road from Buckden to Hawes for stunning views. Gail and Ann bake their own bread, make jams and marmalade and cook very good sausages. Their dinners are prepared with fresh, local produce and are utterly delicious. Two bedrooms have four-posters (one very pink) and all rooms have marvellous views of Wensleydale. (The cheese factory has been bought by the locals.) There is no TV.

Rooms: 2 four-posters, 1 twin and 1 double, all sharing bathroom or shower room.

Price: £19-£20 p.p. Single supp. £5-£8.

Breakfast: 8.30am.

Meals: Dinner, 4 courses, £13.50 p.p. (not Thurs).

Closed: 31 October-mid-February.

The house is approx. 320 yards off the A684, on the road north out of Hawes, signposted Muker and Hardraw.

Entry No: 506   Map no: 15

Gail Ainley & Ann Macdonald
Brandymires
Muker Road
Hawes
Yorkshire DL8 3PR
Tel: 01969 667482
Web: www.sawdays.co.uk

The Madells work hard so that "people should not go away unhappy". This is not going to happen! The restaurant has an excellent reputation — you are generously fed and any of the 6,000 bottles in the cellar is served by the glass! The sitting rooms are snug and relaxing. The bedrooms, from large to cosy, each have sherry and a radio; you can hear racehorses ambling past in the morning on their way to the Moor. You can even get married here. But all of this would be blossom in the wind without Everyl's unflagging dedication and kindness.

Rooms: 2 four-posters, both en suite (shower); 1 twin/double and 2 doubles, all en suite (bath/shower).

Price: £37.50-£47.50 p.p. Single occ. £50-£60.

Breakfast: Until 10am.

Meals: Dinner from £24.50 p.p. Lunch from £22.50 p.p. Booking essential for both.

Closed: Never.

Southbound from A1 at Scotch Corner via Richmond and Leyburn. House at top of hill on right, on entering village square. Northbound from A1 on B6267 via Masham. House in right-hand corner of square.

Entry No: 507   Map no: 15

Everyl & Brian Madell
Waterford House
19 Kirkgate
Middleham
Yorkshire DL8 4PG
Tel: 01969 622090
Fax: 01969 624020
Web: www.sawdays.co.uk

Rebuilt in 1810 after the ravages of plague and fire, a perfect Wensleydale village remains forgotten by time. Four 17th-century almshouses have become Rookery Cottage. It faces the village green and its fine, wood-panelled dining room was once the village post office. Spotless bedrooms, with cottage garden views, are decorated with refreshing simplicity; each has a painted basin, lovely linen and dried flowers. There's a conservatory for guests, too. Home-made jams and marmalades for breakfast and, perhaps, a kedgeree made from Ronnie's catch of the day. Dine at the pub opposite — one of the North Country's finest.

Rooms: 1 twin and 1 double, both with basin, sharing bathroom.

Price: £22.50-£27.50 p.p. Single supp. £10.

Breakfast: 8.30-9am. Flexible by arrangement.

Meals: Packed lunch by arrangement.

Closed: Never.

Gerry is the only person to have won th Grand National (1960 on Merryman II), and started it (in 1996). A portrait of the winning pair hangs in the dining/living room. He's a happy man The bedrooms differ — one, a twin, sports an exciting cherry-red wall, the second, cream and peppermint colours A double has a drawn threadwork bedspread. Views are of paddock and moorland. A mecca for real ale enthusiasts, Masham is the home of both Theakston and Black Sheep breweries. It is also boisterous field sports country, so possibly Pasture House is not for the objectors.

Rooms: 2 doubles and 1 twin with basins, all sharing bathroom & wc.

Price: £18 p.p. No single supp.

Breakfast: Flexible.

Meals: Dinner, 3 courses, £10 p.p. B.Y.O. wine.

Closed: Christmas Day.

From A6108 (Ripon to Richmond road), turn off 0.35 miles north of Masham, towards Healey. Continue through Healey to junction signed Colsterdale. Take right fork. House is first on left.

Avril & Gerry Scott
Pasture House
Healey
Masham
Yorkshire HG4 4LJ
Tel: 01765 689149
Fax: 01765 689990

From Masham, take A6108. Leyburn is 8 miles on. House is on left, opposite Blue Lion Country Inn.

Mrs Ursula Bussey
Rookery Cottage
East Witton, Leyburn
Yorkshire DL8 4SN
Tel: 01969 622918
Fax: 01969 622918
e-mail: u.bussey@breathemail.net
users.breathemail.net/u.bussey/

Oriella goes the extra mile for you and her flamboyancy and style make light of the practicalities of having guests. She is arty, fun-loving and kind: she'll leave out fruit cake if you're peckish, provide a driver, sit and chat or leave you to choose some music. There are tapestries, mirrors, thick oak tables and oriental pieces, something to catch the eye at every turn. The bedrooms are big, chintzy/paisley and one has a seven-foot square bed! A Georgian jewel. *Children over 13 welcome.*

Rooms: 2 doubles and 1 twin, all en suite (2 with bath/shower and 1 with bath).

Price: £45-£50 p.p.

Breakfast: Until 10.30am.

Meals: Dinner, 4 courses, £25 p.p.

Closed: Never.

These are the nicest, most genuine, straightforward farming folk imaginable. Even in the mayhem of the lambing season they will greet you with a smile, tea and home-made biscuits. Their farmhouse is as unpretentious as they are: there's one bedroom here and three away from the homely hub in converted outbuildings. Rooms have a mixture of old and modern furniture and have garden views. Light sleepers may notice some traffic noise, but feel that's a small price to pay for being well-placed for the Dales and the Moors. Local sausages, home-made marmalade and own eggs for breakfast.

Rooms: 1 family, 1 twin, 1 double and 1 single, all en suite (shower). Gate Cottage: 1 double, en suite.

Price: £20-£25 p.p. Single supp. £5. Gate Cottage: £25-£30 p.p.

Breakfast: Until 10am.

Meals: Dinner £15 p.p.

Closed: 1 December-28 February.

Leave A1 at Leeming Bar, take A684 to Bedale. 0.5 miles out of town, turn off A684 to Newton-Le-Willows. Right at T-junc., left at Wheatsheaf pub, then immediate right through gates.

Entry No: 510   Map no: 15

Oriella Featherstone
The Hall
Newton-Le-Willows
Bedale
Yorkshire DL8 1SW
Tel: 01677 450210
Fax: 01677 450014

From Northallerton, take A167 north towards Darlington for 4 miles. House is on right, and signed.

Entry No: 511   Map no: 15

John & Mary Pearson
Lovesome Hill Farm
Lovesome Hill
Northallerton
Yorkshire DL6 2PB
Tel: 01609 772311
e-mail: pearsonlhf@aol.com

A peaceful, informal spirit pervades this elegant, bay-windowed farmhouse — it exudes warmth and friendliness. Anne goes to great lengths to make you comfortable and her cooking is delicious. The house, which harmoniously incorporates the former cottage and dairy buildings, has pale, fresh colour schemes, an interesting collection of books and superb views. The big guestrooms face south and you will be drawn to explore the gentle, rolling dales, the moors, the coastline and York and Durham. *Children over 12 welcome.*

Rooms: 1 twin and 1 twin/double, both with private bathrooms.

Price: £34 p.p. Single supp. £10.

Breakfast: Flexible.

Meals: Dinner, £22 p.p., by arrangement.

Closed: December & January.

The views go on forever, the wildlife comes to you. Lose yourself in 164 acres of parkland and woodland: footpaths lead you from the farm to the moors and take you past wild geese on the flight pond, cantering Soay sheep and even comical rheas and wallabies. Martin and Margaret are interested, involved people: you feel your presence counts. Inside, china knick-knacks and florals contrast with the bright whiteness of the rooms. Guests must take dinner. You won't mind in the slightest. *Children over 12 welcome.*

Rooms: 2 doubles and 1 twin, 1 en suite (bath) and 2 with private bath/shower.

Price: Dinner & B&B from £42.50 p.p.

Breakfast: Until 9.30am.

Meals: Dinner, 5 courses, included.

Closed: Christmas.

Going north on A19 take A172 towards Stokesley. Pass sign on right to Busby. House is 0.5 miles further on the left, with two red triangular deflectors on each side of entrance.

Entry No: 512　　　　　　Map no: 15

Anne Gloag
Busby House
Stokesley
Yorkshire TS9 5LB
Tel: 01642 710425
Fax: 01642 713838

Take B1257 south from Stokesley to Great Broughton. Left at village hall onto Ingleby Road to church at Ingleby Greenhow. Entrance opposite church. House is 0.5 miles away.

Entry No: 513　　　　　　Map no: 15

Margaret & Martin Bloom
Manor House Farm
Ingleby Greenhow
Great Ayton
Yorkshire TS9 6RB
Tel: 01642 722384
e-mail: mbloom@globalnet.co.uk

For 250 years this has been a farm, always in the same family. The Kynges, who have sheep and cattle, are in their second year of organic conversion — everything grown in the garden is already chemical-free. It is a splendid country house of the most traditional kind, at the end of a long, tree-lined drive and in very English parkland. A stone-flagged hall leads to an exquisite dining room that holds much family history. The bedrooms have oak chests, deep basins and magnificent wardrobes. Everywhere there is the nobility of wood and fine furniture. Mrs Kynge's cooking has won many accolades. *Croquet and tennis available.*

Rooms: 1 king and 1 double, en suite (bath); 1 twin with private bathroom and separate shower. Self-catering for 4 also available.

Price: £25 p.p. Single supp. £5.

Breakfast: Flexible.

Meals: Dinner £15 p.p.

Closed: 1 December-1 April.

Breakfast on home-baked soda bread, farms eggs and proper bacon and, for dinner, the Kelly's own lamb and beef. You are in a remote valley near the North Yorkshire Moors where the 1800s courtyard is such a rare survivor of local rural architecture that the BBC filmed it for posterity. The rooms, with views to the craggy moor, were being refurbished during our visit but Jill and the unflappable Andrew gave the warmest welcome. A perfect place to feel in touch with the seasons. "Idyllic," wrote our inspector.

Rooms: 1 double, 1 family room and 1 twin, each with private bathroom.

Price: £20 p.p. Single supp. £25.

Breakfast: Flexible.

Meals: Dinner, 3 courses, £15 p.p., by arrangement. Packed lunch available.

Closed: Never.

From A19, A172 towards Stokesley for 3 miles. Turn left and go straight over crossroads. Drive to house is 0.25 miles on, on right.

Entry No: 514   Map no: 15

Major & Mrs Julian Kynge
Potto Grange
Potto
Nr. Northallerton
Yorkshire DL6 3HH
Tel: 01642 700212
Fax: 01642 700978
Web: www.sawdays.co.uk

From Malton, A170 Pickering road to Cropton. Through Rosedale Abbey and up onto moor, following signs for Castleton. At first cattle grid, 2 miles on, turn right. Farmhouse is on right, 2.5 miles on.

Entry No: 515   Map no: 15

Jill Kelly
Stonebeck Gate Farm
Little Fryup, Danby
Whitby
Yorkshire YO21 2NS
Tel: 01287 660363
Fax: 01287 660363

Two of everything for breakfast — eggs, sausages, slices of bacon — and fresh fruit, too. The Cravens' are equally generous of spirit in their welcome. Their new home is of mellow Yorkshire stone, built in 1767 for the estate owner's eldest son. There is an air of quiet repose — traditional furniture, china in panelled alcoves, lovely prints and watercolours and a drawing room with Delph fire surround. Bedrooms are comfortable and snug — none have even floors — and from one there are winter-time views to Pickering Vale. A pretty village and garden and a lovely labrador enhance the enjoyment.

Rooms: 2 twins, each with private bathroom. One on 1st floor, one on 2nd.

Price: £30 p.p. Single supp. £5.

Breakfast: Between 7.30-9am.

Meals: Packed lunch, £5 p.p., by arrangement.

Closed: Occasionally.

Flamborough Head juts out into the storm-tossed North Sea and you can feel the force of nature. The Manor House a lovingly restored refuge: maple flooring, dark green walls and old oak table in the dining room, book-filled sitting room with brocade sofas, oak furniture, shuttered windows. Perhaps a coal fire in your room, or an elaborately carved Portuguese bed. The bathrooms have marble and Victorian fittings (cast iron baths). Geoffrey is a naval historian and the house is stuffed with his books. The coastal walks are out of this world. Unquestionably special. *Children over eight welcome.*

Rooms: 1 double with private bathroom; 1 twin/double, en suite (bath).

Price: £31-£36 p.p. Single supp. £8.

Breakfast: Flexible.

Meals: Dinner £22 p.p.

Closed: Christmas.

Proceed through Thornton le Dale on A170 towards Scarborough. The road rises after village centre. Pass church on left. Hurrell Lane is near top of hill on right. House immediately on right.

Entry No: 516   Map no: 16

Richard & Tuppie Craven
The High Hall
Hurrell Lane
Thornton le Dale
Yorkshire YO18 7QR
Tel: 01751 474371
Fax: 01751 477701

From Bridlington, B1255 to Flamborough. Follow signs to lighthouse, past church on right. House is on next corner (Lighthouse Rd/Tower St).

Entry No: 517   Map no: 16

Lesley Berry & Geoffrey Miller
The Manor House
Flamborough
Yorkshire YO15 1PD
Tel: 01262 850943
Fax: 01262 850943
e-mail: manorhouse@clara.co.uk
Web: www.manorhouse.clara.net

A northern city base that made our hearts soar — this modern cottage is an excellent alternative to corporate hotels. Both Stephanie's daughters are designers and an innate sense of style clearly runs in the family. You'll love her use of strong colour — the tiled hall with Chelsea Green walls, the bold yellow drawing room, the 'Madder Red' garden room, the intense blue single room which has a patchwork throw made from the daughters' childhood dresses. The Hornbys have a great sense of humour and love good food. From here you can catch daily ferries to the continent. You'll want to return.

Rooms: 1 double with private bathroom; 1 single also available to members of same party.

Price: £28 p.p.

Breakfast: Flexible.

Meals: Supper, £12 p.p. and dinner, £18 p.p. (includes wine).

Closed: Never.

Only the Moors lie behind this solid, stone farmhouse, five yards from the National Park, in farmland and woodland with fine views... marvellous walking country. The house is full of light and flowers. The pretty sitting room has deeply comfortable old sofas, armchairs and fine furniture. Rich colours and hunting prints give the dining room a warm and cosy feel. The Orrs have poured affection into this house, and the result is a home that's happy and remarkably easy to relax in... wonderful.

Rooms: 2 twins/doubles, 1 en suite (shower), 1 with private bathroom.

Price: £30 p.p. For 3 or more nights, £27.50 p.p. Single supp. £10.

Breakfast: Until 9am.

Meals: Dinner, 3 courses (including wine), £24.50 p.p.

Closed: Never.

Where the M62 becomes the A63, follow Humber Bridge signs. At large r'bout north of bridge, take left exit, A164 to Beverley. 3 miles on, right to Kirk Ella. Pass golf course and post office on right. Drive is first on right after Hogg Lane.

Entry No: 518   Map no: 16

From A170 Kirkbymoorside/Pickering road, turn into Sinnington. On village green, keep river on your left and fork right between cottages. Turn up lane, bearing right up hill. Farmhouse is past church, signed.

Entry No: 519   Map no: 15

Stephanie Hornby
Box Cottage
2 Hogg Lane
Kirk Ella, Hull
Yorkshire HU10 7NU
Tel: 01482 658852

John & Jane Orr
Hunters Hill
Sinnington
York
Yorkshire YO62 6SF
Tel: 01751 431196
Fax: 01751 432976
e-mail: jorr@btclick.com

Drive through a stone archway into an old courtyard. A grandfather clock, whose mythological figure blows a furious wind, then greets you. This is a 17th-century, beamed, working farmhouse, once attached to Ampleforth Abbey. The three uncluttered, flowery bedrooms are frilled and co-ordinated and have lovely views. There is a half-tester brass and iron bedstead with a soaring, awning-like canopy in the double. A true, bluff Yorkshire farming welcome from Andrew and graceful efficiency from Margaret. *Children over 10 welcome.*

Rooms: 1 twin and 1 double, both en suite (shower); 1 twin with private bath and shower next door.

Price: £24-£28 p.p. Single occ. £30. Cottages £200-£560 per week.

Breakfast: 8.30-9.30. Flexible by arrangement.

Meals: Not available.

Closed: 22 December-2 January.

Look at the beams — the structure is based on a 400-year-old cruck house and it was restored in the early 1900s using Arts and Crafts features. The dining room, hall and lounge were refurbished with oak panelling salvaged from one of Victoria's decommissioned Royal yachts and oak parquet floors were laid. There is well-loved antique furniture, together with a Victorian half tester bed; each room faces South over the tree-lined cottage garden. The Williams used to run Newstead Grange near Malton — they will look after you here equally well. *Children over 11 welcome.*

Rooms: 1 double and 1 twin, both en suite (1 shower and 1 bath).

Price: From £26-£29.50 p.p. Single supp. £5

Breakfast: 8.30-9am.

Meals: Available locally.

Closed: Occasionally.

A170 from Thirsk for 12 miles. Turn right onto B1257 1 mile before Helmsley. 50 yds on, turn left by church. House is at end of no through road.

Entry No: 520   Map no: 15

Margaret & Andrew Wainwright
Sproxton Hall
Sproxton
Helmsley
Yorkshire YO62 5EQ
Tel: 01439 770225
Fax: 01439 771373
e-mail: info@sproxtonhall.demon.co.uk

From Thirsk A170 towards Scarborough. Ampleforth is signed right after 7/8 miles. Daleside is 70 yards east of White Swan Inn, on same side of road in village centre.

Entry No: 521   Map no: 15

Pat & Paul Williams
Daleside
East End
Ampleforth
Yorkshire YO62 4DA
Tel: 01439 788266
Fax: 01439 788266

This spot, on the edge of the North York Moors National Park, was chosen for its views and Shallowdale House was arranged to soak up as much of the scenery as possible, from the Pennines to the Wolds. Although built in the '60s, the house, which has two and a half acres of mature hillside garden, is stylish and elegant. Bedrooms are soothingly decorated, uncluttered and comfortable. Phillip and Anton love what they are doing, so you will be treated like angels, served freshly-cooked dinners of outstanding quality, with those sublime views thrown in for good measure. *Children over 12 welcome.*

Rooms: 2 kings/twins, en suite (bath); 1 double with private bathroom.

Price: King-size £40 p.p.; double £32 p.p. (less for 3 nights or more). Single occ. £55/£44.

Breakfast: 8-9.30am.

Meals: Dinner, 4 courses, £21 p.p. Packed lunch by arrangement.

Closed: Christmas & New Year.

A superbly solid Georgian house with sweeping views across the Vale of York, yet only three minutes walk from the heart of the village. Set in 28 acres that run down to the River Swale (fishing available), it has black sheep, ducks, horses and ponies, a croquet lawn and a tennis court. The house — largely renovated by the amusing Sam and Annie — is a treat: the large, stylish rooms are all extremely cosy with quirky touches, and the big beamed bedrooms have lots of books, antiques, window seats. One has a four-poster.

Rooms: 1 twin/double, en suite (shower); 2 doubles, 1 en suite (bath) and 1 with private bathroom.

Price: £30 p.p.

Breakfast: Until 9.30am.

Meals: Dinner, £25 p.p., by arrangement, or good food available at four pubs a walk away.

Closed: Occasionally in winter.

From Thirsk, A19 south, then 'caravan route' via Coxwold and Byland Abbey. First house on left, just before entering Ampleforth.

Entry No: 522   Map no: 15

Anton van der Horst & Phillip Gill
Shallowdale House
West End
Ampleforth
Yorkshire YO62 4DY
Tel: 01439 788325
Fax: 01439 788885

From A1(M), take Boroughbridge exit. At North side of Boroughbridge follow Easingwold/Helperby sign. In Helperby, right at T-junction, right up Hall Lane. Left in front of school.

Entry No: 523   Map no: 15

Sam & Annie Atcherley-Key
Laurel Manor Farm
Brafferton-Helperby
York, Yorkshire YO61 2NZ
Tel: 01423 360436
Fax: 01423 360437
e-mail: laurelmf@aol.com
Web: www.sawdays.co.uk

A perfectly proper house run with faultless precision by John and Harriet — wine buff and interior decorator respectively. Right next door to Fountains Abbey and Studley Royal (here are the most complete remains of a Cistercian abbey in Britain), you are spoiled for things to do and see; consider your options in the manicured garden. Deer may wander up to the fence as you drink your tea. Just two beautifully decorated bedrooms and bathrooms that are enough to make you want to put down roots. *Golf, riding and clay pigeon shooting can be arranged.*

Rooms: 2 twins, both en suite (bath).

Price: £45 p.p. Single supp. £15.

Breakfast: Flexible, by arrangement.

Meals: Dinner, £25 p.p., by prior arrangement.

Closed: Christmas & New Year.

A stream runs through the garden and there's wildlife all around: very peaceful indeed. Only a mile from the spa town of Harrogate, this old mill cottage is a good base for sight-seeing. Over 200 years old, it has oak beams and an old stone arch that used to be the dairy and is now the breakfast corner. Peter and Marion are quiet hosts, their only concern being your rest and well-being. Peter was a professional golfer for 20 years and can arrange for you to play. There's a small library, and a guest sitting room. *Children over 12 welcome.*

Rooms: 2 twins, 1 en suite shower and 1 private bath/shower; 1 double, en suite (shower).

Price: £22.50 p.p. Single supp. by arrangement.

Breakfast: Until 9am.

Meals: Available locally.

Closed: Occasionally.

A1 to Ripon. B6265/Pateley Bridge road for 2 miles. Left into Studley Roger. House is last on right.

Entry No: 524   Map no: 15

John & Harriet Highley
Lawrence House
Studley Roger
Ripon
Yorkshire HG4 3AY
Tel: 01765 600947
Fax: 01765 609297

Off the A61 north of Harrogate, signed on the road.

Entry No: 525   Map no: 15

Peter & Marion Thomson
Knox Mill House
Knox Mill Lane
Harrogate
Yorkshire HG3 2AE
Tel: 01423 560650
Fax: 01423 560650
Web: www.sawdays.co.uk

Chris Knowles-Fitton's father was a devotee of Canada and built this timber-framed house in 1938 in the style of a log cabin. The solitude is restorative; the sitting room gives onto the wooden terrace whence views of the River Wharfe and the Dales Way — stupendous. There are books, rugs and oak furniture in the sitting room and glass doors lead through to the bright dining room. Bedrooms have pastel colours with splashes of cheerful floral chintz cushions; curtains and bathrooms continue the theme. A relaxed atmosphere prevails, and there are great walks all around; you can fish for trout, too.

Rooms: 2 doubles and 1 twin, all en suite (bath & shower).

Price: £25 p.p. Single supp. £5.

Breakfast: Flexible.

Meals: Dinner, £15 p.p., by arrangement. Packed lunch £4 p.p.

Closed: Christmas & New Year.

From Ilkley towards Skipton. Right at Addingham for Bolton Abbey, and straight on at r'bout. After 4 miles, pass old castle and bear right. Down steep hill, over bridge, up hill and on for 0.5 miles. At bottom of hill, cross bridge & immediately left to house.

Entry No: 526   Map no: 15

Pam & Chris Knowles-Fitton
Knowles Lodge
Appletreewick
Nr Skipton
Yorkshire BD23 6DQ
Tel: 01756 720228
Fax: 01756 720381

Some 'guests' had to sleep outside when it was a children's hospital. Dulce and Ian took seven winters to restore the Hall to its former beauty. The house now feels very much like a family home; big, comfortable bedrooms with armchairs, fresh flowers and excellent bathrooms. Another labour of love is the two-acre walled garden which includes a nursery and 'potager'. The flowerbeds are a gardener's dream, the lawns are sweeping and there is a grass tennis court. Dulce is a liveryman of the Worshipful Company of Gardeners.

Rooms: 2 twins/doubles, both en suite (bath & shower); 1 twin with private shower. Family suite on request.

Price: £30-35 p.p. Single supp. £10.

Breakfast: Until 9.30am.

Meals: Dinner, 4 courses, £25 p.p. Supper £17.50 p.p.

Closed: Never.

From Bawtry, east on A631. Approaching Gringley on the Hill, 1st left after school sign. Continue for 150 yds. House on left with iron gates.

Entry No: 527   Map no: 15

Ian & Dulce Threlfall
Gringley Hall
Gringley on the Hill
Yorkshire DN10 4QT
Tel: 01777 817262
Fax: 01777 816824

Scramble down from your balcony at a moment's notice, bound gracefully into the sea, become a hero. Return refreshed, then take the lilo out for an afternoon nap. Only one small room, but what views and you can fall asleep to the sound of crashing waves. No electricity, but a nearby lighthouse flashes every ten seconds. The wearing of swimsuits is compulsory at all times and you may be required to perform heroic acts in ice cold water.

Rooms: 1 wood-panelled single.

Price: Your dignity.

Breakfast: With the seagulls.

Meals: Fish suppers.

Closed: Ice ages.

Head for the horizon. Stop where dry land ends. Parking at low tide.

Entry No: 528   Map no: 15

B. A. Watch
Water's Edge
Waverly
Yorkshire
999 SOS

SCOTLAND

*Great things are done when men and mountains meet; this is not done
by jostling in the street.*

William Blake 1757-1827

The Taylors moved to this creeper-clad old manse after retiring from farming. The rooms are large and bright, there is a fine cantilever staircase up from the hall, and the dining room's long windows frame good rural views. The big comfortable bedrooms, with shutters and long curtains, have more character than luxury. The colourful walled garden, full of clematis, honeysuckle and roses, hides a small vegetable garden, orchard and ornamental pond. Beyond, fields rise and there is deep rural seclusion. Genuinely nice people and good, easy conversation. *Children over 12 welcome.*

Rooms: 1 twin and 1 double, both with private bathrooms.

Price: £23 p.p. No single supp.

Breakfast: Flexible.

Meals: Dinner, £12.50 p.p., by arrangement.

Closed: Christmas & New Year.

From A1 towards Duns on B6438 for 5.5 miles. Left at church noticeboard. On for 0.25 miles. After Bonkyl church, 2nd right through black gate.

Entry No: 529   Map no: 19

Libby & Martin Taylor
Kirkside House
Bonkyl
Nr. Duns
Berwickshire TD11 3RJ
Tel: 01361 884340
Fax: 01361 884340
Web: www.sawdays.co.uk

Borders and Lowlands

A 50-ft drawing-room with Venetian glass windows and Adamesque ceiling, Arts & Crafts carvings on the wood-panelled stairs and original cast radiators in the dining room... the small Georgian mansion with neo-Jacobean additions is full of historic surprises. One bedroom has a flash jacuzzi with gold basins to match; all come with their own grand balconies overlooking gardens and fields. Work up your appetite in hunting, shooting and fishing country: Joan is a brilliant cook (*Cordon Vert*) and her veg is organically home-grown.

Rooms: 1 double and 1 twin, en suite; 1 double with private bathroom.

Price: From £27.50 p.p. No single supp.

Breakfast: Flexible.

Meals: Packed lunch and dinner on request.

Closed: Never.

"Leave it better than you found it" — your hosts' philosophy of land ownership applies equally to improvements wrought for their guests' well-being. As soon as you round the bend and see their secluded Georgian farmhouse, wrapped in the bubbling Bowmont's river valley, the magic begins its work. Peace, informality, an immaculate interior of gentle taste and genial hosts who enjoy company. Cheery bedrooms with good beds, crisp linen, flowers and books overlook the garden, fields and Cheviot Hills. Ann cooks most ably with fine, fresh ingredients.

Rooms: 1 twin and 1 double, both with dressing rooms and private bathrooms.

Price: £30 p.p. Single occ. £35.

Breakfast: Until 9.30am

Meals: Dinner £20 p.p. 24 hours' notice needed.

Closed: Occasionally.

From Edinburgh A68 for Jedburgh. Left at Carfraemill, A697 for Duns. Left in Greenlaw, A6105 for Duns. There, pass Jim Clark Museum, and left at Preston-Grantshouse road. House 600 yds on right.

Entry No: 530   Map no: 19

John & Joan Bimson
Wellfield House
Preston Road
Duns
Berwickshire TD11 3DZ
Tel: 01361 883189
Fax: 01361 883189
e-mail: john.bimson@virgin.net

From Kelso, B6352 to Yetholm. Bear right down High St (B6401). 1 mile on, left to Belford-on-Bowmont. After 3.5 miles, house on right by phone box.

Entry No: 531   Map no: 19

Ann & Peter Mather
Belford-on-Bowmont
Yetholm
By Kelso
Roxburghshire TD5 8PY
Tel: 01573 420362

A hands-on farm, undergoing organic conversion, made for children to wander or work: pitch in — milk a cow, watch the lambing and collect eggs. Simple, comfortable rooms, bright from big windows and, everywhere, an eccentric 1700s nooks-and-crannies mood prevails. From the family room — pink floral walls and pink carpet — you can see old Border keeps and a spider-web of stone walls. In nearby Melrose, beneath the Eildon Hills, Robert the Bruce's heart lies buried. A peaceful and romantic spot.

Rooms: 1 family with private bathroom; 1 double, en suite (shower).

Price: £23 p.p. Single supp. £5. Family room £55.

Breakfast: Normally 8.30am, but flexible.

Meals: Dinner from £12 p.p. Packed lunch available.

Closed: Never.

Mary Queen of Scots was here, inevitably, and so is the warrant for her execution; 26 other monarchs have visited since the 12th century. There is so much of interest here that the house is open to the public, but Gail, the housekeeper, will make you especially welcome. There is a fascinating old laundry, a private chapel, fine furniture, porcelains and pictures, and Traquair sells its own beer. A tour of the house — Scotland's oldest inhabited — is included. You can wander the vast gardens and use the lower drawing room.

Rooms: 2 doubles, en suite (bath).

Price: £65 p.p. Single occ. £80.

Breakfast: 7-10am.

Meals: Lunch in Cottage restaurant in grounds. Dinner by arrangement.

Closed: 22 December-5 January.

From Galashiels, A7 past Torwoodlea golf course and right to Langshaw. After 2 miles, right at T-junc., then left at Earlston sign in Langshaw. House is white, in trees, signposted at farm road.

Entry No: 532   Map no: 19

Sheila & Martyn Bergius
Over Langshaw Farm
Galashiels
Selkirkshire TD1 2PE
Tel: 01896 860244
Web: www.sawdays.co.uk

From Peebles, take B7062. After 7 miles, left signed Traquair.

Entry No: 533   Map no: 19

Catherine Maxwell Stuart
Traquair House
Innerleithen
Peebleshire EH44 6PW
Tel: 01896 830323/830647
Fax: 01896 830639
e-mail: enquiries@traquair.co.uk
Web: www.traquair.co.uk

You can roam over 1,300 acres with sheep, cattle, horses and abundant wildlife. An excellent base for families: Arran, in Spring, encourages children to bottle-feed lambs. Rooms are comfortable, not grand, with silk flowers, patterned carpets and rugs and, in the bedrooms, wooden floors and reproduction furniture — but the surroundings are what you came for and the views will make your heart soar. Fishing, walking and pony-trekking are yours for the asking or you can relax in the walled garden. The silence at night is disturbed only by wildlife. Nearby is Lyne Fort, a major Roman encampment.

Rooms: 2 doubles and 1 twin, sharing 2 bathrooms.

Price: £18-£20 p.p. Single occ. £22.

Breakfast: Flexible.

Meals: Packed lunch available.

Closed: Christmas Day.

However elegant and lovely the house may be, delightful David and Sue bring it down to earth; you will enjoy good conversation with them. The best room is the drawing room, formal but seductively so, with a log fire, family furniture, a great old atlas lying open. From the handsome hall rises the cantilevered stone staircase to the bedrooms, two of them elegant with writing desks and high ceilings, one of them more country-comfy, with lots of books and old pine furniture. Sue is a trained cook and uses home-grown organic veg; her porridge is delicious. *Children over 12 welcome.*

Rooms: 1 twin, en suite (bath), 1 twin with private bathroom and 1 double, en suite (shower).

Price: £33 p.p. Single supp. £10.

Breakfast: Until 9am.

Meals: Dinner, 4 courses, £22 p.p., by arrangement. Packed lunch from £10 p.p.

Closed: Christmas & New Year.

2.5 miles north of Earlston on A68, turn east for Birkenside. 150 yds after narrow bridge, at right-hand bend, straight on and immediately left through stone archway.

Four miles west of Peebles on the A72, signed on right-hand side of main road.

Entry No: 534   Map no: 19

Arran & John Waddell
Lyne Farmhouse
Lyne Farm, Peebles
Peebleshire EH45 8NR
Tel: 01721 740255
Fax: 01721 740255
e-mail: awaddell@farming.co.uk
Web: www.sawdays.co.uk

Entry No: 535   Map no: 19

Sue & David Sillar
Birkhill
Earlston
Scottish Borders TD4 6AR
Tel: 01896 849307
Fax: 01896 848206
e-mail: birkhill@btinternet.com

Purest Walter Scott — castles, abbeys, keeps, gardens, salmon and trout rivers — here are the wild, rolling Borders at their most romantically beautiful. The rooms at Ancrum Craig are part 18th-century, part Victorian, and the views are stupendous. Johan will tell you all about the best walks, but don't dash off to explore until you've eaten Jill's sustaining Scottish breakfast with haggis; her smoked salmon and scrambled eggs are equally delicious.

Rooms: 2 doubles and 1 twin, all en suite (1 bath & 2 showers).

Price: £23-£25 p.p. Single supp. £12. Discount for longer stays.

Breakfast: Flexible.

Meals: Walker's supper by prior arrangement.

Closed: New Year.

Highland cattle graze lazily as you drive up to the early 17th-century laird's house, the oldest in the parish. It has been done up recently to make it lighter and brighter, and elegant. You breakfast in the big kitchen at one large table and have your own sitting room with woodburning stove, tartan carpet, red sofa, leather chair and pine furniture. Dinner is served in the cosily elegant dining room. There are 60 acres of woodland and grazing, so you are undisturbed by the noise of the 20th century. It is a lovely house, in a superb setting, with a big welcome attached.

Rooms: 1 twin and 1 double (with extra bed), each with private bathroom (1 shower, 1 bath).

Price: £35-£40 p.p. Single supp. £10.

Breakfast: Until 9.30am.

Meals: Dinner by arrangement.

Closed: Never.

From Jedburgh, A68 for Edinburgh. Left after 3.5 miles to Ancrum. Fork left to Denholm before village. After 1.75 miles, right signed Lilliesleaf. Bear left, then left to Ancrum Craig.

Entry No: 536   Map no: 19

From Hawick A698, right on A6088 signed Bonchester Bridge. Follow road into village (6 miles), sharp right-hand bend at foot of hill. After 100 yds, 1st turning on right before little bridge.

Entry No: 537   Map no: 19

Jill & Johan Hensens
Ancrum Craig
Ancrum, By Jedburgh
Scottish Borders TD8 6UN
Tel: 01835 830280
Fax: 01835 830259
e-mail: ancrumcraig@clara.net
Web: www.ancrumcraig.clara.net

Christopher & Jacqui McLean May
Hobsburn
Bonchester Bridge, Hawick
Scottish Borders TD9 8JW
Tel: 01450 860720
Fax: 01450 860330
e-mail: b+b@mcleanmay.com
Web: www.mcleanmay.com

In a peaceful village, this former manse is a happy and much-loved house; energy and affection have been poured, too, into the lovely and once-derelict garden. You have the drawing room — with old pictures and a log fire — to yourselves, and if you stay for dinner you'll eat good country food, maybe fish or game. Your hosts are keen on country sports, although no longer take part. Some amazing floral wallpapers and comfortable bedrooms. The rooms are all let to just one party, so you can make up your own rules.

Rooms: 2 twins and 1 single, let only to members of the same party, sharing bathroom.

Price: £25 p.p.

Breakfast: Until 9.30am.

Meals: Dinner, £17.50 p.p., by prior arrangement.

Closed: Occasionally.

In utterly quiet and peaceful surroundings overlooking the River Annan, this old sandstone house reveals, astonishingly, the remains of a medieval motte within its big walled garden. The house is ideally placed on the route halfway between deep south and far north — explore the ancient church or the wetlands bird sanctuary nearby. The bedrooms are big and pristine and so are the bathrooms. There is a warm family air to it all, and furniture is a mix of old comfort and old elegance. *Children over 10 welcome.*

Rooms: 1 double with private bath; 2 twins, both en suite (bath).

Price: £30-£32 p.p. Single supp. £5.

Breakfast: Flexible.

Meals: Dinner £20 p.p.

Closed: Never.

From A74M, take junction 20 onto B722 to Eaglesfield. Second left after 350m, signed Middlebie. There, house and gate are next to church.

Entry No: 538 Map no: 19

J. Milne-Home
Kirkside of Middlebie
Lockerbie
Dumfries & Galloway DG11 3JW
Tel: 01576 300204

A74 (M) junc. 17 to Lockerbie, then B7076 to Johnstonebridge. First right after approx. 1.5 miles, and 100 yds on, left back over m-way bridge. After 1 mile, right at T-junc., then 2nd left to Church. House next to church.

Entry No: 539 Map no: 19

Frank & Jane Pearson
Applegarth House
Lockerbie
Dumfries & Galloway DG11 1SX
Tel: 01387 810270
Fax: 01387 811701
e-mail: jane@applegarthtown.demon.co.uk

"Too small for envy, for contempt too great" — the 17th-century motto is written above the door through which Robbie Burns entered when he came to stay. Knockhill is superbly authentic and architecturally impressive. Great stone stairs, carved oak furniture, lovely rugs, grandfather clocks, smooth grass tennis court and croquet lawn. The beamed and eaved attic room has a door that's 4.9 feet high — your stoop is rewarded with long views. Grand farming feel and the Morgans are the easiest of hosts. "These are top people doing B&B in the very best way," says our inspector.

Rooms: 2 twins, 1 with private bath and 1 with private shower.

Price: £25-£30 p.p. No single supp.

Breakfast: Flexible.

Meals: Dinner £18 p.p.

Closed: Christmas & New Year.

The Victorian billiard table is full-size, there are 20 acres of rhododendrons and woods, a turf-and-gravel maze, a croquet lawn, lots of books, some fine paintings and sculpture, and the log fires are lit for breakfast. Christopher is a vintage car enthusiast and keen gardener; Mary is an excellent cook, using food from their own garden. They are warm hosts and the house feels relaxed, even with a formal sitting room. The bedrooms are large, bright, and well-furnished, with good rugs, old long dressing mirrors and the odd *chaise longue. Children over 12 welcome.*

Rooms: 3 twins/doubles, all en suite (bath/shower).

Price: £30-£33 p.p. Single occ. £38.

Breakfast: Until 9.15am.

Meals: Dinner, £17.50 p.p., available on request. Packed lunch from £3.50 p.p.

Closed: 1 November-Easter.

From M74 junc.19, take B725 for Dalton for 1.5 miles. Right at x-roads to Lockerbie, 1 mile on, right at small stone lodge. House is at top of long, unsurfaced drive.

Entry No: 540　　　　　Map no: 19

Yda & Rupert Morgan
Knockhill
Lockerbie
Dumfries & Galloway DG11 1AW
Tel: 01576 300232
Fax: 01576 300818
Web: www.sawdays.co.uk

From Dalbeattie, south-east on B793. Auchenskeoch is 7 miles down this road on right. Turn right and, after 30 yards, left through gate posts.

Entry No: 541　　　　　Map no: 18

Christopher & Mary Broom-Smith
Auchenskeoch Lodge
By Dalbeattie
Dumfries & Galloway DG5 4PG
Tel: 01387 780277
Fax: 01387 780277

You can sink into the sofas without worrying about creasing them; it is a beautiful 18th-century Scottish Georgian house, yet there's not a hint of formality. The Dicksons, engaging and sociable, are at ease here and so will you be. The sitting and dining rooms connect through a large arch; family pictures, rugs on wooden floors, a feng shui cabinet. In the bedrooms: a cast-iron bed, elegant linen, excellent furniture and masses of light and good books. There are 200 acres of grazing land, a dog, cat, donkeys, and free-ranging hens. The place and the people are among the best.

Rooms: 2 twins, both with private bath and shower. Cot etc. available.

Price: £36 p.p. Single supp. £6.

Breakfast: Until 10am.

Meals: Dinner, £20 p.p., may be available on request.

Closed: Christmas.

Polished oak furniture, high-backed chairs, silver — it's traditional and smart, yet not grand and Ginny and David seem to enjoy having guests. Bedrooms — one is a fresh yellow with marine-blue Nepalese bedspread — have fresh fruit, flowers and mineral water with cut-crystal glasses, mohair blankets and comfortable beds. Even within the house you know that you are in deep countryside — walking sticks and fishing nets stand by the door and you can hear the rush of the tumbling stream that cuts through the private glen. The Southern Upland Way goes past the door.

Rooms: 1 twin and 1 double, both with private bathroom.

Price: £27.50 p.p. Single occ. £32.

Breakfast: 7.30-9am.

Meals: Dinner, 4 courses, £19 p.p.; supper, 2 courses, £12.50 p.p. by arrangement. Packed lunch £5 p.p.

Closed: Christmas & New Year.

A75 Dumfries ring road towards Stranraer. Through Crocketford to Springholm & right to Kirkpatrick Durham. Left at village x-roads, after 0.8 miles, go up drive on right by white lodge.

Entry No: 542   Map no: 18

Willie & Catriona Dickson
Chipperkyle
Kirkpatrick Durham, Castle Douglas
Dumfries & Galloway DG7 3EY
Tel: 01556 650223
Fax: 01556 650223
e-mail: dickson@chipperkyle.freeserve.co.uk
Web: www.sawdays.co.uk

A75 towards Stranraer. In Castle Kennedy, right opposite Esso station. Approx. 1.25 miles on, after right bend, right signed Chlenry. Continue down hill, farmhouse is on left after 300 yds.

Entry No: 543   Map no: 18

David & Ginny Wolseley Brinton
Chlenry Farmhouse
Castle Kennedy
Stranraer
Wigtownshire DG9 8SL
Tel: 01776 705316
Fax: 01776 889488
e-mail: WolseleyBrinton@aol.com

"One of the loveliest houses I've seen," said our inspector. The owners have real warmth and interest to match the vibrant, multi-hued brightness of their generous William Adam house. They also have ancestors to oversee the dining table, a club fender before the drawing-room fireplace, a garden room with masses of books and one bedroom described as a "green-combed retreat with a Rajahstani bedhead". All the bedrooms feel private (around corners, in other wings), beautiful and different with superb décor. And adjective-defying Galloway is all around.

Rooms: 1 double, en suite (bath/shower); 1 double and 1 twin, en suite (bath).

Price: £27 p.p. Single occ. £33.

Breakfast: 7.30-8.30am.

Meals: Dinner, 3 courses, £19 p.p., by arrangement.

Closed: Occasionally.

From Stranraer, A77 towards Portpatrick for 1.5 miles. Straight on at A716 towards Drummore. Drive is on left after approx. 1 mile, at junction with B7077 signed Newton Stewart.

Entry No: 544   Map no: 17

Peter & Liz Whitworth
Kildrochet House
By Stranraer
Wigtownshire DG9 9BB
Tel: 01776 820216
Fax: 01776 820216
e-mail: kldrochet@compuserve.com
Web: www.sawdays.co.uk

Sir David Hunter Blair, in 1821, razed the old castle to create this magnificent Regency one, cared for with affection by James and much of it unchanged. It is too rich a treat to fit this brief passage; bring your friends and have the whole place to yourselves — it is worth the considerable cost. The rooms are huge, the furniture is original, the library has walls of leather-bound tomes, there is a billiards room on the expected scale, a family museum, an art gallery full of Scottish colourists and 2,000 acres. A castle, yet still, exquisitely, a home.

Rooms: 4 four-posters, 2 doubles, 5 twins, 6 singles, all en suite bathrooms or sharing bathroom with 1 single.

Price: £110 p.p. Bookings made only for one party at a time. Minimum 4 people.

Breakfast: Flexible.

Meals: Dinner, £70 p.p., includes all drinks. Lunch from £20 p.p.

Closed: Christmas.

From Maybole, south on B7023 through Crosshill, then left onto B741 towards Straiton. After 2 miles, estate wall. Lodge and gates on left and signed.

Entry No: 545   Map no: 18

James Hunter Blair
Blairquhan Castle
Straiton, Maybole
Ayrshire KA19 7LZ
Tel: 01655 770239
Fax: 01655 770278
e-mail: enquiries@blairquhan.co.uk
Web: www.blairquhan.co.uk

They are kind, relaxed and interesting. Our inspector hugely enjoyed them. It is a fine house, too, with views to the River Doon flowing past the garden. The atmospheric drawing room is stately and half-panelled. There is a lot of oak, plus cream colours, bay windows, oils on the walls, and large sliding doors to the dining room. The bedrooms are done in fresh colours — blues and whites — with good linen and towels, fine furniture, decorative wash bowls, shutters rather than curtains. Easy elegance and wonderful people and the sea is only a mile away. *Children over 10 welcome.*

Rooms: 1 double with private bath; 1 twin, en suite (shower).

Price: £35 p.p.

Breakfast: Until 9.30am.

Meals: Evening meals by arrangement.

Closed: Never.

You'd hardly believe that you are 30 minutes from Glasgow. The hamlet used to house the furniture makers of nearby Beith — each cottage is white-washed and immaculate and there's absolute peace. Aileen loves her 1800s mini-manor and sharing the house and the garden; she's a Blue Badge guide and therefore full of excellent, original travel ideas. The bedroom is under the eaves with chintz poppy curtains and bedspread and views to garden and fields one way and to Loch Winnoch the other. Magazines and flowers, conservatory and drawing room, orchards and fields — a real retreat.

Rooms: 1 double with child's bed available.

Price: £25-£27 p.p. No single supp.

Breakfast: Flexible.

Meals: Available locally.

Closed: Christmas & New Year.

A719 into Alloway on south side of Ayr. Follow Tam O'Shanter signs. House is opposite Burns Monument by church.

Entry No: 546   Map no: 18

John & Moira Pollok-Morris
Doonbrae
40 Alloway
Ayr
Ayrshire KA7 4PQ
Tel: 01292 442511
Fax: 01292 442511
e-mail: doonbrae@aol.com

Glasgow-Irvine, A737, bypass village of Howwood, sign on left to riding stables and B&B. Follow road through stables and farm. Signed, 2nd on left.

Entry No: 547   Map no: 18

Aileen Biggart
Glenshian
Newton-of-Beltrees
By Loch Winnoch
Renfrewshire PA12 4JL
Tel: 01505 842823
Fax: 01505 323242

Beside the green in a Borders sheep-farming village, Skirling House is imbued from top to bottom with the spirit of the Scottish Arts and Crafts movement; it has innate grace of space and form in its one-room-thick layout, and gathers its beautiful gardens in a peaceful embrace. The harmony goes on inside, where soft colours and superb design are enhanced by Bob and Isobel, whose eye for complementary ancient and modern is acute. Sleep soundly in your bright, comfortable bedroom, and awake to stunning views.

Rooms: 1 twin and 3 doubles, all en suite. 2 self-catering cottages: 1-bedroomed and 2-bedroomed.

Price: £34 p.p. Single supp £10. 5% discount for longer stays. Self-catering: £200-£450 p.w.

Breakfast: 8-9.30am.

Meals: Dinner £20 p.p.

Closed: Christmas, January & February.

You'll be serenaded by the birds and the bees. The infectiously vibrant Carina and Jim have poured energy, affection and an artistic streak into their lovely 18th-century family home: Turkish rugs, ethnic cushions and intriguing knick-knacks everywhere. A comforting hubbub emanates from the kitchen — Carina is an excellent cook and you'll be chatting easily before you know it. With table-tennis, snooker and a trampoline in the garden, this is a great base for families, as well as for those looking for a country retreat. Glorious views, too.

Rooms: 1 double and 1 twin, en suite (bath and shower, respectively).

Price: £30-£40 p.p.

Breakfast: Flexible.

Meals: Lunch, packed lunch and dinner by arrangement.

Closed: 20 December-6 January.

From Biggar, A702 for Edinburgh. Just outside Biggar, right on A72 for Skirling. Big wooden house on right facing village green.

Entry No: 548   Map no: 19

Bob & Isobel Hunter
Skirling House
Skirling, By Biggar
Lanarkshire ML12 6HD
Tel: 01899 860274
Fax: 01899 860255
e-mail: enquiry@skirlinghouse.com
Web: www.skirlinghouse.com

From Edinburgh A1 for Berwick-upon-Tweed. Left for East Linton, left again under r'way bridge and through village. After 0.5 miles, left for Markle. First white house on right.

Entry No: 549   Map no: 19

Carina & Jim McGuinness
Markle House
East Linton
East Lothian
Tel: 01620 860570
Fax: 01620 860937
e-mail: mcguinness@marklehouse.fsnet.co.uk

A Georgian farmhouse surrounded by 350 acres of undulating countryside — and so close to Edinburgh! The farm has won awards for conservation and Michael is deeply committed to the countryside. Barbara is a gifted hostess. Gardens are informal and pretty and you may roam on the farm or play tennis. On sunny days, breakfast is served in the lovely conservatory full of fragrant climbing geraniums and jasmine. Co-ordinated bedrooms with inspired use of fabric and colour, great views and lots of space. The coral drawing room with log fire is most striking.

Rooms: 2 doubles, both en suite; 2 twins sharing bathroom (other bathrooms are available, too).

Price: £20-£27 p.p.

Breakfast: Flexible.

Meals: Available locally.

Closed: Christmas.

From A1 at Haddington take B6368 south signed Bolton & Humbie. 2.5 miles on through Bolton, at top of hill, fork left signed Eaglescairnie. Entrance 1.5 miles on left.

Entry No: 550   Map no: 19

Barbara Williams
Eaglescairnie Mains
Gifford
Haddington
East Lothian EH41 4HN
Tel: 01620 810491
Fax: 01620 810491
e-mail: williams.eagles@btinternet.com

This 1780s Georgian manse is a real family home, where Gwen and Jake welcome guests who either want the peace of a charming country town or city convenience (Edinburgh is a 30-minute drive, or regular trains will take you to the foot of the castle). The house is elegantly furnished and retains many original features; the bedrooms are well-proportioned and beautifully decorated (one with four-poster bed). The sea is two-minutes from the house and this is a haven for golfers — there are 18 courses within easy reach. Potato scones for breakfast, lots of attention to detail.

Rooms: 1 double, en suite (shower); 1 four-poster, en suite (bath/shower); 1 twin with private bathroom.

Price: £30-£35 p.p. Single supp. £10.

Breakfast: Flexible.

Meals: Restaurants in town.

Closed: Christmas & New Year.

From Edinburgh, A1 signed Berwick. Left onto A198, follow signs into North Berwick. Right into Station Rd signed 'The Law', to 1st x-roads, left into town centre — house on left behind wall.

Entry No: 551   Map no: 19

Gwen & Jake Scott
The Glebe House
Law Road
North Berwick
East Lothian EH39 4PL
Tel: 01620 892608
Fax: 01620 892608
e-mail: j.a.scott@tesco.net

High on Edinburgh's most exalted Georgian escarpment, this eyrie mixes 19th-century elegance with Danish and Middle Eastern style. Brass beds, burnished pine floors and a vast hall with a stairway that floats regally above a magnificent sitting room; the Castle can be glimpsed through the trees. Erlend swapped the rigours of daily deadlines (he was a Scottish Correspondent) for freelancing and advanced egg scrambling. Breakfasts are a full Franco-Scottish affair with oak-smoked salmon and home-made Auvergne jam. The Cloustons will meet you from the train or take you on a tour. It's relaxed and fun.

Rooms: 1 twin with basin and private bathroom (Victorian bath & shower); 1 double with basin, next to private shower.

Price: From £40 p.p. Single occ. £55.

Breakfast: Flexible.

Meals: Available locally.

Closed: Hardly ever.

Heriot Row is parallel to Princes Street, three major blocks north.

Entry No: 552   Map no: 19

Erlend & Hélène Clouston
41 Heriot Row
Edinburgh EH3 6ES
Tel: 0131 225 3113
Fax: 0131 225 3113
e-mail: erlendc@lineone.net
Web: www.sawdays.co.uk

There are secrets sealed at Inveresk — from the heavy long-locked safe to the still-hidden Roman tunnel. Two enormous bow-fronted pine-floored rooms are in the tower. Built in 1596 on an ancient Roman site with Georgian and Victorian additions, Cromwell plotted his siege of Edinburgh Castle from the house. The dining and drawing rooms are huge and you can play the grand piano; panelling cloaks the hall and wide 1643 staircase. Modern flower paintings adorn the bedrooms; a 19th-century Italian mahogany bed with matching wardrobe and washstand dominate the suite.

Rooms: 1 family room, 1 double and twin, all en suite.

Price: From £35 p.p. Single supp. £5.

Breakfast: 8.30am.

Meals: Available locally.

Closed: Never.

From Edinburgh, A199 (A1) to Musselburgh. There, follow signs to Inveresk. At top of Inveresk Brae, sharp right into cul-de-sac. 2nd opening on right, bear right past cottages to house at right end of drive.

Entry No: 553   Map no: 19

Alice & John Chute
Inveresk House
3 Inveresk Village, Musselburgh
Edinburgh EH21 7UA
Tel: 0131 665 5855
Fax: 0131 665 0578
e-mail: chute.inveresk@btinternet.com
Web: www.bitinternet.com/~chute.inveresk

Only the tick-tock of the grandfather clock disturbs the peace as you lounge in armchairs after breakfast with the papers, or discuss the cultural delights of the city with your friendly, multi-lingual hostess — Gillian is a blue-badge guide. Bedrooms (below stairs, looking on to an attractive patio garden) are decorated harmoniously in cerise and cream: Farrow and Ball paints and Nina Campbell fabrics are standard here. Scottish shortbread and books in the bedrooms, local artists' paintings on the walls and the Meadows opposite — a seductive city base indeed.

Rooms: 1 twin, en suite (bath/shower); 1 twin and 1 single, sharing en suite (bath/shower).

Price: From £30 p.p. From £40 p.p. during Edinburgh Festival.

Breakfast: Until 9am July-August. Flexible rest of the year.

Meals: Not available.

Closed: 22-27 December.

From centre of Edinburgh (West End), Lothian Rd to Tollcross (clock) and Melville Drive. At 2nd major traffic lights, right into Argyle Place and immediately left into Fingal Place.

Entry No: 554   Map no: 19

Gillian Charlton-Meyrick
2 Fingal Place
The Meadows
Edinburgh EH9 1JX
Tel: 0131 667 4436
Fax: 0131 667 4436
e-mail: bleish1936@aol.com

A rare thing in Edinburgh, an entire, undivided, Georgian house, in a lovely terrace (1821) very close to the city centre. The house is blessed with fine features: a cantilever staircase and cupola, a bow-walled dining room, spiral stairs that lead down to the basement where the guestrooms are. Susie and Andrew have done everything well and brightly-coloured rooms will be better kitted out than most poly-starred hotel rooms. But the comfort here comes with a personal touch, very nice hosts who can give you inside knowledge of this most beautiful of Scottish cities.

Rooms: 1 twin and 1 double, both en suite (shower); 1 single, en suite (bath).

Price: £35-£45 p.p.

Breakfast: Flexible.

Meals: Huge variety close by.

Closed: Christmas.

Take Queensferry Road out of Edinburgh towards Forth Road Bridge. Travel 250 yards along Queensferry Street. Before Dean bridge, bear left.

Entry No: 555   Map no: 19

Andrew & Susie Hamilton
16 Lynedoch Place
Edinburgh EH3 7PY
Tel: 0131 225 5507
Fax: 0131 226 4185
e-mail: susie.lynedoch@btinternet.com

Sarah is one of the nicest people we have met; she is genuine, enthusiastic and humorous and treats you like a friend. The house, 1830s Georgian, buzzes with life — it's homely, yet stylish. Lots of the decoration is extraordinary, some of it inherited from the previous Italian owner — terracotta meets muddy pink, gold cornicing, murals — unusual but stunning. A cupola lights the stairwell and, in the bedrooms, striking colours; one room has an enormous bathroom, one a sitting area (pictured). Guests have no sitting room, but the kitchen is huge and welcoming, so it doesn't matter a jot. This, after all, is Edinburgh.

Rooms: 1 twin and 1 double sharing bathroom; 1 double with private bathroom.

Price: £28-£45 p.p. Single occ. £28-£45.

Breakfast: Flexible.

Meals: Available locally.

Closed: Never.

American Clarissa has lost none of her enthusiasm for her adopted city. The house is handsome, the atmosphere is easy. From the sitting room you look onto pear tree and clematis and, in the distance, the rolling Pentland Hills. The terrace and south-facing garden are perfect for relaxation and reading. Guests have a study/sitting room — complete with log fire — to themselves and an apple-green painted bedroom with antique American-style four-poster bed. Fling open your shutters in the morning, then breakfast in the elegant dining room. Clarissa is involved in the arts and can help plan your day.

Rooms: 1 double, en suite (bath).

Price: £30-£40 p.p. Single night supp £5.

Breakfast: Flexible.

Meals: Available locally.

Closed: 23-29 December.

In Edinburgh, 500m north of Botanic Gardens.

From centre of Edinburgh, take A702 south, signed to Peebles. Pass Churchill Theatre (on left), to traffic lights. Albert Terrace is first right after theatre.

Entry No: 556   Map no: 19

Entry No: 557   Map no: 19

Sarah Nicholson
44 Inverleith Row
Edinburgh EH3 5PY
Tel: 0131 552 8595
Fax: 0131 551 6675
e-mail: inverleithbandb@yahoo.com
Web: www.sawdays.co.uk

Clarissa Notley
1 Albert Terrace
Edinburgh EH10 5EA
Tel: 0131 447 4491

A 10-minute stroll through some of Europe's finest classical architecture is all that stands between you and the centre of Edinburgh. What a city base! The 1825 house is a showcase for Fiona's professional interior design talents. Impressive features — cantilevered staircase, marble fireplaces, double-barrelled cupola and soaring ceilings — sit with lavish design, designer fabric, real candle chandelier and four-poster or canopied beds. The self-contained flat is equally sumptuous.

Rooms: 2 doubles and 1 single, all en suite. Self-catering: 2 doubles in separate flat, both en suite.

Price: £50-£55 p.p. Check for self-catering prices (3 days minimum).

Breakfast: Flexible.

Meals: Great selection nearby.

Closed: Christmas Day.

From Edinburgh, Queensferry Rd for Forth Rd Bridge. 3rd right after Dean Bridge into Dean Park Crescent, then 2nd right into Danube St.

Entry No: 558　　　　　Map no: 19

Fiona Mitchell-Rose
7 Danube Street
Edinburgh EH4 1NN
Tel: 0131 332 2755
Fax: 0131 343 3648
e-mail: seven.danubestreet@virgin.net
Web: www.sawdays.co.uk

For those who love independence, this is perfect; you have your own entrance, wing and patio and utter privacy. Michael and Anne are committed hosts, nonetheless. Breakfast is served in the main house and you'll enjoy chatting to the newly-settled couple about their travels (Michael was in the Army). The feel is traditional: white candlewick bedspreads, lovely paintings on the walls, rugs on wooden floors. *Children over nine welcome.*

Rooms: 1 twin and 1 double sharing bathroom. Separate bathroom also available.

Price: £28-£30 p.p. Single supp. £10.

Breakfast: 8-10am.

Meals: Packed lunch and dinner occasionally available.

Closed: 22-29 December.

From city bypass, A702 north to Fairmilehead. Past Buckstone, shops and sunken gardens on left. 2nd right (Riselaw Place) leads to Riselaw Road. House is on corner on left with white garage.

Entry No: 559　　　　　Map no: 19

Anne & Mike White
Hillcroft
2 Riselaw Road
Edinburgh EH10 6HR
Tel: 0131 447 2825
e-mail: hillcroft@zoom.co.uk
pages.zoom.co.uk/hillcroft/index.html

There are only around 20 complete Georgian houses left in Edinburgh and this is one of them. *And* it's only five minutes walk from the city centre. Despite the numbers — nine guestrooms and a dining room to seat a house-party of 20 — the scale remains human and the antiques breathe family history. From some top rooms — many have opulent drapes and all have lovely linen — you can see over to the Forth, Fife and the sea; the private garden over the road is yours to wander in. You are the guest of a bright, easy-going, chatty hostess. This sophisticated base once belonged to William Playfair, Edinburgh's famous Georgian architect. *Off-street parking available.*

Rooms: 2 triples, 2 twins, 4 doubles and 1 single, all en suite.

Price: £45-£60 p.p. Single supp. by arrangement.

Breakfast: 8-9am Mon-Fri; 8.30-9.30am Sat-Sun.

Meals: Available locally.

Closed: Never.

Abercromby Place lies parallel to Queen Street just north of the city centre in 'New Town'. Private parking.

Entry No: 560   Map no: 19

Eirlys Lloyd
17 Abercromby Place
Edinburgh EH3 6LB
Tel: 0131 557 8036
Fax: 0131 558 3453
e-mail: eirlys.lloyd@virgin.net
Web: www.abercrombyhouse.com

For nearly 200 years, Annie's terraced fisherman's cottage has stood beside a salmon and trout river. Even today, you can catch your own breakfast in the river, and Annie — a professional cook who conjures up the most delicious breakfasts, including her own home-made mushroom scones, bread and marmalade — will prepare it for you. Bedrooms are fresh, airy and very comfortable and the whole cottage is full of light, flowers, books and original watercolours. No wonder people from all over the world keep coming back to visit. *Children over six welcome.*

Rooms: 1 double, en suite; 1 twin with large private bathroom (down narrow stairs).

Price: £18-£20 p.p. Single supp. £25.

Breakfast: Until 9am.

Meals: Good restaurants nearby.

Closed: Never.

From south A1, exit for Musselburgh. Through town and cross bridge. Eskside West is first left. From Edinburgh, A199 (A1) to Musselburgh bridge. Eskside West is on right, just before bridge.

Entry No: 561   Map no: 19

Annie Deacon
53 Eskside West
Musselburgh
Edinburgh EH21 6RB
Tel: 0131 665 2875
Web: www.sawdays.co.uk

Although you're within hailing distance of Edinburgh city centre, you can add a rural footnote to the metropolitan delights. The front door opens onto a mosaic-tiled entrance hall. From the bay-windowed breakfast room, light and airy and with original cornice and plasterwork, you look out over the garden; the patio catches the evening sun. Breakfasts are something special — Cola makes her own bread and jam and offers the full Scottish feast. Bedrooms are fresh, welcoming and blissfully quiet.

Rooms: 1 twin with private bathroom; 1 double and 1 twin with shared shower.

Price: £26 p.p. Ask about single supp.

Breakfast: Flexible.

Meals: Available locally.

Closed: 23-26 December.

Enter Edinburgh on A702. 0.5 miles from bypass, fork right down Braid Road, after pedestrian crossing. House 0.5 miles on left after mini-r'bout. Free on-street parking.

Entry No: 562   Map no: 19

Cola & Michael Fass
50 Braid Road
Morningside
Edinburgh EH10 6AL
Tel: 0131 446 9356
Fax: 0131 447 7367
e-mail: fass@dial.pipex.com

Hop off your winged monster at the airport and take brief flight to Ratho. It is spectacular, built in 1798 in classical Georgian proportions. The architectural elegance is inevitable, as are the Adam fireplace, the ornate plasterwork, the mahogany furniture, and, perhaps, even the grand piano. But there is more; a large dining room for groups, and a smaller one too, and bedrooms that encourage indolence. White linen, rattan and mahogany, a four-poster, and a sofa in each one where you may recline. The 22-acre garden is another escape — and all so close to Edinburgh.

Rooms: 1 four-poster, en suite; 1 twin and dressing room, en suite; 1 twin with private bathroom.

Price: £35-£45 p.p. Single supp. £20.

Breakfast: Flexible.

Meals: Packed lunch and dinner, by arrangement.

Closed: Never.

A8 from Edinburgh. At large airport sign, immediately left to Gogarstone Rd. At end, right into Freeland Rd. Follow to end; sign for Ratho Hall 1.5 miles on. Take care crossing road to driveway.

Entry No: 563   Map no: 19

Janet & Freddie Small
Ratho Hall
Baird Road, Ratho
Midlothian EH28 8QY
Tel: 0131 335 3333
Fax: 0131 335 3035
e-mail: ratho.hall@btinternet.com
Web: www.countrymansions.com

A comfortable old manse — no slave to 'chic'- offering warmth and tranquillity behind its handsome stone exterior. The dining room has a large Victorian sideboard, pine floors, Indian carpet, family portraits and the morning light. Bay windows in the drawing room with an open fire, impressive gilt mirror, good furniture, Persian rug, green carpet and family photos. One bedroom has Chinese yellow rugs and a power shower; another has a kidney-shaped dressing table and mahogany pieces. Explore the garden or relax with a whisky in front of the fire.

Rooms: 2 twins, both en suite.

Price: £25-£30 p.p. Single supp. £10.

Breakfast: Flexible.

Meals: Available locally.

Closed: Never.

Life here tends to centre around the kitchen table and the Aga — which is not to say that the dining room isn't peaceful, with its family paintings and country views, nor that the drawing room isn't inviting, with its log fire and comfy sofas. You'll get a big and totally relaxed welcome from the Westmacotts. Bedrooms are prettily decorated and kitted-out with comfort in mind — basins and bathrobes, for example. Only 10 minutes from Edinburgh airport with a train from nearby Dalmeny village to the city centre every half hour. Louise may even be able to meet you.

Rooms: 2 twins/doubles, 1 double and 1 single all share a bathroom and separate wc.

Price: £25-£30 p.p. Single supp. £5.

Breakfast: Flexible.

Meals: Available locally.

Closed: Christmas.

From Edinburgh, on A720 bypass, leave on A71 towards Kilmarnock. Through Wilkieston; 0.75 miles on, left onto B7031 to Kirknewton. Left at T-junc. and over crossing. House first on left opposite church.

Entry No: 564　　　　Map no: 19

Jill Hunter Gordon
Highfield House
Kirknewton
Midlothian EH27 8DD
Tel: 01506 881489
Fax: 01506 885384
e-mail: hhunterGordon@compuserve.com
Web: www.sawdays.co.uk

From lights in centre of Kirkliston, follow sign for Forth Rd Bridge (A8000) & continue at r'bout. Approx. 0.5 miles on, 1st right after Milton Farm. Down lane, over small bridge & right before cottages.

Entry No: 565　　　　Map no: 19

Louise & Michael Westmacott
Craigbrae
Kirkliston by Edinburgh
West Lothian EH29 9EL
Tel: 0131 331 1205
Fax: 0131 319 1476
e-mail: westmacott@compuserve.com
Web: www.sawdays.co.uk

Glasgow is only half an hour away, yet here you cannot hear a single car. You can see the ruins of Lennox Castle on a forested hillside, and behind you are the Campsie Fells; pretty, gentle hills that even the unfit can manage. Lochs, monuments, castles — the Henrys can help you plan an itinerary that takes them all in. The drawing room is warm terracotta with open fire and plenty of comfortable seats; the conservatory catches the afternoon sun through Gothic windows and has lovely rattan and wooden seats and inspiring views of the large garden and countryside. *Children over eight welcome.*

Rooms: 1 double, en suite (bath & shower); 1 twin and 1 double, each with private bathroom.

Price: £30-£40 p.p. Single supp. £10.

Breakfast: Until 9.30am.

Meals: Dinner £25 p.p. (children under 16 half price.)

Closed: Christmas & New Year.

A setting that townies dream of — 170 traffic-free acres that wrap around the house, and majestic views of the Lake of Menteith, Campsie Fells, Dumgoyne, the Trossach Hills and Ben Lomond. This is an excellent base for families, with sheep, horses and cows and masses of opportunity for fishing, walking, cycling and climbing. Your pine-clad, cathedral-roofed sitting room is sunny and south facing and has a gallery landing with two single beds. Val, generous and infectiously enthusiastic, will collect you from the airport or the station; she cooked professionally, so the food's great.

Rooms: Barn: 1 king-size and 2 singles, with shower room and sitting room. House: small double, en suite (bath).

Price: £30 p.p. 3+ nights, £25 p.p. No single supp. Reduced rates for children.

Breakfast: Flexible, by arrangement.

Meals: Dinner, £15-£20 p.p., packed lunch and afternoon tea, all by arrangement.

Closed: Rarely.

Eleven miles north of Glasgow, Strathblane is at junc. of A81 and A891. Turn onto A891 at Kirkhouse Inn. 3 miles on, cream gateposts on left just before Haughhead.

Entry No: 566   Map no: 23

Sally & Gerard Henry
Glenmiln House
Campsie Glen
By Glasgow
East Dunbartonshire G65 7AP
Tel: 01360 311322
Fax: 01360 310501
e-mail: glenmiln@aol.com

A81, 3 miles south of Aberfoyle. 0.5 miles north of Gartmore House, over River Forth and 1st private road to right. Look for blue & white house sign.

Entry No: 567   Map no: 23

Val Willis
The Barns of Shannochill
By Aberfoyle
Stirlingshire FK8 3UZ
Tel: 01877 382878
Fax: 01877 382964
e-mail: shannochill@aol.com

Likeable and energetic, Colin and Fiona combine informality with luxury in peaceful, rural, central Scotland. Colin, piper, is a trilingual tour guide while Fiona is a wine buff and talented cook (shortbread, ice-cream, jam and bread are all hers). Imaginative dinners are served in the conservatory with views to Stirling Castle; the fine, organic garden gives the fruit, the river yields its salmon, the moors provide game in winter. The two bedrooms in the house have gigantic beds and large bathrooms.

Rooms: 1 double, en suite (bath & shower); 1 twin with private bath and shower.

Price: From £35 p.p. Single supp. £15.

Breakfast: 8.30-9am.

Meals: Dinner £22 p.p.

Closed: Never.

East Scotland

From M9, north, junc. 10 onto A84 towards Doune. After 5 miles, left on B826 towards Thornhill. Driveway on left after 2.2 miles, turn right off farm drive to house.

Entry No: 568   Map no: 23

Fiona & Colin Graham
Mackeanston House
Doune
Trossachs
Perthshire FK16 6AX
Tel: 01786 850213
Fax: 01786 850414
e-mail: mackean.house@cwcom.net

You will love Kippenross, a superb example of William Adam's Scottish Georgian country house architecture. It might be the fruit and flora of the Italian-inspired plasterwork in the duck-egg blue morning room that captivates you. It could be the polished and creaking mahogany staircase that springs from the oak-parqueted hall past ancestral portraits to the delicately printed Colefax and Fowler bedrooms. Or the stunning grounds, which are almost an arboretum, landscaped nearly 200 years ago; there are miles of river to splash and fish in, too.

Rooms: 1 twin with private shower; 2 twins, en suite (bath/shower).

Price: £38 p.p. Single supp. £10.

Breakfast: Flexible.

Meals: Dinner, £24 p.p., by arrangement.

Closed: Never.

Under five miles from the motorway is this lovely manse, tragically burnt down but rebuilt with great taste, elegance and style. A light-coloured wood predominates and rooms are warm with cornicing, thick carpets, combed ceilings, lots of space... very comfortable in every way. Joanna and Duncan clearly enjoy the world of B&B, and will greet you without pretension. Guests eat in the wonderful country kitchen, which is always informal and fun, or in the conservatory in finer weather. A genuine welcome here.

Rooms: 1 double, en suite (bath/shower); 1 large single with private bathroom.

Price: £28 p.p. No single supp.

Breakfast: Flexible.

Meals: Dinner, £15 p.p., by arrangement.

Closed: Christmas & New Year.

From junction 11 of M9, B8033 towards Dunblane. Get in right hand lane and take first right across reservation to lodge. Keep on drive, over bridge, up hill to Kippenross.

Entry No: 569   Map no: 23

Sue & Patrick Stirling-Aird
Kippenross
Dunblane
Perthshire FK15 0LQ
Tel: 01786 824048
Fax: 01786 823124
Web: www.sawdays.co.uk

From Edinburgh, cross Forth Road Bridge. Follow M90 to junc. 8 (Glenfarg) — 3 miles to village, through village and first right, signed Arngask. 1st large house on right.

Entry No: 570   Map no: 23

Joanna & Duncan Cameron
The Old Manse
Arngask
Glenfarg
Perthshire PH2 9QA
Tel: 01577 830394
Fax: 01577 830394

A long, tree-lined drive leads to an elegant farmhouse, good furniture, space, fun and a huge welcome. The double-ended drawing room has two large log fires, bow windows, pine floor and flowers from the garden. The farm runs down past tennis and croquet lawns almost to the Rock and Spindle beach, the views are spectacular, the coastline walks exhilarating, the cooking (by both hosts) excellent; they love to use local produce. They are easy hosts who know how to look after you. Come join the family.

Rooms: 1 twin, en suite; 1 twin/double with private bathroom; 1 twin/double, en suite (shower).

Price: £28-£32 p.p. Single supp. £10.

Breakfast: Flexible.

Meals: Dinner, £25 p.p., by arrangement.

Closed: Never.

From St. Andrews, A917 for 2 miles towards Crail. Kinkell's drive is in the first line of trees on left after St. Andrews.

Entry No: 571   Map no: 24

Sandy & Frippy Fyfe
Kinkell
St. Andrews
Fife KY16 8PN
Tel: 01334 472003
Fax: 01334 475248
e-mail: fyfe@kinkell.com
Web: www.kinkell.com

Borrow a bicycle made for two (or one) take a packed lunch and explore; there are masses of birds and wildlife to spot, or you can wander dreamily amid the glorious profusion of the garden. Rosie, *Cordon Bleu* trained, loves cooking, using produce from her own garden. You eat in the sitting room of this converted 18th-century smithy; it has family paintings, antiques and a real pipe organ. No fear of night starvation, either — in the bedrooms, which have stencilled cornices, there are delicious home-made biscuits.

Rooms: 2 twins, en suite (1 shower, 1 bath/shower).

Price: From £25 p.p. Single supp. £5.

Breakfast: Flexible.

Meals: Dinner by arrangement.

Closed: Occasionally.

From St. Andrews, A917 for Crail. After 4 miles, ignore turning for Boarhills, and continue to small river. Over bridge; house 2nd on left.

Entry No: 572   Map no: 24

Rosie & Keith Birkinshaw
Falside Smiddy
Boarhills
St. Andrews
Fife KY16 8PT
Tel: 01334 880479
e-mail: birk@falside.freeserve.co.uk

No fewer than four famous courses, and numerous others, are within a 20-mile radius — this is golfing heaven and there is ample space for storing your clubs. The garden views are towards St. Andrews and the Eden Estuary yet, in all this Scottish-ness, Alison has introduced a certain colour with Chinese and Indonesian exotica. You can use the conservatory (rattan furniture, floral-type cushions), where breakfast is served — and a little sitting room with French doors to the garden. Alison has books, magazines and fresh flowers in the bedrooms. Excellent value.

Rooms: 1 double, en suite (shower), and 1 twin/double with private shower room.

Price: £20 p.p. Single supp. £5.

Breakfast: Flexible.

Meals: Packed lunch and dinner by arrangement.

Closed: Never.

Arrive along a mile of wood and rhododendron to this imposing (if not very beautiful), third house on this historic and fortifiable site. The remains of ramparts from earlier castles rear over the Victorian dell with its ferny burn and waterfall. The gardens are "fantastic" (our inspector) with huge, exotic 200-year-old trees, beautifully laid-out walks, wallaby graves — the usual! The house is magnificent on the inside, too, with beautiful rooms in elegant style. Your hosts are great fun and add delicious food and wonderful bedrooms to the many reasons to stay at Dupplin. *Children over 12 welcome.*

Rooms: 3 twins/doubles, all en suite.

Price: From £65 p.p. Single supp. £15-£65.

Breakfast: Until 9am.

Meals: Dinner, 3 courses, £28 p.p., with 24 hours' notice.

Closed: Christmas & New Year.

A914 to Balmullo. Through village heading north, and 0.25 miles on, turn hard left. Right at top of road and left at red telephone box.

Entry No: 573   Map no: 24

Alison Outlaw
Ashbank
Lucklawhill
Balmullo
Fife KY16 0BQ
Tel: 01334 870807
e-mail: alison.outlaw@talk21.com
Web: www.onward.to/ashbank/

From M90 roundabout, A93 towards Perth for 1 mile, then sharp right onto B9112 for Dunning. After 2.7 miles, wrought-iron gates on right.

Entry No: 574   Map no: 23

Derek & Angela Straker
Dupplin Castle
By Aberdalgie
Perth, Perthshire PH2 0PY
Tel: 01738 623224
Fax: 01738 444140
e-mail: dupplin@netcomuk.co.uk
Web: www.dupplin.co.uk

Anne and David are natural hosts and enjoy sharing their newly renovated, traditional Scottish farmhouse overlooking the River Tay. Through their farm/livery stable yard runs the Coronation Walk used by the ancient Scottish Kings en route from Falkland to Scone. Inside, dusky pink, cream and pale yellow work well with polished mahogany, while the scent of fresh flowers fills the rooms. Anne loves to cook using local produce and fruit and veg from the garden. The A90 (0.5 miles from the house) can be busy during the day but should not disturb you at night.

Rooms: 1 double, en suite (bath & shower); 1 twin, en suite (shower); 1 twin with private bathroom.

Price: From £28 p.p. Single supp. £5.

Breakfast: Flexible.

Meals: Dinner, £20 p.p., by arrangement.

Closed: Christmas & New Year.

Penny is a natural at hospitality and it's not long before you feel fully ensconced in your own wing of her lovely 18th-century farmhouse. There's only one guestroom, up its own staircase with its own bathroom and views of the Vale of Strathmore. Penny is a marvellous cook, and breakfast eggs are laid by her rare-breed hens; fruit and veg are home-grown, too. Everything possible is done to make your stay more comfortable. All in all, this is a really friendly home where you are well looked after. You are also within easy reach of Scone and Glamis Castle.

Rooms: 1 twin, en suite (bath).

Price: £30 p.p. Children £15 p.p. Under 3s free if sharing parents' room. No single supp.

Breakfast: Flexible.

Meals: Dinner £18 p.p. Must be booked in advance.

Closed: Christmas & New Year.

From A90 Perth to Dundee road, take Kinfauns exit (NOT Kinfauns Castle). Drive up hill for 0.25 miles, left, and straight up hill to gates on left.

Entry No: 575   Map no: 23

Anne & David MacLehose
Over Kinfauns
Perth
Perthshire PH2 7LD
Tel: 01738 860538
Fax: 01738 860803
e-mail: maclehose@overkinfauns.sol.co.uk

From Perth, A94 north towards Coupar Angus. After Perth airport, 2nd right signed Rait/Kilspindie. House drive on left after 1 mile, over cattle grid & 200 yds up farm drive.

Entry No: 576   Map no: 23

Penny I'Anson
Montague House
Balbeggie
Perth
Perthshire PH2 7PR
Tel: 01821 640656
Fax: 01821 640788

A 170-acre private loch where birds can be watched and pike fished; a great organ halfway up the main stairs with air pumped from a separate building in the grounds; a 16th-century central building with wings added in 1780 to a design filched from Adam. "One of the prettiest houses in Scotland"? It is a very historic, very traditional country house run by delightful people. The bedrooms are big and utterly charming — our inspector said his was the most comfortable he'd had in Britain! *Children over 12 welcome.*

Rooms: 1 twin and 1 double, both en suite (1 bath & 1 bath & shower). Adjoining twin available for children sharing parents' bathroom.

Price: £30-£40 p.p. Single supp. £5-£10.

Breakfast: Flexible.

Meals: Bistro nearby.

Closed: Christmas & New Year.

The house was begun as a tower in 1585 and added to until Victorian times (with turrets, etc) and into the present century. Inside, it is delightfully old-fashioned. The rooms are large and comfortable with open fires which are lit in cooler weather. Paul is a conservationist and writer and both he and Louise love having guests, whom they welcome with grace and humour. This is a lovely family home and visitors can roam freely on the estate with its parkland, woods and heather moorland.

Rooms: 1 four-poster with private bathroom; 1 double with shared bathroom.

Price: £30 p.p. No single supp.

Breakfast: Flexible.

Meals: Dinner, £15-£20 p.p., by arrangement.

Closed: Christmas & New Year.

From Blairgowrie, turn onto A923 for Dunkeld. Look for sign saying 'Kinloch. Drive safely' and take first entrance on left after sign.

Entry No: 577   Map no: 23

Kenneth & Nicolette Lumsden
Marlee House
Kinloch
Blairgowrie
Perthshire PH10 6SD
Tel: 01250 884216

From Blairgowrie, A926 to Kirriemuir. After 5 miles, left to Alyth. Through town on Airlie St. After 2.5 miles, round sharp left bend. Right into drive.

Entry No: 578   Map no: 23

Paul & Louise Ramsay
Bamff House
Alyth, Blairgowrie
Perthshire PH11 8LF
Tel: 01828 632992
Fax: 01828 632992
e-mail: louiseramsay@bamff.demon.co.uk
Web: www.bamff.co.uk

Rattrays have lived here for five centuries. One forebear escaped death in 1747 because the judges were reluctant to hang the world's best golfer. The gorge view from a circular balcony that rings the drawing room is not just dramatic... it's unbelievable! The 300 acres of deciduous woodland, river and gorge provide fabulous walks. A house full of character awaits you. The French room is pink and has a four-poster. Breakfast is served in the 18th-century dining room and you can use the Regency drawing room.

Rooms: 1 four-poster, en suite (bath) and 1 twin + extra single with private adjacent bathroom.

Price: £35 p.p. Single supp. £5.

Breakfast: 8-9am.

Meals: Available locally.

Closed: 22 December-5 January.

"The people, the setting, the house, are just perfect," wrote our inspector. You might find David casting a line into the River Dee that flows behind the house, or Meg picking flowers for your room; they will stop it all to greet you and soon you'll be having tea on the terrace maybe with binoculars in hand, following a kestrel or an eagle. Your room may be huge — two are — and full of fine furniture, fluffy bathrobes, fresh flowers and, maybe, a balcony. Bathrooms are exquisite with great views, too. There are so many places to visit and Meg seems to know them all.

Rooms: 1 twin/double, en suite (bath/shower); 1 twin and 1 double, with private bathrooms. Separate shower room also available.

Price: £30-£40 p.p. No single supp.

Breakfast: 8-9am.

Meals: Dinner, £20 p.p., by arrangement. Also available locally.

Closed: Rarely.

From Blairgowrie, A93 towards Braemar for 2 miles. Just before end of 30mph limit there is a sharp right-hand bend with drive on right. Drive is 1 mile.

Entry No: 579   Map no: 23

Nicky & Lachie Rattray
Craighall-Rattray
Blairgowrie
Perthshire PH10 7JB
Tel: 01250 874749
Fax: 01250 874749
e-mail: lrattray@calinet.co.uk

From Aboyne, A93 west towards Braemar. Just after 50 mph sign, left down Rhu-na-Haven Road. House is 400 yds on, 4th gateway on right.

Entry No: 580   Map no: 24

David & Meg White
Lys-na-Greyne House
Rhu-na-Haven Road
Aboyne, Aberdeenshire AB34 5JD
Tel: 013398 87397
Fax: 013398 86441
e-mail: dwhite7301@aol.com
Web: www.sawdays.co.uk

When the Minister lived here in the 1820s, he commissioned a builder to add a kitchen for the princely sum of £130. The views beyond the Blanches' eight and a half acres have changed little since then; still no other houses. Sensitively restored, spotless bedrooms are light and airy and Doreen thoughtfully lays out fruit and mineral water. The drawing room has a baby grand and stacks of books. Only an hour from Aberdeen airport and close enough for you to enjoy the little fishing villages of the Moray coast. Look out for the touches of exotica — the elephant lamps and a Burmese temple door. *Children by arrangement.*

Rooms: 1 double, en suite (shower); 1 twin, en suite (bath).

Price: £27.50 p.p. No single supp. £25 p.p. for two nights or more.

Breakfast: Flexible.

Meals: Dinner, 3 courses, £18 p.p.

Closed: Occasionally.

From Keith, take A95 towards Banff. After 3.5 miles, left signed Grange Church. Left again opposite church.

Entry No: 581   Map no: 28

Doreen & Bill Blanche
Grange House
Grange
Keith, Banffshire AB55 6RY
Tel: 01542 870206
Fax: 01542 870206
e-mail: wd.blanche@zetnet.co.uk
Web: www.sawdays.co.uk

The Bishop of Spynie used to row across the lake to 'entertain' at Westfield House. There's stacks of history here, but John and Veronica have underplayed it and the result is a bright, elegant, easy place. John's family settled here in 1862 when the house was 300 years old and the solid oak staircase, hung with ancestral oils, sports a Maclean tartan carpet. Heavy, antique furniture sits with plump sofas and the bedrooms are fun — one is extremely pink — and have lots of books, old bedsteads and lovely views. You can play tennis, walk for miles and buy John's whisky — he grows the barley for it right here.

Rooms: 1 twin, en suite (bath); 1 twin with private bath & shower; 1 single with private bath.

Price: £30 p.p. No single supp.

Breakfast: Until 9.30am.

Meals: Dinner, 3 courses, £20 p.p., by arrangement.

Closed: Never.

From Elgin, A96 west for Forres & Inverness. After 2.5 miles, right onto B9013 for Burghead. After 1 mile, right at x-roads on road signed Westfield House. Continue to sign 'Westfield House and office'.

Entry No: 582   Map no: 27

John & Veronica Maclean
Westfield House
Nr. Elgin
Moray IV30 8XL
Tel: 01343 547308
Fax: 01343 551340

With listed buildings, a sense of history is usually assured; at this 1776 country mansion, history extends into the orchard where King Malcolm was murdered among the windfalls about 1,000 years ago. The stone staircase came from ruined Blervie castle. Paddy and Fiona, who know the area well, are still restoring; there are original doors and shutters, marble and carved wood fireplaces, antiques, antlers, guns, violins, huge painted four-posters. Large, ornate mirrors add sparkle. There's a sofa in the bedrooms, books and flowers. Magical, peaceful.

Rooms: 1 four-poster with single bed and private bathroom; 1 four-poster, en suite (bath).

Price: £35 p.p. No single supp.

Breakfast: Until 9.30am.

Meals: Dinner, 4 courses, £22 p.p.

Closed: Christmas & New Year.

From A96, follow signs to Forres. South at clocktower, straight across at r'bout and take B9010. Pass hospital and 1 mile on, left at Mains of Blervie sign. Right at farm.

Entry No: 583   Map no: 27

Paddy & Fiona Meiklejohn
Blervie
By Forres
Moray IV36 2RH
Tel: 01309 672358
Fax: 01309 672358
e-mail: meiklejohn@btinternet.com

Three generations of women live happily here — when we visited, the family dog had been painted partially pink. Built as a sporting lodge in the 19th century, Garramore sits proudly in six acres, on the road to the Isles that was built to take Highland cattle to Lowland markets. The former youth hostel is the most unpretentious home; sofas with throws, unadorned rooms and tartan blankets to keep out the chill. Excellent value for children; Julia, who grew up on the island of Eigg, gives generous discounts for them. The beach is two minutes' walk away.

Rooms: 1 family (double & single bed) and 1 double, both en suite (bath); 1 twin with private shower room; 3 family rooms (double & single bed) sharing separate shower and bathroom.

Price: £20-£28 p.p. Single occ. £30.

Breakfast: Flexible.

Meals: Dinner, May-September. Rest of year, supper by arrangement.

Closed: Never.

Highland & Islands

From Fort William, A830 to Mallaig. Garramore is approx. 3 miles past Arisaig and 1 mile before Morar.

Entry No: 584   Map no: 22

Julia & Sophie Moore
Garramore House
South Morar
Nr. Mallaig
Inverness-shire PH40 4PD
Tel: 01687 450268
Fax: 01687 450268

On the hillside by the loch, there are great views and no noise. Ponder over breakfast as the boats drift by on Loch Linnhe, then ride the cable car to what seems to be the top of the world, climb Ben Nevis or bag a Munro before returning for a tot of whisky. It's hard to fault what the Campbells have done — everything is just so, from co-ordinated fabrics and wallpapers to the complementary sherry and carved four-poster and French oak bed. The silver gleams, the flowers are artfully arranged. Joan has faithfully kept to a Victorian theme.

Rooms: 2 doubles, both en suite (bath/shower); 2 doubles, both en suite (1 bath, 1 shower).

Price: £35-£45 p.p. Single occ. £70-£90.

Breakfast: Until 9am.

Meals: Available locally.

Closed: Mid-November-Easter.

From Glasgow, take A82 to Fort William. There, turn right up Ashburn Lane, next to Ashburn guest house. House is on left at top.

Entry No: 585   Map no: 22

Joan & John Campbell
The Grange
Grange Road
Fort William
Inverness-shire PH33 6JF
Tel: 01397 705516
Fax: 01397 701595
Web: www.sawdays.co.uk

On 50 acres of wild, ferny lochside grounds is Invergloy, a converted coach house and stables in the beautiful Great Glen. There are lovely views of Loch Lochy and surrounding mountains from the guest drawing room. This is a peaceful, no-smoking home run by Margaret, a professional musician and James, a retired chemical engineer. One room has twin beds foot-to-foot. Guests can play tennis or walk to the private shingle beach on Loch Lochy — wild roe deer can often be seen. There's a rowing boat, too. *Children over eight welcome.*

Rooms: 3 twins, en suite (2 with shower and 1 with bath & shower).

Price: From £23 p.p. Single supp. £10.

Breakfast: 8.30am.

Meals: Good restaurants in area.

Closed: Never.

From Spean Bridge, head north on A82. After 5 miles, house is signed on left.

Entry No: 586   Map no: 22

Margaret & James Cairns
Invergloy House
Spean Bridge
Inverness-shire PH34 4DY
Tel: 01397 712681
Fax: 01397 712681
e-mail: cairns@invergloy-house.co.uk
Web: www.invergloy-house.co.uk

This former ferryman's house is small, welcoming, homely, informal, charming and just 50 yards from the River Spey where ospreys and otters fish and dippers dip. Explore the wonderful countryside or sit in the garden with a pot of tea. The sitting room is cosy with a woodburning stove and lots of books (no television). Elizabeth, a free spirit, lived in the Sudan and still enjoys travelling. You will eat very well here. Heathery honeycomb, home-made bread and preserves, herbs from the garden and fresh veg. A superb base for nature lovers and explorers. Good value.

Rooms: 1 double, 1 twin and 2 singles, all sharing 1 bathroom & 2 w.cs.

Price: £20 p.p.

Breakfast: Flexible.

Meals: Dinner £14.50 p.p. Packed lunches £4.50 p.p.

Closed: Occasionally, please check.

This was once their holiday home and they are delighted to live here properly; there are still holiday touches, like the hot water bottles and electric blankets in the old bedrooms. The house is comfortable without being imposing, an 1850 original with later add-ons, mostly clad in gleaming white wood. Christina is lively, down-to-earth and a great hostess. You will be given home-bee honey, fruit and veg from the garden; and the two llamas add an exotic touch.

Rooms: 1 double, en suite (bath & shower); 1 twin en suite (shower).

Price: £25 p.p.

Breakfast: Until 9.30am.

Meals: Dinner £15 p.p.

Closed: Christmas & New Year.

From B970, take road to Boat of Garten. House on left, just before river Spey. From A9, follow main road markings through village. Pass golf club and cross river.

Entry No: 587   Map no: 23

Elizabeth Matthews
The Old Ferryman's House
Boat of Garten
Inverness-shire PH24 3BY
Tel: 01479 831370
Fax: 01479 831370

North of Aviemore for 16 miles, left onto B851 signed Fort Augustus. Continue over bridge, through Inverarnie to Farr and past children's playground. House is through 2nd gate on left, signed.

Entry No: 588   Map no: 23

James & Christina Murray
Farr Mains
Farr
Inverness
Inverness-shire IV2 6XB
Tel: 01808 521205
Fax: 01808 521466
e-mail: murray@cali.co.uk

You can only reach Skiary by boat or on foot. Enveloped in the wilds of Loch Hourn it is lost to the outside world. No electricity, no roads, no neighbours: just mountains, waterfalls (there is a burn and pool yards up the hill for swimming), otters in the loch, deer feeding along the shoreline. The tiny, pine-lined cottage is the last inhabited dwelling of a once busy fishing village. You will be pampered, with 'hotties', early morning tea and log fires. Wonderful meals are served in the lochside greenhouse dining room. John's ferry service for guests down and across the loch makes spectacular walking accessible from Skiary.

Rooms: 3 twins with shared bathroom.

Price: Packed lunch, dinner, B&B £70 p.p. Full board £425 p.p. p.w.

Breakfast: Flexible.

Meals: Dinner and packed lunch included in price.

Closed: Mid-October-mid-March.

Rural simplicity and elegance in rare harmony... Di and Inge are delightful and deeply committed to the place. They stripped the sitting room to its original stone and pine-clad walls, put i a woodburning stove, brought in sheep goats and chickens and resolved to serv the finest of local and home-grown food. People now come from far away to eat here, and Di and Inge have won accolades galore. Dine (part of the package) with white linen, silver and china; sleep in small but pretty bedrooms. A caring, warm and cheerful haven and hauntingly beautiful views.

Rooms: 1 twin and 2 doubles, each en suite (shower).

Price: Dinner, B&B £55 p.p. Minimun 2-night stay. Singles only taken in April and Oct; single supp. £20.

Breakfast: 8.30am.

Meals: Dinner included.

Closed: November-March.

From Invergarry, A87 N; left after 5 miles to Kinloch Hourn. Continue for approx. 22 miles to Kinloch Hourn, at end of road, where hosts will meet you.

Entry No: 589   Map no: 22

Little Lodge is just off B8021 Gairloch to Melvaig road, shortly after turning to North Erradale.

Entry No: 590   Map no: 26

John & Christina Everett
Skiary
Loch Hourn
By Invergarry
Highlands PH35 4HD
Tel: 01809 511214
Web: www.sawdays.co.uk

Di Johnson & Inge Ford
Little Lodge
North Erradale
Gairloch
Highlands IV21 2DS
Tel: 01445 771237

A stupendous, moated house, in the family since 1780. You get columns, a grand piano, big fireplaces, trophies, a snooker table, massive gilt mirrors, silver candelabras and Elizabeth who, in contrast to the grandness of her home, welcomes you in the friendliest way. Beautifully Georgian, the house sits in its own estate; there are 2.5 lochs to fish, wonderful walks, a boat and 1,000 acres of organically reared cattle. The manor — from the antler-bedecked billiard room to the Italian hand-painted panelling of the drawing room to the huge, stately, four-poster room with its bearskin — generates a sense of life lived to the full. Superb.

Rooms: 2 doubles, both en suite (bath/shower); 1 four-poster, en suite (shower).

Price: £35 p.p.

Breakfast: Flexible.

Meals: Dinner, 3 courses, £22 p.p.

Closed: Occasionally.

From Inverness, A96 towards Nairn. After 9.5 miles right on B9090 through Cawdor. B9090 turns left for Nairn, but continue on B9101. Turn first right. House is up drive.

Entry No: 591   Map no: 27

Elizabeth & Jamie Mackintosh-Walker
Geddes House
Nairn
Highlands IV12 5QX
Tel: 01667 452241
Fax: 01667 456707
e-mail: elizabeth@gedes55.freeserve.co.uk

They know the land and its animals, the people and their ways, the geography and the history of their piece of Scotland. Caroline grew up here and Robert, who used to have Les Ambassadeurs, the Park Lane club, has adopted the place as his own; it would be hard to imagine them or their four dogs ever leaving. Staying here, you will be cared for — extra blankets, torches, wellingtons and rucksacks to borrow, home-grown veg and home-made bread freshly prepared for you — yet not fussed over. It is one of the homeliest of our houses. Two rooms are in the Manse and one in the pine-vaulted studio.

Rooms: Main House: 2 doubles with private bathrooms. Stable studio: 1 double, en suite (shower).

Price: £40 p.p. No single supp. 2% credit card charge.

Breakfast: Flexible.

Meals: Dinner, 2/5 courses, £12/£25 p.p. B.Y.O. wine.

Closed: Rarely.

From Inverness, A9 north. Cross Dornoch bridge. 14 miles on, take A839 to Lairg. Cross small bridge in Rogart and take sharp right turn uphill, signed St Callan's church. House is 1.5 miles on, on right, next to church.

Entry No: 592   Map no: 27

Robert & Caroline Mills
St Callan's Manse
Rogart
Sutherland IV28 3XE
Tel: 01408 641363
Fax: 01408 641313

Loch Duich is sea-fed, so seals come close and if you're lucky you might even see a dolphin. The setting is dazzling — across the Loch sit the Five Sisters of Kintail mountains and the sitting room window frames the view perfectly. You can, if you wander the large garden (complete with burn), or follow the forest or loch walks, see pine martens and deer and even eagles. Dinner is equally interesting, with sushi and Scottish seafood a speciality. Rooms are plush yet uncluttered and Anne thoughtfully lays a tray with spring water, fresh fruit and biscuits. Skye, and its ferry, are easily reached.

Rooms: 2 twins/doubles with private bathrooms.

Price: £34-£38 p.p. Single supp. £12.

Breakfast: Flexible.

Meals: Dinner, 4 course table d'hôte, £28 p.p., by arrangement. B.Y.O. wine.

Closed: November-April. Can open by arrangement.

Down Glenshiel on A87, and left at Shiel Bridge Letterfearn. Over bridge, and on for 1 mile. Right at next sign for Letterfearn. House 3 miles on left.

Entry No: 593　　　　Map no: 22

Anne Kempthorne
Duich House
Letterfearn
Glenshiel
Ross-shire IV40 8HS
Tel: 01599 555259
Fax: 01599 555259
e-mail: duich@cwcom.net

A perfect synthesis of owners, house an countryside; the Robertsons are a youn family — gentle and lively and utterly committed to this part of the world. The house was built as four cottages in the 1800s — in front, 100 acres of pasture and hardwood woodland roll down to the river Skiach where you car fish or swim in the pool where the waterfall lands. Views go on forever. In the house, gumboots by the door, dee sofas, open fires, rugs, pretty porcelain, long views and light flooding in.

Rooms: 2 twins, sharing bathroom.

Price: £25 p.p.

Breakfast: Flexible.

Meals: Dinner, 3 courses, £20 p.p.

Closed: Occasionally.

A9 north for Inverness for 12 miles. Left into Evanton and left again at village shop for Swordale. House at end of road, 3.5 miles on.

Entry No: 594　　　　Map no: 27

Phiddy & Gordon Robertson
Fannyfield House
Swordale
Evanton
Ross-shire IV16 9XA
Tel: 01349 830520
Fax: 01349 830493
e-mail: gar.management.@quista.net

Built up on the hill, looking out over Loch Broom, with windows for walls on the loch side — a superb position and view. Walk outside and you can scramble around on the cliff and discover (in bad weather) a blow hole, or stroll down to the private beach. The weatherboard house is a dream — a huge sitting room with books, CDs, fire and hints of the Orient, a connecting dining room with French windows, lovely bedrooms with rattan furniture, wicker chairs, crisp cotton duvets, great bathrooms and a small balcony on one of the rooms. Anne cooked professionally, so the food's good, too.

Rooms: 1 double, 2 twins, all en suite (bath/shower).

Price: £35-£38 p.p. Single supp. £20.

Breakfast: Flexible.

Meals: Dinner, 4 courses, £25 p.p. Packed lunch from £7.50 p.p.

Closed: Christmas & New Year.

From Inverness on A835. On outskirts of Ullapool left immediately after 4th 40mph sign. Take cattle grid on right and left fork down to house.

Entry No: 595   Map no: 26

Anne Holloway
Tanglewood House
Ullapool
Ross-shire IV26 2TB
Tel: 01854 612059
Fax: 01854 612059
e-mail: tanglewoodhouse@msn.com
Web: www.tanglewoodhouse.co.uk

Masses of thought has gone into this neat, professionally run house, yet Kate fills it with a personal friendliness. Her cooking is legendary; she uses whatever is fresh, local and best, and everything, including bread and the cake on your tea tray, is home-made. You'd expect tartan — and it's here, in one of the bedrooms, along with fresh flowers, fluffy towels and smellies in the bathroom. The whitewashed croft sits in a spectacular position on the edge of the sea with views to the An Teallach mountain range.

Rooms: 1 double, en suite (shower); 1 double, en suite (bath); 1 double with private shower room.

Price: B&B £32-£38 p.p.; Dinner, B&B £56-£62 p.p. Single supp. £5.

Breakfast: Until 9.30am.

Meals: Dinner, 4 courses, included (except Sundays). Packed lunch £6 p.p.

Closed: November-March.

From Inverness on A835, follow signs for Ullapool. Left 12 miles south of Ullapool onto A832 coastal route to Gairloch. 29 miles from this junction, house is last on left in Laide.

Entry No: 596   Map no: 26

Kate & Steve Macdonald
The Old Smiddy
Laide
Ross-shire IV22 2NB
Tel: 01445 731425
Fax: 01445 731696
e-mail: oldsmiddy@aol.com

From motorway cop to Atlantic crofter, John has always believed in lending a hand. He and Dorothy have thoroughly renovated this 300-year-old farmhouse. The modern bedrooms are pinkly squeezed under the eaves, flush with facilities. Downstairs, the sun circles the many-windowed library and its new, well-stuffed leather suite; all creature comforts are here. Beyond the cobbled courtyard wall, and the pasture, breakers smash into granite cliffs: walkers and sheep take care. Six miles to the pub (that's close in Lewis), and eight to the Port of Ness beach.

Rooms: 1 family/double and 2 twins, all en suite (shower) & use of shared bathroom.

Price: £29 p.p. Under 4s free, 4-12s half-price.

Breakfast: Until 8.30am.

Meals: Dinner £16 p.p.

Closed: Rarely.

In the 16th century the MacLeod chief of the day brought the King of Scotland to the top of Macleod's Table to show him the beauty of Skye. They roasted ox under the stars and the King was impressed — he couldn't fail to be. Time has not diminished that beauty. After a lifetime in the diplomatic service, Donald and Rosemary (she is an excellent cook), enjoy putting people at ease. Their former manse and garden is an oasis of comfort and charm encircled by mountains, sea and dramatic lochside beauty. Deeply comfortable beds, pretty china and linen and a warm atmosphere. *Children by arrangement.*

Rooms: 2 twins/doubles, both en suite (bath/shower); 1 double with private bathroom.

Price: From £35 p.p. Single supp. £8.

Breakfast: Until 9am.

Meals: Dinner, 4 courses, £20 p.p.

Closed: Christmas & New Year.

20 miles from Stornoway, on A857 for Port of Ness. House is signed left off main road in village, and 0.5 miles on, by the sea, on the left.

Entry No: 597   Map no: 25

John & Dorothy Russell
Galson Farm
South Galson
Isle of Lewis HS2 0SH
Tel: 01851 850492
Fax: 01851 850492
e-mail: galsonfarm@freeserve.com
Web: www.galsonfarm.freeserve.co.uk

From Skye Bridge, follow signs for UIG to Sligachan Hotel. Left fork to Dunvegan (22 miles). There, left (just before bakery) signed Glendale. White house in trees after 0.75 miles.

Entry No: 598   Map no: 25

Donald & Rosemary MacLeod
Kinlochfollart
By Dunvegan
Isle of Skye IV55 8WQ
Tel: 01470 521470
Fax: 01470 521740
Web: www.sawdays.co.uk

The sky envelops you; sea, lochs and views of distant isles surround you. The 300-year-old Tacksman's house is hidden down a bluebell-flanked private drive — and with what energy and enthusiasm it has been renovated. Marcus is converting the 1.5-acre walled garden into an organic smallholding to supply local homes and restaurants and, within, Linda has created a luxurious retreat. There are wrap-around views in your bedroom and sitting room; both are bathed in an explosion of magnificent golden light at sunset. Fresh flowers, bathrobes and a heated floor in the shower room — you are spoiled. Popular with honeymooners, but use any excuse to come.

Rooms: 1 double, en suite (shower) with private sitting room.

Price: £40 p.p. Single occ. £50.

Breakfast: Flexible.

Meals: Available locally.

Closed: Christmas & New Year.

Cross Skye Toll Bridge and take A87 north, through Broadford and Portree. At Borve, take A850 (left fork) signed Dunvegan. 2.4 miles on you'll see gates and Gate Lodge. 0.5 miles along wooded driveway, house at bottom by sea.

Entry No: 599   Map no: 25

Mr & Mrs M.F. Ridsdill-Smith
Lyndale House
Edinbane
Isle of Skye IV51 9PX
Tel: 01470 582329
e-mail: linda@lyndale.free-online.co.uk

The house, warm and simple, is perfect for the setting — the real star of this place. The water is crystal clear, seals — even dolphins or a whale — swim by. Climb up from the rugged coastline of fell and rocky outcrop and watch the sun set over Iona, Coll and Tiree; then turn round and see the almost heavenly red glow. People sail in just for John's cooking. Eleanor works by day at her silversmithing; you can drop in to see her. They are both free spirits inhabiting a cheerful, cosy and eccentric enclave with cabin-like bedrooms and white walls that reflect the glorious light. Special indeed.

Rooms: 2 twins and 1 double, sharing 2 bathrooms.

Price: From £16.50 p.p.

Breakfast: Until 9am.

Meals: À la carte dinner always available.

Closed: Rarely! Please check.

4 miles beyond Bunessan on road to Iona ferry, take right to Kintra. After 1.5 miles, turn left down track and through iron gate. Cottage is on shore.

Entry No: 600   Map no: 21

John & Eleanor Wagstaff
Red Bay Cottage
Deargphort
Fionnphort
Isle of Mull PA66 6BP
Tel: 01681 700396

You drive through wild and spectacular scenery to discover Tiroran, an oasis of comfort and cosiness. The garden is enchanting with delightful walks, and the burn tumbles down to Loch Scridain, an arm of the sea which separates the Ross of Mull from Ben More (the only Munro on the island). Dinner and breakfast are served in the elegant dining room or adjoining sun room which has a hanging vine. Colin and Jane, from Argyll, are knowledgeable and enthusiastic about Mull and nearby Iona and their interest in boats and sailing is evident — there are nautical photographs and books everywhere. The peace and the woodland walk down to the sea are dreamy.

Rooms: 3 twins and 3 doubles, all en suite (bath).

Price: £38-£49 p.p. Single supp. by arrangement.

Breakfast: Until 9am.

Meals: Dinner from £25 p.p. Packed lunch by request.

Closed: Rarely. Please check.

You can borrow the boat on the loch fo rowing or fishing (brown trout); that is a treat in itself. This is very much a simple family home, run with undue modesty by the gentle and lovely Gill and her ex-rugby pro husband. He is ar oyster farmer, big and full of life. They have the gift of making one feel at home. There are lots of family photos, deep red sofas in the sitting room, rugs plenty of books and games. There's a big old pine double bed in one colourfu and large room, with bright linen and good views across the loch.

Rooms: 1 twin/double, en suite (bath/shower).

Price: £22.50 p.p. Single supp. by arrangement.

Breakfast: Until 9am.

Meals: Available locally.

Closed: November-end of February.

From car ferry at Craignure or Fishnish, A849 towards Bunessan & Iona ferry. Right on B8035 towards Gruline. After 4 miles, left at converted church. Tiroran is 1 mile on.

Entry No: 601   Map no: 21

Colin & Jane Tindal
Tiroran House
Isle of Mull PA69 6ES
Tel: 01681 705232
Fax: 01681 705240
e-mail: colin@tiroran.freeserve.co.uk
Web: www.tiroran.com

A816 north from Lochgilphead to Kilninver, then left on B844 towards Easedale. Farm on right opposite Loch Seil, after 2 miles (signed).

Entry No: 602   Map no: 22

Ms Gill Cadzow
Duachy Farm
Kilninver
By Oban
Argyll PA34 4QU
Tel: 01852 316244
Fax: 01852 316244
e-mail: gillian.cadzow@tesco.net

Farm or manor? On land or on water? The views are stupendous; wander as you wish and admire them. The house is elegantly white, the farm definitely working; yet the eye always comes to rest on the waters and boats of Loch Craignish. The drawing room is the original 16th-century bothy with coved ceiling, four-foot-thick walls and log fire. The Services have a 400-acre hill farm but find time for real hospitality and delicious food, including shellfish from the Ardfern landings, and home-baking. The downstairs loo doubles as the library.

Rooms: 1 double, with sitting room and en suite (bath); 2 singles and 1 double, sharing bathroom and sitting room.

Price: £30 p.p. No single supp.

Breakfast: Until 9am.

Meals: Dinner £20-£35 p.p. Lunch available on request.

Closed: 22 December-3 January & 4th week of August.

From A816, B8002 to Ardfern, and through village. 0.75 miles beyond church, you will see long white house on top of hill on right. Turn right by Heron's Cottage, and up drive to Corranmor.

Entry No: 603   Map no: 22

Hew & Barbara Service
Corranmor House
Ardfern
By Lochgilphead
Argyll PA31 8QN
Tel: 01852 500609
Fax: 01852 500609
Web: www.sawdays.co.uk

The closest thing to being on board ship while not on the high seas — every corner of Fernfield exudes Mike's passion for the sea. Perched above Crinan Harbour, with the most staggering views of the Western Isles, our inspector wrote: "A great place, ten out of ten, and, perhaps, the best view in the book." The light, elegant upstairs drawing/dining room is a perfect vantage point — the sunset often stops dinner in its tracks. Delightfully pretty, spotless and comfortable bedrooms, and one bathroom has a huge stone bath. *Children over 12 welcome.*

Rooms: 1 double, en suite (bath); 1 double and 1 single sharing a bathroom.

Price: £28-£30 p.p. No single supp. in rooms that share a bathroom.

Breakfast: Flexible.

Meals: Packed lunch, by arrangement. Dinner £19 p.p.

Closed: Christmas & New Year.

From Lochgilphead, A813 towards Oban. After 3 miles, B841 west towards Crinan. Pass sign to Crinan Harbour. Pass row of cottages. Take first drive on left and fork left between wooden gates.

Entry No: 604   Map no: 22

Michael & Monica Stewart
Fernfield
Crinan
Argyll PA31 8SW
Tel: 01546 830248
Fax: 01546 830282
e-mail: fernfield@easynet.co.uk
Web: www.sawdays.co.uk

Robert wears his old-school, fishing-mad, gentleman's heart engagingly on his tweed sleeve. This 1960s lodge conceals a rich rococo interior of 18th-century style and comfort. He has dragged and ragged the walls to a warming vibrancy and is the perfect host — turning his gatherings into country house parties. The pretty garden is terraced down to the River Awe with its stone road bridge and lies at the foot of two Munros. He'll gladly brave the evening's midges and take you to the barrage where the salmon leap. The rooms are just what you need — fresh flowers, simply furnished, light and airy.

Rooms: 2 twins/doubles and 1 twin, all en suite (bath).

Price: £35 p.p. Single supp. £7.

Breakfast: 8.15-9.15am.

Meals: Dinner £25 p.p.

Closed: Christmas & New Year

Perfect peace, rare stillness, and nothing to jar the senses. The setting itself is healing and Earle and Stella, with their understated generosity and quiet concern for guests' comfort, fit the place perfectly. At bedtime you will find your covers turned down, a hot-water bottle inside, curtains drawn and the bedside light on; maximum care and minimal fuss. The hills of Glen Etive wrap around Loch Baile Mhic Chailen, in which the house almost paddles (you certainly can) and Glencoe can be seen in the distance. Food is beautifully presented and the bread is home-made; Stella is a wonderful cook. *Children by arrangement.*

Rooms: 1 twin and 1 double, both en suite (bath); 1 twin with private shower

Price: £22-£30 p.p. No single supp.

Breakfast: Flexible.

Meals: Dinner, 4 courses, £17.50 p.p.

Closed: Never.

From A85 (Oban road), travel 23 miles west from Crianlarich. Right signed 'Inverawe Fisheries' just before bridge over river. House 1st on left after high hedge. If you reach Taynuilt you have travelled 3 miles too far!

Entry No: 605   Map no: 22

Robert Knight
Bridge of Awe Lodge
Taynuilt
Argyll PA35 1HT
Tel: 01866 822642
Fax: 01866 822510
Web: www.sawdays.co.uk

14 miles north of Connel Bridge, 20 miles south of Ballachulish on A828, Oban/Fort William/Glencoe rd. At r'bout, continue along lochside rd (disregard bridge). Follow large white signs to Invercreran House Hotel. Cottage is 1 mile on, on right.

Entry No: 606   Map no: 22

Earle & Stella Broadbent
Lochside Cottage
Fasnacloich
Appin
Argyll PA38 4BJ
Tel: 01631 730216
Fax: 01631 730216

Loch Linnhe is 200 metres away, so views are stunning. Light floods in, there are windows everywhere and the walls are white to reflect the sun. The daughter's modern art hangs above a classical marble fireplace in the sitting room, whose ceiling is the roof. The dining room connects open-plan, with good, simple, long oak table. The bedrooms are nicely minimalist, with cool fresh apple greens, light yellows, white, fresh flowers, candles, books and views. The two-acre garden is 100% organic, fertilised by seaweed, the pony and free-range chickens. Relaxed and interesting people.

Rooms: 1 double, en suite (shower); 2 twins sharing bath and shower.

Price: £20-£25 p.p. Single supp. by arrangement.

Breakfast: Until 9.15am.

Meals: Available locally.

Closed: Christmas & New Year.

From Oban north on A85, then A828. Continue up to the village of Duror, then left, signed Cuil. House is on left after 0.5 miles.

Entry No: 607   Map no: 22

Bridget & Hugh Allen
Druimgrianach
Cuil Bay
Duror
Argyll PA38 4DA
Tel: 01631 740286

WALES

A holiday is what you take when you can no longer take what you've been taking.

Early Wilson

Lush fields rise and dip, rivers rush and castles and roman ruins stand proud in the magical border countryside of the Usk Valley. Here there are 10 acres of parkland with rare trees, shady lawns and magnificent rhododendrons. The Countess' home has an easy elegance — a grand piano in the wooden floored drawing room, sofas piled with cushions, and tall sash windows that lead onto the terrace. Bedrooms are large, quiet and restful, each with a basin and chairs. Eggs from the local farmer, meat from the butcher and a smashing swimming pool, too.

Rooms: I double and 1 twin each with private bathroom; 1 single with large, private shower room.

Price: £35 p.p.

Breakfast: 8.30-9.30 am.

Meals: Available locally.

Closed: Christmas & New Year.

South Wales

The Court is on B4233 between Monmouth and Abergavenny, in the village of Llanvapley. Look out for stone gateposts with white railings at drive entrance.

Entry No: 608   Map no: 9

Countess Flavia Stampa Gruss
Llanvapley Court
Llanvapley
Nr. Abergavenny
Monmouthshire NP7 8SG
Tel: 01600 780250
Fax: 01600 780520

One of very few Grade I-listed buildings in the country — this medieval manor possesses staggeringly ancient beauty. Underfloor heating warms the flagstones, the dining room is lit by candles in Tudor candlesticks and some of the stone window frames retain the original 1600 finger moulding. Bedrooms have dramatic mountain views and there is a fascinating herb and knot garden, plus a yew maze. A truly historic house, yet conservation and commitment to the environment are evident everywhere — for example, all the soaps are handmade to traditional recipes in a medieval still room. *Children over 12 welcome.*

Rooms: 1 twin/double, 1 double and 1 four poster, all en suite (bath).

Price: From £40 p.p. Single supp. £20.

Breakfast: 8.30-9am Mon-Sat; 9.30-10am Sun.

Meals: Excellent pubs and restaurants nearby.

Closed: Never.

From Abergavenny north on A465. 5 miles on, left towards Pantygelli. After 0.25 miles, follow signs to Penyclawdd Farm — pass this to stone buildings at top of track.

Entry No: 609   Map no: 9

Julia Horton Evans & Ken Peacock
Penyclawdd Court
Llanfihangel Crucorney
Nr. Abergavenny
Monmouthshire NP7 7LB
Tel: 01873 890719
Fax: 01873 890848

Bring a notebook for Sue's recipes: her vegetarian dishes, with much organic fruit and vegetables, are exceptional. In the attractive dining room, revel in her good food and sparkling conversation and discuss sailing, fishing and country life with Nick. You may lie in a deep bed with embroidered sheets and contemplate the heart-healing view, or wallow in the big bath under the timbers, with one of the books from the bathroom library. The bedrooms in this 200-year-old farmhouse are big and beautifully furnished and Sue will greet you like a dear friend.

Rooms: 1 twin and 1 single, sharing private bathroom (let only to members of same party); 1 double, en suite (bath).

Price: £25 p.p. No single supp.

Breakfast: Flexible.

Meals: Dinner, 3 courses, with wine and coffee, £15 p.p. Packed lunch £5 p.p.

Closed: Christmas & Boxing Day.

From Llandovery, A40 towards Llandeilo. At Llanwrda, right for Lampeter (A482). After 1 mile, first right past M H Evans. Over bridge and up hill; first left. House is 1st on right.

Entry No: 610   Map no: 8

Sue & Nick Thompson
Mount Pleasant Farm
Llanwrda
Carmarthenshire SA19 8AN
Tel: 01550 777537/777877
Fax: 01550 777537
e-mail: rivarevival@aol.com

Dolls' house Regency architecture, Grade II* listed, with sunny hall, oak floors, tall staircase and perfectly proportioned rooms. Lynn teaches the Alexander Technique at home and William, an artist, founded the National Botanic Garden of Wales and set up the Aberglasney Trust. At the stair head, be greeted by a bust of his ancestor, another William Wilkins, architect of the National Gallery. You sleep on comfortable mattresses in Victorian beds — one is cosy with a white painted wooden floor and the other has unparalleled views of Carreg Cennen castle. William and Lynne are delightful, utterly modest movers and shakers in the resurgence of Welsh gardening. *Children over 12 welcome.*

Rooms: 2 twins, sharing private bathroom.

Price: £25 p.p.

Breakfast: Flexible.

Meals: Excellent food available locally.

Closed: 20 December-6 January.

From end of M4, A48 to Cross Hands r'bout. A476 to Llandeilo (about 7 miles). Over x-roads in Ffairfach, signed Carreg Cennen Castle. Right after railway bridge, for Castle. 2 miles on, entrance to Avenue is last on left before Trap. House at top (white gates).

Entry No: 611   Map no: 8

Lynn & William Wilkins
Carreg Cennen House
Trap
Llandeilo
Carmarthenshire SA19 6TL
Tel: 01558 823242
Fax: 01558 823242

The startling shriek of a peacock, soft coo of pigeons, clucking of hens and grunts of contented pot-bellied pigs greet you at this mellow-stoned 1708 mansion at the foot of the Black Mountain. There is a lovely crumbling dovecote and energetic Katy has hacked a path through a jungle of laurels and rhododendrons to a dark, cool, 25-foot-deep icehouse. Follow the river running through the estate to a spectacular waterfall. Indoors, the drawing room has a baby grand. Wallow in the bucolic sights and sounds of a passing pastoral age; you can even get married here.

Rooms: 1 double and 1 twin/double, en suite (shower); 1 double with shared bathroom. Self-catering also available.

Price: From £19.50 p.p. Check for self-catering prices.

Breakfast: Flexible.

Meals: Dinner, 3 courses, from £14 p.p., by arrangement.

Closed: November-February (except for large groups).

From M4 to Pont Abraham services, 2nd exit marked Ammanford. There, left at 2nd set of lights. After 2 miles, take 2nd right after Llandybie sign and house is 1 mile up on right.

Entry No: 612   Map no: 8

Katy & Julian Jenkins
Glynhir Mansion
Llandybie, Ammanford
Carmarthenshire SA18 2TD
Tel: 01269 850438
Fax: 01269 851275
e-mail: glynhir@glynhir.demon.co.uk
Web: www.sawdays.co.uk

Near Dylan Thomas's Laugharne, this unassuming Georgian country house has its own water supply. You can stable your horse, play tennis and revel in 16 acres of beautiful grounds complete with pond and mature woodland; brilliant for bird-watching. Furnishing is traditional; rooms, including bathrooms, are big and light. The oak-floored sitting room has an open fire and French windows onto the walled garden. A hum from the A40 if the wind's from that direction, but this place is good value and 15 minutes from the National Botanic Garden of Wales.

Rooms: 2 large doubles and 1 twin, all en suite.

Price: £22.50-£27.50 p.p. Single occ. £28-£35.

Breakfast: Flexible.

Meals: Dinner, 3 courses, approx. £15 p.p., by arrangement. B.Y.O wine.

Closed: Never.

Heaps of fascinating literary history here — Dylan Thomas used to stay as a house guest of Richard Hughes and he would write in the gazebo of the castle grounds next door. His boat house on the estuary is now open to the public, but with Amanda and Charles you have your own personal guides to the ancient township history of Laugharne. The house, 18th century and Grade II* listed, has been in Amanda's family since 1730; the hall doors are said to be designed by Sir William Clough-Ellis. The feel is homely — not at all hotelly or falsely lavish — and there are wonderful views of the Taf estuary.

Rooms: 2 doubles, both en suite (shower); 1 double with private bathroom.

Price: £25-£35 p.p.

Breakfast: Until 9.30am.

Meals: Meals available locally. Packed lunch available.

Closed: Never.

From Carmarthen A40 west. Turn right for Bancyfelin 4 miles on. After 0.5 miles, right into drive on brow of hill.

Entry No: 613   Map no: 8

Cynthia & David Fernihough
Sarnau Mansion
Llysonnen Road
Bancyfelin
Carmarthenshire SA33 5DZ
Tel: 01267 211404
Fax: 01267 211404
e-mail: fernihough@so1405.force9.co.uk

From Carmarthen, A40 to St. Clears, and turn off for Laugharne. There, pass Browns pub and clock tower. House on left, next to Castle entrance.

Entry No: 614   Map no: 8

Amanda & Charles Mitchell
Castle House
Laugharne
Carmarthenshire SA33 4SA
Tel: 01994 427616
Fax: 01994 427616
e-mail: charles@laugharne.co.uk
Web: www.castlehouse.ic24.net

The Quinns' house is somewhat deceptive. It looks like a neat two-up, two-down from the front, but once inside the front door you need a map! The original early 19th-century cottage has been constantly enlarged and is now delightfully higgledy-piggledy. Guests usually forget about lunch after one of Jennifer's breakfasts, sometimes served in the little garden: Welsh Rarebit, fried laver bread, bacon and eggs any way you like; the Quinns give such a touching level of care. Only 100 yards from the harbour, near the beach and the Quinns will happily arrange lifts to or from the coastal path.

Rooms: 1 twin/triple with shared bathroom; 1 double, en suite (shower).

Price: Twin/triple from £19 p.p.; double from £20 p.p. No single supp. Under 3s free, 3-12s half price.

Breakfast: Fairly flexible.

Meals: Dinner available locally.

Closed: Occasionally.

From Carmarthen, A40 to St Clears, A477 to Kilgetty r'bout. Left onto A478 for Tenby. 1.5 miles after railway bridge, left into Sandyhill Rd (becomes Stammers Rd). House on left at bottom of hill, immediately before junction.

Entry No: 615   Map no: 7

Malcolm & Jennifer Quinn
Primrose Cottage
Stammers Road
Saundersfoot
Pembrokeshire SA69 9HH
Tel: 01834 811080
e-mail: jennquinn2000@yahoo.co.uk

Cresswell House — the old Quaymaster's house — sits on the bank of the Cleddau Estuary which literally laps against the garden wall. Boldly decorated in sympathy with its Georgian interior, the house has excellent river views. Philip and Rhian relish producing imaginative and memorable food for dinner and breakfast; home-made sausages, fishcakes and home-smoked salmon are often on the menu. Then go and walk off the excesses along the miles of river footpaths to watch kingfishers, herons and shell ducks. There's a fine old-fashioned inn a minute's walk away.

Rooms: 1 twin with private bathroom; 1 double, en suite (shower) and 1 four-poster, en suite (bath). Self-catering cottage for 4 with sea views.

Price: £22.50-£25 p.p. Single occ. £27.50. From £200 p.w.

Breakfast: Flexible.

Meals: Dinner £20 p.p. Packed lunches available on request.

Closed: Christmas.

From A477, right onto A4075. Left at the garage selling 4x4s. House is on left after 1.4 miles, just before bridge.

Entry No: 616   Map no: 2

Philip Wight
Cresswell House
Cresswell Quay
Nr. Pembroke
Pembrokeshire SA68 0TE
Tel: 01646 651435
e-mail: phil@cresswellhouse.co.uk
Web: www.cresswellhouse.co.uk

An ancient bluebell wood pulsates with colour in the spring; wild flowers of all kinds bloom generously, and badgers lumber into the lovely garden to feed. This is an impressive, creeper-clad house, filled with family antiques, candles and crystal; one of the bedrooms has a fine, restored half-tester bed and both share a giant bathroom with a big Victorian washstand and wooden floor. Home-grown grapes and tomatoes in season, and home-made marmalade, local free-range eggs and goodies from the WI for breakfast . The Pembrokeshire coastal path runs through the land. *Children over 14 welcome.*

Rooms: 1 twin and 1 half-tester, sharing bathroom.

Price: £22.50 p.p. No single supp.

Breakfast: Until 9.30am.

Meals: Available locally.

Closed: Mid-October-Easter.

The setting is breathtaking: you could take your breakfast cup of coffee to the edge of the cliff and still drink it piping hot. Or you could simply admire the views from the sunshiney dining room. The 60s house is formal, traditional, colourful inside — fitted cupboards and very British, yet surprising. Bird-watching, seal-watching, fishing or just sunbathing — all are possible and the Pembrokeshire Coastal Path runs past the house. Jane and Anthony will give you lifts back from walks or to and from the station; just pick up your rucksack and go! *Children over seven welcome.*

Rooms: 1 twin with conservatory, en suite (shower); 1 double and 1 single, both en suite (bath); 1 single and 1 double with private bathroom.

Price: £20-£30 p.p.

Breakfast: Until 9am.

Meals: 2-course dinner, by arrangement, £12.50 p.p. (Not July & August).

Closed: Christmas.

One mile from Pembroke. Take B4320 from Pembroke Town Centre towards Hundleton. After woods, house is first on right.

Entry No: 617   Map no: 2

Mrs Ann Morris
Bowett Farm
Hundleton
Pembroke
Pembrokeshire SA71 5QS
Tel: 01646 683473

From Haverfordwest take B4341, signed Broad Haven. Right at sea front, then up hill signed Nolton. House 1st on left.

Entry No: 618   Map no: 7

Jane & Anthony Main
Lion Rock
Broad Haven, Haverfordwest
Pembrokeshire SA62 3JP
Tel: 01437 781645
Fax: 01437 781203
e-mail: lion.rock@btinternet.com
Web: www.jpmarketing.co.uk/lionrock

The Flynns took on a huge project renovating a Georgian country house built on to an old Welsh farmhouse. They are energetic, fun and helpful. You can take a packed lunch on a walk and arrange to be collected, or hire bicycles — the house borders the National Park with its Coastal Path. Equally you can do nothing more strenuous than play croquet or take tea on the lawn. There's stacks of room here with various barns and outbuildings, and there are plans to host arts and crafts courses. The large guest bedrooms in the main house all have small bathrooms and views over open countryside to the Irish Sea.

Rooms: 3 doubles, 2 twins, all en suite.

Price: £22.50-£35 p.p. Single occ. £30-£45.

Breakfast: Flexible.

Meals: Packed lunch from £3 p.p. Dinner available some weekends. B.Y.O. wine. Good restaurants and pubs locally.

Closed: Never.

Britain only has one Coastal National Park. The Old Vicarage is in it and the most challenging section of the path — a stunning bay and great cliffs — is just a mile away. Inland there are woodland walks and the Preseli Hills. Set in an acre garden of lawned gardens, the house is Edwardian, full of books and family paintings with glorious sunset views of the sea and there's total peace. The mood is traditional and bedrooms — pink, green and yellow — are large and drink in the sea views. David and Patricia take enormous pride in their cooking and guests rave about the food.

Rooms: 2 doubles and 1 twin, all en suite (shower).

Price: £23-£28 p.p. Single supp. £10.

Breakfast: Usually 8.30-9am.

Meals: Dinner, 3 courses, £16 p.p. Picnic lunches available.

Closed: December, January & February.

From Fishguard A487. Right at Croesgoch x-roads, 6 miles from St David's. After 1 mile, left at Llanrhian x-roads. House on left, 0.5 miles on.

Entry No: 619   Map no: 7

Caroline & Eric Flynn
Trevaccoon, Llanrhian
St. David's, Haverfordwest
Pembrokeshire SA62 6DP
Tel: 01348 831438
Fax: 01348 831438
e-mail: flynn@trevaccoon.co.uk
Web: www.sawdays.co.uk

From Cardigan bypass towards Cardigan at southern r'bout. Left by Eagle Inn to St. Dogmaels. Sharp right at end of High St to Moylegrove. There, first left to Glanrhyd, then up hill. House on right, past church.

Entry No: 620   Map no: 7

Patricia & David Phillips
The Old Vicarage
Moylegrove, Nr. Cardigan
Pembrokeshire SA43 3BN
Tel: 01239 881231
Fax: 01239 881341
e-mail: stay@old-vic.co.uk
Web: www.old-vic.co.uk

It's all there: croquet and boules, a piano upon which to tinkle, a jacuzzi fo one of the bedrooms, log fires in the sitting rooms and acres of gardens to roam. The Brecon Beacons National Park is close and there are some ancient trees (e.g. magnolia) to sit under and stare up at. Inside, it is solid and traditional, rather than informal, almost luxurious: fitted carpets, antiques and modern furniture, big pelmeted floral curtains and perfect comfort — nothing surprising, everything reliable. It is impressive and terrific value.

Rooms: 1 family room and 1 twin, en suite (shower); Master room and West Wing double, both en suite (bath & shower); Twin with jacuzzi room.

Price: From £22.50-£27.50 p.p. Single supp. £30-£35.

Breakfast: 8-9am.

Meals: Dinner, by arrangement, £20 p.p. Packed lunch, £3-£5 p.p.

Closed: Never.

From Abergavenny, A40 for Crickhowell. 2 miles on, pass car sales garage on right and 200 yds on, a county sign. Next drive on right with lodge at gate.

Entry No: 621   Map no: 9

Mrs Christina Jackson
Glangrwyney Court
Crickhowell
Powys NP8 1ES
Tel: 01873 811288
Fax: 01873 810317
e-mail: glangrwyne@aol.com

Mid Wales

With views to Pen-y-Fan, the highest point of the Brecon Beacons, and next to the Monmouth and Brecon Canal, this 18th-century farmhouse has so much to offer the active. Canal boating is the Atkins' passion and they own, maintain and hire out their brightly-painted vessels. Canoes, mountain bikes and pony trekking are available locally. Freshly-painted bedrooms are simple, with new pine, and duvet covers and curtains patterned with small florals. Guests have their own wing of the house with a conservatory and a separate entrance and staircase. Delightful canal-side pubs nearby.

Rooms: 1 double and 1 twin, both en suite (bath); 2 doubles, both en suite (shower).

Price: £20 p.p. Single occ. £25.

Breakfast: 8.30-9am.

Meals: Available locally.

Closed: End of October-mid-March.

Sit at the bottom of the long and expansive walled garden. Behind the Georgian façade is a fine 1620s house with tall-ceilinged, dark-beamed hall and dining room. You creak up the oak stairs to bedrooms, past shelves gratifyingly full of books. Big windows, original pargeted ceilings, views over the garden from two of them. The food has an authentic and innovative Welsh flavour and Helen uses local, organic produce. A delightful place with a most welcoming family.

Rooms: 2 doubles and 1 twin, all en suite (shower).

Price: £25 p.p. Single occ. £30.

Breakfast: Until 9.30am.

Meals: Dinner £15 p.p. Packed lunch £5 p.p.

Closed: December & January.

From Abergavenny, take A40 to Brecon. After 15 miles, left to Talybont-on-Usk, then right onto B4558 to Pencelli. Drive through Pencelli for 1 mile, over canal, then immediately right. Signed Cambrian Cruisers.

Follow one-way system to High St. Left at HSBC bank, and right into Lion St. House is yellow, on left. Parking at rear through green gates.

Entry No: 622   Map no: 8

Entry No: 623   Map no: 8

Nicola & Bob Atkins
Cambrian Cruisers, Ty Newydd
Pencelli, Brecon
Powys LD3 7LJ
Tel: 01874 665315
Fax: 01874 665315
e-mail: cambrian@talk21.com
Web: www.cambriancruisers.co.uk/bandb

Helen & Nigel Roberts
Cantre Selyf
5 Lion Street, Brecon
Powys LD3 7AU
Tel: 01874 622904
Fax: 01874 622315
e-mail: cantreselyf@imaginet.co.uk
Web: www.sawdays.co.uk

Years of restoration and conversion work on the Legges' Grade II*-listed watermill have produced spectacular results. The origins of the building have been honoured, even the dining room has been created amid the corn-milling machinery. Lots of wood, flagstone and terracotta with woodburning stoves, comfortable chairs and a riverside garden. The bunkhouse and camping facilities in the old cider orchard give the mill an informal mood with a planet-friendly bias. Food is vegetarian and truly delicious! A brilliant base for exploring on foot, horseback, bicycle or canoe.

Rooms: 1 twin and 1 double (Continental bath/shower); 1 double, en suite (shower).

Price: £20-£22 p.p. Single supp. £10.

Breakfast: Flexible.

Meals: Vegetarian dinner, 3 courses, £12 p.p.; simple vegetarian supper £5.50 p.p. Available on request.

Closed: Christmas.

12 miles north of Brecon on A470. The mill is set slightly back from the road, on the left, between the villages of Llyswen and Erwood.

Entry No: 624   Map no: 8

Alistair & Nicky Legge
Trericket Mill Vegetarian Guesthouse
Erwood, Builth Wells
Powys LD2 3TQ
Tel: 01982 560312
Fax: 01982 560768
e-mail: mail@trericket.co.uk
Web: www.trericket.co.uk

Penpont is magnificent in its sweeping grounds on the River Usk and folded into the gentle Brecon Beacons' foothills. It has not a whiff of pretension yet a relaxed stateliness of its own: great one-table dining room, grand oak staircase and an oak-panelled drawing room. Large bedrooms (one with tapestried walls) have stacks of atmosphere. An early 19th-century conservatory and two Victorian walled gardens are under restoration and a maze is being nurtured. Overflow into tents (£5), show off on the tennis court fly-fish on the Usk, borrow wellies and just walk — wonderful!

Rooms: 1 twin, en suite; 1 double with own shower & basin; 2 family rooms & 2 bathrooms. Self-contained north wing annexe sleeps 14 in 6 bedrooms.

Price: £30 p.p. Children half price. Cot £5.

Breakfast: Flexible, within reason!

Meals: Available locally (not walking distance).

Closed: Never.

From Brecon, west on A40 through Llanspyddid. Pass second telephone kiosk on left. Entrance to house on right. (Approx. 4.5 miles from Brecon).

Entry No: 625   Map no: 8

Davina & Gavin Hogg
Penpont
Brecon
Powys LD3 8EU
Tel: 01874 636202
Fax: 01874 636202
e-mail: penpont@globalnomad.co.uk
Web: www.penpont.com

This handsome Georgian house with its fine gardens and pillared portico could frame your wedding photographs. The Morrows have brought new life to the old hall, with great decorative flair. The drawing room has Italianate gilded ceilings in contrast to the library which is truly snug. Bedrooms are decked out in a mix of period and contemporary and every piece of furniture is special. Duck-down duvets, oak floors, high ceilings, stone staircases, fruit in the rooms and good, fresh food. Ancient trees in the grounds and a walled garden. Pretty Berriew and Powys Castle are nearby.

Rooms: 2 twins/doubles, 6 doubles and 1 single, all en suite.

Price: £27.50-£47.50 p.p. Single occ. £40-£70.

Breakfast: Flexible.

Meals: Dinner £20 p.p. Hampers also available.

Closed: Never.

6 miles south of Welshpool on A483. Driveway is on the right, 50 yds after the Nags Head Hotel.

Entry No: 626   Map no: 8

Tim & Nancy Morrow
Garthmyl Hall
Garthmyl
Montgomery
Powys SY15 6RS
Tel: 01686 640550
Fax: 01686 640609
Web: www.sawdays.co.uk

Plentiful birdlife adds an audible welcome to Broniwan: tree-creepers, wrens and redstarts all nest in ivy covered walls or mature beech trees. This is a small and peaceful farm, where Carole and Allen unfussily draw you into their home, serving tea and Welsh cakes on your arrival. They are organic farmers, so you will eat well. Wonderful views of the Preseli hills and the rooms are cosy, with warm, natural colours in paintings and woollen tapestries. There is a pretty garden, too.

Rooms: 1 twin, en suite (shower); 1 double with private bath.

Price: £24-£26 p.p. No single supp. Reduced weekly rate.

Breakfast: 8-9.30am generally, but can be flexible.

Meals: Dinner £13.50 p.p. Light supper £8 p.p. Packed lunch on request.

Closed: Never.

From Aberaeron A487 for 6 miles towards Brynhoffnant. Left at B4334 to Rhydlewis; left at Post Office & shop, 1st lane on right, then 1st track on right.

Entry No: 627   Map no: 8

Carole & Allen Jacobs
Broniwan
Rhydlewis
Llandysul
Ceredigion SA44 5PF
Tel: 01239 851261
Fax: 01239 851261
e-mail: broniwan@compuserve.com

Where the Snowdonian mountains come down to the crystal sea, you will hear only the waves on the shore and the sheep on the hill. Pentre Bach promises some of the best sunsets you'll ever see. The Smyths grow their own organic veg and Margaret is an accomplished cook; their dinner menu is worthy of the best restaurants. The large old stone farmhouse has good-sized, warmly-carpeted rooms with great views. The Smyths are committed to conservation and 'green' living: you'll enjoy them.

Rooms: 1 twin and 2 doubles, all en suite (shower) plus extra bath available.

Price: £25-£30 p.p. Single supp. £6 or full-room rate when busy.

Breakfast: Flexible — literally at any time!

Meals: Dinner from £15.95 p.p. Packed lunch available on request.

Closed: December & January. Holiday cottages open all year.

Off A493 Dolgellau to Tywyn coast road, 12 miles from Dolgellau. Entrance 40m south of old stone bridge in Llwyngwril.

Entry No: 628   Map no: 8

Nick & Margaret Smyth
Pentre Bach
Llwyngwril, Nr. Dolgellau
Caernarfon & Merioneth LL37 2JU
Tel: 01341 250294
Fax: 01341 250885
e-mail: sawday@pentrebach.com
Web: www.pentrebach.com

In this superbly-preserved example of neo-Gothic architecture (1861), the hall is dominated by the oak staircase winding to the galleried landing full of pictures, the décor painstakingly restored. Beautiful shower rooms are totally up-to-date and the bright sunny bedrooms, Sunflower, Orchid and Bluebell, give lovely views over the bracken-gilt Berwyn Mountains. There are two donkeys in the garden, a self-catering cottage and a weeping ash that is 138 years old. Pistyll Rhaeadr, Wales' highest waterfall, is just up the lane.

Rooms: 1 twin, 1 double and 1 family, all en suite (shower). Self-catering cottage sleeps 2.

Price: £22-£25 p.p. Single supp. £5.

Breakfast: From 8.45am.

Meals: Dinner, £15 p.p., by prior arrangement; also available locally. Packed lunch available on request.

Closed: Never.

North Wales

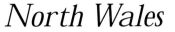

12 miles west of Oswestry on the B4396. In village, right after HSBC bank into Waterfall Street.

Entry No: 629   Map no: 8

Karon & Ken Raines
Bron Heulog
Waterfall Street
Llanrhaeadr Y-M Mochnant
Powys SY10 0JX
Tel: 01691 780521
e-mail: kraines@enta.net
Web: www.kraines.enta.net

Our inspector's arrival was greeted by a toot from the driver of the light railway on his way to historic Bala. This old stone house is 1820s and a former vicarage; Bala Lake — Wales' largest — lies still and shimmering below. Bedroom views — of Lake and mountains — are life-affirming. Bright, fresh and modern bedrooms with palatial bathroom and, downstairs, waxed pine, light colours and unfussy furnishings. Olwen is the kindest of hosts; she loves her cottage garden with its slate terrace, ponds and Welsh poppies — and people and poetry, too.

Rooms: 1 double, en suite (bath); 1 twin with private bathroom. Also self-catering cottage (2 bedrooms).

Price: From £20 p.p. No single supp. Check for price of cottage.

Breakfast: Flexible.

Meals: Packed lunch from £3 p.p.

Closed: Never.

Cotton wool puffs of smoke may emerge from the forest across the lake as steam trains chug through. All very suitable, for the house itself is a heady cocktail of restoration, history and architectural miscellany. Monks built it as a retreat in the 16th century; the Georgians left their mark, as did the 1950s. It is comfortable, dark-wooded, oak-carved, and immensely friendly; fine bone china in the bedrooms, too. The lake is a magnet for birdlife and there are four acres of wood, lawns and uncomplicated formal gardens... and a grass tennis court. Glorious.

Rooms: 1 double, en suite (shower); 1 double and 1 twin, each with private bathroom.

Price: £38 p.p. No single supp.

Breakfast: Until 10.30am.

Meals: Dinner, 4 courses, from £16 p.p.; suppers from £12 p.p., both by arrangement. B.Y.O. wine.

Closed: November-Easter.

On entering Bala on A494, turn left and drive across head of lake. Right on B4403 to Llangower & cross bridge. Look for sign straight ahead.

Entry No: 630   Map no: 8

Olwen Foreman
Plas Gower
Llangower
Bala, Gwynedd LL23 7BY
Tel: 01678 520431
Fax: 01678 520431
e-mail: olwen@plasgower.com
Web: www.plasgower.com

Leave Bala on A494, then 1 mile on, just before 'approaching bend' sign, turn sharply right into first part of triple entrance.

Entry No: 631   Map no: 8

Mair & Jack Reeves
Fron Feuno Hall
Bala
Gwynedd LL23 7YF
Tel: 01678 521115
Fax: 01678 521151
e-mail: mair@moneypennyuk.com

A simple, unpretentious retreat — "the sort of place you come to propose to your lover or to write poetry," wrote our inspector. Just outside the village, the farmhouse sits well in its craggy setting; inside, wobbly walls speak of age and low ceilings cocoon you. There's country and cane furniture, a glazed sun area and the double in the house has its own entrance and sitting room. The self-catering, turf-roofed cottage has direct access to a terrace that gives onto the mountain scene. The Harveys are gentle, kind and unobtrusive.

Rooms: 1 double, with private bath and shower and own sitting room. Also self-catering cottage (2 bedrooms).

Price: £20 p.p. No single supp. Check for price of cottage.

Breakfast: 8-9am.

Meals: Available locally.

Closed: Christmas.

From Beddgelert, south on A4087 for 2.5 miles. In Aberglaslyn Pass, left over stone bridge. After 0.25 miles left into Nantmor. At top of village, left in front of large chapel. House is 300 yds along tarmac road.

Entry No: 632   Map no: 8

Tim & Gay Harvey
Cwm Caeth
Nantmor
Caernarfon
Gwynedd LL55 4YH
Tel: 01766 890408

Gabrielle is brilliant at detail and knows what guests want. She ensures you have comfortable beds, the crispest linen, luxurious towels, excellent showers and super food — maybe roast cod with sun-dried tomato tapenade or lemon ice cream cake with hot gin blueberries... and has created a no-pressure environment in which to savour it all. Fresh flowers everywhere, good paintings, prints and family antiques, and so many beaches and mountains to explore. The house records go back to the 1600s. Guests often book for one night and stay for more.

Rooms: 2 twins, both en suite (bath); 2 doubles, both en suite (1 shower, 1 bath). Self-catering cottage, sleeps 6/7.

Price: £30 p.p. Single supp. £5-£10. Check for price of cottage.

Breakfast: 8-9.30am.

Meals: Dinner, 3 courses, £20 p.p., or light supper, by arrangement. Packed lunch on request, £4.50 p.p.

Closed: Christmas.

From Pwllheli, A499 to r'bout. Turn right onto A497 Nefyn/Boduan road. Turn left opposite church. House is set back, on right.

Entry No: 633   Map no: 8

Gabrielle and Roger Pollard
The Old Rectory
Boduan
Nr. Pwllheli
Gwynedd LL53 6DT
Tel: 01758 721519
Fax: 01758 721519

The timber framing is fascinating and the Grade I-listed 14th-century hall house was once moated; a part of it remains in the garden. Two bedrooms — one has an Edwardian feel and another, downstairs one, is 1920s-style — are blissfully quiet. A cast-iron bath sits under the eaves and out of a low window you can look towards the Welsh Hills. The upper hall, with views of the Welsh Marches, is an airy sitting room with an exposed aisle truss; it feels like a studio. Gill cossets guests and cooks breakfast on the Aga — after butcher's sausages, try her Bara Brith or Welsh cakes.

Rooms: 1 twin/double, en suite (shower); 1 double with private bathroom.

Price: From £25 p.p. Single supp. by arrangement.

Breakfast: Flexible.

Meals: Packed lunch by arrangement, £5 p.p.

Closed: Christmas & New Year.

From Whitchurch A525 to Wrexham. After 4 miles, take second signed turn to Horseman's Green. The farm is first on right, after farm buildings.

Entry No: 634   Map no: 9

Mrs Gillian Huxley
Horseman's Green Farm
Horseman's Green
Wrexham SY13 3EA
Tel: 01948 830480
Fax: 01948 780552

Welcoming spaniels and Welsh air will soothe the weary traveller. So, too, will mountain and river views. Rambling, 18th century, slate-floored, the farm is in the most glorious setting with the River Dee rolling by at the bottom of the valley. Comfortable, antique furniture, old beams and simple, but delicious, food. Most vegetables come from the well-tended garden and you eat in the dining room off the kitchen. Guests have two sitting rooms. There is absolutely nothing here to ruffle you.

Rooms: 1 twin, en suite, 1 twin with private bathroom plus 1 single available for members of same party willing to share bathroom.

Price: £21-£23 p.p.

Breakfast: Until 9.30am.

Meals: Dinner £11 p.p., by prior arrangement. B.Y.O. wine. Packed lunch, £3 p.p. Local pub, too.

Closed: November-March.

From Shrewsbury, A5, right at lights in Llangollen. Over bridge and left onto A542, signed Ruthin. After 1.5 miles, left onto B5103 to Rhewl. On for 2.5 miles. Farm 400 yards on left after chapel, before Sun Inn.

Entry No: 635   Map no: 8

Mary Harman
Dee Farm
Rhewl
Llangollen
Denbighshire LL20 7YT
Tel: 01978 861598
Fax: 01978 861598

Haven't you always dreamed of sleeping in a hayloft? The typical, honey-coloured, former cow byre opposite the 15th-century wattle-and-daub house has been sensitively converted for guests, keeping its low sloping ceilings, beams and small windows; you can still see the outlines of the original thick stone walls. The easy furniture adds to the relaxed atmosphere, the staircase creaks, the sitting room looks over the Vale of Clwyd and your jolly hosts will drop and collect you from Offa's Dyke walks. *Children over 10 welcome.*

Rooms: 1 double and 1 triple, both en suite (shower).

Price: £19.50 p.p. Single occ. £22.

Breakfast: Flexible.

Meals: Packed lunches, £3 p.p. Supper available at nearby inn.

Closed: Never.

Nothing is frilled or flounced — befitting the Arts & Crafts style — but handsome architecture, panelling and solid furniture speak of fine values. The Prices are a Wesleyan family and the house has been theirs for 400 years. A spring runs beneath the dining room and on a beam above the hall fireplace is carved *Aelwyd a gymhell* ('A welcoming hearth beckons'). Upstairs, the feel is fresh and more modern; beds are comfortable and towels are thick. A copper beech rustles in the west wind; views are to Offa's Dyke and there's not another house in sight.

Rooms: 1 double and 1 twin, en suite (shower).

Price: £21 p.p.

Breakfast: Flexible.

Meals: Packed lunch £3 p.p. Dinner, £11 p.p., by arrangement.

Closed: Never.

Take A494 east from Ruthin. Left opposite Griffin Hotel onto B5429. After 0.5 miles turn right to Llangynhafal. After 2 miles, Esgairlygain is signed on right about 100 yds past Plas Draw.

Entry No: 636   Map no: 8

From Chester, A55, then left onto B5122 for Caerwys. There, first right into High St. Right at end, continue 0.5 miles to x-roads. Left past camp, straight for 1 mile. House on left at sign.

Entry No: 637   Map no: 8

Irene Henderson
The Old Barn
Esgairlygain
Llangynhafal, Ruthin
Denbighshire LL15 1RT
Tel: 01824 704047
Fax: 01824 704047

Mrs Nest Price
Plas Penucha
Caerwys
Mold
Flintshire CH7 5BH
Tel: 01352 720210
Fax: 01352 720881

Guarded by a tiny cannon brought back long ago from the Hong Kong Yacht Club, this is the only remaining fortified house on the Welsh/English border and it was built over 500 years ago by the family who occupy it now. The medieval dining hall, in the tower, has a barrel-vaulted ceiling (from which the Mayor of Chester was hanged in 1465), mullioned windows, portraits, coat of arms and family motto: *Heb Dduw — Heb ddim*: 'without God there is nothing'. The tower bedrooms have mullioned windows, portraits, antique furniture and big beds. There are four acres of formal gardens in which to dream.

Rooms: Tower: 1 double, en suite (bath); 1 double with private bathroom. Main house: 1 twin with private bathroom.

Price: £30 p.p. Single supp. £10.

Breakfast: Until 9am.

Meals: Available locally, within 2 miles.

Closed: 22 December-3 January.

Go to traffic lights in centre of Mold, turn into Wrexham street (B5444). After 0.7 miles, fork right into Nercwys. After 0.4 miles, entrance on right, through large black gates.

Entry No: 638   Map no: 14

Charles & Wendy Wynne-Eyton
Tower
Nercwys
Mold
Flintshire CH7 4EW
Tel: 01352 700220
Fax: 01352 700220
e-mail: wynne.eyton@virgin.net

Church records show that the house was built in Elizabethan times with some later Victorian additions — it is beautiful and surrounded by bluebell woods. It also looks like something out of a fairytale and the two-acre terraced garden adds to the magic. Inside there are beams everywhere, open fires and lovely views from all the windows. The bedding is Egyptian cotton, the duvets are goose down and the towels huge and thick; there are bathtime goodies for you, too. Much of the food is locally-grown and Charmian, who spent some years in Mallorca, often adds a Mediterranean touch to her cooking. *Children over 12 welcome.*

Rooms: 1 twin/double and 1 double, each en suite (bath & shower).

Price: £35 p.p. Single occ. £45.

Breakfast: Flexible.

Meals: 4-course dinner, £20 p.p. Packed lunch, £5 p.p.

Closed: Never.

From Mold A494 towards Ruthin. 300 yds past Rainbow Inn, left onto Maeshafn Road. After 1 mile, right at T-junc. into Maeshafn. 100 yds past phone box, left fork through woods. House at end on right, 0.5 miles on. Through five-bar gate.

Entry No: 639   Map no: 14

Charmian & Ted Spencer
Pentre Cerrig Mawr
Maeshafn
Nr Mold
Flintshire CH7 5LU
Tel: 01352 810607
Fax: 01352 810607
e-mail: pentre.cerrig@virgin.net

A magical and intriguing house, Golden Grove is pure Elizabethan, built by Sir Edward Morgan in 1580. Oak panelling and furniture, myriad maze-like passages, rich jewel colour schemes (the breakfast room is red, the dining room a subtle aquamarine). The dogleg staircase is Queen Anne and the hall is hung with family pictures, paintings and prints. The family foursome tend the formal garden and run a farm as well as their excellent B&B. Friendly, fascinating, worth the trip. *Children over 12 welcome.*

Rooms: 1 twin and 1 double, both with private bath & wc.; 1 double, en suite bath.

Price: £37 p.p. Single occ. £47.

Breakfast: 8-9.30am.

Meals: Dinner £22 p.p. Pub food also available locally.

Closed: December & January.

Above you is the Little Orme with stunning views; below, across the main coast road, is the sweep of Llandudno Bay. And, inside, what a surprise! Patricia has given her passion for paint techniques full rein. The Marina Room is fresh yellow with a turquoise ceiling and a painted Neptune on the cupboards; one double has a huge green canopy above it. Colours are bold with golds and creams. You have your own sitting room, bedrooms are double-glazed and the views are lovely. *Children over 12 welcome.*

Rooms: 1 double and 1 twin, en suite (shower); 1 double with private bathroom; 1 double four poster, en suite. Only 3 rooms let at one time.

Price: From £25 p.p. Single supp. £5 or half room charge.

Breakfast: Until 9.30am.

Meals: Available locally.

Closed: Mid-December-mid-January.

Turn off A55 onto A5151 for Prestatyn. At Spar shop before Trelawnyd, turn right. Branch left immediately. Over first crossroads and right at T-junction. Gates are 170 yds on left.

Entry No: 640   Map no: 14

Ann & Mervyn & Ann & Nigel Steele-Mortimer
Golden Grove
Llanasa, Nr. Holywell
Flintshire CH8 9NA
Tel: 01745 854452
Fax: 01745 854547
e-mail: golden.grove@lineone.net

B5115 Llandudno/Colwyn coast road, (sea on left). Continue past turning for Bryn Y Bia on right. House is on right.

Entry No: 641   Map no: 13

Patricia Richards
Lympley Lodge
Craigside
Llandudno
Conwy
Tel: 01492 549304
e-mail: clive@lympleylodge.co.uk
Web: www.lympleylodge.co.uk

"Unbelievable!". Our inspector was blown away by it. An incredible adventure from the moment you leave your car and are taken in the 4x4 vehicle along the cliffs to this isolated outpost on an RSPB Reserve. The old Fog House (a former signal station for Trinity House) is now converted into a bird-watching observatory. Philippa is a painter and will organise painting expeditions on request. She cares deeply about guests, and is generous with everything, food included. The bedrooms, part of the former keeper's quarters, are simple and attractive. Don't forget waterproofs and binoculars. *Advance booking essential.*

Rooms: 1 double next to private shower room; 1 twin, sharing private bathroom.

Price: £20 p.p. No single supp.

Breakfast: Flexible.

Meals: Dinner £15 p.p., including wine. Packed lunch £2.50 p.p.

Closed: November-March.

On Holyhead seafront, take upper road on left. After two bridges, Warden's House at Breakwater Country Park is on left. Wait to be collected. If coming by train or ferry, ring from station.

Entry No: 642   Map no: 13

Philippa Jacobs
North Stack
c/o 4 Lower Park Street
Holyhead
Anglesey LL65 1DU
Tel: 01407 769715
Fax: 01407 761252

Quick Reference Index

Quick Reference Index

CHILD-FRIENDLY

The owners of these houses welcome children of any age, but it is best to phone beforehand to discuss any special needs. Cots and high chairs may not be available.

Quick Reference Index

Quick Reference Index

GROWN

These owners use mostly organic ingredients, chemical-free, home-grown or locally-grown produce.

England

Quick Reference Index

PETS WELCOME

The owners of these houses are
happy to discuss the idea of your
bringing your prize pet on holiday.

Quick Reference Index

Quick Reference Index

WHEELCHAIR

These owners have told us that they have facilities suitable for people in wheelchairs. It is essential that you confirm on the telephone what is available before arrival.

17 • 107 • 213 • 375 • 526

ACCESS

These houses have bedrooms and or bathrooms that are accessible for people of limited mobility. Please phone beforehand to confirm details and special needs.

England

Bristol, Bath & N.E. Somerset
12 • 16

Cornwall
39 • 42 • 43 • 56 • 60 • 63 • 70 • 71

Cumbria
79 • 83 • 84

Devon
108 • 111 • 112 • 139

Dorset
153 • 165

Essex
180

Gloucestershire
187 • 189 • 190 • 191 • 192 • 197 • 200

Hampshire & Isle of Wight
211 • 213 • 221

Herefordshire
225

Hertfordshire, Bedfordshire & Buckinghamshire
246

Kent
249 • 250 • 253 • 263 • 266

Lincolnshire
271 • 279

Norfolk
306 • 308 • 312 • 320

Northumberland
326 • 327

Oxfordshire
342 • 343 • 346 • 349 • 351 • 353

Quick Reference Index

NO CAR?

These owners have told us that their B&B can be reached by public transport and that they are happy to collect you from the nearest bus or railway station - please check when booking. (Other owners not on this list may be just as helpful, so do ask).

England

Quick Reference Index

A short history of the company

Perhaps the best clue as to why these books have their own very particular style and 'bent' lies in Alastair's history.

After a law degree, a stint as a teacher in Voluntary Service Overseas led to a change in direction. He became a teacher (French and Spanish) and then a refugee worker, then spent several years in overseas development work before settling into environmental campaigning, and even green politics. Meanwhile, he was able to dabble - just once a year - in an old interest, taking clients on tours of special places all over Europe. This grew, eventually, into a travel company (it still exists as Alastair Sawday's Tours, operating, inter alia, walking and biking tours all over Europe).

Trying to take his clients to eat and sleep in places that were not owned by corporations and assorted bandits he found dozens of very special places in France - farms, châteaux etc - a list that grew into the first book, *French Bed and Breakfast*. It was a celebration of 'real' places to stay and the remarkable people who run them.

So, this publishing company is based on the success of that first and rather whimsical French book. It started as mild crusade, and there it stays. For we still celebrate the unusual, the beautiful, the highly individual. We have no rules for owners; they do things their own way. We are passionate about rejecting the ugly, the cold, the banal and the indifferent. And we are still passionate about promoting the use of 'real' food. Alastair is a trustee of the Soil Association and keen to promote organic growing especially.

It is a source of huge pleasure to us that we seem to have pressed the right button: there are thousands and thousands of people who, clearly, share our views and take up our ideas. We are by no means alone in trumpeting the virtues of standing up to the monstrous uniformity of so much of our culture.

The greatest accolade we have had was in *The Bookseller* magazine, which described us as 'head and shoulders above the rest'. That meant a lot. But even more satisfying is that we are building a company in which people matter. We are delighted to hear of new friendships between those in the book and those using it and to know that there are many people - among them artists, farmers, champions of the countryside - who have been enabled to pursue their unusual lives thanks to the extra income the book brings them.

Of course we want the company to flourish, but this isn't just about money; it is about people too.

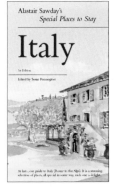

Order Form UK

All these books are available in major bookshops or you may order them direct. Post and packaging are FREE.

Special Places to Stay: **French Hotels, Inns** and other places	Price	No. copies
Edition 1	£11.95	

Special Places to Stay: **Italy** (from Rome to the Alps)		
Edition 1	£9.95	

Special Places to Stay: **French Bed & Breakfast**		
Edition 6	£13.95	

Special Places to Stay: **British Hotels, Inns** and other places		
Edition 2	£10.95	

Special Places to Stay in Spain & Portugal		
Edition 3	£11.95	

Special Places to Stay in Ireland		
Edition 2	£10.95	

Special Places to Stay: **Paris Hotels**		
Edition 2	£8.95	

Special Places to Stay: **British Bed & Breakfast**		
Edition 5	£12.95	

Please make cheques payable to: Alastair Sawday Publishing

Total	

Please send cheques to: Alastair Sawday Publishing, The Home Farm, Barrow Gurney, Bristol BS48 3RW. **For credit card orders call 01275 464891 or order directly from our website www.sawdays.co.uk**

Name:

Address:

Postcode:

Tel: Fax:

If you do not wish to receive mail from other companies, please tick the box ❑

Order Form USA

All these books are available at your local bookstore, or you may order
direct. Allow two to three weeks for delivery.

Special Places to Stay: **French Hotels, Inns** and other places   Price   No. copies
| Edition 1 | $19.95 | |

Special Places to Stay: **British Hotels, Inns** and other places
| Edition 2 | $14.95 | |

Special Places to Stay: **French Bed & Breakfast**
| Edition 6 | $19.95 | |

Special Places to Stay: **Paris Hotels**
| Edition 2 | $14.95 | |

Special Places to Stay in Ireland
| Edition 2 | $19.95 | |

Special Places to Stay in Spain & Portugal
| Edition 3 | $19.95 | |

Special Places to Stay: **Italy (from Rome to the Alps)**
| Edition 1 | $14.95 | |

Shipping in the continental USA: $3.95 for one book,
$4.95 for two books, $5.95 for three or more books.
Outside continental USA, call (800) 243-0495 for prices.
For delivery to AK, CA, CO, CT, FL, GA, IL, IN, KS, MI, MN, MO, NE, NM,
NC, OK, SC, TN, TX, VA, and WA, please add appropriate sales tax

Please make checks payable to: The Globe Pequot Press   **Total**

To order by phone with MasterCard or Visa: (800) 243-0495. 9 a.m. to 5 p.m.
EST; by fax: (800) 820-2329, 24 hours; through our Website: www.globe-
pequot.com; or by mail: The Globe Pequot Press, P.O. Box 480, Guilford,
CT 06437.

Name: _____   Date: _____

Address: _____

Town: _____

State: _____   Zip code: _____

Tel: _____   Fax: _____

The Greenwood Guide to South Africa
Special Hand-Picked Accommodation

Researched and written by Simon and Fiona Greenwood

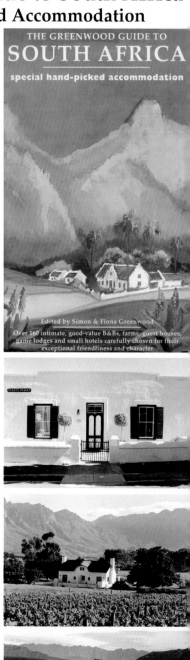

This new guide simply offers you the chance to follow our many footsteps across South Africa, and to stay in B&Bs, guest houses, small hotels, game lodges and farms, all of which we have found, visited and chosen for their comfort, character, interest-value and, above all, enthusiasm and friendliness.

Many of the places in this book can be found nowhere else, partly because they are owned by people whose guests are a pleasurable extra in their lives, not the B&B all and end all.

Stay on a farm, where you can take a picnic and swim in river pools at the top of a 200-metre waterfall; or stay in a cave, a Voortrekker wagon, a castle on a beach; walk through a game park in the company of a tame lion and elephant; walk out of your Cape Town B&B straight into mountain wilderness...

This book has been carefully put together so that you experience great variety, but always in great comfort.

Price £12.95

ISBN 0-9537980-0-3

info@greenwoodguides.com

www.greenwoodguides.com

Report Form

Comments on existing entries and new discoveries.

If you have any comments on entries in this guide, please let us have them.
If you have a favourite house, hotel, inn or other new discovery, please let us
know about it.

Report on:

Entry no: _____ Edition: _____

New Recommendation: _____

Date: _____

Name of property: _____

Address: _____

_____

_____ Postcode: _____

Tel: _____

Comments: _____

_____

_____

_____

_____

_____

_____

_____

_____

_____

_____

Report Form

continued..

_____

_____

_____

_____

_____

_____

_____

_____

_____

_____

_____

_____

_____

From: _____

Name: _____

Address: _____

Postcode: _____

Tel: _____

Please send the completed form to:

Alastair Sawday Publishing, The Home Farm, Barrow Gurney, Bristol BS48 3RW, UK

Thank you.

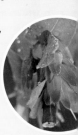

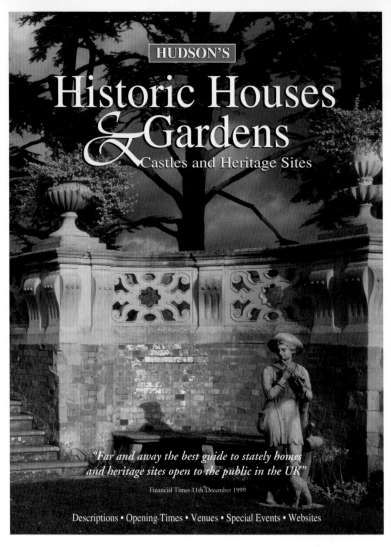

Index of Names

Index of Names

Index of Names

Index of Names

Index of Names

Index of Places

Index of Places

Index of Places

Index of Places

Exchange rate table

£sterling	US$
1	1.49
5	7.45
7	10.43
10	14.90
15	22.35
17	25.33
20	29.80
25	37.25
30	44.70
35	52.15
40	59.60
45	67.05
50	74.50

Rates correct at time of going to press, July 2000.

SPOOFS

All our books have the odd spoof hidden away within their pages. Hot air balloons, sunken boats, telephone boxes and ruined castles have all featured. Some of you have written your own ideas. As such, we have decided to pass the baton on to readers and to hold a competition for the spoof writing every year. The rules are simple: send us your own spoofs, include the photos, and let us know which book it is intended for. We will also send a complete set of our guides to each winner. Please send your entries to: Alastair Sawday Publishing, Spoofs Competition, The Home Farm, Barrow Burney, Bristol BS48 3RW. Winners will be notified by post.

Symbols

Symbols

Treat each one as a guide rather than a statement of fact and check important points when booking:

 Working farm.

 Children of all ages are positively welcomed but cots, highchairs, etc are not necessarily available.

 Pets are welcome but may have to sleep in an outbuilding or in your car. There may be a supplement to pay or size restrictions.

 Vegetarians catered for with advance warning.

 Most, but not necessarily all, ingredients are organic, organically grown, home-grown or locally grown.

 Full wheelchair facilities for at least one bedroom and bathroom and access to ground-floor common areas.

 Basic ground-floor access for people of limited mobility and at least one bedroom accessible without steps.

 No smoking anywhere in the house.

 This house has pets of its own in the house: dog, cat, parrot...

 Credit cards accepted; most commonly Visa and MasterCard.

 The premises are licensed.

25   Entry numbers printed in magenta means premises are uninspected.